The Broken Pearls
CHRONICLES

Pt 1 When the Pearls were Scattered/Pt 2 When the Pearls were Gathered

LILY ANN KEMP

ISBN
978-1-958122-70-9 (Paperback)
978-1-958122-69-3 (eBook)
978-1-958122-71-6 (Hardcover)

Dedication

I'd like to dedicate this book to Nancy and Derrick Kemp, my parents, and to Evelyn and David Dabritz who are some of the best people I have been blessed to know in this life.

Acknowledgments

I happily acknowledge the Gifts which my Heavenly Father has bestowed upon me. One of them, it seems, is writing and telling stories.

Matthew 7:6 "...neither cast ye your pearls before swine, lest they trample them under their feet, and turn again and rend you."

Table of Contents

When the Pearls Were Scattered

Part One

Prologue October, 1985

Lizzie

I passed a stream of urine down into the plastic cup, set it on the bathroom counter next to the pregnancy test kit, and stared at it solemnly.

I hoped there was a God as long as He was going to answer this prayer the way I wanted it, that is.

The instructions said to take a few drops of your urine and place it on the test strip. The advantage of this test was that you got confidential results instantly. Temporarily confidential. As if it wouldn't become obvious to everyone, including my parents, in a few months.

Not, however, confidential from the Almighty Himself. He already knew, since it was His handiwork in the first place.

I was not going to be awestruck by this creation if there was one. I looked at my seventeen-year-old face in the mirror as if it belonged to a stranger. The green of my eyes flecked with brown had a sheen like the first showing of January grass on the hills around Vacaville, one of many bedroom cities northeast of San Francisco where I lived. But the thought of next spring and summer gave me no comfort. Since missing my period two weeks ago, my prayers had become equally bereft of hope. I was used to praying and receiving answers. I was ready for instant gratification, but not instant pink and instant results.

I might as well take the plunge, I told myself. I already had done that in a major way, come to think of it, or I wouldn't be standing here staring at that stupid plastic cup full of golden showers. I picked up the pipette, drew up a few drops from the plastic cup, and transferred them to the test strip.

Pink! Used to be my favorite color but now I hate pink!

I was only ten days late and that stupid test kit was already working.

Hell hath no fury like a woman burned! I scooped the packet into the brown paper sack in which it had been packaged at Rite Aid, dumped the urine back into the toilet, and washed my hands. Then I stuffed the brown paper sack into my backpack because I didn't want to dispose of the incriminating evidence in the waste basket where my younger sister might come across it. I was surprised to find that my hands were shaking. I wanted to be a biology major when I went to college. Now college looked about as likely as toppling the Saddam Hussein regime in Iraq.

I should have been more diligent in my study of the human menstrual cycle. I knew the days of the menstrual cycle that were dangerous, didn't I? Kind of. Sort of. Let's see, 14 days before my last period was supposed to start put conception around the 18th of September, which meant this "little bundle of joy" would arrive around the 18th of June. At least that would be after graduation—if that was even happening now.

I wished I hadn't become infatuated with Jason, but regrets were as useless as life jackets that have slipped into the murky deep with the ship. I should have never dabbled with danger in the guise of swimming-pool blue eyes and Converse tennis shoes.

First date

Lizzie

"Lizzie," Jason said in his usual yet somehow sultry tone that always caught my attention. He had one of those haircuts like Don Johnson of *Miami Vice* fame that tapered around the sides of his head and was just a little too long over the collar. His hair was as sleek as his snazzy Mazda Miata. The famed Converse tennis shoes were navy blue with toothpaste-white soles and matched his crisp white shirt perfectly. His dark chinos sported a sharply ironed crease and his tie was expertly knotted, exactly as they were supposed to look on Sundays, if you were a male member of the Church of Jesus Christ of Latter-day Saints (the LDS or Mormon Church, to the uninitiate). We were taught that Satan assumes many guises – I just didn't recognize them when I saw them. "Hold up, I wanna talk to you."

"I'll be right along," I told Janine, my best girlfriend. We were between church classes on a sultry August Sunday morning, and I was waiting for Jason to catch up to me while Janine brushed her way past mothers and children towards the teen Sunday School classroom. Jason was a senior in our northern California high school, like me. I had been angling to get his attention since the beginning of last school year. I would sit in the row in front of him during Sunday School, preening my hair and kicking my spike heels back and forth, or saunter down the school corridor to class swinging my hips, or pick a lab bench across from his group at school, making sure he got a good view of my rear end in a tight black jean skirt over ankle-length lace-edged pink leggings. I thought I was doing all the right things a fashion-conscious girl does to grab the attention of the boy she desires.

"What's up?" I asked, dropping my eyelids and half-turning towards him. He stepped up right behind me, leaning so close I could feel his breath on my neck.

He lowered his voice. "You wanna come watch me in the first high-school swim meet of the year?" I looked straight ahead of me and saw Janine curling around the door into the classroom.

"Is this like – a date?" I tried to sound coy. I had not realized that my ploys to attract his attention might actually be working, and this could be a bona fide invitation.

"I thought we could go out for ice cream afterwards, seeing it's so hot 'n' all."

I sucked in my breath, barely audibly, and looked away down the hall. I hoped I didn't look too much like a five-year-old gawking as she passed into the turnstiles at Disneyland. I didn't want to think about how many times I'd fantasized going out with him to some swanky restaurant or showing up with him at a high-school dance. I just wished I had paid more attention to the legal brilliance of my father as he tried to teach me how to control my emotions.

I tried to sound casual. "It could work... I guess... when, exactly?"

"First Saturday after school starts."

Which of course meant next weekend. My heart did a few trips on the roller coaster before I took a step sideways and turned back to look at him. I felt safer out of arm's reach.

"You do wanna come, right?" He was flashing that easy smile, looking me up and down, appraising the contents of my carefully accessorized outfit. At lease I was spared the magnetic blue of his eyes that made my mind unable to process speech.

"Sure."

"Just wait for me out back of the pool after the meet's over. Anyway, see ya." He brushed past me and zipped right by our classroom. I was brought back to my senses when a very overweight lady trailing two smartly dressed youngsters in addition to her scriptures and church tote bumped into me.

"Oops, so sorry, dear," she said as she stepped on my toe.

"No problem," I grimaced. I had better get a move on or I would miss the opening prayer. I threaded my way down the corridor, running smack into a white shirt immobilized by the wall next to the classroom door.

The shirt belonged to Michael. We met when he was six and I was five. Michael was as close as I was ever going to get to a brother. We had taken a shine to each other from the outset, even though we were from vastly different backgrounds and our families did not mingle socially. Michael's household was seemingly always strapped for cash while mine was abundantly endowed with worldly goods. The only vehicle Michael ever drove was the family's weathered Chevy Suburban whereas my parents had bought me my own car, even if it was ten years old. Michael was tall and lean, with a thick mat of blond hair coiffed like Paul Michael Glaser of *Starsky and Hutch* fame, but without the manly appeal. I couldn't remember a Sunday when he'd shown up with a hair out of place. Despite the sparse finances, his shirt was always clean, white, and neatly pressed (which I knew he did himself), and his plain black tie was fastened in a tight knot. Michael was anything but flashy. With his thin-rimmed black spectacles and aquiline nose, he looked like a nerd and he was one. Missionaries could take lessons from him in how to dress in the correct and proper attire. I guess he was planning for the future: didn't look like he'd have to change a thing when he went on his mission. All males in our church were eligible to serve a two-year mission when they were nineteen, and all were expected to do so. I often wished I had a brother because then the pressure would be off me. Instead, I had Michael who was in some ways more than a brother to me – he was also my confidante, homework partner, and friend. I'd shared secrets with him I hadn't even shared with my girlfriends—excepting of course, for the way swim team star Jason Dalton made my heart flutter when he breathed on my neck.

The fact that I didn't have a big or little brother had been a sore point to my father for the past ten years. He'd had some major riff with my mother a couple years after my younger sister Lindsey was born about having another baby – and it was one of the rare arguments my mother had won. Thirteen-year-old Lindsey was my only sibling, and she bothered the heck out of me, always wanting to borrow my makeup or clothes.

"Hi," I gasped, "Sorry for running into you. How are you, anyways?"

"I'm fine. Was Jason bothering you?" Michael asked. I could tell he was not pleased from the tense note in his voice. He had never learned to hide his feelings.

"He wasn't bothering me," I replied flippantly, "just being a flirt."

"You shouldn't be flirting with him in church," Michael responded, with a slightly accusatory air. He didn't get that being my friend didn't entitle him to act like my father. "Besides, he's probably going to ditch class."

I already had seen Jason saunter right past the classroom door, but I didn't want Michael to know I'd noticed. "Bishop Dalton ought to get him in line then," I taunted back at him.

"Bishop Dalton's too busy."

"Well, the Young Men are his responsibility," I reminded Michael.

Bishops in the Church of Jesus Christ were charged with many responsibilities, and one of their most demanding roles was to serve as mentors and protectors of the teenage young men, who were more often than not testing the waters of their manhood and generally exhibiting a reckless machismo towards all forms of sensible and safe behavior. That was the problem with being a lay leader: a multitude of responsibilities that included disciplinary counseling, debt counseling, addiction counseling, marriage counseling and just about any kind of counseling you could name. And all this a bishop did without any financial recompense.

In Jason's case, I don't think any amount of counseling with the bishop would have made a bit of difference. Jason had an elevated opinion of himself which was in many ways deserved. He was the golden boy who could do no wrong. He'd suffered a complex fracture of his right femur doing a skateboard stunt at the age of ten, and when he came out of the cast, his leg was noticeably atrophied. His physical therapist had suggested he take up swimming. He hadn't looked back at poolside since. He started winning medals at age eleven and kept going from there. He picked the hardest stroke, the butterfly, because he actually liked doing it better. If there was a race to be won, he was determined to win it. He had more badges in Boy Scouts than the rest of the young men in the Ward's scout troop. He'd made Eagle Scout at thirteen. If you were a betting enthusiast (which, being a good Church member, I wasn't), you'd have put money on him.

·⊹✦✦✦⊹·

Saturday afternoon couldn't come quickly enough. I dressed up in a mid-calf white skirt with a slit up the back that showed my legs nicely when I walked, pulled on a red V-neck T-shirt, and rolled up the sleeves to shorten them. Demure enough to suit my mother, but it set off my figure nicely. I couldn't decide what to do with my hair. I had a thick brown mane well past my shoulders that didn't take well to French braids or being constrained with scrunchies, so I took a couple of sparkly plastic combs and swept it up around the sides. That gave it a breathless, windswept look, exactly what I had wanted to achieve. I lined my green eyes with hazel brown and smeared red lipstick the color of venous blood across my lips. I was hoping I looked at least twenty-one and apparently I did, because my mother was a little shocked at the effect.

"Lizzie, you look so... sophisticated," she gasped.

My father looked up from his *San Francisco Chronicle* which, along with the *Wall Street Journal,* he read avidly. The only other reading material he studied as intently was scripture, which for every member of the Church meant the Holy Bible, consisting of the Old and New Testaments, and the "triple combination," which is the, the *Book of Mormon, Doctrine and Covenants,* and *The Pearl of Great Price.*

I spent the least amount of time studying my scriptures I could get away with. What with seminary every weekday, three hours of church on Sunday, and a weekly Young Women's activity, I figured that was enough already. Piety like my father's was extremism. That's what started wars, I thought.

"You got a date?" my father asked.

"Just going to the high-school swim meet," I answered, trying to sound casual. I did not achieve the effect I intended.

"No one-on-one dates until you're eighteen, remember?" I rolled my eyes. I'd heard this pearl of wisdom so many times it was like a cave echo in my head. My father had the beginnings of a frown in his eyes. "Who is he?"

"Look, Dad, Jason's taking me for ice cream afterwards – no big deal."

"In case you don't remember, I'm still responsible for you and it is a 'big deal' to me where my daughter's going and who she is with."

"Well, unless anyone's holding up the Dairy Queen this afternoon, I should be fine. And seeing as I'll be under the watchful eye of his parents if we go over to his house, you've no need to worry. It's not like we'll be *alone*."

I could tell Dad didn't like my flippant tone, but this time he let me off the hook, which was a rarity in my experience. He probably had some big legal case in the offing and couldn't be bothered with me.

It helped that my father had known Jason's parents for ten or more years and that they moved in the same social circles. I hugged my mother good-bye and danced out the door. My ten-year-young Nissan was parked out on the street. I should count myself lucky to have a car when Michael didn't. His father had started up an auto repair shop and it was taking everything they had to keep it afloat. Michael worked at the local garden store on Friday nights and Saturday afternoons to save money for his mission, since young men planning to serve were expected to provide a portion of the funds required to finance their spiritual endeavors. I was so glad young women weren't expected to serve—and anyway, we couldn't leave until we turned twenty-one. I donned my sunglasses and rolled down the Nissan's window because the air conditioning didn't work and I hadn't gotten around to asking dear old dad if he would pay to get it fixed. I was definitely going for the windswept look.

"Jason – here I come," I said, with perhaps more enthusiasm than needed. I blew myself a kiss in the mirror for good measure.

The Swim Meet

Lizzie

The swim meet was an unmitigated bore, but I played my part and cheered along with the rest of the parents and fans who'd been suckered into showing up. There was a lot of muscled, well-shaped, bare flesh out there, which was interesting at a certain level. Of course, the barely there, skintight swimsuits had me swimming in thoughts I shouldn't have been indulging, but so what? I'm a regular girl and I love to "window shop" as much as anyone. But those goggles and caps didn't work too well as accessories.

Frankly, the ultra-humid air, heavy with the scent of chlorine blowing off the pool, did precious little to endear the event to me. I felt sweat dripping down my neck. My hair was sure to have fallen flat and my make-up felt like it had melted to the consistency of a Napa mud bath by the time Jason came out for his event. He did win his race, albeit by a narrow margin. In the medley relay, however, he struck out ahead of the three opposing teams by a quarter-length, but the last swimmer from our high school was caught before the finish line and we came in second. I could tell Jason was a little miffed as he glared at the scoreboard. Then he disappeared in the tangle of arms and legs and towels of his team.

I escaped from the claustrophobic air of the building to the welcome cooler, drier atmosphere outside with relief. The famous delta breeze was teasing its way around the treetops above the crowd of spectators who waited in cars with humming engines or lounged at the edges of the parking lot. A few children were playing a desultory game of soccer, getting in the way of cars exiting the parking area or tripping over waiting parents. After about thirty minutes, athletes began to exit the locker rooms like bees leaving a hive but I saw no one I recognized. The opposing teams began boarding their school buses to the strident cheers of teachers and coaches. I was feeling faintly annoyed as I waited for Jason to emerge. He was certainly taking his time. I shifted from one foot to the other in my sandals, twirling my foot over the heel, and paced along the edge of the lot under the trees where the shade provided respite from the afternoon sun. I didn't dare sit down for fear of soiling my white skirt.

By the time Jason did show up, the parking lot was empty and the air was stirring faintly, like the insides of my stomach. He seemed to bring with him an aura as visible as the sun coming out from behind a cloud, glowing like Apollo: the dark blonde of his hair streaked with straw-colored highlights, his face ripped with a wide grin and his eyes spilling chips like the sun dancing on water.

"Hey, Liz, sorry it took so long. We got the usual rehash and dressing-down from our coach. That dud on the medley relay team really blew it for us."

Jason's hair was dry and shaped to the curve of his head, so I knew he'd taken the time to blow dry and style it. He was wearing a black T-shirt, light tan cotton khakis and matching sockless Crockett loafers. I managed a smile that melted like ice cream on a hot day as I thought about how long I'd waited in the heat for him. Taking my arm, he said, "Let's take my car – we'll get yours later."

If Jason had an inkling I was miffed, he simply ignored it. He walked over to his snazzy Mazda Miata, gleaming like it had just exited the car wash and fairly reeking of new-car scent and Aramis cologne. He opened to the door for me, and I slid into the seat feeling like a matinee idol. We sailed down the street, breaking the twenty-five-mile-per-hour speed limit, and pulled up at the drive-in window of the Dairy Queen.

"What d'ya want?" he asked.

"A 'blue hurricane,'" I responded.

"You look famished," he added.

"That's because I am," I added petulantly.

He ordered a caramel fudge topped with nuts for himself and my blue creation, which soon floated out the pickup window. I began slurping it down, grateful at last to assuage my hunger. He drove with a careless grace, ignoring the speed limit and bouncing across drainage ditches on the side streets that led to his house. In one of the bounces, I took a nose-dive into the blue goop and he laughingly scooped ice cream off my nose. He licked it off his finger suggestively, rolling his eyes at me. A few more bounces, and we rolled up to the curb outside his house. He leaped out and opened the door for me with a lavish sweep of his hand. If he was trying to impress me, it was working.

"So what are we going to do at your house?" I demanded. My stomach was churning around like a jellyfish in a swell. His parents would be home—of course.

"We have an excellent selection of videos, all rated no higher than PG-13."

Church members had been admonished by their current leader, Prophet Ezra Taft Benson, to refrain from watching R-rated movies. Mindless violence and gratuitous sex in the media were discouraged. I had the distinct feeling Jason was making fun of both his and my family's values. He unlocked the front door and let me in.

The entry way led to a living room that was as immaculate as Michael's hair and clothes. It looked as if the Merry Maids cleaning service had just been by: the carpet didn't show a footprint, the glass was gleaming, lampshades had not a speck of dust, and all wooden surfaces shone like they did in furniture polish commercials. I fully expected a bright young woman to pop up and extol the virtues of Old English orange-scented oil over SC Johnson's Pledge. The sofa, loveseat and three chairs were carefully arranged around a coffee table set with a silver dish of Hershey's Hugs candy, an unspoken invitation to sit down and make myself comfortable.

"Nice," I said. "Where is everyone?"

Jason had three younger siblings: two sisters and a brother.

"They all went down to Walnut Creek to my uncle's house for dinner. Hope you don't mind missing that."

"Not at all," I gulped. I tried to ignore the bird-like swoops in my stomach. Of course I wanted to be alone with the coolest teenager in my high school.

With a broad sweep of his arm like a game show host, Jason indicated a six-foot wide set of wooden shelving almost completely filled with videos. "Check out the video collection. Mom's a little obsessive – they're in alphabetical order, by title."

"Can't beat that," I rejoined. Some might say such attention to detail had something to do with being a "Molly Mormon" (a wife and mother in the Church who does everything perfectly), but the arrangement showed me Jason had a well-organized mother. Maintaining a house of order was essential to the mantra. I stepped tentatively within arm's reach of the video bookcase and began perusing titles, acutely conscious of Jason's presence at my right shoulder, his breath on my neck. "How about *Falling in Love*?"

"That's a chick flick," he snorted.

"It's very romantic," I replied. "*Out of Africa*, then."

"What – are you obsessed with Meryl Streep?" he said as he stepped a tad closer.

"I like her movies. She's a classic tragic heroine, as her roles in *French Lieutenant's Woman, Silkwood,* and *Sophie's Choice* attest."

"Some of those movies are R-rated. Have you seen them?" demanded Jason, leaning around my right shoulder to offer me a sly grin, as if we were conspiring together.

"No, stupid. I read the books." I had read the books, and I wasn't about to admit to Jason that I'd sneaked out to watch my favorite actress bring them to life on the silver screen, in defiance of church and parental standards.

"So R-rated books are OK?" he quizzed me, arching his eyebrows, but it wasn't R-rated books he was thinking about. Jason slid his left arm around my waist, which made me think of sultry places like the jungles of Africa.

"Books don't get R ratings!" I returned.

"So that makes them legit for you?"

"Shut up and let's pick something. Here's *Romancing the Stone.* Got enough action for you?"

"You're the action around here," he teased, leaning in close, enveloping my waist with his other arm, and kissing the back of my neck slowly and seductively. "How about *Red Dawn*? It's a long movie, if you've got time." He worked his hands down to my hips. There were a lot of things I could find time for, I decided, even asinine depictions of the Soviets invading American soil, if I were watching them with Jason. I slipped away from him coyly and headed for the TV console, which was situated to enable viewing from any seat in the room.

"All right. Let's get it rolling," I answered, finding that my hands were shaking as I slipped the video out of its jacket. Jason sneaked swiftly in behind me as I fiddled with the VCR knobs and his lips found a tender spot in front of my ear.

"Ready to shoot," he whispered.

"The movie, Jace."

"Sure, the movie." He was about two moves ahead of me, and whipped the video out of my hand before I had time to consider other alternatives. I stepped away from him, feeling the breath ragged in my throat, while he busied himself with the mechanics of the VCR.

I settled on the sleek damask-upholstered couch in a state of tremulous anticipation. I was sure my red T-shirt clashed with the slate-blue couch and pink walls, and I wished I had worn something more subdued. Jason queued the tape to the start of the movie, fast-forwarding through the ten minutes of trailers, and returned to sit next to me on the couch.

He put his arm around my shoulders in a proprietary manner, but that was as far as it went. I had the feeling he was ready to charge into battle but was awaiting the order. I didn't understand the sortie during the video selection, and this sudden retreat. He was acting as if nothing had happened. I spent the entire movie on edge, waiting for an advance that was not forthcoming. Then, just as the titles were rolling, he leaned across me with his face next to mine, our lips almost touching. I froze like a hare caught in the sights of a rifle. He brushed his lips across mine and I realized my heart was battering against my ribs like a machine gun. He slid the breech, took aim, and homed in for the kill. I didn't have a chance – I was his and he knew it. Even though I didn't surrender my virginity to him then, he knew I would.

Pandora's Box

This road to hell wasn't paved with good intentions, it was simply destined to descend ever downward into an abyss of sin. After our first date, my romance with Jason began a series of sorties and retrenchments. On some occasions he was restrained and considerate; on others, he made shameless advances and sexual overtures. Consequently, I didn't know what to expect from one date to the next. For the two weeks before I submitted myself to him and gave up my virginity, he alternately ignored and cajoled me, but he insisted we keep our involvement clandestine. Considering my father's rules about dating, which meant I couldn't go out on an exclusive date with anyone until I was eighteen, I completely understood Jason's frame of mind.

We met as we could, for Sunday afternoons in the park, on my way back from doing homework at Michael's house, or just about any time we didn't have to account for our whereabouts. Jason's father was completely engrossed with his church calling in his spare time, and his mother was wrapped up with shuttling Jason's younger siblings to their various activities. My parents were no less engaged. My father, when he wasn't traveling on business, rarely arrived home before seven pm and my mother was so frequently busy on the telephone or attending meetings related to her church responsibilities that she failed to register my absences. She assumed I was upstairs in my room doing homework once I'd given her a quick hug after arriving home from school, and she failed to notice me slip out of the side door off the laundry room soon thereafter. I left the light on in my bedroom and my stereo cooing Air Supply to reinforce the impression that I was home. Our families were so preoccupied that once Jason was able to sneak me into his bedroom, and I got him into my father's downstairs home office. I dared not tell Janine or Michael about our relationship because Janine would want to know everything, and Michael had already expressed his disapprobation of Jason's character. And there was no way I was going to let on to either of them what I was up to, because I knew my personal conduct was in complete opposition to all the teachings of our church.

Although skulking around and Jason himself were hell on my nerves, I felt as high as James Belushi on coke without the withdrawal symptoms. But they were coming. Everything that autumn was tinged with a kind of madness. The amber colors of the leaves had a garish dangerous quality to them, as if they were about to burst into flame. The roses in our garden appeared to drip velvet off their petals in vivid shades of magenta, burgundy and scarlet, as if they had just been painted, and the air had a harsh, acrid taste to it from the smoke of wildfires in the Sierras. The sky flung back at me the insolent blue of Jason's eyes.

These external assaults were compounded by internal sensations as brutal and overpowering as electric shock. The breeze on my neck reminded me of the touch of Jason's lips. I ached for him to put his arms around me. The simple touch of his hand sent the blood screaming down my veins like an out-of-control BART train. I was in this psychedelic realm, reminiscent of the Haight-Ashbury 1967 summer of love, when Jason told me he had the key to our community pool where he worked as a lifeguard. He often worked well before sunrise and long after dark. His proposition sounded innocent enough, but it wasn't. I was walking rapidly between classrooms when Jason sneaked up behind me and yanked my ponytail.

"Watch it," I yelped. He was wrapping my hair around his finger and my heart around his ankles.

"Guess what I got?" He swirled me around to face him and dangled a key in front of my nose with his other hand.

"What's that, the key to Pandora's box?"

"You spend too much time studying Greek mythology. It's the key to the practice pool." Like I was supposed to know that.

"I'm not on the swim team so why would I care?"

"After the Saturday away meet, we could hook up and have a swim together." I must have looked unimpressed by the invitation, so he added, "It's not like we're going to vandalize the place. I could ask someone else."

That got my mettle up. "Like you'd want to."

He smirked and said, "Nine pm, Saturday."

"How am I going to make up an excuse to be out that late for my parents?"

"Tell them you're going to the movie with Michael. You're always hanging out with him; you'd think *he* was your boyfriend," Jason smirked.

I drew in my breath and closed my eyes, trying to focus my thoughts, but they were as disjointed as a cubist painting with Jason standing in front of me. I wondered if Jason realized how closely my father held the reins on me and how unlikely it was that he would approve of a one-on-one date. Perhaps for Michael I could get my father to make an exception. Jason took a step back, holding the key at arm's length and wiggling it at me like a worm on a fishhook. I bit. I took it all – hook, line, and sinker.

"Sure, I can manage it," I conceded.

That rendezvous was the start of many such encounters and the key surely did open Pandora's box with all its hellish consequences.

A Solution

October

When I told him about my pregnancy, I couldn't believe Jason actually dumped me. For about a week, I walked around like a person drowning, wishing the waves would suck me under. I kept hearing those words, "You're going to get rid of it, aren't you?" It was expressed like a question, but it was not.

Like what was inside me was not a living being, but an object he could toss away like a ball. I knew I'd broken all those lofty principles about chastity and virtue to mess around with him, but I couldn't compound that with another wrong. I had an obligation now. My senior year of high school was going to be a disaster and Jason didn't care.

He didn't care about 'it' or me.

I guess God had chosen to punish me as I deserved. I hadn't spent much time on my knees conversing with the Almighty before, but my attitude was changing. I spent a lot of time begging for Jason to have a change of heart and an equal amount of time begging for a miscarriage. I didn't really want to accept 'No' from the Almighty, although it looked like that was going to be His answer.

I had to talk to someone. I didn't think I could trust Janine with a secret this big. Worse – I was afraid she would ask me why I hadn't thought about contraception when I knew the church was so staunchly opposed to abortion. She would condemn me for being too stupid to know how to protect myself, not for the act itself. We both had been taught by the Church from the cradle that chastity was God's law, not the part about getting caught. But what I feared most was her condemnation, so it fell to Michael to bear the brunt of my revelations. I'd known him for most of my life, and I felt I could trust him. More than anything, I think I simply wanted a shoulder to cry on.

I flagged him down after church. "Hey, Michael, can you take a ride with me? I gotta ask your advice," I said, grabbing his sleeve as he was exiting the Sunday school classroom on a day in late October.

"Sounds serious," he responded lightly, but he was used to me asking for his advice. Like on how to handle an authoritarian parent or treat my sister Lindsey with greater forbearance. He had no idea what was about to land in his groin with a wallop.

"Meet me out front. I'm in my own car so I can drive myself home. Dad's got some meeting anyway and Mom's staying for choir practice. Lindsey's going to her girlfriend's house for lunch."

"Does this mean you'll drop me home?"

"You bet."

"Let me tell my dad and I'll be right there."

Michael disappeared for several minutes while he went to tell his father I was taking him home from church. I stood by the door, fidgeting and twirling a wisp of hair in front of my ear. Michael returned and held the door for me so I could walk out. It was nice to know that chivalry wasn't dead. I led the way to my Nissan, wishing it didn't look so battered. It didn't have many miles on it for ten years old, only around sixty-three thousand the last time I'd looked, but the black dash had some cracks from too much sun exposure and the gold paint had lost its sheen. I couldn't park it in the garage because my parents' vehicles occupied both spaces, so it had to weather the elements. That was my mom's dream: to own a house with a three-car garage like what we lived in wasn't really upscale. It sure was a helluva lot more upscale than the rat trap Michael occupied.

I unlocked the passenger side door and Michael eased himself in, leaning across the seat to release the lock on my side. I scooted into the driver's seat and revved up the engine.

"Sounds like you might have a loose belt," he said. I guess he ought to know, seeing as his father was an auto mechanic. But Michael had no intentions of following in the family business, and his parents didn't want him to. They had aspirations for Michael of going to college and becoming like my parents.

"If that's a belt, it's been like that for ages," I replied defensively.

"Yeah, well, you should let me take a look at it."

"If you really want to, then OK," I conceded testily.

"What's wrong, Lizzie? You seem uptight."

He knew me too well. Even though I was trying to play it cool, it wasn't working. "Let's talk when we get to the park."

"You look like someone died or something," he added.

I only wish, I thought. I drove the rest of the way in silence because I didn't have words for what I needed to say. There was no going back. I'd missed my exit off this freeway with Jason and I couldn't go back, no matter what I did.

I pulled into the curb between a truck and a Toyota Celica when we reached the park. People used the grounds for walking their dogs and an exercise route, but this was Sunday afternoon and it was quiet. A mother was pushing her children on the swings and over at the far end, a couple was watching their dog anoint a tree. I killed the engine, stepped out simultaneously with Michael, and slammed the driver door closed with hard smack. Michael raised his eyebrows and stared at me.

"That's not going to help her last," he said.

"I was hoping she wouldn't," I responded.

I'd been angling my father for a new car since July, with the intention of passing the Nissan on to my younger sister Lindsey, but Dad was a hard sell.

"So what's got you all upset?" asked Michael.

I ignored his last question, walked around the car, and headed into the park, not looking at him. I wished I could feel as serene as the setting. Michael caught up to me.

"You're acting like it's the end of the world."

"It is." This was probably a bad beginning.

"It's not like you're pregnant. 'Cos if you are I'm gonna shoot you," he said, trying to lift my black mood.

"Does your dad own a gun?" I retorted swiftly.

He grabbed my arm and swung me around to face him, staring me down. "This isn't funny, Lizzie. You are kidding me, right?" The expression on my face must have told him otherwise.

"We can run another test, if you like. Instant results," I added, sounding like a doctor telling a woman the lump in her breast is cancerous. Then the tears that had been lying in wait all morning started up, and Michael put his arms around me and let me sob mascara all over his best Sunday shirt.

"Oh, God, Lizzie, I can't believe you've got yourself into a mess like this." I was trying to remember if I'd ever heard Michael take the Lord's name in vain. It was probably a first for me. That made it one of many firsts today, like crying on Michael's shoulder and telling him I was going to have a baby.

Michael put his arm around my shoulder and walked me to the nearest bench. I sat down, beginning to feel nausea in the pit of my stomach, and wondered if I was getting morning sickness in the early afternoon.

"Who's the lucky father?" He hadn't chided me for the fact that I had not told him anything about seeing someone. We used to share all our secrets. That was before I surrendered my virginity to Jason.

When I continued to sob, he tried another tack. "Does this guy know you're gonna have his baby?"

"Yeah," I blubbered. "He wants me to get rid of it."

"Slick mover, isn't he? Please don't tell me he's a church member."

That was the question I'd been dreading. "You don't think I'd date a non-member, do you?"

"Doesn't look like it made much difference," he chastised.

"Look, Michael, the deal is, I'm not telling you who he is, OK? He dumped me when he found out."

"Love 'em and leave 'em," Michael added wryly.

"Thanks, Michael. So I'm screwed. I know that."

"Haven't you been listening to anything we've been learning in church?"

"Obviously not," I responded, jerking my head up from his shoulder. I saw a young mother place her toddler in a stroller. I sighed, thinking of what I had to look forward to. "I want to keep this baby, Michael." I sounded like a child begging for candy.

"You should really be talking to Bishop Dalton, not me." His voice was more conciliatory now, and he was staring off into the grass beyond the baseball mound.

"But I am talking to you." I wiped my eyes with the back of my hand, leaving a black line from my eye makeup. Then I felt Michael stiffen by my side.

"Fortunately for you, since my father's been in the bishopric, I can tell you what advice Bishop Dalton would be giving you." He threw a look at me then, reminding of the picture of Jesus Christ that hung in our living room. It was said that in the painting Christ had one condemning eye and one forgiving one. I bit my lip, but held his gaze. "You have two options. Option one: you marry the father of the baby."

"All right, so option one is out of the question. Give me option two."

"You're not going to like option two." He paused. "You have the baby and give it up for adoption to Church Social Services. That means at least your child will be raised in a good home with a loving mother and father. That's what I'd recommend for you."

"I'm not giving up this baby," I said firmly. Didn't Michael get it? This wasn't a thing we were talking about. It was a real live person growing inside me – the only piece of Jason I would ever have. I couldn't help it, I still wanted Jason as much as ever.

"That's what Bishop Dalton will tell you. Then he'll tell you to go away and pray about what you should do, not to mention repenting for breaking the law of chastity." Michael was sounding like my father now. One knee was jiggling as he adjusted his glasses. He always did that when he was nervous. He waited, giving his words time to sink in. What I didn't realize was that his mind was racing and he was miles ahead of me.

"There is a third option," he began thoughtfully.

"Now you have my attention," I rejoined, feeling like I was about to exit a bad dream.

"*I* could marry you."

I was so shocked I felt like I'd had the wind knocked out of me. I hoped I wasn't going to throw up all over him. "You'd do what?"

His words started tumbling out now, like water rushing over pebbles in a stream. As he spoke, he avoided my eyes. "We get married. Everyone thinks it's our baby. We've been friends forever. No one realized we were dating, so no one was paying attention to what we were doing. They thought we were doing homework in my room. Now they know different."

"But they'll think it's your baby."

"Yeah, well, that's part of the deal, since you won't tell me who the father is." Then he turned to me with a fierce expression in his eyes, and I felt like I'd walked out of a dark cave into the glare of the noontime sun.

"I thought you were going on a mission, then college." I stammered. He couldn't be serious. He wasn't thinking straight.

"Does this mean you're considering saying yes to my proposal?"

"Slow down, Michael." I drew my hand through my hair. "If – and that's a big if – we decided to do this, then you'd have to take the heat for getting me pregnant and raise a kid that doesn't belong to you. That's not right."

"Don't think it gets you off the hook."

"It's ridiculous to confess to something you didn't do. Besides it's wrong."

"At least I'm not guilty. God knows that. He's the only one that matters. You're the one who has to square things with the Almighty."

"Lying's a sin, too."

"It's for a good cause."

"Doesn't make it right."

"So what makes you an authority on matters of religious doctrine, Lizzie? If you'd been paying any attention – whatsoever – in Sunday school, you wouldn't be pregnant."

Michael did know how to put me in my place, I thought. I wasn't getting anywhere with my arguments because I was playing from a position of weakness. Then I realized we shouldn't be arguing about this at all because I didn't love Michael and there was no way I was going to spend the rest of my life with someone I didn't care about in a deep and sincere way.

"Michael, it's just that I don't really –"

Then, in spite of my intention to firmly refuse, I found I couldn't get the words out. I had to get a grip on myself.

What he had offered was foolish and reckless and utterly unthinkable. He was willing to sacrifice his reputation, his mission and college to make me happy. What planet had I been living on? Michael, my childhood playmate, surrogate brother, friend, and homework partner couldn't really be in love with me, could he?

"Why are you doing this?" I asked, twisting my hands in my lap and avoiding his eyes.

"You can't bring this baby into the world without a father and mother. You owe it to the kid. I just want to make it right for him – or her."

"That's not why you're doing this," I went on.

Now Michael was the one struggling for words. "I've known you since you were five. You're a special person to me; you always have been my special pearl of great price. I don't want you to ruin your life over this."

Michael placed his hands gently over mine and stilled their motion. His fingers were thin and sinewy, and his nails had a soft, white sheen like pearls. Jason's hands, on the other hand, were large, square, and suntanned, the wrists tough as ropes from working out in the pool. I wanted those hands, not Michael's. But it was difficult not to start to see those hands in a new light at this moment.

"Yeah, so you're going to ruin your life as well," I grumbled, pushing his hands off my lap and inclining my shoulder away from him. I didn't want to sound ungrateful, but that's how it came out.

"My pearl, I want to make things right for you."

Then he surprised me by seizing my shoulder and turning me toward him. We were face to face with each other and only the sun-soaked air and our breath hung between us. I wanted to be mad at him, but I wasn't. I wanted to say no, but I couldn't. He had never called me "my pearl" before – and neither had anyone else.

Much later, I learned that he would only use "my pearl" in his most tender moments, but it was the title he used in his mind and heart every time he had thought of me. I was supposed to be Lizzie – frivolous, swift-tongued, barefaced, lighthearted Lizzie. But she had vanished in that park in the bright sunshine when I told Michael I was pregnant. My life was never going to be the same. Michael was my friend, but I didn't know if I could ever think of him as my husband. I felt as if I were going to be sick.

"You should pray about this. You don't have to decide right away," Michael said softly.

My eyes were stuck on his lips and I still couldn't give him an answer. He ought to be praying about this, too, I thought, but I believe he had made up his mind the moment he threw the proposition out there into the quiet afternoon.

"I do have to decide right away," I said. Then I turned away from him, put my head between my knees and tossed up the remnants of breakfast. Michael, however, didn't flinch. It was a quality I would later come to admire in him.

"Morning sickness," I said, when I could speak again. My mouth tasted bitter, like the fruits of sin. Michael rested his hand lightly in the center of my back.

"Why don't we go over to the fountain and get you a drink?" he suggested.

The Savior had said, "If you drink of My cup, you will never thirst." Oh, how I wished I had followed my Savior. Michael took my hand and I followed him like a lamb to the slaughter. I knew what I was going to do. Satan had me in the chains of sin and there was a price for my release. We reached the water fountain, Michael depressed the spigot, and water sprayed out.

"Drink," he told me. "You'll feel better soon. You should be home eating lunch. Don't you know you're not supposed to miss meals when you're pregnant?"

Michael would know. He had four siblings, the youngest only five. I gulped down some water and the acrid taste in my mouth dissipated. I gulped some more water, grateful for its cool, sweet taste. Then I stood up, feeling stronger.

"I'll do it," I said, facing Michael squarely.

"Do what?" he asked.

"Marry you." I could hardly believe what I was saying. This was a dream, I told myself. More like a nightmare, actually. I thought maybe he'd whoop for joy, or hug me, or somehow express his undying devotion to me, but he didn't. Perhaps he was in as much shock as I was.

"Right then, my pearl, we'd better see Bishop Dalton today."

"Why today?" I asked.

"Time waits for no man – or baby," he said matter-of-factly. Then he put his hands on my shoulders and looked me down sternly. "I hope you've got the courage for this."

I wanted to tell him to take his hands off me and I was going to talk to the bishop when I was good and ready, but there was something about the firmness of his grip that stopped me.

"Let's go back to church and see if he can meet with us," I said, realizing that of the two of us, Michael was the only one who had a true grasp of what was going on.

"Not so fast, Lizzie. we're going to my house and have lunch. Then we're going to sit down with my folks and tell them the son their hopes are riding on is going to disappoint them in a very major way." There was that hard stare again.

"OK, it's your call," I said meekly.

Then he took his hands off my shoulders, turned, and started walking briskly out of the park and back towards my car. For a moment I hesitated to meet my destiny, but it was like the tide coming in –no way to stop it.

"Michael," I called, running after him. "Thank you. You have no idea what this means to me."

"That's because you have no idea what you're doing," he threw over his shoulder, his feet crunching on the sandy pathway that led out of the park. He kept walking and I quickened my pace to catch up with him. I couldn't imagine why he was being so churlish. I didn't like being treated like a two-year-old.

"Let's have the keys," he said as we drew level with my car. It would have been nice if he'd said "please." I wasn't used to a Michael who was this ungracious. I avoided his gaze, dug the keys out of my purse, and unceremoniously dropped them into his outstretched palm. He unlocked the passenger door, held it open, and waited.

"Aren't you getting in?" he asked, extracting the keys from the lock and jiggling them impatiently.

I hesitated, realizing he was intending to drive, but my parents didn't allow any of my friends to drive my Nissan.

"My parents don't let anyone but me drive this," I protested.

He raised his eyebrows and cocked his head. "I'm eighteen, and I've got a license. Wanna see it?" He was already fumbling in his back pocket for his wallet and I didn't like the way he was playing "in your face." I wondered if my parents would have different rules for a fiancé.

"Don't," I said, touching his forearm to stop him from getting out his wallet. Suddenly the autumn air felt as hot as an August heat wave. There was sweat in my armpits and between my shoulder blades. "It's my parents. I don't wanna upset them."

"Upset them? You should hardly be worrying about that now. You've got a lovely surprise for them in your belly, don't you? Now get in or you can walk to my house. I'm driving this thing."

We faced off for a second, our noses six inches apart above the door jam. Then I ducked my head and got in on the passenger side. If he was as set on driving me to his parents' house today as he was on marrying me, I would demur for the moment, even though I wanted to slap him. The only other person I'd wanted to slap before was my little sister Lindsey.

"Fine, have it your way. But I'm not gonna be responsible if anything happens."

"Evading responsibility does seem to be something you're familiar with," he retorted. Before he had time to shut the car door for me, I grabbed the inner door handle and slammed it shut, ripping the door trim a little further apart from its housing around the edges. I cursed inwardly. This was not an auspicious beginning to a marriage. I guess being pregnant before the day never was. Michael shrugged his shoulders at me, walked around the front end, unlocked his door, and got in. After fastening his seat belt, he started the engine and fumbled with the knobs for the air conditioning.

"I'll do it," I said curtly.

He gave me one quick glance, sharp-edged like an eagle's claw, his hand poised in front of the dash, thought better of it, and pulled away from the curb without speaking. I worked on the appropriate AC adjustments and deliberately avoided looking at him.

Unlike Jason, Michael did observe the speed limit and maneuvered the corners carefully. I realized he'd never driven me anywhere because up until now, it had been my car and my rules, but this game was about to change. As we progressed towards the undersized house where he lived, I cast furtive looks in his direction. I could see the muscles around his mouth had slackened and he had loosened his rigid grip on the steering wheel. He appeared to have recovered from his outburst. His next words confirmed my observations.

"Anything you don't like to eat?" he asked. "Mom will have a whole spread like she usually does on Sundays."

"Just pickles and ice cream," I replied. That actually got a smile out of him. It was good to see the Michael I had always known was still there, along with this new person of whom I was wary.

"Lizzie, sorry about back there. I wasn't quite ready for this."

"Me, neither. Are you really sure you wanna do this, Michael?"

"I'm sure if you're sure."

"You bet," I said. I wasn't at all sure, but I couldn't tell him that. I couldn't imagine how we were going to break this to his parents or how they were going to react, but I knew it wasn't going to be pretty.

The Kerry's

Patrick and Anne Kerry lived in a nondescript house in one of Vacaville's moderately desirable neighborhoods between I-80 and Monte Vista Avenue. Twenty years ago, these homes had been popular housing for families fleeing the urban sprawl of the San Francisco Bay, but now they were beginning to show the inevitable signs of age. Families who had become more affluent had moved further out, north of I-80, but the Kerrys hadn't gone with them. They'd been making babies instead of money; raising a family instead of investment accounts.

Michael had four siblings: Rachel, sixteen; Sarah, fourteen; Edward, ten; Alison, five. I figured Alison must have been an afterthought or worse, an accident. Michael, being the eldest, had contrived to have his own room, or maybe his parents had decided to compensate him for babysitting his numerous siblings. The three sisters shared a bedroom, and Edward slept in the fourth bedroom, which was large enough to accommodate Edward's bed and not much else. Supposedly Patrick Kerry had added on this room during his wife's fourth pregnancy. Its meager size was hardly a drawback for Edward because he spent most of his time in the garage tinkering with engine parts and helping his father fix cars. It appeared that Edward's destiny lay in the direction of auto mechanics, unlike Michael's loftier aspirations to a career in engineering. I wondered if they had given any thought to family planning but decided that was a subject on which I ought to keep silent at this point in my life.

The house was orderly and neat but frankly, with the number of humans living there and the limited space, projects and activities frequently gave it a cluttered look. But every evening before the family retired for the night, everything was shoved under tables or onto shelves, giving a semblance of order.

Alison's dolls and play cooking utensils were strewn about the living room, along with various Lego and Capsela parts from projects Edward was in the process of building. But all had containers for them to go into, so the clutter was temporary. Anne Kerry's sewing and crafts projects ended up on various tables or shelves while she set them aside to make dinner or help her children with homework. She did have a knack for sewing, unlike my mother, who spent more time perusing Chadwicks and Land's End clothing catalogs for the most up-to-date styles than she did reading her scriptures. Anne Kerry's most famous attribute was her ability to cook – the more mouths there were to feed, the more food came out of her kitchen. She could make dinner rolls, cinnamon rolls, meat casseroles, stuffed cabbage, the tastiest black-eyed peas I ever had, and cream of chicken soup to die for, none of which came out of a can. All of which came from recipes long ago memorized and tweaked until they were perfected. She wasn't one bit afraid to try new recipes, particularly if they included beans. I couldn't begin to remember the last time my mother had made beans, probably at one of those ward BBQs last summer when they'd given her an assignment. I guess it was hard to put enough protein on the table with seven family members in the household, and even with my privileged upbringing, I knew beans would go a long way toward making up the difference when money was tight.

Michael was compulsively neat, a characteristic sorely lacking in the rest of his family members. This necessitated owning containers for all his possessions despite occupying a small bedroom. I'd never been into his personal space without seeing the bed made, his shoes neatly tucked at its foot, and his schoolwork organized in orderly piles on his desk.

I realized I spent so much time at the Kerry's that Michael's parents hadn't taken time to notice that we spent a lot of hours in Michael's room, all by ourselves. This would, of course, be a plus now that we needed a plausible explanation of how

I'd gotten into this predicament. We mostly did homework together, because Michael was so much smarter than me, and he'd help me with physics and chemistry. I knew I'd need those subjects if I was going to become a biology teacher. I doubted I'd need them anymore. Sometimes, we'd kick our shoes off, lounge on the floor with tapes strewn around us, and take turns picking our favorite artists to insert into the portable cassette player. Michael liked the B-52s, Talking Heads, Oingo Boingo, Dire Straits, Huey Lewis and the News, and Duran Duran, but I was more Madonna, Eurythmics, Rod Stewart and Air Supply. We'd gossip about church and high-school life, speculating about who was dating who, who'd broken up, who was going to be king or queen at the prom, and who'd be the next Deacon's Quorum leader. I didn't know what we were going to find to talk about after the confidences we'd shared this afternoon.

I was scared and exhausted and pining for Jason, and somehow I had to act like I was madly in love with Michael. I would have to pretend not to be in love with a scoundrel, while simultaneously pretending to be devoted to someone whom I'd never regarded as more than a friend.

As Michael opened the door for me, the aroma of some kind of vegetable stock or soup enveloped me. I realized I was insanely hungry. Maybe Michael was right about not skipping meals.

"Hey, son, home at last," called out his father. "Hello, Lizzie. How's life treating you?"

"Great, thanks, Brother Kerry," I responded. I stepped into the living area and followed Michael into the kitchen. Patrick Kerry was sprawled on a sofa that was upholstered in fading plaid print and had arm covers that were wearing thin. He had short-cropped curly dark hair graying at the temples, piercing blue eyes rather like Michael's, and a nose that kinked sideways as if it had been broken when he was younger. He had removed his tie, and his shirt was open at the collar. His wife Anne certainly would have passed for very attractive in her teens, but children, hard work, and age had worn her features like the wind and weather etching the face of a cliff, hollowing her eyes and drawing creases from the thin nostrils of her nose to her mouth. Her hair had faded from the golden blond of young adulthood to a shade somewhere between ash grey and mink, was slightly mussed, and had lost the curls she'd sported this morning in church. She was wearing an apron patterned with daffodils in dull gold over her Sunday dress.

"You two are late," she said from the kitchen, which adjoined the dining and living areas. "We've already finished lunch but there's bread and minestrone soup on the stove-top. Then you can have some leftover lemon meringue pie or cake for dessert."

"Thanks, Mom. Sit down and I'll fix it," he indicated to me.

I pulled a chair out from the dining room table and sat down, trying to ignore the pounding in my temples. When Michael brought me the bowl of steaming soup, I downed it quickly, hardly registering its flavor. It seemed to settle my stomach. I imagined my own family, barely home from church and fixing hot pockets or quiche in the microwave. Mom never cooked lunch on Sunday. We always ate something expensive and microwavable from the freezer for lunch and a casserole made the day before for dinner. My parents probably wouldn't even realize I hadn't made it home. I usually arrived before them, heated up my lunch, and disappeared into my room to read or study because we weren't supposed to watch TV on Sundays. Other than that, as long as my mother knew where I was, she rarely limited the range of my activities.

When I was finished eating, I turned back to survey the living room and saw that Michael's father was on his knees on the floor, fixing what appeared to be a locomotive from Edward's train set. The track, miniature station, farm animals, fencing and railroad crossing gates were spread out across the autumn-gold shag carpet. Edward looked on intently. Luckily Michael's three sisters were nowhere in sight. They were probably crammed into their room doing appropriate activities for Sunday afternoon: writing letters to friends or missionaries, preparing lessons for family home evening, or studying scriptures. That was the stuff my father expected my sister and me to be doing.

"Hey, Dad," Michael began, after cleaning up a large slice of lemon meringue pie, his favorite dessert. "Lizzie and I want to talk to you and Mom. You got a moment?"

"Kinda busy now, son – can it wait?" He looked up from the miniature locomotive.

"It's kinda important, Dad. Can we go up to my room?"

In this house, I knew there was no private space where we could visit, and Michael's room, crowded though it would be for four adults, was the most logical choice for what were likely to be heartbreaking revelations. It was at this moment I realized I didn't have a clue what Michael and I were going to say, so I decided to follow his lead.

"All right, then," Patrick Kerry replied. To his younger son, he said, "Edward, I'll get back to this. Keep tweaking these wires – maybe we can get this little guy back on the tracks later this afternoon."

Patrick Kerry looked up at his wife, scrambled to his feet, and motioned her to follow us. She was still cleaning up lunch in the kitchen. Michael took my hand and we walked up the stairs together with his parents following. I wonder if they noticed that Michael had never been a hand-holding kind of friend, and this was the first time I could think of that it had happened. He swung open the door and we sat down on the bed side by side. Anne Kerry took the seat by the desk and Patrick Kerry leaned slightly against the closet door.

"What's on your mind, kids?" Patrick Kerry began.

I realized that Anne Kerry was staring at our intertwined fingers, while Patrick Kerry regarded me with a quizzical air. My heart started beating the way it had done on the day Jason and I met up after the swim meet, but with trepidation rather than the fervor of virgin love.

"Dad, I know you won't understand or believe this, but Lizzie and I need to get married," Michael said.

There was a moment of stunned silence, then the Kerry's exchanged glances with one another before fixing their eyes back on us. I wilted under their intense scrutiny.

"I didn't realize you and Lizzie were an item, son," said Patrick Kerry.

"Well, we are, Dad," Michael went on in the same steady voice, devoid of emotion. He was holding it all in, squeezing my fingers so tightly that he was cutting off the circulation.

"Is there some reason you can't postpone this until after your mission?" Patrick Kerry asked. "You're both young, you've got plenty of time. I wouldn't want you to rush into anything. No offense to you, Lizzie."

"None taken," I said. My voice sounded wobbly.

"Actually, there is a reason," Michael went on.

I think Michael's father knew what was coming then. He said heavily, "There usually is."

"Lizzie's pregnant." I put my head down This was the part I didn't want to see, like the moment in a horror movie when the creature is about to pounce on the unsuspecting victim. Michael continued, "I'm sorry, Dad. It's all my fault. I should've known better."

We hadn't paid any attention to Michael's mother. When I did raise my eyes, during the long silence that followed, she sat looking at me like she'd caught me in the act of stealing her firstborn child. Patrick Kerry sighed and regarded his son with sad eyes. I felt a wave of emotion from him, but I could not intuit its meaning. Oddly, he did not seem angry, which would have been easier for me to bear. It was probably the way Jesus would have looked at Michael if He were here. No, I had that all wrong – it was the way Jesus would have regarded me. Jesus would have known Michael was innocent.

"Have you talked to Bishop Dalton yet?" asked Patrick Kerry.

"No. We wanted to tell you first, and we're planning to see him right away. Today, if possible."

"What about Lizzie's parents?" This was an event I wasn't looking forward to with joyful anticipation.

"We'll tell them after we talk to Bishop Dalton," Michael jumped in.

I hadn't anticipated this, but considering Michael was making this up as he went along, it sounded like a wise move.

"Lizzie," said Patrick Kerry, "I take it you're expecting your parents to be pretty upset."

"Well, wouldn't you be?" I said, instantly regretting my flippancy. "I mean, I..." I let out a sigh and regained my composure, "we knew you'd be more understanding." I glanced over at Michael to see how he was taking this and he gave me just the slightest nod of encouragement.

"When is the baby due?" asked Anne Kerry.

I did some fast mental math. After all, I was going to be a biology major and I knew my gestation periods. "Late June, after graduation."

"Are you both really sure you want to do this?" said Patrick Kerry. "I don't have to tell you how bad the statistics are on the success of teenage marriages. I want to know you're both committed to making this work if we're going to help you get through it."

"Absolutely, totally committed, Dad," Michael responded with a confidence I wasn't sure at that moment he felt. "I love Lizzie and I want to make this up to her."

I wished I wasn't hearing him say these words to his father instead of me, and I wished he was looking at me when he spoke them, but I just sat there mute, feeling only the sweat in his palm.

"When are you planning the happy event?" asked Patrick Kerry. I was glad someone was thinking practically.

"December, as soon as school is out," Michael said, without missing a beat.

That was news to me, but I guess it would be best if we got it over with as soon as possible.

"Where are you going to live?" asked Anne Kerry.

"My parents have plenty of room," I blurted out before Michael had time to answer, "until we can save for a place of our own."

"I'm going to use what I've saved for my mission to get us into an apartment," Michael added. The sacrifices kept coming, but I hadn't seen anything yet. "Dad, if you'll take me, I'll work with you at the shop."

If there was anything I knew Michael hadn't wanted to do, it was going into his father's line of business. His father could hardly turn him down – and he didn't.

"If that's what you want, I can arrange it," Patrick Kerry said.

"There's no way I can ever thank you enough for all of this, Dad."

Me neither, I thought.

"Look, son, it's your decision. If you're willing to accept responsibility for Lizzie and the baby, then I gotta go with that."

I wished I didn't feel like such a worm.

Michael blundered on. "I'm sorry, Dad. I know you had dreams for me."

"Life has a way of intruding on dreams," added Anne Kerry.

It was all my fault, I thought. If it weren't for me, we wouldn't be here. I was the bad apple in this barrel.

"It's not his fault," I interrupted.

"Look, Lizzie, we're not here to assign blame," Patrick Kerry countered. "There was two of you, so the way I figure it, if you want to get technical – which I don't – then it's fifty-fifty."

"No, it's not," I protested, but Michael squeezed my hand even harder and gave me a look to melt glass.

"Well, whatever," I muttered, dropping my head and staring at our intertwined fingers as if they were some kind of alien creation. There was an awkward silence before Anne Kerry came to the rescue.

"Why don't you call Bishop Dalton?"

"Good idea, Mom," Michael replied.

I wished the earth would swallow me up right now. I was the wolf in a pen of sheep. I swore to myself I would make it up to them, somehow, as God was my witness. I would never have made that unspoken vow if I'd known I'd have to keep it.

Bishop Dalton

Bishop Dalton

I got the call on a late fall Sunday afternoon. Lizzie Sherringdon and Michael Kerry requested an interview. Despite his usual composure, Michael sounded nervous. I didn't think he had anything to worry about. His father had served with me in the bishopric prior to his calling to serve on the Stake High Council, and a man of Patrick Kerry's character wouldn't have a problem with his son. Michael was earnest, hard-working, and intent on serving a mission. I knew Patrick Kerry's family didn't have the resources to fund Michael's mission, and the kid was working weekends at a garden store and putting everything except his tithing into savings for his mission fund. Most of the kids in the ward owned a car, but not Michael. His parents couldn't afford to buy him one and he was determined to set aside most of his earnings for his mission fund.

It was expected that young men and women planning to serve a mission paid for a portion of it themselves. It strengthened their testimonies and taught them the concept of sacrifice. And it weeded out those who weren't ready to dedicate themselves completely to the Lord. Furthermore, Michael wouldn't work on Sundays, even though his refusal to break the Sabbath had caused a disagreement with his employers. But the Lord blesses those who are committed to His principles. Somehow Michael had kept his job. I had to admire that kind of commitment.

Lizzie Sherringdon, on the other hand, had challenges at home. Derek Sherringdon her father outwardly obeyed the principles of the gospel. He was personally and professionally not a man to be reckoned with. It had, I assumed, something to do with what happened a couple of years after the birth of their second daughter, Lindsey. Derek had wanted another child; no, he wanted a son. He'd held numerous leadership positions in cub scouts and was always talking about the day he'd have a son to take camping and hiking. But Sally had different plans. She wasn't ready to have more children. I couldn't remember who'd been the bishop at that time, but if it had been me, I'd have told Derek to be patient, pray, and wait for the Lord to touch Sally's heart. Derek did not suffer Sally's rebuff lightly. Her refusal to change had created a rift in their marriage. When several years had gone by and it became apparent that Sally had no intentions of bearing another child, Derek had begun devoting more hours to his work in the city and fewer to his family at home.

He had become driven in his quest for financial success and accolades in the corporate world. It was at this time that his firm rose to lofty heights, but it appeared sank in the esteem of his wife. He had not been the same man since. I credited my understanding to the inspiration of the Holy Ghost, because I had not become aware of Derek Sherringdon's deficits until I was ordained a bishop six years ago. Each time his name had been proposed for a calling on the High Council, I had been restrained from recommending him. This, too, I credited to the Holy Ghost.

I wondered what could be wrong now, because as soon as Michael spoke to me on the phone, I knew something was amiss. I knelt on the floor beside my desk, and found myself overcome with humility as I prayed to the Lord for guidance and inspiration. What could these two young souls be in need of, and how could I help them?

<hr />

They arrived promptly at four pm. Patrick Kerry accompanied them, and immediately I sensed Lizzie's distress. She and Michael were holding hands tight. They'd been childhood friends, so it didn't strike me as out of the ordinary. I knew they were close like brother and sister. In fact, I sometimes wondered if Lizzie didn't spend more time at Michael's home than her own. I had always thought the Kerry's were a refuge for her.

"Welcome, Lizzie and Michael," I said, trying to sound reassuring as I met them in the foyer. Lizzie looked positively frightened. "I'm not the ogre you believe me to be."

"Bishop, I'll just wait out in the hallway, if you don't mind," Patrick Kerry added.

"Thanks, Brother Kerry. Nice of you to bring them."

I walked into my office and Michael drew two chairs up to the desk, one for himself and the other for Lizzie. He seemed unusually solicitous about her comfort. She sat down, not saying a word.

"Perhaps we could begin with a word of prayer," I began. "Brother Kerry, would you like to offer a prayer for us?"

"Sure, Bishop," Michael responded.

For several moments, he did not speak. I waited, knowing that when we are wrestling with a problem, we must wait for the Lord to give us the words. Michael's prayer was simple and sincere. He thanked the Lord for his blessings, his family, and Lizzie's friendship. He asked the Lord to endow me with the spirit of understanding and compassion for his problems. He pledged to follow the Lord's counsel in all things. Finally, he begged for forgiveness of his sins and for mercy towards those who have sinned and repented of their wrongdoings. I was impressed by his poignancy and the force of his words. I looked forward to the day when I would submit his mission papers, which I hoped would not be long in coming.

We arose from our knees. Lizzie looked pale and vulnerable.

"So what can I do for you today?" I asked.

I noticed that Michael took one of her hands between his and held it gently in his lap. It was a gesture signifying compassion and protection.

"Bishop, I'm really sorry to be here today. You're not going to be happy with what I'm about to tell you," Michael started.

I have sometimes felt Satan lurking outside the walls of my office, and I felt him now. I prayed for the Lord to protect us.

"Lizzie's pregnant, and I'm the father," Michael said flatly, looking me right in the eye.

There are times as a bishop that I wish for a release from my responsibilities, and this was one of them. I wanted to say – no, no, not you. It can't be you, not Michael Kerry. I was there when they blessed you as a baby. I remember the day you were baptized and gazed up at me with the rapture of heaven in your eyes. I ordained you to pass the sacrament. You were supposed to go on a mission, for heaven's sake. Oh, how thou art fallen, son of the morning!

Then I understood the heavy expression on Michael's father's face as he waited for them in the hallway. Michael's parents already knew.

"We want to get married, and we'd like your blessing," Michael continued. "But I know we've done wrong, and I'll do whatever it takes to make it right with the Lord."

I nodded slowly. I dragged my gaze from Michael to Lizzie.

"What do you have to say for yourself?" I asked. When it came to serious violations of the Lord's commandments, I needed to hear from each individual. No one could speak for another because salvation was a personal matter.

"It's not his fault at all. I take responsibility for what happened."

There was something in her eyes that made me stop and ponder. What was I missing? If they were passionately in love, I didn't see it. This was the kind of couple who'd wait for each other on missions. It was my unfortunate experience in this type of situation to see one party accuse the other, and yet here they were, trying to absolve each other. What did that mean? I needed more time to consider their case, but they needed words of advice right now. prayed that the Lord would not fail me.

"How are you planning to support Lizzie and the baby, Michael?" I asked, directing my attention back to him.

"My dad's agreed to take me on at the shop."

"I see. Are you planning to finish high school?"

"Yes. He'll carry me 'til then, and I'll start part-time. We haven't worked out the details yet, but the ball's in play."

"Where will you live?"

"With my parents," Lizzie interjected.

"Only until we can afford to move into a place of our own," Michael added. "I want to stay in the ward."

He had used "I," so I assumed he hadn't consulted Lizzie about all their future plans.

"Sounds like you've thought it through." I turned to Lizzie. "You OK with all this, Lizzie?"

"Sure." Her tone belied her confidence, but there would be time for them to negotiate. That's what marriage was, an endless series of negotiations, agreements, breaches of contract, and reconciliations. It evolved and changed like a lengthy court case. Sometimes you had to battle upstream and sometimes you just rolled with the flow.

"Marriage should not be taken lightly," I said, selecting my words carefully. If you are absolutely sure this is the right thing for you and you've prayed about it, then I'll support you. But I want to meet with you weekly to talk about your spiritual progress and what you're doing to strengthen your relationship with the Lord."

Finally, I got a rise out of Lizzie. She looked like she was about to spit at me. Even Michael noticed her reaction.

"Do you have a problem with that?" I asked, directing my question at her. Her reaction was hardly a surprise. The rebellious do not take rebukes meekly.

Her answer surprised me. It gave me hope for them. "I'll do whatever it takes, even if I don't like it."

At least she was being honest, which was more than I could expect from some of our youth.

"We're not here to like it," Michael interposed. "We're here to repent and be counseled. Lizzie's really worried that her parents are going to be super mad about this. I just gave my parents the biggest disappointment of their lives, but they're taking it in stride. I know I can never make it up to them, but I'll try to be a good father to their grandchild."

I knew then what I could do to help them. "Would you like me to be there when you talk to your parents, Lizzie?"

It was the first time she'd stopped looking like a deer caught in the headlights since they'd entered my office. "Bishop, that would be wonderful."

"My secretary will set up an appointment for Tuesday evening." That was my night for evening counseling appointments. "And I'd like to see the two of you, together, next Sunday before church. You may not take the sacrament, say public prayers, or hold a calling until this matter has been resolved with the Lord. And I don't suppose I need to tell you that whatever physical relationship has existed between you must stop, if it hasn't already."

"We've taken care of that, Bishop," Michael reassured me.

I didn't think they would be here if they hadn't ceased the error of their ways. I still couldn't fathom Michael. He just didn't seem the type to take a girl down the wrong road and get her pregnant. Lizzie, on the other hand, might be looking for the approval she hadn't found at home. Seeing them, sitting there with such earnest faces and interlaced fingers, made me feel old. It was getting harder for me to remember what it had felt like to be eighteen and in lust. When I was tempted, I'd devoted myself to intense scripture study and prayer, praying to the Lord to forgive my weakness and strengthen me against temptation. If I did these things, He had promised me, "Ye may not be tempted above that which ye can bear." Sure, I'd had opportunities before marriage, but I hadn't crossed the line. I had been saving myself for that special someone who would be my wife. I hadn't regretted that decision for a moment. It was on days like this one that the Lord affirmed I'd made the right choices as a young man. But how could I counsel those who had made less wise choices?

We closed with a prayer, offered by Lizzie at my invitation. Patrick Kerry hugged his son when they came out, and then hugged Lizzie too. I was glad to see she was going to be getting support from somewhere. She was going to need it.

Tuesday came all too quickly. Derek Sherringdon and his wife Sally were early. I was hoping Michael Kerry wasn't going to keep them waiting because Derek was a stickler for punctuality. I guess it had something to do with being a lawyer. Based on his tithing checks, Derek was a wealthy man, a corporate tax attorney who found lucrative tax shelters for his clients. He would have done better to have devoted his time to sheltering his daughter from the evils of the world. As well as I knew Lizzie, who'd moved into the ward when she was three before Derek's meteoric rise in the corporate legal world, I couldn't imagine her instigating the events that had led to her pregnancy. But then, I couldn't imagine Michael as the perpetrator.

I had been turning my head around the knot of their involvement and I still couldn't unravel it. Though none of those present knew it, I had opened my fast at sunrise with a prayer. My wife Becky was worried that I didn't grab my sack lunch on the way out, but I told her there was an important spiritual matter about which I needed an answer, and I was determined to do everything in my power to learn the Lord's will. At lunchtime, I'd closed the door to my office and knelt in prayer again.

"Brother Sherringdon, thanks for coming out," I said warmly, as I walked out of the bishop's office and into the hallway.

I shook his hand, his wife Sally's, and finally Lizzie's. "We're still waiting for one other person to arrive," I went on.

I hadn't told them Michael Kerry would be present. At that moment, he flew in through the door.

"Hi, Bishop, hope I'm not late," Michael said. I shook hands with him and directed them all into my office. Lizzie sat next to Sally who was next to Derek, and Michael was on the opposite end so that Lizzie's parents were sitting between them. Derek threw a suspicious look at Michael as if to ask why he was here, but Derek was savvy enough to know that I would provide a full explanation at the appropriate time.

As usual, I began the meeting with a prayer, asking Derek to offer it. I paused for a few seconds to study Derek and Sally's expectant faces. Derek was a handsome man with a fine head of grizzled hair, a square jaw, and shoulders like a quarterback. He was thickening at the middle, no doubt as a result of power lunches with his clients, but his custom-tailored dark blue suit and crisp white shirt minimized the weight gain. He looked as if he'd arrived directly from the office. His wife matched him for attention to detail. She had a doll's face framed by huge swathes of gently waved dark hair that fell over her shoulders. Her lips were daubed with some variety of red lipstick. The striking nature of her green eyes kind of popped with the black eyeliner and carefully manicured eyebrows. She wore a dark blue suit that was obviously expensive and a lace blouse.

They had no idea what was coming. Lizzie looked positively terrified and Michael was averting his eyes from all of us, waiting for the bombshell to hit.

"I've asked you here tonight to discuss a spiritual matter concerning Lizzie and Michael," I said. I couldn't mince my words with this one, but I spoke deliberately so they would not misinterpret me. "Lizzie is pregnant, and Michael is the father of her baby."

"You can't be serious! She wouldn't do a thing like this to us," cried out Sally. Then, turning to Lizzie, she added, "Tell me it isn't true, Lizzie."

"I am, Mom. I'm quite sure," Lizzie said, not looking up.

"What will all our friends think? They'll blame it on bad parenting," Sally whined.

I could see this was going to be a long night for Lizzie and Michael.

"You mean to tell me you've gotten our daughter pregnant?" demanded Derek, grabbing Michael's arm. Michael winced from the force of Derek's anger-enhanced grip. Michael raised his head to look Derek squarely in the eyes, and I saw him momentarily flinch under Derek's unrelenting gaze, which he quickly replaced with his resolute stare. I bet Derek Sherringdon was formidable in a courtroom. I wouldn't want to be on the wrong side of the bench when he was arguing a case.

"Yes, sir, it's my fault," Michael said flatly, looking him straight in the eyes.

"What were you thinking?" yelled Derek.

"I wasn't, sir – that should be quite obvious," Michael replied with a stern and resolute tone of voice that he must have been practicing.

"Folks," I quickly interrupted, "we're not here to argue, we're here to talk. I am representing the Lord in regard to Michael and Lizzie's repentance. You will recall that 'the Lord will forgive whom He will forgive, but men must forgive all.' Jesus's Atonement provides a way for Michael and Lizzie to receive mercy from Heavenly Father. Right now, Michael, I'd like you to explain what you and Lizzie are proposing."

Derek released Michael's arm and all eyes turned to Michael.

"Lizzie and I would like to get married as soon as possible, but since she's not yet eighteen, we'd need your permission on the marriage certificate."

Michael must have been doing his research over the last two days, carefully practicing what he needed to say. He seemed more assured today, as if he'd had time to get used to the notion of a shotgun wedding.

"We'd like to get married right after school's out in December," he went on.

"That gives me barely six weeks to plan a wedding! How am I possibly going to manage that?" rejoined Sally. I tried to conceal my annoyance.

"We haven't decided there will be a wedding yet, dear," jumped in Derek.

I began to think it not so surprising that Lizzie was pregnant, given her mother's preoccupation with worldly concerns and her father's indifference to her feelings. Neither of them had expressed the appropriate parental concern over her physical or spiritual well-being.

"I think what Michael is trying to say, Brother Sherringdon, is that they would like to get married before Lizzie is showing. That would shush the gossip, and give them time to work on their relationship before the baby comes. There's no need for the ward to know Lizzie's expecting now. I'm quite sure it won't escape the notice of our Relief Society sisters in a few months, but if she and Michael are married by then, it will be less traumatic for both of them."

"It ought to be painful for both of them," interjected Derek. "Their sins should be flaunted as an example of the consequences of unrighteousness."

"Derek, I really think that's unnecessary," begged his wife.

"I hardly believe that would serve any worthy purpose, Brother," I enjoined. "I am quite sure they are suffering enough remorse already. I suppose you do understand that if Michael marries Lizzie, he will be expected to support her and the baby. That means getting a job as soon as he's out of high school. No mission, no college. I think he's sacrificing enough."

"It will never make up for what he's done to my daughter," grunted Derek.

"Let he who is without sin cast the first stone," I said simply. "I ask you to look into your hearts, Sister and Brother Sherringdon, and see if forgiveness may be possible, in time. Lizzie and Michael have taken the first steps on the road of repentance:

they have acknowledged their sins, they have confessed to the appropriate authority, and they are going to suffer the consequences of their actions. I am going to meet with them weekly to set spiritual goals and offer them guidance."

"Dad, I was stupid, and I know it. It's a lot to ask, but I want to know if Michael and I can move in with you and Mom after we get married," interjected Lizzie.

"I haven't said I'll agree to let you marry him yet, young lady, so don't jump the gun." Derek Sherringdon pursed his lips. Again I saw the persona of Derek Sherringdon the lawyer, and it intimidated me.

To Michael he said, "Michael – I hate to be tough about this, but moving into my home is not in the cards. You marry Lizzie, you'll have to support her. Our medical insurance will be in effect until she graduates high school. She can keep her Nissan and I'll cover her auto insurance – which I've been doing already – until she's out of high school. Aside from that, you've made your bed, you'll have to lie in it. I'll give my permission for you to marry not because I think you two have the least chance of success, but because we want our grandchild to have a mother and father. But you may not live in our house. It would be a bad influence for Lindsey."

His eyes were as hard as flint. I didn't think I would get anywhere trying to dissuade him from this course. In time, I hoped he would back down. Grandchildren had a way of softening the sins of their parents.

"But where are we going to live, Dad? Don't you care what happens to me?" pleaded Lizzie. I felt my eyes growing moist. I knew there were many callings and tasks I could persuade Brother Sherringdon to take on, but I didn't think accepting the young man who got his daughter pregnant into his home was one of them. I knew the Sherringdon's had space, but that house would be as close as a ship's galley with Michael and Derek in it. The Spirit touched me, and I realized Michael and Lizzie would have a better chance if they temporarily moved in with Michael's parents. The Kerry's were bursting at the seams, but they were overflowing with love and that's what Michael and Lizzie needed most.

"Lizzie, I'll come up with something else, don't worry," said Michael gently. I could see she wasn't convinced.

"Then are we agreed that you'll give your permission for Lizzie to marry Michael?" I said, in an effort to redirect the subject. I turned my attention to Derek Sherringdon.

"I'm not happy about it, but, yes, you have it," he acquiesced.

"I want all of you – that goes for Michael and Lizzie too – to keep this matter confidential. You are not to discuss this with anyone but Michael's parents, and myself. Is everyone clear on that?" There were nods and murmured assent all around. "I'll not have this ward become a rumor mill. We have been counseled to avoid gossip, speculation and idle chatter. I expect you to adhere to the Lord's admonition."

"I'll follow your lead, Bishop," said Derek Sherringdon. And if I hadn't been his bishop, I doubted he would have. There were some advantages to being in a position of authority, if one exercised that authority with discretion.

"I guess that means you have a wedding to plan, Sister Sherringdon," I said to Derek's wife. She smiled at me ruefully.

"Mom, let's not do the wedding thing right now, OK?" Lizzie pleaded. "Michael and I need to talk first. We'll get back to you."

"Folks, I think we should close with a prayer. I'm going to ask Lizzie to offer it."

Lizzie flashed anger briefly, but her emotion disappeared as quickly as a storm on a summer day. I can't remember what she said, only that the words were abject and monotone.

As they stood up to leave, Michael crossed over to where Lizzie stood and took her hand.

"Hope you don't mind, Brother Sherringdon," he addressed his future father-in-law who'd just denied him practically all financial support after Lizzie and he married, "but Lizzie and I are going to my house to chat."

"It better not be anything else," warned Derek.

"There's no need to get paranoid," I interjected. "I don't think these kids are going to get into more trouble than they are already in. They need to spend some time talking and working out their future."

"They've gotten in enough trouble already," retorted Derek. "You, young lady," he directed at Lizzie, "had better learn to straighten up and fly right."

"Yes, Dad," she responded meekly, dropping her head to contemplate her toes like a lily drooping in a vase of flowers.

"I'll be watching, you can rely on it!" he added with unnecessary emphasis.

Despite Derek Sherringdon's lack of trust in his daughter and future son-in-law, there was no doubt in my mind that Michael and Lizzie were going to keep their end of the bargain. If my faith in them was unfounded, then I shouldn't be a bishop.

"Brother Sherringdon, we're all entitled to second chances. That's what Jesus taught us. I'm giving them the benefit of the doubt." Then I turned to Michael. "Your parents are home, right?"

"Of course, Bishop."

"Then get Lizzie home at a decent hour. She needs her sleep."

"My Mom will drive her home. Sound all right to you, Mr. Sherringdon?"

Derek Sherringdon reluctantly acquiesced. He took his wife by the arm and headed out for his car. I could hear her complaining about such short notice to arrange her daughter's wedding, and how in the world were they going to get the dress made and the invitations out in time? I wouldn't want to be in their bedroom tonight.

"Drive safe, Michael," I said, patting him on the back. "It'll all work out. Just be patient."

My words didn't seem to fortify him.

"Bye," said Lizzie, shaking my hand. She looked so young and vulnerable. She was the same age as my son. I couldn't imagine him being a father. She smiled up at me like a puppy dog.

"I really appreciate what you did for us in there, Bishop."

"Anytime, Lizzie," I responded warmly. I hoped a repeat performance of this didn't happen again next week. I didn't think I could do this more than once in a decade.

Michael and Lizzie headed out the door, hand in hand, and I had a fleeting mental image of Becky and me, in our early twenties, going out to a dance for young adults. It was good to be young and foolhardy, even if you were marked with the stain of sin.

Making Plans

Lizzie

"So where are we gonna live?" I demanded of Michael. It was most annoying that he wouldn't look at me to answer my question. He was still holding my hand and I withdrew it.

"Give me time to think, all right?" he said, stepping ahead of me to open the door to the outside. I walked through, my heels clicking smartly on the concrete, and headed toward the car without speaking. The cold air bit into my lungs and I drew my scarf more tightly around my neck. By some amazing feat of persuasion, Michael had finagled his father into loaning him the family car.

It was a "Mormon-mobile," AKA a Chevy Suburban, and it looked older than Patrick Kerry. It wasn't locked – no one would want to steal the decrepit monster – so I swung open the passenger door myself and hauled myself up into the front seat. There were no running boards to aid getting in, so it felt like I was pulling myself over a ledge. The inside was even less promising than the exterior – everything you would expect from the Kerry family: clean and orderly, albeit dated and worn.

Michael turned the ignition key and the engine grunted to life. He seemed to let it idle for a long time while I stared out at the lights in the parking lot.

"Lizzie, I was thinking we should ask my parents if we can move in until I finish high school," he began tentatively. He sounded like he was asking his parents if he could stay out until one am, just this once. He backed out of the parking space and turned onto the quiet streets in the direction of his house.

"You are kidding, aren't you?" I replied, digging my hands into my pockets. "I'm not moving into that dump."

He gave me a furious glare, jerked the wheel, and pulled over to the curb, barely missing two parked cars. Perhaps I should rethink my positive appraisal of his driving skills.

"Don't you ever – I mean, EVER – talk about my family like that again. Do you want me to make it any clearer or should I cut your tongue out right now?"

I had to admit, Michael did have a testy side to him. "Don't take it so serious."

"I'd rather live in the darkest, most miserable cave in the universe than move in with your parents, but I would have done it to make you happy. And I would have never said one word about how I felt, to spare your feelings. My home may not be fancy like yours, but it's got what we need. I'm in charge of us now. So listen up."

"You sound like my father," I said sullenly. Michael was in the driver's seat, both physically and metaphorically, and I didn't like it one bit.

"Stop sulking, Lizzie. We're going to ask my parents if we can stay with them until after the baby comes, because I'm going to have to finish high school and work part-time at Dad's shop while I'm doing it. I can't afford to put us into even the crummiest apartment while we're both at high school. I checked around. Bite your tongue and let me handle this. If we're really lucky, my parents will agree and we'll have a place to stay."

"Where am I gonna sleep?" I asked. They only had four bedrooms – and Edward's bedroom hardly qualified.

"Are you dumb or what, Lizzie? Did you lose your brain after getting pregnant?"

"No, just my charm," I snapped back.

"We'll be married. We'll sleep in my room."

Oh my freaking goodness, I thought, let's not go there. Why hadn't I considered this facet of my future relationship with Michael until just now?

"Where am I gonna put my clothes?"

"Don't worry about your damn clothes. You won't fit in any of them very much longer."

I slammed my hand on the dash. I hadn't thought about not fitting into my clothes, either. There were aspects of my situation that just didn't bear examination and I had no desire to confront them.

"I wanna go home," I whined.

"Sorry, Lizzie, you got me into this, and we're not turning back now. We're going over to my parents and we're gonna act real humble and ask them if they'll take in another mouth to feed."

"Two," I interrupted, just to mess with him.

"One-and-a-half," he conceded, and I saw the faint outline of a smile.

"I hate this," I said.

"So do I."

I didn't have a clue how hard it was going to be.

When we pulled up at Michael's house, the wind had come up and was whipping amongst the trees. I wanted to lash out like the wind, but the stern set of Michael's face told me I'd better keep my mouth shut. He opened the door for me unceremoniously and I stepped out, avoiding his eyes. I strode up to the doorway ahead of him and stepped aside to let him open the front door for me. I think he liked doing it because it put him in control.

"I'm home," he yelled over my shoulder as we entered the maelstrom of the living room. This time the whole family was present. Edward and Alison were in pajamas, and Rachel and Sarah were scrunched up on the couch watching TV.

"Hi, Lizzie," called out Anne Kerry. "How're you doing?"

"Fair to middling."

"How'd it go?" asked Patrick Kerry from the kitchen table where he was poring over some kind of paperwork. He was probably scrutinizing invoices and work orders from his shop, which seemed to be an almost nightly ritual.

"Better than expected," said Michael. "Bishop Dalton was a help."

"Come sit down, Lizzie. You look all in," said Anne Kerry. That's because I am, I thought. I guess we weren't going to congregate in Michael's room this time. I sat down in silence at the table opposite Patrick Kerry, and the glum look on my face must have helped them realize we had some more bad news. Anne Kerry pulled up a chair next to her husband while Michael sat next to me and took my hand again. That was something I was going to have to get used to.

Anne Kerry joined us. "So, what's the scoop?"

"Lizzie's father won't take us in," Michael began. Fortunately Michael's siblings were paying no attention to us, oblivious of the extra person who was about to attach herself to the household, not counting the baby, of course.

Patrick Kerry scratched his chin. It was disconcerting that my future father-in-law could read ahead. "And you want to move in with us."

"That's the long and short of it," said Michael.

"Your Dad pretty mad, Lizzie?" Patrick Kerry asked me.

"Yeah, so what's new?" I said. I was tired of covering up for my father's totalitarianism.

"I reckon I could save up enough for a place by late summer, soon as I'm at the shop full-time," Michael said.

I didn't share his optimism. We were going to be stuck in this dump with a newborn baby and no money. Neither of us was going to college. I was going to be married to an auto mechanic who hated what he was doing, was supporting a child that wasn't his, had in-laws that despised him for the damage he'd inflicted on their daughter, and had a wife who might be, no, absolutely was, still in love with the child's father. I couldn't go there. Our prospects were as dismal as a coffin.

"We're a pretty tight ship, already," interjected Anne Kerry. "We're going to be on top of one another." What we were going to be, I thought, was stacked up like the Old Woman and her children in the Shoe.

"We've got my room," said Michael.

"Your parents intending to give you any financial support?" Patrick Kerry, ever the pragmatist, asked.

"They're expecting Michael to handle that, once we're married, except for medical expenses," I responded. I ought to have scheduled a doctor appointment by now, but the thought of it just made me more miserable.

Patrick Kerry nodded his head gravely. "I think we can cover the cost of food – that is, if Michael will provide whatever else you need – school stuff, clothes..."

He was interrupted by Alison, who clambered up onto Anne's knee and gazed around the table at us, examining each face in turn. "Why does everyone look so serious, Mom?"

"We're not, sweetheart," Anne Kerry said quickly. "We're just sorting out a little problem. Nothing to worry about. Why don't you go up to your room and bring down a book for your bedtime story?"

Maybe a little problem for, you, Anne Kerry, but a big problem for me. Big enough to keep me up all night fretting. Alison hopped down off her mother's lap and trounced upstairs. I wished I were five years old and as innocent as Alison.

"Lizzie, we may not have a fancy place like your family, but we'll make sure you don't go hungry." Patrick Kerry was trying to sound reassuring. "I'd like you to come for Family Home Evening next week and give us a lesson on the Atonement. Think you can manage that?"

I stared at him, numb with disbelief. I was not even living here yet and they were already sucking me into their lives. Like an automaton, I said, "Sure, I can."

"We want you to feel like part of the family," added Anne Kerry.

I spent enough time here already that I was practically a fixture, I thought.

"We'll use the occasion to tell the kids what's going on, and that you'll be staying here soon," said Patrick Kerry. He had it all figured out, didn't he? "We like to let everyone have their say at Family Home Evening. If anyone's got issues, we sort them out then. Sound like a plan?"

Issues, I thought. I had lots of issues, but I definitely wasn't going to share them with anyone, least of all my family-to-be.

"Yes, it's a plan," I said wearily. Then, feeling that I should somehow express the undying gratitude I didn't feel, I added, "You've been very kind to me in spite of what I've done, and I appreciate it."

"You're most welcome, Lizzie," Patrick Kerry responded.

"Dad, I want to talk to Lizzie up in my room before she leaves. Just five minutes, OK?" asked Michael. Patrick Kerry nodded his assent. I stared at Michael with raised eyebrows, trying to imagine what he wanted with me. He took my hand and we walked up the stairs together. After closing his bedroom door behind us, he put his arm around me. I would have liked to back off, but I was up against the door. I wasn't used to being this up-close-and-personal with Michael, but since I was going to be his wife shortly, I thought I'd better get used to it.

"Before you go home, I just want to make sure you're OK with this." His words brushed past my ear, making the hair on my neck stand up.

"Yeah, of course." Like what other choice did I have? I thought.

He took a step back, giving me room to breathe. "Now tell me what you really think."

"As long as it isn't a prison or a Nazi death camp, I can get used to anything."

"Why don't you just say what you mean?"

"Your parents are decent, God-fearing people. Your mother would give me her last piece of bread if it came down to it. Your father would probably fight to the death to protect me. I don't deserve to be treated this well. So I'll handle it. I don't know how, but I will."

"Don't ever let on, for my sake. It would break their hearts, as if it hasn't already. That's our agreement, OK? We're madly in love and you're thrilled to be moving in here after we get married."

I wondered if I should take up acting. Sure seemed like I was going to need the skills. I looked around his room, realizing that I would be sharing it with him in less than six weeks. It must have dawned on him what I was thinking. He stepped in close and pinned my left shoulder gently against the door with his right hand. He smelled of Zest soap and chamomile shampoo.

"Oh, my precious pearl," he whispered, and kissed me swiftly and lightly on the lips. I felt a rush of blood in my veins. His kiss was so unexpected and so startling. I realized I'd drawn in my breath and my mouth was gaping the way it would if I got an unexpectedly bad grade on a test.

"I should not have done that," stammered Michael, stepping back.

"It's your prerogative," I said wryly. "I am your fiancée."

My lips were still burning. Pregnancy hormones, stress, I told myself. This was not acting.

"So, umm… Chemistry homework on the usual day?" he queried. There was a soft flush of pink on his face like the blush before dawn and he was blinking rapidly behind his glasses.

"Yeah, right, Thursday. We can talk about arrangements for the wedding." Just the wedding, I told myself, I won't think about the wedding night.

"I'll be seeing you, then."

He turned away from me, went over to his desk, settled his gangly frame into the chair, and began shuffling papers on his desk. I stared at the back of his neck where light brown hairs were pricking up out of the skin. I wanted to say something like "thank you" or "I love you" but I was neither grateful for what was happening to me nor in love with him. But I did wish I could tell him that on some level I appreciated what he was doing for me.

"It's all good, isn't it?" I said. His head shot around in my direction with a look as intent as a knife blade to the throat in a mugging. He stared at me as if he were waiting for something, and it felt as if he were shredding my clothes in preparation for a meticulous dissection of my innards.

"Good?" he asked, with a slight tweak of his head.

"What I mean is... Oh, hell, I don't know what I mean," I stuttered. Then I grabbed the door handle, flung open the door and fled down the stairs, not daring to look back at my fiancé. All the way home in the Suburban with Anne Kerry behind the wheel, I couldn't stop thinking about being backed up against the door face to face with him and the sudden brush of his lips against mine, like the brief flirtation of a spring breeze against the down-drooping globe of a daffodil. My feet were lighter as I stepped out of the intrepid vehicle onto the driveway and waved good-bye to Anne Kerry, but I couldn't for the life of me fathom why.

The Pearls

Michael Kerry

My "most precious pearl," my *Pearl of Great Price*, is now my fiancée. I hardly can believe it. I've been calling her my "precious pearl" in my head and heart for several years. It all started when my mother gave me the pearls her mother gave to her just before her wedding day, like her mother before her. She, my great-grandmother, received them just before her wedding day from my great-grandfather.

As the story goes, my great-grandfather was called to go on a Church Mission to northern Japan in 1919. He stayed there for three years, and baptized an entire family of pearl farmers, who made their living harvesting Akoya pearls. To show their gratification, they gave him a strand of thirty-eight of their most precious, saltwater, natural Akoya pearls, pink-colored with rosé luster. There was one pearl for each person baptized in the family. The value of that strand of pearls was incalculable at the time, but after my grandmother gave it to my mother, she had the strand appraised at just under $112,000.

I had spent years telling Mom how I felt about Lizzie. One day, when I hit my teens, the changes in my own body caused changes in my feelings for my precious pearl. Mom picked up on those changes and tried to keep me from getting my hopes up too much. I knew my chances of marrying Lizzie were small, but if I could keep showing her that I was a good member of the Church, then maybe—just maybe—when I returned from my mission, she would want to marry me.

My grandmother died when I started high school, so my mother took the strand of pearls and the treasure box she kept them in and gave them to me for my "eventual wife." She was trying to prepare me for finding someone else besides Lizzie, but it didn't work. From that moment until this week, I called Lizzie "my precious pearl" in my head. I started say it out loud after Lizzie accepted my offer to marry her and keep her from facing her illegitimate pregnancy alone.

When she starts to sound like she is happy about the marriage, I will present her with the pearls. Until then, they stay well hidden in my footlocker.

Preparations for a wedding

Lizzie

On Wednesday, I was clearing up the dinner dishes with Lindsey when my mother asked to speak to me 'in the study' when we were done. I knew that meant she wanted a private conversation with me away from Dad and Lindsey.

"Bet you're in trouble, Lizzie," Lindsey spoke up mischievously, loading the glasses into the dishwasher. She smirked at me with the same tweak of the lips as my father. She had his steel-blue eyes and square jaw, a head of dark wavy hair much like my own, and some day she would be called attractive. But she would never, ever, have my allure. That came from my mother.

"You keep your mouth shut, you're the trouble," I said.

When we were finished with the dishes, I straightened the chairs around the table, shook out our hand-embroidered tablecloth, and replaced it with a clean one. Everything had better be immaculate for my father at breakfast time.

"I'm ready, Mom," I called. She had already gone into the room we called the study to wait for me. It would have been more properly called our home office, because one of our four computers was housed there, on a replica of an antique mahogany desk with all the trappings necessary to accommodate a modern computer and its accoutrements.

This was not Dad's office; it was the home office, and we called it the study to minimize confusion. This was the place where Lindsay, my mother and I would use the computer. It was also where Dad did work associated with his church calling in the Elder's Quorum and the "real work" he brought home from the office.

Mom also used the study for her own projects. In reality, this would have been a fourth bedroom for the third child who never came. Lindsey and I both had personal Apple computers with printers and this new software for composing documents. We were probably the first teenagers in the ward to get computers. Dad had spent several hours with a senior computer consultant from his law office setting up our systems and making sure we had access to educational data that you could buy on disk. Lousy investment that turned out to be, I thought, since the prospects for me attending college were about as likely as a reunion with Jason.

I wondered what my mother wanted with me. I soon found out. "Lizzie, I think we should talk about the wedding arrangements," she said as soon as we were ensconced in the two wing armchairs in the study. I had a brief, emotionally flustering flashback to Jason sprawled in the chair where my mother was sitting, not more than a month ago, with a lazy insouciant smile playing about his lips, and I went weak at the knees. I forced myself to focus my mind on the present so that my mother could tell me what she was planning. I was sure she had it figured out to every last inconsequential detail. Mom was mostly show and no substance, so this wedding would be right up her alley.

"Have you decided on your colors?" she asked. Funeral black would be appropriate, I thought.

"My colors?" I asked vaguely. I found myself tumbling into the wild blue of Jason's eyes, a mess of intertwined arms and legs splayed across the light gold rug, pooled in sunlight.

"You need to choose two colors, sweetheart. The bridesmaids will be in one of them; the other is to offset the first color. The bridegroom's vest should match the bridesmaids' color."

I hadn't given a single thought to bridesmaids, let alone the color of their stupid dresses. I felt like I'd been assigned a term paper on a topic about which I knew nothing.

"Who's paying for this, Mom?" I began. I was picking up some of my future father-in-law's pragmatism.

"Lizzie, the bride's family always pays for the wedding. You don't expect Michael's family will contribute, do you?"

"I guess Michael's sperm is enough, isn't it?" I retorted.

She glared at me. "Lizzie, I'm not going to take that kind of nonsense from you. You pay attention, d'you understand?"

"So what do you suggest, Mom?" I asked with a weary toss of my head, because doubtless she already had a master plan as elegant as Einstein's derivation of $E=mc2$ and I didn't really care. It wasn't like the wedding day was going to be the culmination of my life's ambition.

"It's close to Christmas, and they'll be lots of burgundy in the stores. I thought you might like burgundy and pink. Then even if the bridesmaids are overweight, it won't stand out too badly in your photos."

"None of my friends are fat," I stated pointedly, knowing she'd overlooked the obvious. "Unless there's someone else you want in the lineup?"

Mom always had hidden agendas. I was waiting to find out who she was proposing for a bridesmaid and she hadn't spat it out yet.

"Whom do you want, dear?" Mom went on, not missing a beat.

"Janine and Shannon... and Michael's sisters." I couldn't believe I proposed Rachel and Sarah, but there it was. Perhaps I did it just to spite Mom.

"I thought we might invite your cousin, Celia." Now Cousin Celia made you want to redefine obese. She was a cousin on my mother's side via her unfortunate sister, and Celia had never gone on a date in her life. My mother was probably doing this to give the poor girl a chance because girls always looked more attractive at weddings, even without the champagne.

"That's a bad idea. We hardly know her," I responded.

"We hardly know Rachel and Sarah," my mother replied coolly.

"You want burgundy, Mom, that's fine. But no Celia. It'll be Janine, Shannon, Rachel and Sarah – that's it." I rarely stood my ground against my parents, but this was a time for kicking up my heels. To my surprise, she conceded.

"All right. Just those four in burgundy and pink," she said.

"Not pink. Burgundy and white."

"White?" She acted as if she'd seen a rat in the family dining room during an elegant dinner.

"It is a color, Mom," I retorted.

"The bride wears white. You can't have it as the second color at a wedding, Lizzie."

"I'll be wearing it, so what's the big deal? We'll have arrangements of burgundy and white roses on the tables with white table cloths and burgundy napkins. It will all look very chic and stylish." Burgundy to represent the stain of sin, and white to represent the pure in heart, I thought. Burgundy for me, white for Michael.

"So do you intend for Michael to be wearing a white tux and burgundy vest?" she asked. I couldn't envision Michael dressed in a white suit, let alone a burgundy tux. It was enough to make me puke.

"How about a black tux and a white vest?" I suggested. "A classic look."

She smiled at me, so at least we'd made progress. I had my bridesmaids selected along with the bridegroom's outfit. The problem was that I now had to supply bridesmaids' dresses for four girls and that was going to cost a fortune. I wondered who Michael was going to choose for his best man.

"What about your dress?" my mother asked. I wondered how much Dad was going to be willing to shell out for a bridal gown. I thought we'd better talk to him first. I was sure Mom could get away with the decorations because Relief Society had lots of stuff stashed in cupboards around the building, but a wedding dress was going to be a big investment. Given my father's gloomy view of my upcoming nuptials, I doubted he'd be enthused about forking out money to satisfy my personal whims, but it was worth a shot.

"We'd better talk to Dad first," I suggested. "Let's move on to the invitations. Burgundy on white?"

"Nice, dear, classy," she responded. "They should go out as soon as possible. I'll put together the invitation list for the bride's side. You need to get names from Michael's side this week. Can you do that? Then you and Michael need to draft the text so I can take everything down to Kinkos."

It was so nice to know my mother had her act together as far as wedding planning went, especially as we didn't yet have the date. I guess I would have to figure that out with Michael tomorrow while we were doing our chemistry homework. Now we just had to tackle Dad about my dress.

"Can you find Dad, and we'll figure out my dress?" I asked.

She swept out of the room, looking happier than she had yesterday evening in the bishop's office, and I heard their footsteps returning up the stairs. The door swung open.

"So, Lizzie, you're really going to do this, huh?" he said as he came in.

"Yup," I replied, folding my arms across my chest and trying to convey the confidence I did not feel.

"We need to talk to you about Lizzie's dress," interjected my mother. Dad knew what was coming. He didn't bother to give her time to say anymore.

"And you want to know how much I'm going to fork out for it, don't you?"

"That's the crux of it, yes," I added. I looked up at him and gave him my most demure and sweet smile, but it wasn't sweet enough.

"You understand the meaning of the word 'nada,' I take it," he responded dryly.

"Totally, Dad," I said. I bit my lip and drew my knees up to my chin. I hoped I was not going to cry in front of my father because there was a lump building in my throat and the sight of tears was sure to send him off into a tirade.

"You've made your choices, young lady – you live with them. I told you I would sign your marriage certificate and take care of your medical and auto insurance, but that's where my support ends. It's your dress, you make it. Isn't Sally Kerry something of a seamstress?" Then he turned on his heel and marched out. I had heard he was a bear in the courtroom, and today I believed it. I looked up at Mom and she shivered.

"That didn't go very well, did it?" she said.

"I'll figure something out," I replied, with a confidence I didn't feel, because I had not the faintest clue how I was going to sew my own wedding dress. My mother couldn't sew a stitch, though she was great at nails, hair, and makeup. I guess that those skills would be useful too, what with getting four bridesmaids and me ready in one day. But no matter how prepared everyone else was, there was no way I was ever going to be ready for what was to happen on my wedding day.

———— ·•✦✦✦•· ————

Thursday came quickly. My mother was downstairs working on a flower arrangement for the wedding when I told her I was going over to Michael's as usual to do chemistry homework. For Lindsey's benefit, I didn't mention the wedding. Mom, Dad and I had decided to break the news to her on Sunday after we got home from church.

"How late will you be coming home from Michael's?" she asked.

"Like normal, Mom, about nine," I responded gruffly.

"Then drive careful and we'll see you about nine, sweetie."

I flounced out the door and shot my car out the driveway. I could imitate Jason, too, I thought. I was filled with a sudden recklessness as I navigated the streets to the Kerry's in my ailing vehicle. I whipped around turns and blatantly ignored the speed limits. I rolled down the window and let the wind tear through my hair. Autumn leaves scuffed across the windshield and a ground squirrel skittered away from my tires. I was going to make Jason regret throwing me away like a takeout container when he'd done with me. I was going to look so good on my wedding day that he was going to want to eat me up along with the wedding cake. I was going to show Jason what he was missing and I was going to make him burn and burn and burn with wanting me. He was going to know what it was like to be filled with a desire so terrible and cavernous that it yawned up at me from my pillow in the night, soared and moaned through my dreams, and found me prostrate at its feet in the grey light of dawn.

The flapping of my car's loose belt, which Michael had pointed out to me earlier in the week, brought me back to more immediate concerns. I reminded myself to ask him to fix it as I arrived at my destination. The Kerrys' house looked squat, quiet, and in need of a fresh coat of exterior paint, preferably in some shade other than mud brown. The lawn was neatly trimmed, but there were virtually no shrubs adorning the flower beds. The Kerrys really needed to invest some money in home maintenance and landscaping instead of children, I thought. But, really, what did I know?

The ancient Suburban was parked in the driveway and I pulled in behind it. I suspected no one would be going anywhere tonight. It wasn't a night for Mutual or Scouts, and I doubted Alison was in ballet class, though she'd probably like to be. I was later to realize my inspiration about Alison was one of my first experiences with the Holy Ghost.

I walked up to the door lugging my backpack on my shoulder, and Michael flung it open before I had a chance to ring the bell. I guess he must have been watching for me. This was another aspect of the new Michael I would have to get used to – the new Michael I wasn't in love with but was planning to marry.

"How was your day?" he asked.

"Better than some, worse than others," I said flippantly. He ought to know – we'd been in chemistry lab together today, though we weren't lab partners. Then he stepped outside and gave me this long bear hug.

"I missed you."

I couldn't quite think of an appropriately impudent response for that. Still feeling rash, I said, "Me, too," and the words came out sounding lame rather than sincere.

"Let's go upstairs and work on our assignment," he said, pulling me along behind him.

"Hi, Rachel. Hi, Sarah," I called out to the girls, holding Michael back to observe the tableau. They were sitting at the dining table, doing what looked like homework. I doubted there was space for a desk in their bedroom. I couldn't imagine how two teenage girls could fit in a room together, let alone a baby sister with Barbie dolls, strollers, and dress-up clothes. There was no sign of Patrick or Anne Kerry. He was probably in the garage with Edward. I didn't notice Alison curled up on the couch, watching TV. Rachel and Sarah looked up when I came in and both instantly noticed that Michael was holding my hand. Here we go, I thought.

Rachel, the sixteen-year-old with the dark curly hair and mischievous eyes of her father, said, "So, are you two guys like dating?"

"Yeah, we are, actually," said Michael with a proprietary air. He put his arm around my shoulder and hugged me to him. I felt like I'd been hit with novocaine. "Right, sweetheart?"

"Yes, we are," I affirmed. At least I could still talk.

"That's so sweet," said Sarah. "You guys have been friends forever."

"I'm just here to do homework," I added.

"Bet me," said Rachel. I couldn't believe she was going to be my bridesmaid. I could fix her dress so it split during the first dance, I thought, and that would wipe the glib smile off her face.

"Do Dad and Mom know about this?" asked Sarah. She was the steady one, I decided.

"Of course," I reassured her. "They're totally over the moon about it."

Technically, I figured they'd gone around to the dark side, but what did Rachel and Sarah know?

"Does that mean you'll be coming over more often?" piped up Alison from the couch. That was the last thing I needed. "I like you, Lizzie Sherringdon."

It wouldn't be Sherringdon for long, I thought. "I guess it does."

"She practically lives here, anyway," rejoined Rachel. I hoped Satan would cut her tongue out.

"Let's go, honey," said Michael. He gave me an easy smile and I realized that he must actually be enjoying this. We made our way upstairs like a pair of drunken sailors because he wouldn't leave hold of me.

As soon as we were inside the door which, mercifully, he closed behind us, I disentangled myself from him and said, "No need to overdo it for your family, you know."

He was grinning. "Don't be a stick-in-the mud, Lizzie. You want them to believe us, don't know? In four days we're gonna tell them we're getting married and you're gonna move in after the wedding. We ought to make it look real, huh?"

He could be a son-of-a-bitch when he wanted, I thought. I didn't like him taking advantage of me, especially as Jason had done his fair share of it. Then, trying to change the subject, I said, "I picked the colors for the big day – burgundy and white."

"So?"

"Why don't you just pretend you care? We wanna make it *look real*, right?"

He stared me down. "Lizzie, do anything you want. You want me in a clown suit, fine. What makes you think I even care about that stuff?"

"You're supposed to care – it's our wedding day," I whined. I was wondering why I was making such a big deal of it when I didn't care either.

"Here's the plan," I continued. "I've decided Janine and Shannon and your two sisters will be bridesmaids."

"Rachel and Sarah!" he exclaimed. It was his turn to be taken aback. "That's really sweet of you, Lizzie."

"Seeing as I'm going to be part of your family 'n' all, I thought it best," I said. Actually, I had no clue why I was going to include them as a part of this special ceremony. It just seemed to be the right move. "And will you be OK in a black tux and white vest?"

"Lizzie, I already told you – whatever you want. It doesn't matter."

"It will when you look at our wedding portrait twenty years from now."

This time, he was the one who had a hard time finding the words. "Right, then. Black tux, white vest."

"I need a list of the people you want to invite."

"We need a date first," he interjected. He sat down at his desk, grabbed a pocket calendar off it, and flipped through the calendar to the month of December. I edged towards him for a better look. "First Saturday after school is out. Sound good?"

It didn't sound good at all to me, but I wasn't about to argue. "Sounds great."

"Let's work on the guest list Monday night, with the rest of the family."

"OK, but it better be quick. My mom wants to get the invitations out next week." I was thinking that weddings developed a life of their own, and I already had a tiger by the tail. "Can you talk to your mom before Monday?"

"Sure, Lizzie." He looked nonplussed. "Is that all for now?"

"No!" I exclaimed. "We need to make up the text for the wedding invites."

"Can't you do that?"

"Fine, I'll sit down at your desk right now and do it."

I walked deliberately over to his desk as he moved away to let me sit down. I saw what looked like a journal lying open on the desk.

"Hey, keep your hands off of that!" he said. I had finally found a sensitive spot. He practically swiped me in the head to whip it away from me.

"Secrets, huh?" I teased.

"I'm just telling you, right now, that this is off limits. Got it?"

"If you say so," I replied with a mutinous look.

"I mean it! You promise that you'll never read this unless I give you permission." He had the precious calendar tucked under his arms against his chest and he sounded as serious as my father when I was instructed never to let anyone else drive my Nissan.

"Wanna seal it in blood?" I asked, holding out my hand.

He gave me a withering look. "Just promise."

"I swear it," I replied solemnly. "Satisfied?"

"Do you keep a journal?" he asked, mollified.

"As a matter of fact, I do," I replied. "Isn't that something all church members do?" Keeping journals was as natural to members of the Church of Jesus Christ of Latter-day Saints as making the sign of the cross was to Catholics. If it had not been for faithful "journal keepers" in the ancient Americas, the *Book of Mormon* itself would not have come to light.

"Just wondered," he mused. He turned away and stowed his journal in a bookshelf alongside his bed. While he busied himself stashing his personal secrets, I drafted the public announcement of our marriage.

**Sally and Derek Sherringdon
are delighted to announce the marriage of their daughter,
Elizabeth Dawn Sherringdon to Michael Kerry,
son of Anne and Patrick Kerry
on December 14, 1985 at 1 P.M.**

**The pleasure of your company is requested at
the ceremony and reception immediately
following. R.S.V.P.**

I held it up for Michael to read. "My middle name is John," he said.

I might have known that, back the past, but it had slipped my mind in the pressures of the present.

"I'll add it," I said. It was all lies, I thought, a pack of lies. My parents weren't delighted, they were furious. And I couldn't say I was looking forward to my nuptials either.

"How big is this going to be, anyway?" he asked. Not small enough, I thought.

"Who knows what my mother is going to do? At least Cousin Celia's not going to be a bridesmaid." Michael knew who Cousin Celia was.

"That's a relief. You'd need a tent just for her."

"At least we can cut down on the cost of material for the bridesmaids' dresses," I said suppressing a giggle. Then, trying to sound casual, I added, "Oh, here's the deal. Dad won't pay for my dress, so would you?"

He looked taken aback. "Can't you make a dress? It'll cost more than $300 in the store and you'll only wear it once."

Men could be so callous sometimes. "This is my big day, I want to look good."

"Talk to my mom, maybe she'll help you make it."

"Make my own dress?" I was incredulous.

"What about the four bridesmaids? You're going to have to make their dresses, too, right?"

I stared up at him. I didn't have spare time for this many wedding projects.

"Who's paying for the bridesmaids' dresses?" he asked. "And my tux? It's like $100 to rent an outfit."

I wished I'd started on the chemistry homework first, I thought. At least maybe that math would add up. "All right, so I'm making the dresses. With your mom's help – that's assuming she can fit it into her spare time and assuming I can sew five dresses in five weeks. That's only one dress a week." I hoped my sarcasm wasn't escaping his notice. "If my mom buys the fabric at the sewing store, we can probably slip it by my dad."

"Good plan," he said. Did he mean it was a good plan to sew the dresses or slip the cost of the fabric by my Dad? Oh, hell, why didn't we elope and we wouldn't have to do any of this?

"Don't look so desperate, Lizzie. Everything will work out."

"I am not desperate," I snapped. Michael's eyes widened behind his glasses and I couldn't be sure if he was sympathetic or surprised.

"Get my sisters' dress sizes on Monday night, and you can get started. I'm sure they'll be ecstatic to be a part of our wedding."

It was good to know someone was going to be ecstatic about being a part of it, I thought.

"In case you didn't know, we need to go down to the courthouse with your dad and mom to apply for the marriage license. Let's do it next week."

"You mean we're going to have to skip school?" I asked.

"For a smart girl, Lizzie, you sure act dumb sometimes. Yeah, we gotta all go together."

"That's a party I'm looking forward to."

"Can you please ask your parents what day?"

"If you absolutely insist," I responded churlishly. "Got a preference?"

I realized my brusque attitude wasn't endearing him to me, so I softened.

"Sorry, Michael. I'll do it, all right? By the way, who's gonna be your best man?"

It took him so long to answer, I realized he hadn't even considered it. "Jeremy."

"Jeremy Stein?"

"I only know one 'Jeremy.'"

"He's Jewish."

"I know that, Lizzie. And he's my best friend. Ever heard of missionary opportunities?"

"Since we're such a fine example of upstanding young Latter-day Saints, it's a 'golden contact,' isn't it?"

"Lizzie, stop the sarcasm and stop acting like you're planning your own funeral. It's your *wedding*," he said. He looked so serious that I decided not to answer. "Where's the damn homework, anyway?"

"Don't swear, Michael." I began unpacking my backpack while Michael retrieved some papers from his. Then he slammed them down on his desk right under my nose.

"Here's what I did. Unless you need help on a problem, don't talk to me." I heard him bounce onto his bed.

"That's not how we usually do it."

"It is now," came the speedy rejoinder.

"You know I can't just copy off your answers," I complained, feeling the quick salt of tears behind my eyelids. A couple of them dropped onto the open page of my notebook. I sniffed and wiped my eyes. I didn't want Michael to see me crying because I despised this weakness in myself and I didn't want him to know I found chemistry problems so dauntingly difficult without his help.

"Shut up, Lizzie, I'm studying."

I was hopelessly outmaneuvered and I couldn't conceive any way to bring Michael around, so I began balancing equilibrium equations by myself. The chemistry that Michael and I had shared for most of our lives seemed seriously lacking and I wondered if we were ever going to reach equilibrium.

Two Promises

Lizzie

The following Sunday, Michael and I had our first follow-up meeting with Bishop Dalton. He asked us to pray morning and evening, and read at least one chapter of the *Book of Mormon* every day. That seemed overzealous to me, but I wasn't about to argue with him because he hadn't threatened to excommunicate me and he'd helped me break the happy news to my parents. And I was betting his all-seeing eye would discern if I wasn't following his directions, and I couldn't bear the thought of lying to him. It was OK to conceal the identity of the baby's father, because I didn't see that as coming under the category of lying, exactly – more like disinformation. But when it came to my personal righteousness, I didn't have the gall.

I doubted Michael was having the same challenges as me, because I knew he was doing all this stuff already I must try to think of it as a way to prepare for being married to Michael, I told myself. Because come December 14, the day of infamy, I had better have my act together. I didn't know anyone who could fake sincere religious faith, and since I was marrying Mr. Built-on-a-Firm-Foundation, I had better start setting some cornerstones for myself. At least if I became a disappointment to him, let it not be on grounds of religion, I thought. I could fake the other stuff, couldn't I?

The weekend had been stressful for me. Lindsey had confronted me Saturday afternoon and asked if Michael and I were an item. I could hardly deny it. Sarah had mentioned it to one of her girlfriends who had gossiped to one of her girlfriends and so forth, until the news reached Lindsey.

"Yes, we are, Lindsey," I said.

"I thought you said you wouldn't go out with him unless he was the last guy on earth."

"I changed my mind."

"So that's why you've been mooning around and not telling Mom and Dad where you're going."

"Have not."

"I know you have, but I won't let on."

I wondered what she was planning on blackmailing me with.

"How come you spend so long in the bathroom in the morning?"

Because I'm throwing up, you little sicko, I thought. "That's none of your business, you little snot. You stay out of my room and out of my life, got it?"

"You're so mean to me," Lindsey whimpered. "I always try to be nice to you."

I thought that when she got her heart broken for the first time, then she would see how blissful self-assurance could turn to miserable self-doubt in a single day. Then I went back to my room, got on my knees, and repented for being so nasty to my little sister. Being pregnant was sure making me as prickly as a pear cactus. Or perhaps it was working out all the details for the wedding. I hadn't anticipated it was going to be such a production.

Less than half-an-hour later, Janine called. I guess she'd been hooked into the grapevine too.

"Lizzie, is it for real? You and Michael are dating?"

"Yes, we are." I hoped I sounded more convincing than I felt.

"Why didn't you tell me?"

"It happened fast. I've been swept off my feet."

"No wonder you're acting so strange lately. You look like you're sick or something."

"The homework for math, physics and chem is killing me. I'm short on sleep."

"Sooo," she said suggestively. "Is he keeping you up late?"

"No, he's not. You know my parents," I said, smiling at the magnitude of my deception. It sounded compelling even to me.

"How does he kiss?"

"Janine, why should I tell you?"

"Because you used to tell me everything," she said emphatically. "Now I hear you're going out with Michael Kerry from my little sister – you owe me."

"He's a gentleman, through and through. That do it for you?"

"And what do you mean by that, Lizzie? Hasn't he kissed you yet?"

"Of course he has," I went on bravely.

"So tell me how it is."

"It's fine, absolutely fine."

"That's it?"

Janine was beginning to be exceedingly tiresome, and I wanted to get back to my homework. I was getting way behind on everything having to read my scriptures every day, meet with the bishop before church on Sunday, and compose Family Home Evening lessons, not to mention the extra fifteen minutes spent in the bathroom each morning tossing up my insides.

"He's a wonderful kisser, all right? Enough already. I got stuff to do. 'Bye."

Mollified, she too said good-bye, and hung up. I should have known the gossip wouldn't end there.

Sunday morning had a similarly inauspicious beginning. It started with a row between my parents and me about sitting with Michael in Sacrament. I thought since Michael and I were about to announce our nuptials, we ought to look like we were dating. I told them I could either sit with Michael and them, or sit with him and his parents. I had a pretty good notion it was going to be the latter. There's nothing like woman's intuition.

So, for the first of many Sundays, I found myself squeezed on a bench with the seven members of Michael's family. At least I wouldn't be getting phone calls from any other girlfriends. It was patently obvious to all that Michael and I were together. He even put his arm around me and played with the hair at the nape of my neck. He had abandoned the idea of the direct frontal assault for a rearguard action about which I couldn't do a dang thing in the middle of Sacrament meeting. I sat next to him, head bent, kicking my feet under the pew and making a fist with my right hand. I was ready to strangle him for acting like my boyfriend.

I had driven my own vehicle in to church because I was now leaving for services at least an hour before the rest of my family, and I had to pick Michael up on the way. Out of the generosity of my heart, I'd told him I'd take him home too. That gave us all of ten minutes to talk in private. I confronted him before we got into the car.

"What do you think you were doing in Sacrament?" I asked.

"Acting like your boyfriend," he responded coolly.

I wanted to scream that he wasn't that kind of friend, in any sense of the word. With difficulty I restrained myself.

"Why are you so upset, Lizzie? I'm just trying to act like a normal guy."

"I can't do this," I said helplessly.

"Of course you can. You don't have to do anything. Just sit there and keep quiet. Let me hold your hand."

"You weren't holding my hand," I protested.

"Lizzie, just play along with me. You're taking this way too serious."

"It is way serious." I was in so deep, I might just suffocate, I thought.

His mouth twitched and he adjusted his glasses. "We need to get to know each other."

"We do know each other!"

Michael looked away and stuck his hands in his pockets. "No, we don't."

"Why we can't be friends like before?" I asked.

"Because we are not friends!" he spluttered.

I stared at him, feeling like I was trying to read a foreign language that I had never studied. I turned smartly on my heel, strode over to the Nissan, unlocked the door, threw my

Sak's Fifth Avenue purse across onto the passenger seat, and installed myself behind the steering wheel. The heat inside the vehicle was suffocating so I unwound the window.

"Are you coming?" I called out. He didn't answer. He just walked around to the passenger side of the vehicle with his hands still in his pockets and his head hanging. He opened the door, picked my purse up off the passenger seat, and sat down with the purse on his lap. I was tempted to snatch it away from him, but I forced myself not to.

"Lizzie, where you and I are headed is way more than friends," he said softly. "Is there something wrong with me wanting to touch you?"

My fingers trembled as I stuck the key in the ignition and revved the engine. Michael was one of the few people on earth who could make me feel small. I was asking him to tarnish his reputation, renounce mission and college, and raise a child he hadn't fathered. He had offered everything and I had given nothing. I gripped the steering wheel tightly, steeling myself. "I'll make you a promise. After we're married, you can touch me as much as you want."

I turned my head towards him and leaned against the back of the seat, gazing at him through my lashes. Michael was blushing the color of a red anemone. I forced myself to breathe deeply and evenly, because I had obviously and completely lost my mind. Of all the dumb and stupid promises I could have made, this had to be the dumbest! I could just hear Janine and Shannon laughing about my naivety. We pulled out of the church parking lot and drove to Michael's house in a silence as round and as full as the moon. We had turned the corner onto his street and pulled to a complete stop alongside the curb before Michael spoke. He took my head between his hands and held it so that he could look me straight in the eye.

"Lizzie, whatever you may think about me, I'm not the kind of guy who would force himself on a girl. You ought to know me better."

He held me, mesmerized, like I was suspended between heaven and earth. My nails made a nervous patter on the steering wheel. The sound of the blood in my ears was like the drone of insects on a summer night, with the solid thump-thump of my heart playing bass underneath. Under his fingertips, my veins pulsed. We had entered no-man's land and I did not know if we would press forward across the barbed wire or retreat to the waterlogged trenches. It was Michael who took us back because he knew I did not have the heart for it – not now, not today.

"My precious pearl, it'll be just fine. Don't get all worked up like this." He released his grip from the sides of my head and drew his fingers through the tresses of my hair.

"Don't ever cut your hair. Please. It's so beautiful."

"Promise I won't," I whispered. It was the second promise I'd made to Michael that Sunday. At least it was going to be easier to keep than the first. I leaned back against the seat, drawing in a long slow breath. I think Michael was as much afraid of touching me as I was of being touched. It was easier in public when we could claim we were pretending.

"I think you better go, Michael."

He nodded, unlatched the door, and stepped out into the sunlight. I couldn't look at him because I couldn't face certain facets of our relationship. It was like a crystal that I could not examine for fear of what I might find, and I was both fascinated and repelled by it. I held it softly in my hand to protect it from breakage because I knew I had it in my power to smash it into thousands of pieces. I felt the tears rising up again, so I put my head onto the steering wheel and let them roll out of my eyes. I told myself I was crying because I was pregnant and seventeen and scared, and everyone knows women go to pieces when they're expecting. But no matter how much I wanted to delude myself, in the dark places of my soul I knew it was because I was still desperately and hopelessly in love with Jason, and I wanted Jason to look at me and touch me the way Michael did.

Family Home Evening at the Kerry's

Lizzie

By sheer dint of will, or was it fear of embarrassment, I'd been diligent in preparing the lesson for the Kerry Family Home Evening the following night. I'd hunted down an article in the *Ensign* (our church's monthly magazine) about the Atonement, read a bunch of scriptures in Alma, checked out a couple of conference talks from my father's video collection, borrowed the picture of Christ in Gethsemane from the church library, and copied a line drawing so Alison and Edward would have pictures to color. I even dug out an almost-new box of coloring pencils. I didn't expect Alison or Edward would be able to find any on short notice, and I didn't want the distraction of folks looking around.

I didn't know which was coming first – my lesson, or the news that Michael and I were getting hitched and I was moving in – but I was hoping to get through the lesson before the kids were hit with the news of our wedding.

The Kerry's had invited me not only to give the lesson, but to share dinner as well. I sat next to Michael and kept quiet as the family chatted about the latest luxury car that came into papa's shop, the next ward activity, homework, and the million other details that occupy a family dinner. We had crab cocktail for hors d'oeuvres served over lettuce. I knew this was a special treat in the frugal Kerry household, and that it was not crab at all but that flaked pollock that my mother would have been shot for if she'd have dared to serve it at my father's table. It was followed by a big pot of beef stew with turnips and potatoes. They were saving dessert until after my lesson. That was a Family Home Evening tradition, not only in their home, but in many church members' homes. I always knew two things about Monday dinner time: the Kerry's would always expend extra effort and funds to feed a guest, and that no matter what, Family Home Evening would be followed by a special dessert.

Rachel cleared the table and loaded the dishwasher. Apparently it was her turn to do after-dinner chores that night. I had spent a lot of evenings at the Kerry's, but I didn't usually stay for dinner or remain there for their Family Home Evening nights. I was expected to be spending them at home with my family, even though we did not actually do anything. That made it even more significant that I was at the Kerry home tonight. When Rachel had finished cleanup duty, I went over to the couch to retrieve my backpack and gather up my lesson materials. Patrick Kerry opened the Family Home Evening by thanking me for accepting the teaching assignment and asking Michael to give the opening prayer.

"Lizzie, what song did you pick out?" he asked.

I gulped. I didn't have a song.

Realizing I hadn't been totally informed about their expectations, Anne Kerry jumped in with, "Let's do 'Families Can Be Together Forever.'"

"That's my favorite," piped up Alison. Obviously they sang this one a lot, I thought.

Edward, who was apparently in charge of the musical accompaniment and proud of it, pushed back his chair, bent down to the floor, and hit some buttons on what must have been a cassette tape player. We waited while he fussed with the controls to cue the tape to the correct song. He obviously knew where to locate it on the tape. I heard the familiar notes of the intro. They all sang, and so did I. Rachel had the prettiest voice. I tried to remember the last time we'd had a song or hymn to open Family Home Evening at our house, but I couldn't. The singing helped settle my nerves.

"I invited Lizzie to teach our lesson tonight," said Patrick Kerry after the singing had died down. "Go ahead."

He smiled at me and I gave him a fragile smile in return.

"My lesson tonight is on the Atonement. That's a big word. Does anyone want to tell me what it means?" I asked

Rachel replied, "That Jesus died so we could be forgiven of our sins."

"Good," I said.

"It was on the cross," chimed in Alison.

"And why is that important?" I asked. I kicked Michael under the table and he jumped. He had better help me out here.

"He suffered on the cross," Michael said, picking up the thread and not looking the least bit upset that I'd nailed his right foot. I was later to see the bruise. "He suffered the pains, both in Gethsemane and on the cross, of everybody who had lived, is living, and will live so that we could return to our Heavenly home."

"I have a scripture about that. Sister Kerry, would you mind reading it? It's in Second Nephi, chapter 9, verse 21." I handed her my scriptures where I'd bookmarked the page.

"'And He cometh into the world that He may save all men if they will hearken unto His voice; for behold, He suffereth the pains of all men, yeah, the pains of every living creature, both men, women, and children, who belong to the family of Adam,'" she read.

Like Jesus would actually know how miserable I am, I thought. And even if He did feel my pain, He knows I earned it.

"That's why Jesus can help us, because He knows how we feel," I said. My eyes started tearing up and I swallowed hard to stop myself of breaking down in front of them. I had to keep it together tonight. Patrick Kerry came to my rescue.

"Jesus does know," he said, looking pointedly at me. Michael magically produced a crumpled tissue from his pocket, handed it to me, and I dabbed my eyes. I was glad I was wearing waterproof mascara. "To be free of our sins, we must give them up to Him. That is the power of the Atonement," he continued.

"Right," I went on, regaining my composure. "Now who can tell me why Jesus has the power to save us, while others do not?"

"That's easy," answered Sarah. "He lived a perfect life. And only someone who is absolutely free of sin can atone for our sins."

I really didn't need to teach this lesson. They had the answers already. Something I knew all along, but it took Sarah's comment to hammer it into my brain was how wonderful Patrick and Anne were. They knew their "real treasure" was in Heaven with their family, and that is where they poured their love. I guess I should have realized that it was their sublime example that drove Michael to pour all of his love into me, but that level of introspection was beyond me at that moment.

"I've brought a picture of Jesus praying in the Garden of Gethsemane. He knew His death was near." I wished mine was, I thought. "He prayed to His Heavenly Father to give Him strength to face what He was chosen to do. He knew He was going to die a terrible death on the cross. He wished He might not have to go through with it."

"Was He afraid?" asked Edward.

I looked to Patrick Kerry for help again. "Edward, He wouldn't have asked for 'this cup to pass from me' if He hadn't been afraid," Patrick Kerry said gravely.

"What does that mean?" asked little Alison. She was looking at me.

"Jesus wanted Heavenly Father to tell Him what He should do. If He didn't have to, He didn't want to die on the cross."

"And what did Heavenly Father say?" asked Alison.

"Jesus must do His Father's will, which was to die an awful death," I responded. It was probably the same awful death I deserved, I thought. "We sometimes want to shirk our responsibilities – like not doing our chores or our homework. But we have to do them, don't we?"

And how I wanted to shirk my responsibilities now, I thought. How I wanted to be somewhere else doing something else with Jason. "Heavenly Father," I silently prayed, "please don't let me be tempted above what I can bear. Don't allow me to let this wonderful family down."

"I brought a picture of Jesus in the Garden for Edward and Alison to color," I continued. I handed them across the table and spilled the coloring pencils out in a heap.

"Oh goodie," cried Alison. At least somebody was happy, I thought.

"Finally, what is necessary for us to receive the Atonement?" I asked.

"We must confess our sins, and have a broken heart and a contrite spirit," replied Sarah.

"Very good," I said. I knew I'd confessed my sins, I thought, and my heart was broken in a thousand pieces, but I didn't know if my spirit was truly contrite.

"Lizzie," interjected Michael. "Can you explain 'contrite spirit' for us?"

I wished Michael wouldn't be such a jerk and would stop reading my mind.

"It means being humble enough to accept punishment," I replied.

Anne Kerry added, "Jacob, Nephi's younger brother, wrote about that."

"What did he say?" I asked.

"Let's see." Anne Kerry shuffled some pages in her scriptures. "Jacob 2, verse 16. 'Listen unto the word of his commands, and let not this pride of your hearts destroy your souls.'"

"The proud don't like to be reprimanded," Michael explained.

"I think you're talking about Helaman, chapter 12," interjected Anne Kerry. "The proud are slow to remember God and set his counsels at naught."

That struck right to the heart, I thought. I wondered who this lesson was for. I looked over at Alison, who was busy coloring the picture of Jesus in Gethsemane. "Whatever happens to me, whatever He did," I prayed to Heavenly Father, "please never let that little girl be drawn into temptation like I was; and the same goes for Rachel and Sarah."

"Shall we close with a scripture to summarize the lesson? It's in Alma 42, verse 15. Michael?" Anne Kerry handed her scriptures over to my fiancée. He took my hand and kissed the back of my fingers. This gesture of affection escaped no one.

"'And now, the plan of mercy could not be brought about except an atonement should be made; therefore God himself atoneth for the sins of the world, to bring about the plan of mercy, to appease the demands of justice, that God might be a perfect, just God, and a merciful God also'," he quoted.

There was a brief silence while Patrick Kerry allowed the importance of these words to sink in. Then he invited Sarah to give the closing prayer.

"Now, before we serve dessert," said Patrick Kerry, and there was a perceptible sigh, because dessert was to be delayed, "Michael and Lizzie have an announcement to make."

"Dad, why don't you do it?" interjected Michael.

"All right." Patrick Kerry's gaze swept around the table and I was struck by its warmth. "Lizzie and Michael are going to get married."

There were gasps all around. Rachel and Sarah were looking at me like I'd come to life out of a fairytale.

"I thought you just started dating," commented Rachel.

"It may not have been obvious," replied Michael calmly, his hand firmly clasped over mine, "but we've been in love for a while."

I rolled my eyes at him. He ought to get an award for improvisation. He could definitely be a cool customer when he needed to be.

"I heard he's a 'wonderful kisser,'" Rachel said with an impish grin.

Those were the exact words I'd used to describe Michael to Janine only two days ago. I looked over at Patrick and Anne Kerry and they were trying really hard not to lose it, but their shuttered smiles and half chuckles escaped, nonetheless. I was hoping Janine suffered a long and painful death for this betrayal. Michael, on the other hand, was boasting a self-satisfied grin, and I just put my head in my hands to avoid looking at them all. If Alison asked what a "wonderful kisser" meant, I was going to leave right now.

"When's the wedding?" asked the more practical Sarah. I was grateful that at least one family member had the tact to change the subject.

"December 14," I replied, hoping everyone had forgotten about the "wonderful kisser" line, especially Michael.

"That's soon," said Edward

Yeah, well, we were in a hurry, I thought. Babies couldn't wait.

"And I want Rachel and Sarah to be bridesmaids," I added.

"Cool!" exclaimed Rachel.

"That's very sweet of you, Lizzie," said Sarah.

"Does that mean we get new dresses?" asked Rachel. Boy, these girls moved fast, I thought.

"You bet," I replied. "Actually, I was hoping your Mom might help me with them if I bring the material."

"Of course, Lizzie," said Anne Kerry warmly. "I'd be delighted. Sarah and Rachel will pitch in, too."

"I know it's short notice," I said forlornly.

"We'll manage, dear," she said. It was nice to know one member of the family wasn't in the least daunted by this shotgun wedding.

"Lizzie needs a dress, too," interposed Michael.

"I have an idea for that," replied Anne Kerry. "My wedding dress is in great shape, and I think we're about the same size. Would you like to take a look at it some time, Lizzie?"

The dress had to be almost twenty years old, but I wasn't in a position to turn it down. I tried to sound enthusiastic. Maybe I could dye it scarlet so it would match the color of my sins. "OK, I'll find out how soon I can come over and try it on."

"Later this week?"

"Yes, probably Thursday. I'll be over to do chemistry homework." I sighed at the thought of yet another set of homework problems from Mr. Crowle.

"There's one other thing," added Patrick Kerry. All faces turned expectantly toward him. "Lizzie and Michael are going to be living here after they get married."

Indrawn breaths all around for the second time.

Little Alison clapped her hands, jumped up from her chair, and hopped onto my lap. "That is the bestest news!"

"Where's she going to sleep?" asked Sarah.

"We'll be in my room," responded Michael, glaring at his sister. Was it really necessary to state the obvious?

"I'm going to call Serena right now and tell her I'm going to be a bridesmaid," cried out Rachel, jumping up from the table.

"Sit down, young lady. We haven't finished Family Home Evening yet," interjected Anne Kerry. "First, Alison is going to help set out dessert and you're going to wait until the weekend before you call anyone, because Lizzie wants to tell her friends first. I better not hear that Lizzie's friends heard it from anyone else but her." Anne was, in all ways, a wonderful and loving person, but when she gave "the look," nobody balked.

I was glad someone was looking out for my interests. I had a ton of phone calls to make. The first was going to be Janine to rip her to shreds about the "wonderful kisser" story. That would teach me to make up inane stories about making out. Alison danced off to get dessert – home canned pears doused in homemade chocolate mousse with a dollop of cream on top. Anne Kerry brought out two bottles of Martinelli's sparkling apple cider and a set of fancy-looking glasses so the family could toast the wedding. I felt guilty knowing they were splurging their much-needed food budget on frivolities like sparkling apple cider. I didn't deserve all this brouhaha, I thought. But I smiled through it all and prayed the wedding dress would be gorgeous. All this attention was making me giddy.

When it was time to leave, Patrick and Anne Kerry thanked me profusely for providing the Family Home Evening lesson. I headed for the door with Michael following. We stepped outside and the crisp air cut my breath. He pulled the door closed behind us.

"'Wonderful kisser,' huh? Quite a compliment from my pearl, isn't it?"

You bastard, I thought. "Janine was pressing me – I had to make up something."

"Let's not make it up."

I shook my head and backed a step away from him into the rough surface of the stucco under the overhang where my eyes were cast in shadow. "Have it your way then, Lizzie. What day did your parents want to go to the courthouse?"

"Wednesday," I responded glumly. The headiness I'd felt earlier was wearing off in the face of the grim realities. "I'll be seeing you, then."

"You gave a beautiful lesson in there, you know," he added, placing the first two fingers of his right hand under my chin.

"I can fake it if I have to," I said evenly, twisting my head away from him.

"You weren't faking it." Then he turned my head toward him, crushed me up against the wall and kissed me very briefly, just long enough for me to seriously wonder just how much "practice" he had before. It was hard to imagine that the two kisses he had given me were his first, but I couldn't for the life of me think of how, or who, he might have kissed before. I turned my head away from him and wiped my lips with the back of my hand. It made me tremble all over.

"I was faking that," I said, slipping away from him and running for the sanctity of my car. I didn't turn to look back at him. It served him right, I thought, getting fresh with me when my defenses were down. I had told him he could touch me as much as he wanted *after* we were married and I was sticking to it.

If I had turned back, I would have seen him hang his head, remove his glasses, and wipe his eyes.

Battles

Lizzie

On Wednesday afternoon in a pouring rain, my father and mother came by the high school to pick up Michael and me. Michael's father had written him a note excusing him from school for a "legal matter," while mine simply said "doctor's appointment."

"Hello, I hope you've got your driver's licenses with you and a certified copy of your birth certificate like I asked you to bring, Michael," said my father as he pulled up in his swanky Audi with the white pearl paint. He was clad in a sleek grey pinstripe suit, matching silk tie, and a white shirt imprinted with barely visible grey lines. The sapphires in the wedding ring on his left hand flashed as he opened the rear door for us and the raindrops in his hair glittered with diamonds. He looked as handsome and self-assured as I had ever seen him.

"You bet," said Michael. I was sure my mother had all my paperwork.

The Audi's interior was upholstered in white leather. The car had a cassette, radio and four stereophonic speakers. My father had it washed every week and it was nothing less than immaculate. He checked it out for dents and scratches each time we came home from church and enjoyed showing our family off in it. I had come to believe that darned car had become the apple of my father's eye in place of the son he'd always wanted.

Michael and I scooted into the back seat, hand in hand. My mother was in the front passenger seat, dressed to the nines in a navy suit with white trim along the collar, white pumps sporting navy buckles and trim, and a white purse with a navy bow that matched its straps. She looked like she was going to church. I felt down-to-heel in my faded jeans and striped black and grey sweater. I was glad to see Michael was wearing a shirt and slacks, even if he hadn't had the good sense to remember a tie for this ill-fated occasion.

We drove in silence. The rain continued to batter against the windows and I was hoping Mom and Dad had remembered extra umbrellas. As luck would have it, we found a parking place only a couple of minutes from the Registrar's Office and were able to make a dash for it, falling in line behind my parents. My father had made it obvious he was going to be in charge by taking Michael's birth certificate and identification from him. Michael set his backpack down on a chair, took my hand, and pulled me down beside him. My mother took out a certified copy of my birth certificate that had been slipped in between a clear sheet protector.

"Your driver's license, please, Lizzie," my father indicated to me. I dug it out of the pocket of my jeans, where I had temporarily stashed it for convenient access. Then my father motioned for us to remain where we were while he went up to the window in the small outer office. A lady with spectacles attended to him. She recognized him, of course, and they had a few moments of animated conversation. After their pleasantries, she briefly stopping to look at us over her glasses, while she compared our faces to the pictures on our licenses. Her stare was not encouraging. She shoved a stack of forms under the glass. When it appeared that she was about to expound the lengthy explanation about marriage requirements for minors, she said something about since Derek was an attorney, that would already understand it all. He sat down and began filling out forms on a clipboard provided for the purpose. My mother stood a few paces away from him, fidgeting. Michael was clasping and unclasping his fingers as he held my hand. I took that as a sign that Michael was acting a whole lot calmer than he felt.

"OK, Michael – you fill out the stuff pertaining to you. You two do know you'll need to see a counselor and have a Superior Court judge sign off on this?" he said shortly.

I didn't know, but it was good to be informed.

"Not that I expect you'll have any problem," he added. "You seem pretty set on this."

"I brought money..." Michael said, digging around in his pocket for his wallet.

"That won't be necessary," intervened my father brusquely, handing Michael the clipboard. I guess Michael figured it would be useless to argue with his future father-in-law, the attorney. I realized I hadn't even thought about paying for the license. I hadn't a clue how much a marriage license cost in our county. I stared down at the form, looking at the place where my father and mother had to write their signatures.

"Is it expensive?" I whispered to Michael.

"Yeah – like fifty bucks. Shush," warned Michael, pressing hard with the ballpoint. He was filling in information about his parents' birthplaces and names. I saw his mother was born in Ohio and his father in Iowa. He signed his name in the box "groom" and gave me the pen so I could sign under "bride." And into the fire I go, I thought. Then he silently handed back the clipboard to my father, who shot it back to the efficient woman at the counter. She bade us wait and disappeared in the labyrinth of the offices beyond the glass partition.

It was a long time before she came back. She had written on a slip of paper the name and number of the court-appointed counselor we would need to see and told my father that after we'd completed a satisfactory interview, an appointment would be scheduled with the Superior Court judge. It seemed like a whole lot of rigmarole to me, but I guess the state didn't like minors getting married, so they made it as difficult as possible for us. Not that the residents of legal age in our state were any better at deciding who to marry, the national divorce rate hovering around forty percent and probably a lot higher in California, I'd learned in my sociology class. Maybe they ought to start premarital counseling for everyone.

Finally, we emerged out of the lackluster building into the rain and made another dash for the car. I hoped water wouldn't spoil the leather seats.

"The invitations are going to be ready tomorrow," I reminded Michael after we were safely ensconced in the vehicle and belted up. "You need to meet me at Kinkos at four and I'll drop you home. My mom wants to make sure everything's correct in case they have to reprint them."

Michael readily agreed to meet me, though I knew he didn't want to. Then he began fumbling around in his backpack and pulled out a small velvet box

"Here, this is for you, now that we're official," he whispered.

He popped up the lid of the small black velvet box. I stared down at a delicate gold ring. A ruby glittered at the center of a swirling design encircled by minute diamonds. I hoped they were diamonds, anyway. I blinked.

"That is, wow, impressive," I breathed.

I flashed a look up at the rearview mirror and could see my father furtively trying to work out what kind of sordid activities were taking place on the back seat of his pristine vehicle. Nothing like what happened on the floor of your home office with Jason, I thought, so there!

"It was my grandmother's. Mom said you should have a ring and she wants you to have this."

"I don't think I can accept a family heirloom like this," I said softly. I had been a wicked slut and I didn't deserve this, I thought. This baby was not even the Kerry's grandchild.

"Come on, Lizzie." He didn't give me a chance for further protest; he simply slipped the ring onto my finger. The obligations were getting deeper and deeper. I was already in up to my neck and sinking fast.

I had to admit the ring looked pretty on my finger. I smiled foolishly at Michael, whispering "I can't thank you enough."

I would be eternally grateful, I thought, and eternally damned for this. We drove the rest of the way in silence, listening to the sound of raindrops chattering on the roof and windows, and it made me feel smug that my father spent the whole journey trying to figure out what we'd been pouring our heads over in the back seat of his car. I wasn't about to enlighten him.

———— ⋅⊹✦⊹⋅ ————

The next evening, I swung my Nissan into the Kinkos parking lot and rammed it into a parking space. I was anxious to see how the invitations were going to look. Could it be that I was getting sucked into the excitement of the preparations for my own wedding? Weddings were like whirlpools, I thought, eventually it was impossible to resist the suction and the pull of your family's expectations.

I entered the store and walked up to the pickup counter, where a pimply young man was tapping away on a computer keyboard. I gave him my name and explained what I was there for, and almost instantaneously an official-looking box appeared. He handed me a second one and I took that as well. I set them on the counter, pried up the lid, and checked out the card. My mother had selected the emblem of a rose for the front side of the invitation card. It made me think of the Wars of the Roses in medieval England.

I told the counter attendant I was waiting for another person, and he set the boxes aside so he could attend to another customer while I waited. Michael was late. I paced around and spent twenty minutes perusing the different paper colors and font styles for wedding invitations. It was almost 4:45 and Michael still hadn't shown up. I was betting he'd forgotten. By this time, I was fuming so I told the attendant I'd take the invites anyway, they looked fine, and thanks very much. Then I spun on my heel and did a balancing act trying to hang onto my purse and the boxes getting out the door. It had started to rain outside, which didn't improve my mood because I didn't want my mother's precious invitations getting wet.

I was intending to stop by Michael's place later for our usual Thursday night chemistry homework session, but I thought perhaps I ought to swing by now and give him the full force of my temper while it was good and hot. So I made a U-turn and began driving in the direction of his house. It was almost five when I screeched into his driveway. The Suburban was not in evidence. I again juggled backpack and boxes out the door and marched up the driveway in high mettle. I ran the doorbell insistently since they couldn't be expecting me. Michael answered it. He looked surprised to see me.

"You forget something?" I demanded.

"And, hello, I hope your day is going all right, too," he replied with aplomb. "What can I do you for?"

I could have cursed him for having such a cool head. "You were s'posed to meet me somewhere, remember?" I hissed.

The light finally came on. "Right, Kinkos, four."

He looked at his watch. "I screwed up on that one, didn't I? I'm real sorry, Lizzie. No offense intended."

"Offense taken," I snapped back.

"Again, I'm real sorry. Why don't you come in out of the rain and we'll look at those invitations right now?"

"We were supposed to look at them an hour ago, but fine, we'll do it now."

I swished by him and marched up the stairs to his room. I hardly acknowledged Rachel and Sarah who were at the dining room table doing homework, while Alison and Anne Kerry busied themselves in the kitchen. Patrick Kerry hadn't yet arrived home from work. Michael followed me up the stairs and into his room. I dropped my backpack in the middle of the floor and confronted him, shoving the boxes at him.

"You know, when something's important to me, at least you can pretend to care about it," I yelled.

"This wedding is important to me. But I don't think a minor detail like these invitations is a reason for you to lose your temper in a major way."

I narrowed my eyes and practically spat out my next words. "It's not a minor detail to me. It shows me you don't really care."

"Stop acting like a spoiled brat, Lizzie," he came back, stepping right into my strike zone. "Let me put this into perspective for you. You screwed some guy in our ward –"

"I never said he was in our ward..."

"You were fornicating with some guy – maybe in our ward, maybe not – breaking the law of chastity, and you are stunned, shocked, to find out you're pregnant. Like you're not smart enough to figure out that's a possible consequence. Then you have the good fortune to find another guy who's willing to accept the responsibility and take the fall with you – which your lover wasn't – even though this other guy is totally innocent. Then you have the audacity to whine about some freaking wedding invites that mean absolutely nothing in the grand scheme of things."

It was really nasty how Michael could ball up the truth sometimes.

"So you're saying I messed up, and I deserve this?"

"Yeah, you do," he yelled, and his eyes had a wicked glint to them.

"Everyone will think it was you now, even if we don't get married, so you'll just have to deal with it," I retorted.

"I should've never got myself into this," he blazed.

"You're telling me you're regretting it?" I blasted back.

"When you act like this, yeah!"

"Well, I hate it, too; and I wish we weren't doing it either."

Then I unceremoniously tipped the boxes upside-down above his head and the contents went flying everywhere. Now his perfectly pristine room looked as trashed as I felt.

"You can have this back, too," I said, tearing the ring off my finger and flinging it at him. I whipped around and grabbed the door knob. I thought Michael would come after me, but he didn't. I opened the door, went through it, and slammed it as loudly as I could.

To my horror, I saw that Patrick Kerry had just arrived home. He was still in his mechanic's coveralls. He sprang up the stairs and barred my escape.

"Good afternoon, Lizzie, pleasure to see you."

"Let me pass, please," I said, avoiding Patrick Kerry's eyes.

"Not so fast, young lady." His voice was firm but without ire. I chanced a look at him and winced. "You're going to turn around and go right back in there."

He took my arm and guided me back to the door. His hands were rough and stained with grease. He smelled like he'd spent the entire day under a diesel engine. I had no choice – he was going to make me go back in there. Gingerly, I opened the door to Michael's room. Michael was still standing in the pile of spilled wedding invitations, unmoving, as if he were lost and seeking directions. When he saw me enter followed by his father, he bent down for my backpack and held it out.

"Forget something, Lizzie?" His voice was shaking, but whether from anger or pain, I couldn't tell.

"Put that down, please, Michael. Lizzie doesn't need it right now."

Michael noiselessly obeyed.

"I want both of you to get on your knees," he went on. His voice was soft and low, but yet authoritative. Michael dropped down instantly, clearing a space on the rug amongst the white envelopes. When I hesitated, he added, "That goes for you, too, Lizzie."

I followed suit, flashing Michael an irate glance as if to say, see what you got us into. If anything, Michael gave me a warning frown. Michael and I were facing each other, on our knees, and Patrick Kerry was a shadow by the door. I heard rustling behind us and realized the diesel fuel and automotive grease had sunk to the carpet as well. I didn't know what was coming.

In my home, Dad just let his top blow off and we ended up in our bedrooms without dinner and grounded for as long as Dad thought necessary, which was usually longer than my mother thought necessary.

"Michael, you may begin your repentance, now. I'll wait as long as you need."

I still didn't understand what Patrick Kerry was doing, but Michael surely did.

"Lizzie, please be still and reverent," Patrick Kerry interjected for my benefit.

I bent my head sullenly. Fine, I could wait, whatever. Several minutes went by as Michael struggled to find the words for his Heavenly Father, but I didn't dare move. I sneaked a look over at him but his head was bowed and his eyes were closed. When he did at last begin to speak, he expressed his sorrow to his Heavenly Father for losing his temper, for being harsh with me, for not adequately understanding my feelings, and for sinning against the light and truth of the Holy Ghost. He begged both Heavenly Father and me for forgiveness, promised to work harder at keeping the spirit of contention out of his heart, and asked the Savior to have mercy on his miserable soul. Then he thanked his dad for intervening, for his wisdom, sensitivity, and support, despite the grave sins he had committed. Finally, he asked the Savior for mercy and acknowledged the Savior's sacrifice on the cross.

I told myself I could not be hearing this. Everything that had happened had been my fault. If I hadn't been in such a foul mood when I walked in the house, Michael wouldn't have reacted as he did. We wouldn't even be here today but for the fact that I was a wretched sinner and didn't keep Heavenly Father's commandments. This was ludicrous, I thought. I was playing in a farce and no one was laughing.

When Michael had ended, Patrick Kerry said, "Lizzie, it's your turn, now."

There was no way Michael's father could possibly mean me, could he?

"We'll wait as long as you need."

Right, I thought. They could wait all night, but I had no intention of participating in this little "atonement ceremony," if that's what it was. The minutes fell away while the rain pattered against the window, and still I didn't speak. I peeked at my watch and saw they'd been kneeling there more than twenty minutes, waiting for me to acknowledge my deficits and ask forgiveness. I was reminded of Anne Kerry's words at Family Home Evening, just three nights ago: 'The proud are slow to remember God and set His counsels at naught.'

After a few more minutes, Patrick Kerry spoke up from behind us. "Lizzie, I know this may be hard for you, but we will wait – all night, if necessary."

I had underestimated the strength of my future father-in-law's resolve. The quiet resilience of his words helped me to realize that I wasn't going to worm my way out of this as easily as I'd thought. Patrick Kerry had broken my will as surely as Jason had broken my hymen. One was a righteous man, helping me come closer to Christ; one pushing me further away.

When I did, at last, begin, my voice sounded small and disconnected. I said that it was not Michael who had started the argument, but me. I was at fault for being petty and unreasonable, and picking a fight because I was unhappy about my condition. I had too much pride, and the Lord had chosen to humble me. I was focused too much on the outward trappings of the wedding and not enough on its inward significance. I had wronged the Lord by my actions, and then wronged Michael by deliberately trying to hurt his feelings. I didn't deserve to be Michael's fiancée at all. I didn't deserve the love and consideration his family had shown, and was still showing, me. I apologized for throwing the family heirloom on the floor. I acknowledged that although I had taught the lesson about the Atonement in Family Home Evening only that week, I had not understood it. I prayed that my understanding might grow and that I might have more desire to study my scriptures with real intent to learn, rather than to meet a goal the bishop had set for me. Finally, I asked the Lord for forgiveness and, if it were possible, for Michael to forgive me also. I thanked the Savior for making mercy possible through the Atonement. Then I stopped. To my chagrin, I began to sob violently. I felt two arms wrap themselves around my shoulders – Michael's and Patrick Kerry's.

"You should throw me out of your house," I sobbed.

"I'm not a throwing-out kind of a guy," Patrick Kerry responded quietly.

He was so unlike my father, I thought.

"I spend my days fixing broken-down cars. Some are old. Some are new. I figure most of 'em are worth the trouble of fixing. You know why a lot of 'em break down?"

"No, why?" I asked weakly. I glanced up at him, and saw that although his eyes were tinged with sadness, a slight smile played on his lips.

"The owners don't maintain 'em like they should. Change the oil, rotate the tires, change the air filters. You're just in need of some maintenance, Lizzie."

"More like a major overhaul," I said wryly.

"I think you've already done that. You get back on the road and you'll see."

He certainly had more confidence in me than I did in myself, I thought.

"Dad," interjected Michael. I had barely realized Michael was there, I'd been so engrossed in listening to my future father-in-law. "Can you give us a minute, please?"

"You bet. Do you want to stay for dinner, Lizzie? Anne's probably been holding it up for us. I can call your parents and let them know you're here."

"I hope my dad doesn't chew you out."

"I'll see to it he doesn't, how about that?" he responded warmly.

Patrick Kerry didn't know my dad, I thought, but he seemed undaunted by my trepidation. He rose slowly to his feet and went out the door.

I looked at Michael, feeling like a mouse in front of a big alley cat. He had a pained expression on his face but was trying hard to keep his composure.

"I'll look for the ring," I said tremulously. I began scrabbling around in the fibers of the rug amongst the invitations. "I am honored to be wearing it."

"Thank you," he said softly. "I hope you mean it."

My fingers ran across it. I scooped it up into the palm of my hand and held it there, staring at it and thinking about what it symbolized: the circle of life, the bond between two people, the long line of love from which it came. A love that stretched into eternity without beginning or end. I slid the ring back onto the finger of my left hand, and thought that I must never, ever, misuse or abuse the trust that Michael had placed in me.

Misguided trust, perhaps, but trust nonetheless.

I hesitated to assume such a formidable responsibility. If this cup may pass from me, I thought, but I already knew the Lord's answer. I had accepted it when I said I would marry Michael and he had agreed to share the stain of my sin. We couldn't turn back now.

Michael interrupted my train of thought. "Lizzie, I have a scripture I think you should read."

He scrambled up to his feet and picked his scriptures up off the stand next to his bed. I watched him expectantly as he went to the Topical Guide at the back of the Bible to search out what he wanted. He found what he was seeking, and turned to it. Then he paused and said, "You will recall that after Moses died, Joshua was called to lead the Israelites into the Promised Land. The Lord knew Joshua was afraid, and this is what He told Joshua: 'Be strong and of a good courage; be not afraid, neither be thou dismayed: for the Lord thy God is with thee whithersoever thou goest.'"

And I wondered, looking at the stoic expression on his face, whether he needed these words more than I did.

"We should read the whole chapter," I suggested, trying to lighten his solemnity.

"Good topic for a Family Home Evening lesson, I wouldn't doubt," he added, but his tone was no less somber. "I'll mention it to Dad."

"Want to go down to dinner?" I asked.

"I expect they're waiting on us."

"I'll help you clean up this mess afterwards."

"It doesn't matter. I can handle it," he replied forlornly.

I got to my feet and stretched my hand outward towards him. He took it, staring at the ring glinting so hopefully on my finger.

"It's a beautiful ring, Michael. I'm not worthy of it," I said, biting my lip.

"Then I guess you'll have to work on that," he suggested.

"You've been so much more a friend than I could ever have imagined." I felt the words stumbling out, failing to express what I intended.

He stood up, still gazing at the bright spark on my finger. "Don't start, Lizzie. I don't need your platitudes now."

That left me groping for words I didn't have. I grasped his hand and walked out of his room and down the stairs ahead of him. If I had only known, it would have been so easy to give him what he did need.

The Dress

Lizzie

Dinner was a quiet affair. Two places had been set apart for us next to each other and I gladly took my spot next to Michael. Anne Kerry had made a meat pie and it hadn't suffered from being served fifteen minutes later than she'd anticipated. Sarah offered grace, and everyone anxiously awaited their plates of food. Michael hardly touched his. I had never seen him this down and out.

This was another Michael I didn't recognize. By the time dessert (apple pie with ice cream) showed up, a less strained atmosphere prevailed. Alison, however, managed to dispel the charade.

"Lizzie, if you were mad, why have you been crying?" she asked.

Sarah knocked a glass of water right into Alison's lap – intentionally. The little girl let out a yelp and Anne Kerry flew to her rescue. I silently thanked Sarah for her quick thinking. But I didn't believe the question should go unanswered, so I collected my thoughts while they were cleaning up.

"I made a mistake," I said quietly. "I lost my temper and I'm sorry about that. And I'm sorry that I made you wait on dinner."

"You slam doors really hard," interjected Edward.

I rolled my eyes at him. "Yea, I can. But I'll try not to do it again."

"That's enough, kids," interrupted Patrick Kerry from the far end of the table. "Let's not put Lizzie and Michael on the spot. They've had a fight, they've made up. Clear?"

No one was going to contradict him, so we resumed our destruction of the apple pie. Only Michael had declined dessert.

"So when are you going to start on our dresses?" asked Rachel, deciding it was time to discuss the banalities.

I sighed. "I'm going to try on your mom's wedding dress tonight, and I'll buy the fabric for the other dresses over the weekend. Want to have a sewing session Tuesday night?"

"Awesome!" exclaimed Rachel.

"Can we watch you try on Mom's dress?" asked Alison.

If I had thought I was going to be able to blend in and disappear in this family, I'd been wrong.

"Girls, I know you're excited about your brother getting married 'n' all," interposed Anne Kerry, "but you can see Lizzie in her wedding dress after we've decided what she's going to be wearing."

"All except Michael," said Rachel. "It's bad luck for the groom to see the bride in the dress before the big day."

"Rachel, that's superstition," protested Sarah. "You shouldn't believe in that stuff."

Superstition or not, I told myself, I was not letting Michael see me in my wedding dress ahead of time.

"What's 'superstition?'" asked Alison.

"When you believe in stuff that isn't real, like the bride and groom heading off into the sunset to live in wedded bliss," answered Michael.

Oh Michael, what have I done? I asked myself.

"So what's 'wedded bliss?'" Alison went on, not realizing that Michael was at the edge of his limits of tolerance.

I jumped in before Michael had time to answer. "It means when you live happily ever after, in spite of your differences."

That got a real laugh out of Patrick and Anne Kerry as well as Rachel and Sarah. Alison looked around the table, slightly bewildered, and my remark went right over Edward's head. I glanced at Michael to see how he was taking it.

Michael's eyes glittered, and he said, "Witty, Lizzie. Very witty. It's nice to know I'll have a wife who'll entertain me on those long, dark nights."

OK, Michael, so you won this round, I thought, but I'm up for the challenge. Don't count me out of the running yet.

"Lizzie, let's go up to my room and check out the dress," said Anne Kerry, sensing that an unseen drama was about to be played out on the family stage when it had barely recovered from the scene earlier. I took her cue.

"Don't get too lonesome for me, love," I tossed at Michael, pushing back my chair. Before I could stop him, he took the hand with the ring on it and kissed my fingers in an exaggeratedly gallant gesture. He looked up at me with the same hard glitter in his eyes, while I tried to shield my embarrassment.

"I'm going to try that dress on right now, so I'll see you all later," I jettisoned as I hopped up and started away.

Michael released his grip on my fingers, and I flew up the stairs in what I was hoping was an impressive exit. It hadn't been half as impressive as slamming that door earlier, I thought. Anne

Kerry was right behind me. I stopped at the top of the stairs so she could pass by me and lead me into her bedroom.

The room was tastefully decorated, although the paint looked as though it had been fresh about twenty years ago. The bed had an old blue and yellow hand-made quilt with stars and various geometric shapes on it that had been made as a wedding gift by Patrick Kerry's mother. A wedding picture in a gold frame boasting a merry looking Patrick Kerry and Anne as the sweetly smiling bride, wearing a gorgeous pearl necklace with a delicate pink luster to it, stood out above the bed. Next to it was a picture of Jesus Christ, and a print of the Oakland Temple. One knew where this couple's priorities lay.

The dress lay across a chair in the corner of the room in a great bundle of shimmering white. Though its whiteness had faded with time, it was in remarkably good condition. The whole skirt and bodice were overlaid with lace. Anne Kerry lifted it up so I could see it more clearly, and I smiled.

"It's a lovely dress," she said. "I had it professionally cleaned and packaged right afterwards to make it last. I was hoping one of the girls would want to wear it someday. So you'll be the first. Why don't you try it on?"

I stripped down to my underwear and stepped carefully into the gown. I had to admit I was shaking a little. The responsibility I was about to take on seemed even more daunting in Michael's mother's dress. It wasn't just about him, I thought. His family had expectations, too. Then I tried to remember the scripture Michael had read to me earlier, but the only words I could think of were "be strong and of a good courage." I guess that would work for the time being. I repeated it several times in my head while Anne Kerry buttoned up the dress. It must have had a million buttons, because it took her ages to fasten them.

I was beginning to sweat when she said, "That's the only drawback about this dress. It's got about thirty buttonhole loops and they're a bit tricky. Must have been the style, or someone wanted to make sure I didn't get this off in a hurry." She smiled a warm, knowing kind of smile that told me she was excited for us about the pending intimacy after the wedding.

I gulped. I hoped it wouldn't come off in a hurry either.

"Poor Patrick. His hands were trembling so badly he could hardly get me out of this thing on our wedding night." But your son has nerves of steel, I thought, and I didn't anticipate it being a problem for him.

I heard Anne Kerry giggle softly behind me and tried to see the humor in it. I tried to imagine Patrick Kerry without the assuredness he now possessed, and I couldn't summon the image.

"All right, turn around and let me take a look at you," she said.

I obediently swished and the dress twirled with me.

"My goodness, Lizzie. You look stunning." There were tears welling up in her eyes as she looked at who she recognized as the new woman in her family.

Satan was an expert at making bad things look good, I thought, while my future mother-in-law fussed with the sleeves, which fell softly from the elbows, sixties-style, like a wizard's costume. Satan certainly knew how to conjure up a tempting bride.

"I think I'll redo the trim using lace sewn with pearls," she said. "Patrick and I got married in the temple and my mother thought what with the family pearls and a lot of lace, the dress would be too flashy. But I always secretly dreamed about having them."

So even the righteous sometimes entertained frivolous thoughts, I mused.

"Honestly, the trim looks fine," I said, thinking I ought to focus on the spiritual rather than material aspects of this dreaded event, now that I'd finally seen the light. I couldn't bear the thought of Michael making a sarcastic comment about me being preoccupied with 'levity and light-mindedness' on our wedding day. Still, new trim would set me off in the dress and I wanted him to be impressed. More than that, I wanted to dazzle Jason, because I knew he'd be there.

"Do you have any pearls to match?" she asked.

"I do have a little something," I responded. I did have real ones that were made into a choker. "With matching earrings."

"Wonderful, we'll do it," she exclaimed, enchanted.

I was weaving my spell on them all, I thought, except Michael. He could see through me as easily as he could solve a chemistry problem.

"Thanks a million, Anne," I said. "Now please get me out of this dress because I've got to start on that beastly chem homework."

"Turn around then," she said, and began the arduous task of unlooping all the buttons.

It wasn't long before I was skipping down the corridor to Michael's room. I wanted to tell him how proud he was going to be of me in that dress. The door was ajar when I poked my head around it. Michael was at his desk, bent over his journal, scribbling furiously. The invitations had all been retrieved from the floor and were neatly stacked in their boxes.

"Hey!" I called softly.

He looked up briefly, just long enough to acknowledge me, and then returned to his writing. Something about his posture told me to hold off regaling the splendor of the dress for now.

"I fixed that worn-out belt in your car," he said.

"You shouldn't have done that – or this," I said, indicating the boxes of invitations.

"Well, I did," he continued, without looking up.

"Look, Michael, if there's anything I can do –"

"Lizzie, can't you see I'm busy? Now get started on your chemistry homework. Mine's done, so if you can't figure it out, check out what I did."

I hoped this was not going to be a repeat of last week. Michael had set my backpack down on his bed and placed his homework folder neatly next to it. I set his work aside and started on the problem set. Pressure, temperature, volume – it was all getting mixed up in my head. I didn't dare interrupt him to ask him for help, not when he was so absorbed in whatever it was he was penning for future generations. I flung my papers down hopelessly and picked up his scriptures. They lay open at a text in Moroni 3. Michael had underlined verse 20 in red: "Wherefore, there must be faith, and if there must be faith there must also be hope; and if there must be hope there must also be charity."

I couldn't understand why Michael was reading up on faith when he had enough of it for both of us. I was the one lacking faith. I couldn't conceive that Michael would be searching for faith. I should have realized it wasn't faith he sought. His need was more fundamental, but I wouldn't know it until months later. I flipped back to the first chapter of Joshua and read about Joshua's call to lead the Jews and the parting of the River Jordan in chapter 3. It gave me the courage to keep going. My situation seemed unimportant and petty compared to leading a rabble of rebellious wanderers into a land of inimical strangers. After I had lain on Michael's bed for a while comparing my plight and Joshua's, I realized Michael had stopped writing and was watching me.

"Must be earth shattering reading," he remarked.

I jumped.

"Finish your chemistry homework already?"

I gave a perceptible sigh. "No, I haven't. Just thought I'd look at the chapter where you found that verse about Joshua. It's inspiring."

"Planning to go into battle sometime soon?" he asked derisively. "Or was it the parting the waters of the Sacramento River you were intending?"

I stared at him in dismay.

"You're not going to get pious on me now and spoil things, are you?" he went on in the same ruthless manner. "I was so looking forward to wrestling with Satan."

I snapped his scriptures closed. What was his game now?

"It's pretty late, Lizzie. You better go home. You can't be sleeping in my bed – at least not for a few more weeks."

I wished I had the power to strike people dumb, I thought.

"Quite right, I should be leaving," I said, trying to avoid his mocking eyes. I hastily stashed my unfinished homework into my backpack, threw the assemblage on my shoulders, and picked myself up off the bed. "See you tomorrow, or whenever." I made my way out the door without a backward glance and thumped down the stairs in a thoroughly bad humor.

Love you, too

Lizzie

The next morning, I awoke to the phone ringing at 6:30 downstairs. My mother picked up the receiver in her bedroom, probably wondering why someone had chosen to die at such an early hour. Then I heard her feet shuffling down the hallway and a knock sounded at my door.

"Lizzie, dear," she called.

I clambered out of bed, pushing the hair out of my eyes. I wanted to go into the bathroom and practice my throw-up routine before I talked to anyone. I wished my friends didn't have the audacity to call at this hour, especially as I'd been up past midnight struggling through the chemistry problems and I hadn't made it halfway.

"It's Michael," said my mother.

The bastard, I thought, didn't he have the decency to allow his pregnant fiancée to have her little vomiting fit in the bathroom in the morning?

"Thanks, Mom," I said, taking the receiver from her.

"Don't you have clocks at your house?" I demanded. My mother raised her eyebrows, shook her head, and closed my bedroom door softly. She probably figured it was a lover's tiff.

"Good morning to you, Lizzie, and how are you doing today?"

"Spare me the niceties, jerk. D'you know what time it is?"

"Of course."

"Then what the hell are you doing calling me at this hour? Don't you know I need to spend fifteen minutes with my head in the toilet bowl every morning?"

"Poor Lizzie, we'll have to fix that."

"Yeah right, so let's go to the abortion clinic, then," I retorted.

"Boy, you are testy in the morning, Lizzie. I hope you're not going to be like this after we get married."

"Look, lover boy, hurry up and spit out what you're going to say, otherwise I'm going to contaminate the receiver with vomit and my father will give me all hell about it." I could feel the bile rising already.

"Meet me in the cafeteria in half-an-hour and I'll help you finish your chemistry problems."

I drew in my breath. "You called me for that?"

How in the hell did he know I hadn't finished them?

"I'm sorry. I wasn't paying attention last night and I'm trying to make it up to you."

"What makes you think I can be there in thirty minutes?"

"I'll buy you breakfast, and you care more about your precious grades than anything."

"I'm gonna look awful. I won't have any time to fix my face and hair."

"I don't care how you look, Lizzie. C'mon, just show up."

"I'm glad to know that love is blind," I retorted.

"Just get down here."

Then I realized that he was already at the cafeteria waiting for me and must've got up before first light to walk to school. Hell, I wanted the grades, didn't I? "OK, I'm on my way. 'Bye."

Before I hit the "Off" button I had time to hear him say, "Love you, too, Lizzie." He always had to get the last word in, didn't he?

Final Logistics

Lizzie

I hoped Michael wasn't going to be so offhand when we appeared before the court counselor. That was sure to be a red flag. We duly presented ourselves at the courthouse the following week to see the court psychologist, missing yet more time from school. Michael took my hand when we walked into the office. I wanted to snatch it away, but I restrained myself.

"Good afternoon," said a well-dressed Hispanic woman from behind the desk.

"I'm Veronica Bahia. I'll be talking to you today. Michael Kerry and Elizabeth Sherringdon, right?"

"Call me Lizzie," I said. I held out my hand and we shook across the desk. Michael followed suit.

"Please have a seat," she said, indicating the chairs on our side of the desk. She reached for a file on her desk, opened it, and made a few notes. "I'm here today to ask you a few questions about your decision to get married and provide you with some information about options for contraception."

"I'm already pregnant, so it's a bit late to worry about that now," I interjected.

Her head shot up from the notes she was writing. "You'll still need to use contraception after you have the baby."

I hadn't thought about that or anything else beyond the wedding ceremony. I decided to keep it that way.

"I hope you're not rushing into this because you are pregnant," she said, directing her attention toward me.

"We love each other," Michael interrupted. "We've known each other since kindergarten. We've been friends for a long time."

"I'm glad to hear that. When is the baby due?"

"Late June," I answered.

"Make sure you go to all your prenatal appointments and get information about taking care of the baby. Being a parent is a tough job. I suppose you know the statistics on marriages for under twenty-fives aren't encouraging?"

"We're Mormon," interposed Michael. "We're very committed to making it work."

"We counsel with our bishop every week," I added.

"Having religious convictions in common is important. I want to be sure both of you are doing this of your own free will and you know what you're getting into. I'm going to give you some leaflets on sexually transmitted diseases and contraception."

She handed a packet of literature across the desk. I took it.

"Are you being married by a priest from your church?" she asked.

"Yes," said Michael.

"And the information I have says you're getting married just before Christmas?"

"Correct," replied Michael.

"Do you have any questions for me?"

We shook our heads.

"All right. I'm going to complete the paperwork and authorize you to go ahead with your plans. That means you'll get a court date with the judge in about a month. It will basically be a formality, but you both need to appear and bring your paperwork with you."

She made a few more notes in the file and dismissed us.

"That was relatively painless," I remarked.

"Let's get out of here," Michael added, obviously more uncomfortable with the ordeal than I was.

While we were on our way home, Michael dropped yet another imposition on me.

"Mom's got a friend who teaches dance. So I've set up for us to spend an hour a week getting lessons so we'll know what we're doing on the big day."

I knew very well he wouldn't know what he was doing on the big day, but I wasn't thinking dancing.

"And you didn't ask me first?" I replied incredulously.

"I thought you'd be excited."

"What kind of dancing, anyway?" I asked, trying to hide my interest.

"Ballroom – like swing and cha-cha. I dunno exactly, that's why we're taking lessons."

"Sounds wickedly romantic," I said sarcastically.

"At least if you're my partner, I can count on the wicked," he shot back without missing a beat.

"I don't see how I'm going to find time for all this," I complained.

"I'm counting on you to rise to the occasion."

"I wish they weren't so many people counting on me."

"Have a little faith in yourself, Lizzie," he said gently.

And for some inane reason, I had to blink back tears.

"You're not the one who screwed up, are you, Michael? As if you had a problem reminding me of that."

He reached over from the steering wheel and squeezed my hand. "You need to stop looking back. It isn't an irredeemable mistake."

"I don't think you or I can undo this baby."

"Someday you'll see it as a blessing in disguise."

"I wish I could see that now," I grumbled.

"I do."

Michael would, wouldn't he, seeing as he was keeping the prize.

"Then you'll have to keep the vision alive for both of us, Michael."

"You have faith in me, then?"

"You've certainly proved to be the go-to guy," I replied wryly.

I hadn't, however, been expecting Michael to go from friend to fiancée in a matter of days. But seeing that Jason had whizzed from distant idol to lover in only a couple of weeks, perhaps Michael wasn't so different.

"I don't intend to let you down," Michael added.

I was sure he wasn't going to, but I wasn't guaranteeing I would be returning the favor. I gave him a quick, brittle smile as we pulled up outside his house, where I was once again invited for dinner. Over the previous weekend, my mother and I had purchased the material for the bridesmaids' dresses and the back seat of the car was covered in shimmering wine-colored cloth. I was supposed to start cutting out dresses today with Michael's mother. Sarah and Rachel were planning to help too, and I wasn't sure whether they'd be an asset or a liability. I hoped Anne Kerry had cleared a spot on the living room floor, because I had no idea how I was going to lay out the yards of cloth in the diminutive space of the living room. I'd never cut out a dress before.

We were greeted warmly on our arrival, and Rachel and Sarah helped bring in the cloth and trim from the car. Edward was doing homework rather than working on a model train for once, and the couch and chairs had been pushed back to make room for my sewing project. I hoped someone had thought to vacuum, because I didn't fancy groveling on the shag carpet in the dust.

Michael went upstairs to start on his homework, and I opened one of the packets with the dress pattern. There were several sizes marked on the tracing paper, and I had to make this pattern do for two of them, so Anne Kerry told me to cut the pattern to the larger of the two sizes and fold over the edges when I was cutting out the smaller size. I thought I'd be lucky to get one dress cut out in an evening, but I discovered that cutting out a dress went fast if you were diligent about following the cutting la4youts. Sarah helped lay out the material for me and explained that you cut with the right sides folded together, unless the pattern showed otherwise.

The dress patterns seemed to have an awful lot of pieces. Anne's assessment was the pattern looked pretty straightforward and wouldn't take long to sew. I wished I could believe her.

I decided that since Sarah was helping me, we'd cut out her dress first. By five-thirty, I had it all done and my back was aching from stretching and cutting on the carpet. Mercifully I hadn't cut any pieces of carpet along with the dress. I started on the second dress, the one for Shannon, who was only one size bigger than Sarah. I was concentrating so intently I didn't notice that Anne Kerry had dinner on the table and the entire family was assembled when they asked me to join them. I flushed in embarrassment and took my place next to Michael at the table. Sarah blessed the food and Anne set down a casserole of beef stew topped with biscuits. The family began helping themselves to portions from the stew in the center of the table.

"How are the bridesmaid's dresses coming, Lizzie?" asked Patrick.

"Good, actually," I responded through a mouthful of food. "I'm doing better than expected."

"Lizzie's good at following the directions," commented Anne.

"That must be a first," interjected Michael.

I flung him a look of remonstration.

"Michael..." warned Patrick.

"I should probably come over tomorrow night and help you sew," I said to Anne, ignoring the confrontational looks interchanged between Michael and his father.

"You're welcome anytime," she said.

"I just don't want to impose."

I would, of course, be doing a lot of that in the coming months, I thought.

"Feel free to impose on us anytime," added Michael. His sarcasm was unmistakable. Another long look passed between Michael and his father. "You gonna do any homework tonight, Lizzie, or are you too involved in planning this wedding?"

"There's a lot to get done," I snapped. He could have said *our* wedding.

"Glad to know you've got your priorities straight," he went on.

"I'm going to finish cutting out dress number two after dinner and then I'll come upstairs. Is there something you need to talk to me about?"

"Nothing important – I mean, nothing more important than sewing those dresses."

I had the feeling that Michael was feeling undermined by the magnitude of the preparations for our nuptials. Hell, I was feeling beleaguered by them myself. I'd set the wheels in motion and they were moving too fast, but there was no going back. In addition to everything else, now that Michael had decided he wanted to dance with me at our wedding, I had to find a DJ to play music and no clue how to pay for it.

My mother had reminded me the previous night that we needed to decide what we were making for hors d'oeuvres, not to mention ordering the cake. I thought finger food, like raw vegetables with ranch dip and fresh fruit with yogurt dip would suffice. I was sure my mother had more elaborate plans and I was counting on her to pull them together. As for the cake, I figured I'd let her pick it out. She seemed to care more about it than I did. She'd said something about buying Martinelli's sparkling apple juice, but the plethora of items needed was getting mixed up in my head.

We spent more than an hour at the craft store talking about table decorations, and we finally decided to partially fill glass bowls with white marbles, cover the marbles with water, float a swan holding a lit candle on the water, and lay a wreath of dark red silk roses around the outside of the bowl. It sounded elegant and romantic to me, and my mother assured me it would be. With Michael being so maddeningly flippant about the arrangements, I didn't dare ask his opinion. I just won't think about it, I told myself, I don't want to think about any of it.

"Thank your lucky stars all you have to do is show up in a tux," I reminded Michael.

"I was thanking my lucky stars for snatching you up before anyone else did," he came back with an insolent smile. He put his arm around my waist and I squirmed.

"You may live to regret it," I teased.

"Kids, are you ready for dessert?" interjected Anne.

She brought out a cherry pie and set it in the middle of the table.

"Is there whipped cream?" I asked eagerly.

Anne turned back to the refrigerator, retrieved a large plastic container of Cool Whip, and set it down in the center of the table. I should have known it wouldn't be the real thing like we had at my house, but I would have to make do. Michael released his hold on my waist, reached over for the container, and snapped open its lid. Then he stuck his finger in it, scooped up a dollop, and stuck it right in front of my nose.

"I am not going to eat that with your cooties in it," griped Sarah.

"Michael –" remonstrated Anne, "we have spoons for serving that – "

"Here's your whipped cream, Lizzie," Michael went on, undeterred by the complaints from his sister and mother. I scrunched his foot under mine and temporarily silenced him.

"I think she'll need some pie to go with that, Michael," Anne said lightly as she started serving up pieces of pie, setting mine in front of me first. Michael rolled his eyes at me and licked some of the cream off his finger.

"Good stuff, want some?" he asked mischievously.

"No, thank you!"

"You just said you did."

I hoped Michael wasn't deliberately testing my forbearance. "I've changed my mind now that your cooties are in it."

I threw a sympathetic glance in Sarah's direction and she smiled at me, then I began attacking my pie, furious that I'd painted myself into a corner and I couldn't now ask for the Cool Whip even though I wanted it. Out of the corner of my eye, I watched Michael load up on Cool Whip, this time using a spoon instead of his fingers. He was doing this just to goad me, I thought.

"Are you absolutely sure you don't want some?" he asked.

I dropped my spoon into my bowl, but I couldn't speak because my mouth was full of tangy cherries.

"Michael," interjected Patrick. "That really is enough."

If there was one person Michael didn't want to test, it was his father. "Sorry, Dad."

Then Michael scooped half his Cool Whip onto his spoon and dropped it on top of the remaining pie in my dish.

"I don't – " I began.

"Yes, you do, so don't argue about it." He leaned toward my ear and the unexpected rush of his breath on my neck sent the blood rushing up to my face.

"Sorry, Lizzie," he whispered. "I was out of line. Pax?"

"Only if you stop teasing me," I said softly.

"You're so fun to tease."

In the past we ribbed one another and made jokes, but it had never bothered me before. I wondered why his behavior was putting me out of joint now. Probably because I was pregnant and his parents knew it, and I was as embarrassed as hell about ruining their expectations for their son, especially when he had nothing to do with the miserable state that I was in. Rachel brought me out of my unproductive reverie.

"Lizzie," asked Rachel. "Are we going to have flowers?"

"The bridesmaids all get posies," I replied.

"She'll probably buy out the flower store," added Michael.

"Twenty years from now even you will remember our wedding was beautiful," I retorted.

"Twenty years from now I hope you'll still look as beautiful as you do right now," he returned disarmingly. I flushed for the second time in as many minutes. Michael was more adept than a sailor at taking the wind out of my sails. I started back into what remained of my pie, now adorned with Cool Whip. It was infinitely easier than dealing with Michael's backhanded compliments.

After dinner, I finished cutting out the second dress in less than thirty minutes and decided to make haste for home. I ought to go upstairs and bid Michael farewell, I thought. It wouldn't look right if I didn't, seeing that I was now his fiancée. I dragged my feet up the stairs reluctantly and opened the door to his room.

"Just want you to know I'm leaving," I said.

Michael was lying on his bed, reading his scriptures.

"Good night, then. Drive safe." He lounged nonchalantly on his bed, not looking up.

I didn't get it. At dinner he'd gone out of his way to get my attention and now he wasn't giving me the time of day. I walked over to the bed and leaned over him as though I were about to kiss him, showing as much cleavage as possible.

"Lizzie," he said, barely flicking me a glance, "that may have worked for your lover, but it won't work on me."

"Don't bring him into this."

"But he is in this. Right there." He stuck a finger into my belly. "Don't tell me he doesn't occasionally cross your mind."

I sat down on the bed, inclining away from him. That was one thing Michael had a talent for, knowing just where my weaknesses were. I closed my eyes and tried to sound convincing. "It's over, Michael. I'm done with him."

"Done with being in love with him or just done screwing him?" he demanded. He swung his legs off the bed and leaned forward with his elbows on his knees.

If Michael kept going, he would see my guts spilled out all over the floor.

"I told you already."

"But you didn't answer my question, did you?" he remarked. "And you've never told me where and when you did the evil deed – or was it deeds as in plural?"

Did it always have to come back to this? I wanted to cry but the tears wouldn't come. I put my head in my hands and spoke through cupped palms.

"You've no right to ask me anything. And you promised not to interrogate me about his identity."

"I don't care who he is – "

"Of course you do!" I exclaimed, turning the full blaze of my anger on him.

"And I haven't asked you. I was wondering about the gory details – how you got away with it."

"In the park, in the car, anywhere we could," I replied, flipping up my head and looking down nose at him. I left out the pool. That was cutting it too close.

"Trying to impress me with your creativity?"

"I was in love."

"Must've been good while it lasted."

"It didn't last," I said flatly.

"So it was good, then?"

"It wasn't good," I spat back.

"Then why were you doing it?"

"I mean it wasn't right."

"So it was good?"

"If you're asking me if I liked it, yes I did!" I yelled.

"Except, of course, for the getting pregnant part," he added. His eyes were as smooth as a lake on a windless summer day.

I wanted to break something valuable he owned. I wanted him to know how much it hurt and hurt and went on hurting for hours and days and weeks. He hadn't been rejected in love. He hadn't a clue. I got up and whipped my backpack onto my shoulder. "I was in love. I did some crazy things. It's done. Deal with it."

I shouldn't have used the past tense. I spent too much time thinking about Jason; longing for him, wishing he would come back to me; dreaming magic spells I might weave to get him back. I was both completely love-sick, and at the same time sickened from loving him. I was filled with desperate longing, and desperate to forget. I hated obsessing over him and was scared to death I might forget. But none of it would bring Jason back. I should have accepted that fact long ago, but I couldn't. I only hoped attempting to banish Jason from my thoughts counted for something, even if I was doing a supernally lousy job at it.

Michael's eyes flashed up at me. "Then I'm sorry for you. Being in love but not being loved in return, that's a kicker." I wondered if he realized how hard it was for me to hear the truth and, if he did know, whether he understood how completely and utterly broken up about Jason I was. I wondered if he felt sorry for me or if he was saying this stuff deliberately to hurt me.

"You wouldn't know anything about that, would you?" I cried, dropping my backpack and jabbing my finger in his face.

He grabbed my wrists and forced me to the floor. "Oh, wouldn't I?" he said, leaning in so close that his features were out of focus.

"Get your hands off me," I hissed, backing off and struggling to get away from him. He released me and I fell awkwardly back onto the rug on my rear end. My wrists were marked with pale red welts where his hands had been. I rubbed them defensively. I felt shattered and spent and furious. "We are *not* going to have this conversation again on our wedding night, are we?"

"Hopefully we won't be talking at all," he responded, narrowing his eyes and weighing me.

"Good, because at least we won't be arguing," I replied.

"It's going to be a long night if you're gonna spend the whole time talking," he countered.

"Speak for yourself, Michael Kerry."

"I'll just have to think of some way to shut you up," he came back softly. He was very still, like a mountain lion poised before a kill, every muscle taut.

"I'm sure you will," I taunted back.

I swear I saw his lips curl slightly at the corners, as if he were about to smile. I drew in my feet, hugged my knees, and got awkwardly to my feet.

"I gotta go," I said. I tried to keep my voice steady, but his immobility was unnerving. Only his eyes shifted, following every nuance as I reached for my backpack, adjusted it on my shoulders, and flipped up my hair.

"Good night, my most precious pearl. Sleep easy."

Sleep was never easy for me now. I was plagued with fears about what was happening to my body, inundated with the pressures of organizing a large wedding, haunted by the stern faces of my parents, disturbed and dismayed by Michael's unpredictable moods, and obsessed – completely obsessed – with images of Jason.

"I never sleep easy," I said under my breath.

I ducked my head, went out the door without a backward glance, and dragged my weary feet down the stairs into the Kerry living room I stopped only briefly to wish them goodnight. I was confused and exhausted and thoroughly fed up with Michael's questions. I was tired of being chided and upbraided and interrogated and the good-cop bad-cop games Michael was playing. I wished Michael would tell me what was bothering him instead of taking out his frustrations on me with so mercilessly. I was tired of being the butt of some joke I didn't understand.

Marching to the Wedding

Lizzie

The days marched inexorably forward towards the wedding.

I spent most of my spare time sewing the bridesmaids' dresses and not much of it with Michael, except for our weekly meetings with the bishop, chemistry homework, and the dancing lessons. By a miracle, all the dresses were finished and fit their respective owners one week before the fateful day. Rachel looked particularly stunning in the rich wine color of her dress, with part of her hair swept up and the rest curling and cascading over her shoulders.

Michael and Jeremy had been measured for their tuxes.

The flowers were ordered, the table settings prepared and stacked in boxes in my parents' garage, linen table clothes and burgundy napkins rented, and the preparation of the hors d'oeuvres assigned to a group of Relief Society sisters. I'd even convinced one of our Young Men to act as DJ and play classic rock and current pop hits for free. I was thinking Madonna, Air Supply and Phil Collins.

My mother had invited the entire ward, as I expected, and we were anticipating at least a hundred guests counting relatives and Michael's family. Cousin Celia had naturally accepted. The size of the event was way bigger than I wanted, but I didn't want to object to anyone my mother invited because she'd finagled the finances so that my father was paying for almost everything, except my dress.

As for my dress, adding the pearl and sequin trim had been a stroke of genius on Anne's part, and set off my pearl choker. She'd also sewn sequins randomly into the lace overlay so the dress sparkled as I walked and made me look like a fairy princess. Only Anne Kerry had seen me in my dress; we'd decided we wanted to keep it a surprise for everyone. She'd also fashioned a diaphanous veil for me adorned with a spray of cranberry and white-colored roses.

I decided that mothers relived their own weddings by becoming obsessed with the nuptials of their daughters, rather like playing an adult game of doll dress-up with the daughter standing in for the doll.

Because Michael and I were taking dance lessons, Alison decided she wanted to learn as well, so we commandeered Edward as a partner for Alison and the four of us showed up on Wednesday evenings right after school at Jean Gurnsey's house. Alison was decidedly the more apt student of the four, but Edward kept pace with her just to prove he had more talents than building model trains and cars. It took some adjustment to become accustomed to Michael leading me in the dance, but we could make a few impressive moves in spite of ourselves. Michael liked the swing best and I was sure it was because he liked to fling me around and make me dizzy.

The hour we spent learning to dance was about the only time we could relax around one another. On other occasions, we were in the presence of parents, classmates, the church congregation, or up in Michael's room doing homework together. Normal activities, but the dynamics had seriously changed. He hadn't tried to kiss me again since that night I gave the Family Home Evening lesson. In fact, he hadn't tried anything – he avoided physical contact with me, even when we were alone. When we sat at his desk poring over chemistry problems, he kept me at arm's length. He apologized if his arm brushed mine when he leaned in to sketch a solution. He stopped playing with the hair at the nape of my neck in Sacrament. He asked no more questions about my premarital forays. He asked no more questions about anything.

I wasn't sure if this new aloofness was a benefit or a detriment because I was beginning to feel I didn't know Michael at all. I should have seen it. I should have recognized what was happening. I was losing my best friend. No, I had already lost him. I had driven him out with a mace and chains, and built the Wall of China around myself. He was out in the cold, and it was my fault just like the rest of this farce we were playing.

But I was so preoccupied with the arrangements for the wedding and so infatuated with Jason that it went completely over my head.

Wedding Pearls

Michael

I went to visit Lizzie, my precious pearl, on the evening before our wedding day. I had a gift to present to her, and it had to be now or never. I had been debating "never" for several weeks but decided that I should do it. It was my act of faith about our future.

My great-grandfather's pearls, now going to the fourth generation of the first bride of the family: my future wife, my most precious pearl, Elizabeth.

When she told me she was pregnant, I completely panicked.

I was already very worried that she would be married or at least hopelessly in love with someone else when I returned from my mission, and that I'd never get the chance to ask for her hand. I never considered that her morals would slip to the point where she would be fooling around enough to get pregnant. When she told me, and then told me the father would not marry her, I saw my only chance to guarantee that not only would she be my wife, but that she would love and honor me for the sacrifice I was making.

One nagging question keeping me up at night: was the reason the "father would not marry her" because there were too many options and nobody would take responsibility? I couldn't imagine that – but then again, I couldn't imagine she was having sex with anyone, so what other reason? Elizabeth Sherringdon was the most knockout girl in our high school. How could any self-respecting young man toss her aside?

Was it one person, one time? Lots of times? Was she forced? Was it voluntary? Was she drunk? She would give me absolutely NO information on those nagging questions, so I was, naturally, left to my own thoughts. Those thoughts grew to become a daily, haunting nightmare that scrambled along the hallways and wove through my footsteps.

But in my panic, I also saw my opening. If I married her, and took responsibility for her and her baby, then she'd see I was worthy of her love and honor, and we'd have the wonderful marriage I had always dreamed of.

So I made the offer. To my wondrous joy, she accepted!

I then experienced a range of emotions for which I was absolutely and totally unprepared. And none of them were love, honor, or joy. I cannot say how many times I regretted making the offer. Or how many times I scolded myself for that regret.

So here I sit, in the Sherringdon's living room, the night before our marriage, with this honored family heirloom. I wish I could have told my mother all my thoughts because I know she could have helped me make the decision. But this one is on me, and I have struggled with it. I wished I had more time, but I don't. So I have made the "default decision," and decided to give her the strand of pearls. Lizzie's friends came over earlier for a hen gathering and they've finally left. That's what she told me on the phone. Her mother has gone to the church to set up something for tomorrow's reception, Lindsey is staying over with a friend, and her father has secluded himself in his home office. I must grasp these few precious minutes with Lizzie alone. I've been carrying the pearl necklace with me for days trying to find the right moment and summon up the courage. It's now or never.

"Lizzie," I start, "my great-grandfather was given a strand of thirty-eight perfect pearls by the families he baptized on his mission to Japan. He presented them to his bride just before their wedding. She gave them to her daughter, my grandmother, just before her wedding, and my grandmother in turn gave them to her daughter, my mother, just before hers. Mom gave them to me so I could present them to you. Tradition says that the first bride in the family should wear them on her wedding day. These are our only family heirlooms..."

Lizzie's face is nearly devoid of color. She sits in shocked silence as I hand her the old, handmade, velvet-lined box that contains the strand of pearls. "Elizabeth, my love, please accept these pearls as a token of all I hold dear. You are my most precious pearl, and you deserve to wear these. Please wear them tomorrow for me."

She is silent as she carefully opens the box and draws in her breath when she recognizes their magnificence. I see tears welling up in her eyes as she runs the pearls through her fingers, their luster silken as the moon, and I am hoping that these pearls will heal whatever is between us.

"I do not deserve them," she whispers, "so I cannot accept them."

A single tear drops from her cheek onto one of the lustrous gems.

"But you do," I say. "You are my most precious pearl. You always have been. There is nobody who deserves them more than you do. I have loved you for as long as I can remember."

She sits there gazing at the pearls in her hands, lifts her glistening eyes to mine, then drops her lashes. She does not weep openly, but I see tears withheld. I hope they are tears of joy.

An abiding silence layers the air between us, thick with hope and dread, happiness and pain, memories of childhood games and teenage teasing, and this new tenuous connection, as delicate as the string of gleaming pearls.

She murmurs low, and I strain to catch her words. "That must be why Anne wanted to put pearls and sequins on my wedding dress. She knew about this all along."

"She has known how much I loved you for a long time," I confess.

The wall cracks behind us and Lizzie leaps up from the couch with a start, spilling the box and its precious cargo out onto the thick carpet at her feet. I start scrambling to retrieve the pearls and prevent the box from being broken.

"What the hell are you doing here?" bellows my soon-to-be father-in-law. I can't imagine what distracted him from his office or how he knew we were in his house.

"Get out!" he yells. "It is too late for you to be here." Then, directed at Lizzie, now as white as the plush carpet, "And why the hell did you let him in?"

Lizzie drops to her knees next to me on the floor as I scoop up the pearl necklace and return it to the safety of its box. I set the box gently on the table. Our eyes meet as we scrabble on our hands and knees, and hers are lit with unexpected merriment, as if we were two kids who'd successfully pulled off a prank. In a second the lightness slips away and Lizzie hustles to her feet.

"I'm so sorry, Dad, we didn't mean to upset you," she intones. She's almost taunting him with the contrite tone, but he's too enraged to figure it out.

She turns her back on him, pulls me to my feet, and walks me to the front door. She leans up and kisses me on the cheek, ignoring the ongoing rant from the office. A slight smile plays on her lips.

"OK, I'll wear them," she whispers.

Perhaps the pearls have worked their magic.

Wedding Day Eve

I didn't want to flirt with tradition, so I hadn't planned to see Michael the night before our wedding day. But he had come by and presented me with a family heirloom – such an impressive strand of pearls, that I am going to have to take some serious time to digest what it means. His precious gift and declaration of his feelings for me have changed things. But I'm not sure how. So I'm filing it away for the time being.

Before Michael arrived unexpectedly, Shannon and Janine came over to my house to celebrate my nuptials and make wisecracks about getting hitched. We spent the time gossiping about which high-school girlfriend would end up with which guy and trying to imagine who Jeremy Stein was going to dance with at my wedding. I observed that the best man always danced with the bridesmaids, but they said all four of them couldn't have him at once, so I proposed they take turns. They laughed about him being "too short for any of us!" and collapsed into giggles over the dining room table, evoking enough noise to disturb my father from his home office. He admonished us to "keep the noise down or you'll be waking the dead!" As soon as he'd re-ensconced himself back in his man cave, they burst into raucous laughter over his outburst. They renewed their speculation as to which bridesmaid "almost cute enough to be a Hobbit" Jeremy Stein was going to pick for the first dance. Whoever he picked, they were going to take it as a sign and I admonished them for being 'sign seekers,' which elicited further spasms of laughter, albeit muffled so as not to awaken the bear who lived in my father's home office.

They both tried on their burgundy bridesmaid's dresses and tried to outdo each other, parading around my room like models on a runway. They begged me to give them a sneak preview of my dress. I stood firm and claimed it would be bad luck for them to see me in it before the big day. In truth, I wasn't ready for anyone to see me in it yet.

They dropped innumerable innuendos about my "deflowering," and I decided not to enlighten them with my greater light and knowledge.

All in good time, I thought.

Janine wouldn't let up on my "wonderful kisser" description of Michael and I chastised her for levity and light-mindedness and starting rumors, which did little to deter her. Just before ten, my mother appeared to tell the girls it was time to leave and to inform me she was headed over to our chapel building to put the finishing touches on table displays for the reception. Janine and Shannon planned to be back at nine in the morning, giving us over three hours to prepare for the first day of the rest of my life as Mrs. Lizzie Kerry.

After the girls and subsequently Michael had left, I pulled on my pajamas and checked my suitcase to make sure I had everything packed for our three-day jaunt up the coast. I set the box of pearls out on my dresser so that I wouldn't forget to don them for the ceremony. Michael had not told me exactly where we were going, but it was somewhere up north. This did nothing to allay my anxiety. He was going to spirit me off like the Pied Piper and there was nothing I could do about it. I'd packed a Sunday dress, because if Michael had any say in the matter, which no doubt he would as my husband, we'd be going to church in the morning. There were worse ways I could be spending tomorrow morning, I told myself. Too bad we didn't have church on Mondays.

I lay in bed thinking of Jason, wishing sorely I could hold him one more time.

Then I chastised myself for being so bloody stupid to even be wanting him at all!

I tried to mull over every detail of the wedding reception that had been organized, from the bridal bouquet to the bowls with swans floating in candlelight.

I thought of how I'd sewn the pieces of the bridesmaid's gowns together under the watchful eye of Anne. How Rachel and Sarah had gasped to see their luminous gowns emerge from the scraps of material.

How I'd fixed Rachel's hair and turned her into a ravishing young woman.

How Edward and Alison had shown me their latest dance steps, impressing me to the max.

How Michael had stayed in the background, watching the preparations. It felt to me like he was a mountain lion waiting in the sagebrush, biding his time. He wouldn't have to wait much longer.

Then I cried for innocence lost, and hopes dashed, for the unborn child whose father had demanded him dead, threatening to destroy me in the process.

For the world's best friend, Michael, who seemed to be dead and gone, and for Michael, the soon-to-be husband.

For the love I was stupid enough to think I had found, and for the love I may have always had, and forfeited.

For the woman I must become, and the faithless girl I was leaving behind.

Sleep was long in coming and served only to deepen the dark torrent of my thoughts.

Wedding Day Morning

Lizzie

I awoke long before the dawn broke and curled into the sheets, wishing the dawn would never come and I could remain in limbo in the shadows of the night. It didn't matter that the darkness brought its own horrors and memories that plagued my sanity. The days, and the coming day especially, seemed like a bad dream.

As the light sneaked in between the slats of the blinds, I crept out of bed and peeked in my closet to reacquaint myself with my bridal gown. It hung in my closet with the four bridesmaids' dresses, gleaming in the gloom, like the pearl necklace waiting to be taken out of its box.

Today I would dazzle my friends and relatives, but it would be a false depiction. Even Michael did not know the illicit desires of my heart; at least I hoped he did not. I should certainly not be dreaming of another on my wedding day. I fell to my knees and prayed for the strength to overcome the sinful yearnings of the flesh, and that such lusts would not fool me again.

I passed an hour in soft light of dawn contemplating the ill-fated events that had led up to this day, until I heard my mother stirring down the hallway. Quietly I stole back into bed and pulled the covers over me. Minutes later she tapped on my door and asked me if I was ready for breakfast. For once I had been spared morning sickness, so I responded in the affirmative and, still dressed in pajamas, made my way to the kitchen.

She offered me a cup of orange blossom herbal tea and anxiously inquired if I was still sure I wanted to marry Michael. If I was certain of one thing, it was that I couldn't allow an unborn baby to grow up without a father, and I was determined to do whatever was necessary for the baby's happiness – Jason's baby. If that meant giving up what I wanted, then so be it. I wished I could learn to believe my own credo. If I only had more faith, I would feel less trepidation about what was in store for me today.

My father came downstairs in slacks and a casual shirt, took his habitual place at the kitchen table, and disappeared into the *Wall Street Journal*. At least he was his usual self.

My mother hovered over us, calming her nerves by fussing over everything. She whipped up scrambled eggs and served them up with a plateful of fancy muffins from in the Albertson's bakery.

Thankfully, Lindsey had gone to spend the night with a friend, and I had a couple of hours before Janine, Shannon, Rachel and Sarah descended on our household. I decided I would take a long soak in the tub and wash my hair to help myself relax before they arrived.

My mother assumed my disinclination for conversation was due to a bad case of nerves. She could hardly have expected her daughter to be nursing a furtive longing for another man on her wedding day.

They say love and hate are opposites, but that is not now, nor has it ever been, true. The opposite of love is indifference. This is why when you both love and hate someone, the hate causes the love to become an all-engulfing inferno of anguish and pain. It might be easy to forget someone you once loved, eventually thinking of them less and less, until you no longer do. But once hate has cemented the emotional state, the process of forgetting becomes almost impossible. While my love might have, at one time, just been lust on steroids, the emotions that hammer on my psyche today are love and hate, battling for supremacy over my psyche. That was the battle my mother mistook for nerves, which should, at some level, qualify me for an acting award.

"I'm fine, Mom," I said flatly, "I'm just going upstairs to take a bath." I finished up the last crumbs of my cranberry-nut muffin.

"Good idea. Try to relax, sweetheart, everything's going to go off without a hitch," she reassured me.

I smiled at her, wishing I felt more anticipation and less dread. "I'm sure it will, Mom, especially since you're in charge. Thanks for everything – I truly mean it!"

I jumped up and kissed her. She had shown her love in the only way she knew how: by planning a stylish wedding and giving me everything she would have dreamed about having twenty years ago. I could hardly fault her for fulfilling her fantasies in her daughter. I was sure I would do the same for mine.

"I'll be in the bathroom, then," I threw over my shoulder as I began climbing the stairs. My feet were reluctant to obey my directions, and my stomach wasn't feeling as peachy as it had before breakfast. Please not today, I thought.

In the tub I stared at my belly, wondering about the life inside it. I speculated about whether the nameless 'it' would be a girl or boy, and when I would first feel its movement.

It seemed incongruous that one created life during a moment of passion, and then would nurture it through years of mindless drudgery.

I didn't know if it would be possible for me to feel the kind of love I felt for Jason ever again – something so out of control that it consumed my days and nights, leaving me aching and hollow when I awoke to the knowledge that he was gone. I wished the water in the tub would rise over my head and I could sink into oblivion, but that was not the Lord's will.

He preferred us to face our demons. We were promised His help when we did, and perhaps I was receiving that help, but it certainly did not feel that way on this momentous day.

I heard a commotion downstairs and realized I must have dozed off in the tub. In the interim, my bridesmaids had arrived. Quickly I stepped out, drew a towel around me and dried myself off. I wrapped my hair up around my head in a second towel and threw on my robe. That was when the first wave of nausea hit. I really didn't want to contemplate cranberry muffin in the toilet, so I closed my eyes as I hung my head over the bowl. The storm had broken although the rain hadn't started falling yet. I was dreading the rain.

I heard someone banging on the bathroom door, opening it, and Janine's voice calling down the stairs from the hallway, "Lizzie's throwing up in here."

I retched again. Janine leaned over and pulled the handle to flush the toilet. My eyes were still closed.

"What the hell, Lizzie? Got a raging case of the nerves, or what?"

I had got a case of "and baby makes three" and I wasn't even married yet, I thought. My throat felt dry and raspy. The toilet finished flushing and I opened my eyes.

"I guess."

"I'll get you some water."

"Yeah, sure," I replied, hoping I wasn't going to lose it again.

I stood up, flipped down the toilet lid, and sat down on it with my head between my knees. I heard footsteps scampering downstairs and Janine giving directions. She came back with a glass of ice-cold water and handed it to me. I drank eagerly.

I thought of Michael in the park on the day he proposed pressing the button on the water fountain and quenching the bitter taste of bile, and Jason swimming laps ferociously in the high-school pool. I wanted all of those mind-wrenching images to go away.

"You gonna be OK, Lizzie?" Janine asked.

"Give me five minutes to figure it out," I said, taking another deep gulp from the glass. Five minutes, five hours, five days – like I was going to figure it out by then. "Just go in my room. The dresses are all hanging in the closet."

After a few minutes, when it appeared the nausea had passed, I stood resolutely and headed up the stairs.

My mother had set up her electric hot rollers on her dressing table along with an assortment of pins, ties and ribbons. Her makeup kit was strewn on the spare bed. She'd brought up extra chairs from the dining room, so the girls had a place to sit. Rachel and Sarah were staring up at me from their positions in two of the chairs as if I were an apparition. Janine was absorbed in checking out the dresses and Shannon was brushing out her long golden hair.

"You gonna be all right, Lizzie?" asked Sarah.

"Of course," I lied.

"You don't look so good," added Rachel.

Neither would you if you'd just chucked up your eggs and muffins in the toilet, I thought.

"I feel fine," I said, hoping Michael wouldn't get word of the morning's events from one of his sisters.

"Let's start with Sarah," suggested my mother. She'd wisely picked the least vain of the four bridesmaids.

The electric rollers were already heating up when they began brushing out Sarah's shoulder-length hair. When they had her hair all fixed up, my mother did her makeup. I definitely had an appreciation for ugly ducklings that turned into swans after seeing the transformation. Makeup softened Sarah's thin nose and brought out her deep-set eyes. I realized they were the same pale blue as Michael's. The rich burgundy of the dress enhanced her fair coloring, and she looked as delicate as a painted china doll.

Shannon went next, followed by Janine and finally Rachel. With her springy dark curls and apple-red cheeks, Rachel glowed in her bridesmaid's dress. She would turn heads at my wedding today. Shannon and Janine were as impressive as I had expected them to be. They looked confident and excited, feelings I did not share at the prospect of my imminent nuptials.

Around eleven am, my father knocked on the door to announce the arrival of the flower bouquets and left them on the floor outside. Shannon retrieved them and our entire company marveled at the balls of burgundy and white lilies interspersed with baby's breath. There were single white carnation boutonnieres for Michael, Jeremy, and both of our fathers, as well as purple orchids for both mothers. My bouquet was the most splendid of all, boasting cream and burgundy lilies along with baby's breath and two single red roses of perfect shape and size, and merlot-colored ribbons that trailed almost to the floor.

My turn to be coiffed came all too soon. My mother spent an eternity fixing the hot curlers in my hair to make sure she achieved exactly the effect she was intending. It took a long time to pin in the veil, and I was betting I wouldn't be taking it out until I was alone with Michael tonight. Half of my hair was up and half down. It cascaded over my shoulders in big rolls, reminiscent of a 1940s hair style. Sarah kept walking around me, fingering my flowing dark hair, and getting in the way. I was glad my mother didn't seem to mind. One of my mother's more endearing qualities was patience, a virtue I unfortunately had not acquired from her.

"You're so beautiful, Lizzie," Sarah said. "I wish I could look this good."

"You will – on your wedding day."

"Thanks, Lizzie. I'm glad you're going to be my sister."

"You're welcome."

"Will you fix my hair on Sundays?"

"Sure." Making Sarah beautiful would be infinitely preferable to what Michael would want to be up to with me on Sunday mornings, I thought.

Having finished my hair, my mother went downstairs to take a break and bring up refreshments, which consisted of apple juice, granola bars and melon slices. I was hoping I could keep them down.

The girls and I sat around in our slips crunching granola and sucking melon pieces. I imagined we'd be reapplying our lipstick. I was starting to feel better. Lounging on the bed and floor with my bridesmaids, I could almost believe everything was going to turn out all right. Must be something to do with safety in numbers, I thought. Too bad Michael and I couldn't bring the girls up the coast with us.

Then my mother had picked up the plates and glasses and carried them all downstairs, leaving us alone to finish up. The bridesmaids donned their gowns and I helped smooth out ruffles and make final adjustments to hair and ribbons. They all had long, dark red ribbons fastened in their hair. They were an impressive group. If I were Jeremy, I'd have a hard time deciding which bridesmaid to ask out on the dance floor first. Luckily, Michael wouldn't have that problem.

Finally, it was my turn to put on my gown—and those wretched pearls. Shannon and Janine held the dress while I stepped into it. Sarah knelt behind me and began fastening the loops up the back.

"You're fidgeting, Lizzie," she remarked.

"Sorry."

Everyone waited with breath drawn while Sarah finished the loops. She stood up and stepped back from me.

"Let's take a look at you," said Shannon.

I made a dramatic, sweeping turn.

"Jiminy Christmas!" exclaimed Janine.

"You look like a fairy princess," breathed Sarah.

"You're gonna knock Michael's socks off," said Rachel softly.

Probably more than his socks, I thought.

Too bad Michael wasn't the person whose socks I was dreaming about. I turned toward the floor-length mirror hanging on the back of the door. Even I had to gasp. The dress sparkled and twinkled like the sky on a clear night. The pearl and sequined trim set off my wrists and neckline, and Michael's strand of pearls around my neck shone with an alluring luster. With my pallor and the blue rings under my eyes, I gave the impression of a tragic heroine like Ophelia in Hamlet. I looked as brittle as the thin ice overlaying a lake in springtime, ready to break the moment anyone dared set foot on me.

"There is one last thing I need," I said to Janine, "that wooden box on the dresser."

Janine opened the wooden box, showing the velvet-lined interior and the strand of perfect pearls. "Oh, my word," she cried, "these are the most beautiful pearls I have ever seen! Where did you get them?"

"They are Kerry family heirlooms. Michael gave them to me last night. His mother wore them on her wedding day, and her mother, and her mother. It's a family tradition."

Janine brought them to me while the other girls looked on, gasping at the contents. She stood right there in my face, looked me in the eyes, and declared, "You had better be the best wife any man has ever had!"

Her words stabbed me with a reality I could not deny, no matter how much I tried. Michael was the best husband on earth, and he was marrying the most heinous bride, a witch in white clothing.

Janine fastened the pearl necklace around my neck, and I turned to look at myself in the mirror again. As stunning as the dress and veil looked, the pearls bloomed against my skin. I was aghast at the value of this treasure I had been given. How could I ever be the wife Michael deserved? Especially since I couldn't stop dreaming about my baby's worthless sperm donor?

Time to get Married

Lizzie

"What time is it?" I asked.

"Twelve-thirty," answered Rachel.

"Time to go, right?" ventured Shannon.

"Yes. Can someone go down and tell Dad we're ready?" I asked.

He was taking Shannon, Janine, and me in the Audi. Sarah and Rachel were relegated along with my mother to my Nissan, which Michael and I would be driving away from the chapel when we set out on our honeymoon later in the afternoon.

I did not want to think about it.

"Let's get the flowers," added Sarah.

She began collecting the posies off the dresser and gave each bridesmaid one. She handed me my handsome bouquet with its trails of ribbons. My hands were shaking when I took it. Meanwhile, Shannon had gone downstairs to find my mother and father.

"Showtime, girls," I announced, trying to sound braver than I felt. We marched down the stairs like soldiers going into battle.

Rachel remembered to fetch the suitcase from my bedroom on the way down. I stared at it gloomily as she set it down in our lobby. My mother picked it up and took it with her out the front door to load into my car. She was dressed in a cream suit with a burgundy blouse, fishnet white stockings, and cherry-colored spike heels the color of black Tartarian cherries. I knew that she was a looker in her day, but it still surprised me how she could pull off a glamour shot. Most of the time the smile on her lips never reached her eyes, but today might be an exception to the rule. She was in her element organizing my wedding.

I heard my father roll up the garage door and back out onto the driveway. Shannon flung open the front door and the troop of bridesmaids traipsed out across the stepping stones. I followed behind, glancing around one last time at the vaulted ceilings and glass chandelier hanging in the entry way, realizing I didn't live here any longer. I locked the front door and turned towards the Audi. My car was parked out by the curb, my mother already at the wheel, and Rachel and Sarah were getting in.

My father actually whistled. "Aren't you the queen of the show today, Lizzie?"

I found myself smiling. It usually took a major win in a corporate lawsuit to see my father looking this self-satisfied. He got out of the driver's seat, walked around to the passenger's side, and held the door for me.

"If you intended to dress to impress, Miss Lizzie, you surely succeeded," he added.

"Thank you, Dad," I said.

Thanks for nothing, I thought, remembering that he hadn't been willing to pay for the dress but was going to take full credit for my appearance today. Fortunately, he didn't know how much he'd actually contributed to the wedding, thanks to my mother's wangling. I carefully picked up my skirts and settled myself in the seat. Shannon and Janine were already installed on the back seat. I twisted my head to look at them and gave them a mischievous grin.

"Let's knock 'em dead, girls."

They giggled. My father closed the door, walked around the hood and slipped into the driver's seat.

"Anyone missing anything?"

Nothing vital, I thought, other than my sanity.

"We're all set," I said boldly.

The trip to the chapel passed all too quickly. We went in by a side door and convened in the Young Women's classroom. Rachel and Sarah were already there. My mother had disappeared to make the final touches to the refreshment tables.

"I'll let you know when they're ready for us," said my father, making an elegant exit. He was clad in a black suit with the faintest pinstripe and looked impressive himself. I started pacing up and down, and Shannon and Janine said I really ought to sit down. They probably figured I was going to toss up the granola bars.

"I'm fine, leave me alone," I said, twisting the bouquet.

"Let me fix this lock of hair," suggested Sarah. "Stand still a minute."

She laid a roll of dark hair over my left shoulder to match the right one.

"Now don't toss your head."

"You're gonna mess up your flowers if you keep doing that," added Janine. "You've got the ribbon all twisted."

Sarah stepped aside while Janine took my flowers, rearranged the flowing ribbons, and handed them back to me.

"For goodness' sake, Lizzie, stand still."

"You're not the one getting married," I protested.

"You want me to redo your lipstick? Shannon has some stashed in her posy," Janine asked.

"Bad idea," remarked Rachel. "When she kisses the groom, it'll smudge."

I really wished my future little sister hadn't made that helpful suggestion, I thought.

"Good point, Rachel," answered Janine, her opinion of Rachel having risen considerably as a result of this insightful observation.

"They're ready for us!" called my father as he opened the door. "Don't all of you look lovely? Take my arm, Lizzie."

I walked up to him with an impressive swagger. I could lay it on too, I thought.

"Ready, Dad."

I took his arm. We exited the classroom with the foursome of bridesmaids on our tail and made our way down the hallway and into the Cultural Hall. I had no idea how they were going to place the chairs for the brief ceremony, but as it turned out, the chairs were set around tables which were ranged around the side of the hall. The company was standing below the stage with an aisle down the center. Michael and Jeremy were waiting at the end of it. I gripped my father's forearm more tightly and stared at the floor.

I was skating down the ice and I could see the water swirling beneath it, like the tumult in my ribs. I hadn't seen Jason yet, but I knew he was in the crowd somewhere gawking at me. Eat your heart out, you worthless, piss-ant punk.

I glanced over my shoulder at my bridesmaids to make sure they were still with us. Maybe they'd fallen through the ice. Sarah flashed me an encouraging smile from the rear. Our DJ hit a button and Vivaldi's Spring Concerto began to play. My father started walking again. I finally raised my eyes from the lines of the basketball court and swept the crowd. I saw Cousin Celia in a dark blue tent, but no sign of Jason.

I located Michael and fixed my gaze on him.

Please don't let me fall, Michael, don't let the river take me. You're the only one who can get me through this. Be strong for me because I don't know what I am doing here.

I was walking up to them, gripping my father's forearm like it was the lifeline between the shore and a thick sheet of ice, and I was staring at Michael and Jeremy as if I'd never seen them before – Michael with his lustrous, immaculate blonde hair; Jeremy with his dark Arabic looks and the curls ringing his forehead – Michael lean in his black tux and Jeremy fidgeting with sleeves that were a tad too long.

One moment I was hanging onto my father's arm, the next he had merged into the background and I was hopelessly plunging into the freezing darkness of the black water of my future. I stood next to Michael, my eyes locked on his. This could not be happening to me. The ice encompassing me melted as a wave of genuine affection for Michael swept over me. He took my hand and his touch was such a shock I thought I had lost it in the icy water. Don't let the river take me, I silently begged him, still fixed on his gaze, don't lose me in the blackness.

He turned me to face Bishop Dalton, whose presence I had hardly recognized. I smiled, feeling as numb as a frozen river. Bishop Dalton bestowed us the slightest of smiles in return. He began the ceremony, following the standard wording for marriages sanctioned by the State of California. For the benefit of the company, he said that rings were external symbols and that, as members of the Church of Jesus Christ of Latter-day Saints, we did not place value on these worldly demonstrations of spiritual unity. Bishop Dalton wasn't speaking for me, of course. Those damn pearls were worth a fortune, and they were as much a curse as a blessing.

He ended with the fateful words, "I now pronounce you husband and wife. You may kiss the bride."

Thank God Rachel had made that comment about the lipstick. Michael gently put his arms around my waist and gave me a lingering, tender kiss. I turned hot and cold. This is not happening to me, I told myself, and I was not supposed to be kissing my best friend while the cretin who took my virginity watched us.

"Lizzie, you look fantastic," he whispered in my ear as he released me. "Thanks for wearing the heirloom."

Bishop Dalton shook hands with us. Michael hugged Jeremy and I got congratulatory hugs from all four bridesmaids. Then Jeremy took the portable microphone from the bishop and announced that we were going to stand under the arch with our families for photographs. After that, members of the ward could personally wish us their best in the lineup.

It was going to take a lot more than wishes to make this a happy marriage.

While the photographer shot pictures for our wedding album, Jeremy suggested the guests make themselves comfortable in the seating provided and avail themselves of the refreshments. By this time. I was wishing I'd been able to keep down more than granola bars and melon slices earlier in the day.

Michael led me over to the white arch I'd seen employed in numerous ward functions, including weddings. This time it was draped with garlands of leaves and crimson roses. We stood in the center. I was on Michael's right followed by my father and mother and the bridesmaids, and Michael's parents were to his left. The camera flashed and my mother worked me in-between shots, checking my hair, flowers, and dress. There were pictures of me with the four bridesmaids, with Michael and Jeremy, both of us with each set of parents, and a group picture. In the shot Michael and I later picked for our bedroom, I was staring up at him with an anxious expression on my face, barely smiling, and he was grinning down at me confidently. The necklace shone. In the picture of me and the bridesmaids, my eyes looked dark and hollow, and everyone but Sarah was showing lots of teeth. She was furthest from the center of the tableau, smiling shyly at the camera. Michael and I looked more relaxed in the snap with his parents than my own, understandably so, as Patrick Kerry had made a wisecrack that caused me to giggle. It was the picture in which I looked the most at ease.

After the photos, I endured endless handshakes and hugs from friends and relatives, including Cousin Celia, most of whom passed by in a blur. Suddenly Jason was shaking hands with Michael and I thought I'd been plunged into the river of ice water again.

"Looks like you got the hottest girl in the ward," he said under his breath to Michael, clapping him on the back in congratulatory fashion.

"I'm a smooth operator," replied Michael with a self-satisfied grin. If I were really a witch, I would have turned them both into frogs.

Jason moved down the line and took my hand. "Well, if it isn't the delectable Liz Sherringdon. Err, I mean Sister Liz Kerry, of course. Congratulations." I shuddered at the enunciation of my new name. Others may have said it, but his was the first time I remembered hearing it: Sister Liz Kerry. Whatever have I done?

He put his arms around me, held me next to him momentarily, enough to cause me to feel my insides heave, and breathed into my ear, "You are a spectacular woman. I'm eternally grateful for what you did."

He might be eternally grateful, but I was praying he would be eternally damned. His lips brushed my neck and I felt tempted to shove him onto the floor, but since his father was shaking hands with Michael, and Michael and I were practically touching, I restrained myself. As he released me, Jason ran his hand down my back and along the curve of my waist.

"You look lovely, Lizzie. Your husband is a lucky man," Jason expressed his words in a way that made me realize he had practiced them until he had it down pat.

May your soul rot in hell, Jason Dalton, I thought.

I smiled sweetly at him. "Thanks, Jace. Glad you could find the time to make it."

I hoped the irony was not lost on him. Before I knew it, he was gone and Bishop Dalton was shaking my hand and hugging me.

"You made the right decision, Lizzie. Keep the faith," he said under his breath.

It was gonna take a lot more than faith, I thought, but I could go for a miracle. Anytime would be great, Lord, like—now.

"Thanks, Bishop – for everything."

That's when I thought I was going to lose the melon and granola bars, all over Bishop Dalton. I prayed fervently to God that, because this was my wedding day and I'd done the right thing for the life inside me, He would please help me keep my lunch down. I would do anything, I begged, to make Heavenly Father happy, but I couldn't embarrass myself in front of everybody today. If I threw up, I reasoned, somebody would be sure to figure out I was pregnant.

"You all right, love?" whispered Michael in my ear.

"Hold my hand," I responded.

He did, tightly. The swaying universe slowly came back to equilibrium. Jason was out of range, chatting with Rachel somewhere further down the lineup.

"I'm OK now, thanks. You're a rock," I said under my breath to Michael.

He brought my fingers to his lips and kissed them softly. "Everything's going to be fine, my pearl."

"I know," I replied.

"Hey, you two, just want to wish you the best," came the voice of Becky, Bishop Dalton's wife. She drew us back to the present, as if Michael and I had been in a time warp.

She shook hands with Michael and hugged me, then moved on. The line of people waiting to congratulate us was getting shorter, and soon petered out. Michael slipped away to the refreshment tables and brought me something to eat, then disappeared again to speak to Joey, our DJ. Jeremy told me it was time to start dancing. Then Michael returned to Jeremy and the bridal party. Both sets of parents wished us well and went to find seats at the tables. Michael wandered off again, chatting with his parents.

I was munching crackers and cheese when Jeremy asked me, "Lizzie, who's that?"

He was indicating the elegant Rachel, who was chatting amiably with Janine and Shannon to my right.

"Rachel, Michael's sister," I answered.

"Think she'd go on a date with me?" he went on.

"Why don't you ask her to dance first, idiot," I teased.

"Good point."

"If she said yes to the date, you'd still have to deal with Michael's parents. I don't know if they'd let her go out with a guy of a different faith."

"We have similar values and all that," he said earnestly.

"What d'you mean?" I inquired.

"I'm Jewish."

"I know," I responded.

"We believe in chastity before marriage, too."

I flushed and stammered, "Why, of course."

Realizing he'd caught me unawares, he added, "Sorry, guess I shouldn't have brought that up on a day like today."

"And what secrets are you two sharing?" came Michael's voice and I jumped, nearly dropping my plate. He slipped his arm proprietorially around my waist. I squirmed but he held me firmly.

"Jeremy's trying to figure out which bridesmaid to dance with," I said lightly, as Michael leaned into me and brushed his cheek against mine.

"I think it's time I took my wife out on the dance floor, don't you?" said Michael.

"Sure," I whispered. Jeremy took my plate.

"Have fun, guys," Jeremy threw after us.

I didn't know Michael had set me up, but the minute we walked out into the open space in the center of the floor, Air Supply's "Every Woman in the World" hit the air waves.

"I think we do a slow rumba to this," he said. The rumba was, after all, the dance of love.

He took charge of the dance and started me off in a box so that we could fall into the rhythm. He was holding me more closely than our instructor had taught us, but I figured it wasn't a position I should argue on our wedding day. I saw Jeremy dancing with Rachel out of the corner of my eye. I could see Jeremy's soft eyes going all mushy. I smiled.

"Did you pick this?" I asked.

"What makes you think that?"

"You don't like Air Supply – you say it's elevator music. This song is kinda romantic."

"This is a wedding, Lizzie. For my sake, you could pretend."

"I was saving that for tonight, lover boy," I returned.

If he was miffed, Michael didn't show it, unless the barely perceptible tightening of his jaw was anything to go by.

"Don't you want to impress this crowd, Lizzie dear?" he went on lightly. "Or is it your father you want to annoy?"

He knew very well I'd smile as wide as a Cheshire cat if I could find a way to irritate my father. What he didn't know was that impressing Jason with our dancing prowess would be even more gratifying.

"Let's show 'em, then, my love," I replied with a toss of my head.

I tried to slip away from him into the standard dance hold, but he was having none of it. He started moving then, sliding his hips into mine, and I'd never known him to dance so suggestively before. He whirled me around from one fluid movement to another. He was showing off and loving every second of it. I saw the white-covered tables with their candlelit swans and the faces of the guests and the present table piled high with boxes adorned with silver ribbons and the garlands of crimson flowers reeling by. Then my eyes caught Michael's as he swung me out and there was such a challenge in them that I found myself laughing and wanting to dare him right back. So I played to his moves and hung on his eyes, so that every time he wheeled me around, I locked onto his torrid gaze and returned fire for fire. I found myself caught up in an intricate play of legs and arms and hips and always the smoke of Michael's eyes; then the flash of his teeth and my own laughter as he caught me to him when the music faded and teased his lips against mine, just for an instant, to let me know that if I thought this was a game, he was going to play for keeps.

I heard applause from the guests, and Michael and I took an elaborate bow. Jeremy came up to us, holding Rachel's hand.

"You're stylin', man," he began. "Mind if I have the honor of a dance with the bride?"

"You'll have a tiger by the tail, but you're welcome," Michael said, handing me off with a flourish. I glared at him. "Don't miss me too much, Lizzie. I'll be back."

I flashed Michael a sultry look and batted my eyelids, just to let him know I could play at his level. Dire Straits' "Money for Nothing" began to boom out of the speakers.

"Let's do it, Jeremy," I said. Out of the corner of my eye I was watching Michael. He was leading Janine out to dance. I decided I really ought to get to know more of this cougar's slicker moves or he was going to catch me unawares someday.

Jeremy and I danced opposite one another, occasionally touching hands and sharing friendly smiles. I was beginning to like Jeremy more and more, in a best-man kind of way. After Jeremy, my father stepped up to dance with me. To my surprise, he was an accomplished dancer, and we did a foxtrot to Phil Collins' "One More Night." My father was followed by Patrick Kerry, who was all bounce and fun. When Patrick Kerry left to dance with his wife, I turned away from him and walked straight into Jason Dalton. I nearly cursed.

"Liz, think I could have this dance?" he asked.

He knew I couldn't refuse. I didn't want to arouse suspicion, so I allowed him to take me in his arms and dance with me while the room reverberated with Gloria Esteban's "Bad Boyz," which Jason certainly was.

I am falling into the river and Michael isn't here to save me. Jason has me and he knows it. Even though I belong to Michael now, Jason still moves me and I want him in the worst kind of way. Every cell in my body is crying out to know him one more time, but I must let him hold me and pretend he means nothing. I must be an ice queen with blue water for blood and crystals for eyes and a stone for a heart.

Jason held me lightly as if he'd never known me more intimately, and I ached for him and ached for the dance to be over so that I wouldn't have to endure his nearness and the lust it evoked. As the music faded, someone tapped Jason on the shoulder. It was Michael, and the stone I had for a heart rolled over and over in the torrent of ice water flowing through me.

"Mind if I take my wife back?" Michael said unsuspectingly.

"She's yours, man," replied Jason, letting me go.

"Can't wait," I interjected, placing my arms around Michael's neck and giving him a sultry smooch. My intensity took Michael by surprise. I wished I could have seen Jason's expression.

We started a swing, Michael's favorite, which was no mean feat in a bridal gown. I lost sight of Jason in the melee of the crowd.

"Honey, I hope that wasn't pretending," he said as we came together. He swung me out and around.

When he reeled me back in, I said defiantly, "Don't count on it."

He tossed me out and back, bringing me in with my back to him. "With you, Lizzie, I don't count on anything."

Now he'd made me mad. I was about to protest his assessment of me when he threw me out around him in a circle and I had to wait until I'd made it back to the starting point before I could respond.

"I'm not a flake. I keep my promises. You'll see," I flashed.

"Can't wait," he returned suavely. He whipped me out and back again and I was beginning to think he was handling me wildly on purpose. I was trying to remember how we'd been in practice, but we were moving so fast I could only concentrate on the steps, or I was going to missing the timing.

"I'm sure you won't," I fired off as I flew by him.

He gave me a wicked grin and I couldn't help but respond. I would show him tonight. I would show him. He knew *nothing* about the real stuff that happens between a man and a woman.

"So which is it, Lizzie?" he went on, tossing me out again.

"Which is what?" I flung at him as I swung by.

"Are you really an angel –" Swing out, rock step, back together, " – or am I dancing with the devil?"

Out again but he was twirling me in the opposite direction and I almost missed his cue.

I was so out of breath by the time I was close enough to speak on the next step that I couldn't get the words out.

"Or do you like to keep me guessing?" he tossed out after the next turn before I had a chance to interject. White table cloths and burgundy napkins and candlelit swans flew by.

"Both!" I managed on the next go round.

Out again, feeling my head spin, then he drew me in with my back to him, our arms crisscrossed in front of us, and rocked me.

"I'm keeping you here 'til you explain."

"Face of an angel, heart of the devil," I croaked breathlessly.

"I'm not buying that."

"You will."

He kept hold of me and was still doing steps to the swing. I was going to nail his foot if he didn't release me, I thought, and these spike heels would hurt. But I kept time with his beat, making small steps to avoid stepping on his toes.

"Then I have one piece of advice for you, Lizzie," he said, suddenly lifting his arms and twirling me back out. I swung back in, facing him.

"What's that, lover boy?" I sassed.

The music was fading out when he reined me back in.

"Work on the heart."

He put his arms around me and hugged me as he had done when he was only a friend. If we could just go back to what we had been, we would be all right, I thought. And, unexpectedly, I felt a yearning as deep as a glacial crevasse to have him hold me like this for a long time, and to have all the people go away, so that it could just be us, alone, and there would be no more Jason and no more fear and no more contention and he would know everything in my heart and he would understand.

"Michael, I'm sorry."

"Sorry for what, precious?"

"Sorry for getting you into this mess," I gulped.

It had come out all wrong, I thought. I was sorry for betraying him in my heart and sorry for pretending to be something I was not and sorry that I could not tell him.

"Shhh." He stroked my hair. "It was my choice, too."

But it was not his choice to be number two on our wedding day, I thought miserably; the guy I was marrying was supposed to be up there at number one.

"Michael, are you happy?" I asked.

"Of course."

"Then that is enough."

I broke away from him and started walking in the direction of the water cooler. He caught up to me and whirled me around.

"It's not enough for me," he said.

"Why not?" I demanded.

"I want you to be happy, too."

I wanted to tell him that I couldn't be, not now, maybe not ever, but I didn't have the heart to say it. He took me by the hand.

"Please go easy on me," I beseeched him.

"Did you mean metaphorically or in a more immediate, physical way?"

Now it was my turn to be nonplussed. Seeing my confusion, he added, "I meant tonight."

"Oh, that," I stammered. "No problem. I got that down pat."

"Then why is your hand shaking?"

"Is not," I protested.

I looked down at the hand he was holding and saw that my fingers were trembling. Michael was way too observant for my own good.

"I need some water," I said, trying to change the subject.

We reached the table, and he picked up a paper cup and filled it up from the cooler.

"Not gonna drop it, are you?"

I snatched the cup away from him and slopped water on my hands. He rolled his eyes and shook his head.

"I know you'll be nice," I said, realizing that I was backtracking. "And I will be too. That answer your question?"

"Now that we've got it sorted out, let's eat. Then you can toss your bouquet, I'll throw the garter, and we can get out of here."

My heart did a slow roll in the swift current along the riverbed, but I wasn't going to let on.

We found Jeremy, who had by now danced with all the bridesmaids and was chatting up Rachel in front of the salmon canapés. His tux still looked too big for him, but he was managing to carry it off. We asked him to assemble the single women for the bouquet toss. I looked out to the dance floor and saw Edward and little Alison in a lacy white frock doing a variation on the cha-cha, and felt a surge of pleasure for Alison. I bet this was the best party she'd ever attended, and she was doing her favorite thing – dancing. Michael led me up onto the stage while Jeremy made the announcement over the microphone and the female guests gathered in a group behind me on the floor below the stage.

"Here it comes!" I yelled and tossed the flowers.

I spun around to see who'd made the catch, and it warmed my insides to see Rachel come up with the bouquet. Janine had barely missed it and was visibly displeased. She would be thanking God for blessings in disguise in no time flat, I thought. Michael dug a white garter out of his pocket (since it wouldn't be proper for him to take one off my leg in the church), and held it up for the guys to see. Jeremy instructed the girls via microphone to make way for the guys. I couldn't help noticing that the guys were slow in coming up, and I started giggling uncontrollably. I yanked the microphone away from Jeremy and spoke into it.

"OK, you chickens. Get up here, just below the front of the stage. You don't actually have to get married until after your missions."

A few more single males joined the group. Jason materialized from the edges of the room and melded into the crowd of young men while my heart fell like a stone over a waterfall. I dragged my eyes away from him. Inwardly, I chastised myself for letting him get to me again.

"They're ready, Michael. Throw it!" I urged.

Away went the white lace garter and I turned back to see who caught it. I knew the hand instantly. I'd watched it flying in the pool on a hot fall evening less than three months ago, on the night I lost my virginity. Jason was grinning up at me with the same mindless expression he'd had on his face when he crawled out of the pool and stripped me of what should have been a sacred possession. I whipped around to Michael, hoping he wouldn't see the mist in my eyes.

"I wanna get out of here right now," I said breathlessly.

"Sure, sweetheart. Whose parents did you want to take the wedding presents home?"

"I don't care, whatever you decide," I replied. I wanted fresh air.

"Then I'll have my parents take them and we can unwrap them when we get home. That OK with you?"

"Yes, anything. Can we please leave now?"

He must have recognized the desperation in my voice. "I think I was too demanding on the dance floor. Kept you up too late last night. You're tired."

I put my arms around his neck and leaned against him. I wanted Michael to keep me safe from Jason – and I didn't. I couldn't figure out what I wanted, except that we needed to get out of here.

In no time flat we'd loaded Michael's overnight bag into the trunk of the car, kissed parents, family and friends good-bye, and were heading out the chapel door in a shower of rice to the sounds of clapping, whistles and whoops. While the wedding reception was in full swing, the Young Men had tied burgundy ribbons on every projecting part of my Nissan including the radio antenna, and the car looked a great deal less dilapidated decked out in burgundy bows. As we walked away from the crowd, Rachel rushed forward and pressed the bridal bouquet into my hands.

"I know it's tradition for me to keep it, but I want you to have this as a keepsake," she said.

"That's sweet, sis," said Michael. He gave her a long hug.

"Know what, Michael?" Rachel went on.

"Don't tell me Jeremy asked you on a date!" I interrupted.

She threw me a triumphant glance and Michael glared me into silence.

"You're gonna have to clear that with Mom and Dad, you know," he said seriously.

"Don't be a wet rag, honey," I remonstrated.

"She's my sister!"

"Mine, too," I protested.

I put my hands on my hips in a defiant stance as we stared each other down and Rachel watched.

"No harm in asking," I went on insolently.

"You stay out of it, Lizzie. It's my parents' decision to make. And you shouldn't be encouraging Rachel. Or Jeremy, for that matter."

"What makes you think I am?" I asked with feigned innocence.

"You two aren't going to have a fight about me and Jeremy, are you?" asked Rachel.

"We're not fighting," I responded impertinently, flicking a sardonic gaze in Michael's direction. He was leaning with one arm on the roof of the car, fuming.

"You're mistaken, Rach. It's called foreplay," he rejoined.

Her jaw dropped and I spun on my heels, mortified, and began fumbling with the door latch. Michael placed his hand on my bare forearm and stopped me.

"I'll do it," I protested.

"No, you won't." He shoved me aside, turned the key in the lock, and opened the door for me with a grandiose gesture. I stood irresolutely, not moving.

To his sister, he said, "Rachel, we'll see you in a few days, all right?"

Before turning back towards the chapel, Rachel called, "So long, Michael and Lizzie. Have a good time."

Michael redirected his attention to me. "Princess Pearl, are you going to get in or are you going to keep me waiting all night?"

I gazed at him sullenly.

"You better get in right now."

"In the interests of preserving the family heirloom," I said stiffly, indicating the pearls, "I'm getting in."

I slid into the seat awkwardly, taking care to protect the gown and flipping the veil over my shoulder. Exercising considerable self-control, Michael closed the door gently and walked around to the driver's side. He turned the ignition key and the engine started.

"I hope you're not going to be this contrary all night," Michael commented darkly.

"I can be anything you want me to be," I replied in a voice that didn't sound like my own.

We were, after all, acting out a fairytale, weren't we?

Wedding Night

As we drove away, I turned to look back at the chapel and felt as if I were Alice in Wonderland falling down the rabbit hole. I was leaving behind familiar territory and about to navigate down passageways I did not know without the benefit of map or compass.

The euphoria I'd felt while dancing with Michael earlier in the day was fading as the raindrops began to fall. Towards the coast where we were headed, the skies looked dark and foreboding. It was close to four pm, and night was coming upon us as fast as the rain. The traffic on I-80 towards Napa moved torpidly, and Michael concentrated on keeping us at a safe following distance. I would just have to get used to him being in charge and driving my car, though this rearrangement of roles did not agree well with me. I had enjoyed the feeling of sitting behind the wheel and being in control of my weather-beaten Nissan. There were no longer any opt-out clauses between Michael and me. I was his wife – with all the complications and obligations that entailed. Every wife goes through this, I am sure, I just wasn't ready for it.

Michael switched on the radio and searched for a while before he found a rock station. They were playing Sade's "Smooth Operator" and I thought dejectedly of Jason and hoped the irony was escaping Michael.

Michael and I hadn't spoken to each other since leaving the building. I still held the wedding bouquet in my lap, and its burgundy ribbons trailed over the gown. I bent my head to smell the lilies again, enjoying their sweet scent. Then I dusted the rice off the lace of my dress and thought about what a pain it was going to be to clean up the car when we got home. Of course, I wasn't going home, I was going to move in with Michael's family.

He glanced over at me. "Tired?"

"Yeah, long day."

"Especially when it starts at five a.m. Guess you were pretty jazzed about us getting hitched."

"Jazzed" hardly described it, I thought, but I'd better not let on.

"My mother had me all stressed out," I said, tearing the petals off one of the flowers and letting them drift to the floor.

"You should take a nap while I'm driving. It's a good four hours to Jenner."

"That's where we're going? Where is that, anyway?"

"North of Fort Ross. Never been up the coast, Lizzie?"

"I went camping with my parents up by Eureka. But I've never heard of it."

"I hadn't, until I did some research. I figure, life's an adventure and I'd spirit you away some I was place beautiful and quiet."

I didn't dare tell him I didn't want to be spirited away anywhere, least of all the coast north of San Francisco in the middle of December in the rain, but I could play act with the best of them.

"So how d' you find it?" I asked.

"That's a trade secret," he said, grinning. It was the first time I'd seen him smile since we hit the road. "I had an idea I'd like to take you up the coast so I checked with Dad and he suggested this place. Supposed to be real romantic."

I didn't want to hear how romantic it would be because I was still recovering from Jason's assault on my heart and I wasn't about to take the plunge again with my best friend... correction, I told myself... husband.

"Let me know if you want to stop for a bathroom break, because we'll have to tank up before we get there."

"That's going to be real easy in this wedding dress," I responded wryly. "I'm staying in this car, no matter what."

He threw me another playful smile. "That dress will definitely get you some attention."

And I was going to get all attention I wanted or needed tonight and then some, I thought. He must have sensed the gravity of my mood because he changed tack and said seriously, "Lizzie, you were dazzling, today. Most beautiful bride I ever saw."

I wondered how many weddings he'd attended, but I didn't want to ask. He paused before going on.

"Lizzie, the father of this baby – he really hurt you, didn't he?"

"Yes."

"So, here's the deal: I'm not him. I'm not like him. I'm your best friend. I always have been. Please give me a chance, all right?"

But Michael was no longer my friend. He had been right when he said it, that day in the parking lot after the first time we sat together with his family in Sacrament meeting. We could no longer be friends – he was my husband. We were coming to a great river and I was terrified of crossing to the other side, but I was going to anyway. "Be strong and of a good courage," I told myself. If Joshua could do it, then I ought to be able to manage it, too.

When I remained mute, staring into my lap and twirling his grandmother's ring, he commenced another line of conversation.

"Were you really in love with him?"

"Guess so," I acknowledged sullenly. "Didn't do me much good, did it?"

I tore the petals off another flower, a really perfect one, rolled them between my fingers and dusted them over my gown like confetti. Then I commenced ripping the leaves off the stem.

"We all take chances. You can't expect to walk through life without pain. That's part of what we come to Earth to learn," Michael continued.

"I've had enough lessons on pain."

"You broke the rules, Lizzie. 'Wickedness never was happiness,' remember?"

"Please don't quote scriptures at me now," I responded testily. "It's not *your* heart that was broken."

"You know nothing about my heart, Lizzie – you're so wrapped up in your own little pool of misery."

I whipped my head up to look at him, but this time it was his gaze that couldn't meet mine. I felt tears sting my eyes.

"Why don't you get to your point?" I demanded.

"If your tongue wasn't as harsh as a whip, I probably would," he responded tightly.

"All right – I'll share if you will," I challenged him.

"You go first, then," he said, not flinching at the gauntlet I'd flung down. I wished I could beat a hasty retreat, but I'd thrown down the glove, so I couldn't back down now. Fine, I'd shove the lancet right down his throat.

"I'm waiting," he scoffed.

"You don't know what it's like to be in love so you wouldn't understand!"

"That is sheer and unadulterated bullshit, Lizzie." He still wasn't looking at me. I stared at the droplets of rain slithering down the windshield and clenched my fists. "Your problem is that you don't know the difference between love and lust, and if you DID, you would have never said something that completely stupid!"

I gulped, leaned back in the seat, and contemplated the incessant assault of rain against the windshield.

"Example: my sister Janine and Jeremy. They've barely met. Suddenly the hormones are blazing. That's not love – it's lust."

"If they never have a chance to get to know each other, they'll never find out if it's love," I protested.

"So you have to know someone to love them?"

"Yes," I responded. Then I hesitated. I was being painted into a corner. "No, not necessarily." I was thinking of Jason, whom I knew most intimately and yet not at all.

"Come on, Lizzie, you can't have it both ways."

"Sometimes two people meet and they know nothing about each other but they know they're meant to be together."

"Lizzie, you've been watching too many Hollywood movies. You know the reason we have so many divorces in the United States?"

"Yeah, people get married for stupid reasons like physical attraction or for financial security or because they're lonely or because their religion says they have to or they want to have kids..."

"Or the girl is pregnant," Michael interjected.

I frowned, feeling suddenly out of my depth. "Anyways, since you have never given in to lust – or whatever you decide to call it –"

"Lizzie, you are so wrong. Didn't you know I had a crush in my junior year of high school?"

"No way, Michael." I took a long look at his profile, but it betrayed nothing.

"Yes, way. Her name was Kathy Foster."

I drew a blank. "Sorry, doesn't ring a bell."

"She's a sophomore on the cheerleading squad."

I closed my eyes and tried to picture the cheerleaders, but I had not been to many of our high-school football games, unless I knew Jason would be in attendance.

"It was her ankles. Ever seen a girl with perfect ankles? And she had these nicely muscled calves..."

I picked up the folds of the gown and contemplated the heels I'd bought at Macy's for the wedding with my mother on a rainy day in late November. I had tried on dozens of shoes until I found a pair that was both comfortable and alluring. They were sparkly and silver, adorned with a silver rosette, and had a single strap that curved up around my ankles. My mother had assured me they were perfect in every way. I glanced up at Michael and realized that he was laughing at me. I slapped his leg.

"You're messing with me, aren't you?" I spat at him.

"Lizzie, I am not messing with you in the least. I used to go to all the high-school football games just to see her. Do you think I care a fig about football?"

"So how did you know it was lust?" I demanded, still clasping the wispy folds of the gown in my hands.

"C'mon. I never met her. I never talked to her. I knew what it was. Sometimes I fought it; sometimes I didn't, but I always knew. She's not in the Church – I would never go out with someone who wasn't. It was a fantasy and it would have been a disaster."

"When did this lovely little fantasy come to an end?" I asked, leaning down to rub my calves. I caught Michael staring at my legs out of the corner of his eye. I quickly drew the layers of my dress down over them, feeling suddenly, inexplicably, self-conscious.

Michael shrugged. "I knew it wasn't going anywhere, so I chose to stop it."

"But you can't just 'stop it,'" I protested. "It doesn't work that way."

"Yes, it does, Lizzie."

I bit my lower lip and crossed my arms over my bosom. The strands of pearls felt cool against my skin. "That's how you knew it was lust. If it was real love, it would have lasted and you would have been broken in a thousand pieces when it stopped."

"Is that what happened to you, Lizzie?" he asked – softly, like herons gliding over the Suisun marsh in the opaque light of a foggy dawn. The car went suddenly quiet, and he was waiting for my answer the way you wait to hear a pebble hit the bottom of a dark deep well. I drew in my breath and toyed with the pearls around my neck.

"You wouldn't understand," I said, watching the rain paint patterns on the passenger window.

"Try me."

"It's not like you think." I twisted and untwisted the pearls around my forefinger.

"It's either love or lust, Lizzie, and it's that simple."

"No!" I cried, "it is NOT that simple!"

My hands had developed a life of their own and they twitched so sharply that the strand of pearls fractured and went skittering all over the car. I was horror-struck. I scrabbled on the floor trying to retrieve some of them, but it was hopeless. I stared at the few pearls I had managed to salvage and began to cry. "Look what I've done now. Your mother is gonna kill me."

"They're very precious pearls, Lizzie. We'll have to find every single one of them and make a brand-new string..." Michael's hand found my thigh and squeezed it, but I jerked when he touched me. I choked back the latest onslaught tears. I would try not to remember this part of my wedding night, I told myself.

"D' you wanna pull over, Lizzie?" he asked.

"No!" I cried. I fumbled through my purse for a tissue, found one, blew my nose, and curled up against the passenger window. "I don't wanna talk anymore. Just drive."

"OK. I'll drive, you cry. Your choice."

I put my left hand up like a stop sign. "I said don't talk to me."

Then I scrunched up against the window with a rustle of skirts and peeked through my fingers at the grim set of Michael's face.

I shouldn't have shut him out like that, but I couldn't accept his dispassionate disavowal of the physical nature of love. It was natural to develop feelings of physical attraction toward the opposite sex. Love had to start somewhere. Whether what I had felt for Jason was lust or love didn't matter because the feelings inside of me felt the same, no matter how Michael wanted to rationalize them. I was furious that he was minimizing the value of a relationship that had affected me in profound and permanent ways. I wished I wasn't still in love with Jason, but I was. I hated him and I loved him, and both drove me nuts.

Seeing Jason again at the wedding, knowing that he was admiring me and wanting me, had illumined those dark corners of my memory where Jason hid. Jason's touch had brought back all the feelings I'd been reining in. The miserable truth was that I wanted Jason just as badly as I had in the beginning, and I did not know how to reconcile the fantasy of those desires with the very real person who had pledged to share his life with me. I had promised myself to Michael and I could no more dishonor his trust than I could convince Jason to come back to me.

"Michael?" I ventured, still leaning my head on the passenger door.

"I thought you said you didn't want to talk."

"I'm sorry. That's all. This has been a difficult day for me."

"It's been a difficult day for all of us," he added.

"I really did try to be nice to you today."

He managed a smile. "You were."

"You'll just have to be more patient with me."

"I will try. But honestly, you are testing my patience, sweetheart."

"It is a virtue, you know." I rested my head on my hand and contemplated him. I just needed to stop wishing for the impossible.

"Truce?" he asked, offering me his hand.

"Sure," I replied. But it wasn't truce I was offering, it was surrender. Instead of shaking on it, I shifted back to the center of my seat, took his hand in my lap and stroked his fingers.

"I'm such a screw-up, Michael. You should never have proposed to me. What the hell were you thinking?"

"I wasn't. Not with my brain. It just sort of happened and I went with it." He squeezed my hand like he did when we were best friends, and he wanted me to know he was there for me.

"I owe you."

"I was hoping I'd get to collect on that debt," he added, squeezing my fingers in a whole new way.

"And you will," I said. "I made a commitment and I'm keeping it."

"Then you're not the screw-up you say you are."

"I'm glad to have your vote of confidence, Michael."

"Let's just say I haven't even come close to giving up on you yet," he added, drawing his hand away from mine and replacing it on the steering wheel. "Go to sleep, Lizzie. It's a long drive and we're going to somewhere really beautiful."

"Even in the rain?" I asked.

"Even in the rain," he assured me. "But with you, my precious pearl, anywhere would be beautiful."

"That's flattery," I said, half-smiling.

"True enough, but it got a smile out of you, didn't it?" he grinned. "Anyway, my dad said this place is awesome, and I can't remember a time when my dad was wrong about anything – even you."

Now my interest was piqued. "So what did your Dad say about me?"

"That's for me to know and you to ponder," he countered.

"You're not playing fair," I complained.

"Your lover gets you pregnant and leaves you – so that's fair?"

"Life isn't fair – I know that!" I exclaimed.

"Then stop fighting the current and go with the flow."

"The last time I did that I got pregnant."

"Bad metaphor. But you knew what could happen if you weren't using protection. What were you thinking?"

"Obviously, I wasn't. D'you wanna know the truth?" I demanded, feeling my mettle rising again. Michael might as well know what a miserable sinner I was, I thought.

"That's what this conversation is about, isn't it?"

"I wanted him and I let it happen. I knew what I was doing and I was a willing participant. I wasn't a victim. Satisfied?"

"Then I'm glad to know that one of us knows what the hell we're doing tonight," he continued smoothly.

"And aren't you the lucky one to reap the benefit of my experience," I said, trying to inject exactly the right quantity of sarcasm.

"I don't think luck has anything to do with it," he came back.

I glared at him, but I couldn't make out his expression in the shifting light as our car sped swiftly up Highway 101 towards the coast.

"You can't stop messing with me, can you?" I said.

"Not when it's so much fun," he countered.

"I'm going to sleep," I said, knowing when I was beaten.

"Good, I was hoping for some peace and quiet." I caught a flash of white teeth as a set of headlights went by in the opposite direction.

Perhaps there was hope for us, if we could still share the easy banter that had characterized our friendship before I informed Michael that I was pregnant and he offered to marry me. I rearranged myself in the seat, resting my head against the window and taking care not to crush the remaining delicate flowers in my lap. I listened to the regular slap of the windshield wipers across the windshield and the swish of water under the wheels of the car. I felt the cool of the glass against my hand where I supported my head and was lulled into sleep by the purr of the engine and the swaying of the car. I gave myself up to slumber gratefully, weary of this long day fraught with conflicting emotions.

Two hours passed before I came to consciousness. When I awoke, I was aware of the moon flitting between tree trunks and the car winding through a forest of shadowy trees. I caught a flash of water through tree trunks and the brief, blinding glare of headlights as we encountered the occasional oncoming car.

"Where are we?" I asked dozily. I stayed curled up against the passenger door.

"You're awake," said Michael, touching my shoulder. "'Bout time. We're almost there. Maybe half-an-hour."

"Are we at the coast?"

"Soon. Look to your left. It's the Russian River."

I uncurled myself in the seat and stretched, with the wedding dress rustling and shimmering as it caught the moonlight. Then I looked out the window beyond Michael's silhouette to a vision of cliffs a few hundred feet away across the river. Mist curled through the trees next to the road.

"It's a long way across," I remarked.

"The river is deep and the river is wide," Michael commented. "Dad told me it can come up over the road."

I shivered, but not because I was cold. I watched the tree trunks whirl by and disappear into the darkness behind us and stretch out into the blackness above. In time, the road dropped in graceful curves towards Jenner, and we came out of the forest at the outskirts of town, which boasted a population of one hundred and seventy, according to the sign. I saw a vast, eerie chasm where the river went out to sea. The ocean was somewhere below us as we began to climb the coast highway, and I could see a car half-a-mile away ascending the cliff face, looking as though it were an airplane taking off into the night sky. The moon was obscured by clouds again. We drove on in silence broken by the occasional splatter of rain on the windshield and the squeal of the tires as Michael navigated the winding curves of Highway 1.

After what seemed like an interminable time interval, but was perhaps only thirty minutes, Michael exclaimed, "I think we're here!"

I did not share his excitement. "Where, exactly?"

I need not have asked, because at that moment, we passed a sign announcing that we were entering Stillwater Cove. Michael made his way around one more hairpin bend, scaled a short hill, and faultlessly maneuvered the vehicle into the driveway of a place calling itself Stillwater Cove Ranch. The car bumped along a dirt road and pulled up outside a stone building with a sign proclaiming it to be the Office. It looked unattended, but Michael jumped out the door and went in. He came back moments later and flashed me a smile across the car, his teeth gleaming in the dark.

"We'll need to go up to the owner's house for directions, but the key will be in our door."

"Whatever," I said, trying to sound nonchalant.

I told my heart to stop beating so fast and and forced my lungs to take in deeper, slower breaths of air. In contrast, Michael appeared calm and confident. He made a U-turn, bouncing me against the passenger door, and pulled up to an impressive stone structure with lights shining in the downstairs windows. He got out, closed the car door gently, and went up to the door. I watched him push the bell, hoping against all odds to delay the inevitable. A shaft of light pierced the dank air, and Michael and the person who opened the door had a brief conversation complete with gesturing and arm waving, so I gathered Michael was getting directions. He came back to the car with a triumphant look on his face.

"Just up the road and through the gate to the right," he said, folding himself into the seat.

"Can't wait," I said sarcastically.

We're Here

Lizzie

Michael shot me a warning look, as if to say it was time for me to stop being so contrary. He revved the engine loudly enough for me to realize I'd annoyed him, made a neat three-point turn, and drove the Nissan up a muddy track. He stopped about one hundred feet from a white-painted building that was situated behind a high wire gate and gleamed against the background of trees. A light was on underneath its small porch. He popped the trunk latch, got out of the car, and unloaded our baggage from the back. Then he walked around to my door, set the cases down in the mud, and opened the door with a flourish.

"OK, my most precious pearl. We're here."

"The grass is all wet and I'm going to get your mother's dress muddy," I murmured, staring disconsolately at the ground under the open door.

"Then pick up your skirts. Let's go!" he replied bluntly, taking my hand.

I stepped out, clinging to my bouquet and still feeling as if I were playing a part in a fairytale. Pearls were falling from my lap, some in the car, and some, I was afraid, in the grass and mud.

The rain had slowed to a lackluster drizzle, and Michael's hair shone with dampness like the glaze on a cake. The ethereal white of the cottage lying so serenely against the obsidian background enhanced my sense of unreality. The grass was ankle-high and wet, but I was able to scoop the skirts of the dress up into a bundle and make a sweeping procession up to the gate. Michael preceded me with my suitcase and a small bag of his own. I noticed he traveled light. That was exactly like Michael – spare and frugal, not wasting space for frivolities as I had.

My mother had packed us a cooler for Sunday with some of the refreshments from our wedding so that we wouldn't have to break the Sabbath by eating out and we could save our money on meals over the subsequent two days, but Michael had left it in the trunk of the car. I suddenly realized I was ravenous, but my guess was that food wasn't on the menu for tonight, and I didn't have the nerve to ask Michael to go back for the cooler. Aside from the breakfast I had tossed up, I had eaten very little all day and my stomach was gnawing a cavernous hole in my insides.

Michael opened the gate and went through ahead of me. I clicked it shut and followed him to the porch, nearly tripping on the slick grass in my heels. He set down my bag to open the door to our cottage, switched on the internal light, and lugged the bags inside. Then he came back out, smiling broadly.

"This is it, kiddo," he said and, to my surprise, swooped me up in his arms, carried me inside and set me down on the bed. My heart did a few perfect back flips. My face must have told him how little I'd anticipated this move.

"Lizzie, it is tradition to carry the bride over the threshold."

"You might have warned me," I replied, recovering my breath.

Then I let my gaze wander around the room and saw that its interior was as charming as its exterior. The fairytale would not end. The ceiling was lined with wooden beams, giving the cottage a rustic air. Each wall had two small windows with pink lace curtains. I was facing a stone fireplace with a box of wood and kindling next to it. There was a basket of fruit and an electric kettle on a small table near the door, along with pink cups and matching napkins. The nightstand featured elegant pastel-pink lamps with burgundy fringes and a small pot of African violets in bloom. A vase of white and pink lilies adorned the bookshelf. A hurricane lamp with wine-colored oil had been set on a shelf between the bathroom door and the door to what I later discovered was a walk-in closet. There were two double beds, and Michael had set me down on the one nearest the hearth. I was deadly sure we wouldn't be using both of them. Michael walked back to the door to close it and stopped to survey the scene with his handle on the door as I stared absently around the room.

"You like it?"

"Seems a little whimsical for someone as pragmatic as yourself," I observed, cocking my head to one side.

"I may surprise you, my precious. Let me get the fire going. It's chilly in here."

I hadn't noticed, but the air was indeed cool. Michael moved the fire screen to the side and knelt down to arrange the kindling in the grate. Matches had kindly been provided to start the fire, as well as a load of logs.

"While I'm doing this, check the thermostat on the heater in the corner," suggested Michael.

"I think I'll check out the bathroom," I responded.

I stood up, stopping to turn up the sheets on the bed, and began looking around for the thermostat. I adjusted it to 69°F, as I wasn't one for sleeping in overheated rooms. I took off my silver heels and tossed them into the corner next to the heater. Then I unzipped my suitcase and rummaged around for my makeup kit.

"While you're at it, Lizzie, please find my toilet bag and stick it in the bathroom," called Michael from the fireplace.

"Sure," I responded.

After finding my toiletries, I opened Michael's bag and located a small blacked zippered case on top, along with his journal. I picked up the journal and turned it over in my hands. I glanced quickly over to where Michael was preoccupied with lighting the fire and decided not to risk it, but I was as curious about what lay within its pages as a child is with a new toy. A white shirt was carefully folded on top of his clothes, all ready for the Sabbath, I supposed. We were not going to miss church, even on our honeymoon.

With the items in hand, I made a sortie into the bathroom, which had new plumbing fixtures with porcelain handles painted in pink and blue flowers. It was spotlessly clean and would have made a great ad in Good Housekeeping for bathrooms designed to fit into small spaces. I put our toilet bags down and opened mine. I set out soap, shampoo and conditioner as well as my toothbrush and toothpaste. Maybe I ought to lay out Michael's as well, but I didn't feel like invading this last vestige of his personal space. I closed the door carefully, brushed my teeth, and used the toilet. I had to practically throw the back portion of the skirt over my head to find the seat, and I imagined how ridiculous I would look if there were anyone there to observe me.

Bridal gowns were entirely impractical, so it was tricky to get my hose, slip and underwear back on. I decided, what the heck, I wasn't going to need them anyway, so I kicked all of them off and tossed them into a corner. Then I examined my face in the mirror critically, noting the dark circles under my eyes. I looked tired and anxious. My veil was still attached to my hair. There was no removing it without taking my hair apart, so I had decided not to make the effort until after we arrived. Despite my haggard appearance, the gown and veil still looked as stunning as they had earlier in the day. Some of my hair was piled up on my head with the veil pinned under it, but the remainder cascaded in huge rolls over my neck and shoulders. I fingered my neck where the strands of pearls had shone softly against my bosom, and thought of Jason's frantic kisses that had started at the neck and worked all the way downward. My eyes dropped to the gown, whose pearl-and-sequin trim fairly sparkled. I still looked like I'd stepped right out of a fairytale, even if I didn't feel like a princess.

"Ready, set, go!" I said to myself softly, but I wasn't in the least ready or set. I turned around with a rustling of skirts, opened the door, and went back into the main room of the cottage. Michael was still messing with the fire, and a few meager flames were dancing in the hearth.

"Almost there," he proclaimed, looking up to see that I had finished up in the bathroom. Using the poker, he toyed with the kindling some more, and the fire began to look more hopeful.

I walked over to the door and turned off the overhead light, throwing the room into semi-darkness. He looked up at me with the firelight throwing shadows up behind him. At that moment I realized he'd removed his vest, shirt, shoes, and socks, and was squatting beside the fire barefoot, in nothing but dress pants.

"You know, this room has no phone or TV," I observed.

"I'm well aware of that. I hope you don't need to call anyone." He stuck the poker into a log and turned it over, sending a shower of sparks into the fire.

"Of course I don't need to call anyone," I retorted. I didn't know of any cottages in fairytales that had phones or TVs, either. "I only thought it would be nice if – if it weren't so isolated."

"We need 'isolated.' I haven't been able to get you alone for weeks," Michael protested.

If this reasoning was supposed to impress me, it didn't, so he tried another angle.

"You sure look gorgeous, Lizzie," he said, taking me in as he twirled the poker. "Come sit by the fire. You cold?"

"Yeah," I lied. I was as hot as that poker in the fire and pulsing with nerves. I felt like I was walking across a lake of cinders as I moved across the room towards him and arranged myself in one of the chairs facing the fireplace. The fire snapped and popped at me encouragingly.

"I'm going to light the hurricane lantern – you made it awful dark in here," he went on.

Darkness was what I wanted. Then I could draw its mists around me and Michael would not see the gloom in my heart. I stared into the flames. hey were beginning to billow and swell like the sails of a ship as it catches the wind.

"I'll be right back," said Michael, startling me as he stood up.

He disappeared into the bathroom, and I remained motionless in the chair, watching the flames skip in the fireplace and the sparks shoot up the chimney. I wished I could transform myself into one of those flames and fly up the chimney as an evanescent spark.

I shouldn't be here.

I wasn't supposed to be married to my former best friend at seventeen and expecting a baby who belonged to someone else.

I wasn't supposed to become a mother when I was barely an adult myself.

I had utterly and completely abandoned all my dreams of the future for this – a wedding night with a teenage boy who was going to take my body and leave my soul crying out there in the rain-swept night for someone else.

I was as love-sick as Ophelia and it would be better for everyone if I threw myself into the Russian River.

Michael, I believed, despised me for giving myself away to another and he would never rest until he knew the bastard's name. He was going to call this child his own but it was always going to be someone else's.

I had disappointed Michael as a friend by failing to confide in him and it was very likely I was going to disappoint him as a wife.

And to add to my chagrin, I had failed to banish lascivious thoughts of Jason from my mind. My bitter reverie was cut short when Michael emerged from the bathroom. He found a match for the oil lamp and lit it. I shuddered, dreading what was to come.

"Let's say our prayers. I'll do it," he said.

"All right."

He came over to the bed and knelt down. I rustled to my feet, trying not to step on the dress, and knelt carefully next to him to the sound of another pearl rolling away.

When he was finished, he said, "Want me to take off your veil?"

"Good idea," I responded, still on my knees.

Michael put his hands on my shoulders and leaned over to kiss my neck. I was going to protest that he was supposed to be unfastening my veil but I didn't want to spoil it for him, so I remained quiet and still. On the inside, my blood was at a slow boil and threatening to breach the confines of my veins. Michael withdrew himself, sat down on the bed behind me, and deftly began removing my hair pins, unrolling my hair as he went.

"I do love your hair, precious pearl," he said, fingering the strands. He finally extricated the last pin holding the veil and swept it off to the side, throwing it over the chair where I had been sitting before I knelt for our night time prayer. I caught my fingers around my throat, trying to still the tumult in my veins. I was hoping he couldn't hear my heart, because it was pounding so hard against my ribs that I thought it would burst from my chest.

"D' you want some help with the dress?" he asked softly.

I nodded my head to acquiesce, half-blinded by tears, my hair falling across my face to shield me. I stood slowly, turning away from him, wiping my eyes, and he got to his feet behind me.

He started unhooking the loops of the buttonholes with fingers that were exasperatingly swift and nimble. He was surer of himself than his father had been, I thought. The flesh of my shoulders felt seared as he raised his hands up to slip off the dress. It fell in a great heap of glitter around me with the sound of yet another of his pearls rolling across the wooden floor. I stepped out of the layers of translucent fabric, not daring to turn around, as the cool air stung my exposed flesh.

"I'm gonna lay this out on the other bed," Michael breathed in my ear, making my hair stand on end.

I heard rustling and scraping and more pearls falling to the floor as he took the dress over to the second bed and spread it out on the coverlet.

I stood there, naked, staring helplessly at the fire, wishing I could burn up in it right now. I saw Michael's shadow cross the room back towards me, and realized my hands were shaking violently. I crossed my arms over my breasts and waited with my back to him. He put his hands on my shoulders and turned me around. I stared numbly at the middle of his chest, afraid to meet his eyes. He took my right hand off my left shoulder and placed it on his left shoulder, repeating the movement with my left hand. I stared at his Adam's apple.

"My most precious pearl," he whispered, "for a woman who's done this before, your hands sure are shaking."

"I know," I murmured, tilting my head up to look into those piercing eyes of his.

His glasses were gone – along with the rest of his clothes. Then he took me in his arms and I went hot and cold all at once at the shock of contact with so much skin.

I wanted to say, I cannot do this, I am not ready for this. The river is too wide and too deep and I cannot go across. "Be strong and of a good courage," whispered Joshua in the recesses of my mind. But I was in up to my knees, and the water was so cold it was like being stung by wasps. Then I was up to my waist in water and Michael was crying my name and the water was rising and I was too far in to go back and I knew it. When we got to the sheets I don't know, because by that time I'd stepped in so far the water went over my head and I was freezing and choking and I thought I was alone being swept away in the flood of a great river. I kept fighting the current, but I couldn't breathe and I had no strength left in my limbs and I thought I should go up for air before my limbs failed me. I rolled over and found my breath and begged for the river to let me go, but it would not, and I saw Michael's eyes in the murky water and I knew the only way to cross was to succumb to the river and let the current take me where it wanted.

Then Jason appeared from the shadowy depths swimming towards me just as he had in the pool, with long savage strokes, and I felt myself torn between them – Michael and Jason – and I gave myself to both of them until the bottom rose up underneath me and I found my footing. My feet scraped against pebbly bottom and my knees shook and I clawed my way out, dragging great breaths of clear air into my lungs, realizing I was on the other side and still alive.

When I found my voice, it was Michael's name I was saying, over and over, and he was telling me please not to cry, please not to cry and I was going to be OK and no one was going to hurt me anymore and please not to cry.

Then objects in the room came sharply into focus and I was lying in Michael's arms, panting, wrapped in the sheets while he cradled my head against his shoulder. My body felt warm and tired, as though I'd been swimming for hours and had finally allowed myself to rest. I drifted into sleep with Michael's arms around me and the knowledge that this time he had kept Jason away, but the Jason in the dark corners of my mind still wanted me back, and I would not banish that unreal and undead Jason easily or soon.

When I awoke, what must have been hours later – for there were no clocks to keep track of the night's progress in the cottage – I lay still, listening to Michael's regular breathing. Our bodies were still in an embrace, with our warm, moist skin glued together.

For the first time I heard the smashing of the waves against the cliffs somewhere below us on the beach, but from which direction it came was impossible to tell.

A terrible restlessness seized me, and I scrambled out from under the sheets – stealthily to make sure I didn't wake Michael – and fumbled in my suitcase to find my floor-length robe. I wrapped it around me, hugging it to me. I walked over to the fire, removed the screen, and added two more logs from the bin next to the hearth. I drifted over to the window nearest the door and looked out at the sky. A three-quarter moon was sailing amidst ragged clouds, and mist dipped and weaved its way through the redwoods. I stared at the moon for a while, wanting to be as serene and devoid of emotion as that cool face.

I began pacing the floor, thinking of the life inside me, and the life in the bed across the room, and the life I had seen in the river, and the lives that were depending on me to "be strong and of a good courage." The Lord would not let this cup pass from me and I had agreed to drink of it if the Lord required it, and I must find a way to go on, even when Jason tormented me and tempted me to go back across the river.

"Lizzie?"

I jumped. I hadn't realized Michael was awake and watching me with his head propped up on his hand, and I had no idea how long I had been pacing or how long he had been watching.

"Are you OK?" he asked.

"Just couldn't sleep," I replied.

"Come back to bed, sweetheart."

Reluctantly I willed my feet to make tracks across the hardwood floor and stood next to the bed, watching Michael.

I let the robe slip from my shoulders, falling to the floor, and felt my face flush. I seriously wondered why I had never felt as naked in front of Jason as I did under Michael's unflinching gaze. It should have been obvious: to Jason, I was an object, but to Michael, I was his universe. One used me; one adored me. One looked at me like a conquest; one gazed upon me with pure adoration.

Still he didn't move. I lifted the edge of the coverlet, folded the blankets and sheets back over it, and slid in beside him. Only then did he reach for me.

"Can I ask you something?" he said, slipping his arm around me, so our bodies came into full contact.

"Ask away."

"May I make love to you now?"

I realized with this query, that he had just laid next to me, holding me in his arms while I cried and struggled to endure crossing the river of my emotions. Simply holding me. Being the man I had never realized he was, as I struggled to cross the threshold to become the wife he deserved, as he held me against his chest.

Outside, I imagined the placid moon drifting amidst the ragged clouds and skeins of mist teasing the redwoods, while I felt the wild beat of Michael's heart next to mine. I had not responded to his question, and I was afraid I was too long in answering.

"Yes, Michael, any time you want," I whispered.

This time when I entered the river, I never took my eyes off Michael, and as long as I held his gaze, I could keep the unreal Jason from coming for me. This time I remembered the lesson I had learned from the moon, that I could be still and dance on the water like a moonbeam, that I could be in motion without feeling emotion, and that I could sail amidst the storms of the night sky but not let them touch me.

When I slept for the second time, I slept peacefully, languishing in the warmth of Michael's embrace.

Sweet Slumber

Michael

After I lost my virginity to the girl I'd dreamed of marrying for most of my teenage years, I laid there watching her sleep. I couldn't take my eyes off the long lashes resting against the pallor of her cheek. I ached to take her into my arms again, but I restrained myself.

I gently pulled myself away, giving her sleeping form a long, slow, adoring once over, then tucked the sheet and blanket around her, and arose from the bed.

If there is one thing I can say about my wife, she is one sound sleeper. I already knew this because there were times when she'd drift off on my bed while we were doing homework, and she could have slept through Madonna's "Material Girl."

Musing on my first sexual encounter, I was struck by the thought that despite being with a girl who had a certain amount of sexual experience, I had the impression she had lacked confidence in bed. I had done some intense research on the matter and had a reasonable idea of the physical mechanics of the various acts. With zero actual experience, I wasn't sure how it would all work. I was counting on her to "help out" in that arena. But she was shaky and, to be blunt, didn't seem like she was really a part of the event. I wondered if she was this unresponsive with her other lovers, or if it was just me?

Stupid to be dwelling on what had just happened between us. I had more important tasks on my plate for what was left of my wedding night. I slipped on my underpants and pulled a flashlight out of my bag. I started looking for the heirloom pearls. There were originally thirty-eight and I'd heard them bouncing off the floor when I helped Lizzie out of her wedding dress. The next few hours were going to be laborious and the thought of scrabbling around on the floorboards of Lizzie's car repelled me. I'd have to look everywhere. This room wasn't large, but there were still hundreds of places to check. I wasn't leaving this place until I found every last one of those precious gems. I looked at my watch, and it was 10:40 pm. I had plenty of time and Mrs. Kerry was blissfully unaware. I knelt down and said a prayer, asking Father to help me find the pearls.

I went into the bathroom and emptied my toiletries bag. After cleaning it out, I started looking for the pearls. I commenced in the bathroom, shone the flashlight down the drain to see if one could be seen down there; nope.

I looked in the toilet; nope. I checked the shower drain, behind the toilet, between the shower curtains, around the floor under the bathroom cabinet; voila, found one. I unzipped the bag a tiny bit and slipped the heirloom pearl inside.

I picked up Lizzie's dirty clothes and shook them out; none. In the trashcan; none. Bathroom done.

I left the bathroom and moved as quietly as I could over to the dress, lying on the second bed. That is where I found the remains of the strand of pearls caught on some of the trim. The string still had sixteen pearls on it, thank heaven. I unzipped my bag and dropped them in: seventeen pearls found; twenty-one to go. I picked up the veil and shook it out; one fell onto the bed; eighteen found.

I quietly shook out the dress, and four pearls fell to the bed. On closer inspection, two were the fake ones mom had sewn in, and the other two were heirloom; I put them all in the bag: twenty heirloom pearls found. Just to be sure, I shook out the dress some more, and nothing fell out. Eighteen left to find.

I hung the dress up on the hanger mom gave me, and carefully tucked it into the hanging storage bag, along with the veil. I then took them out and put them in the trunk. It was cold outside, especially barefoot and in my skivvies, but I didn't care. I was on a mission that was more important than my comfort.

Even though I know it will take a nuclear bomb to awaken Lizzie, I am trying to be quiet. I often dreamed about lying next to her all night, but that's all down the toilet now. I just get madder and madder every time I envision those pearls flying all over the car and possibly missing for *eternity*.

I returned to the cottage, retrieved the pearl bag and flashlight, and headed back out to the car again. I grabbed the trashcan on my way out, just for good measure. I had not locked the car, so I didn't need the keys. I opened all four doors and started working on the front seats.

The car was filled with bits of trash and gunk, which I picked up and threw in the trashcan. There was a movie ticket - almost a year old - and other odd bits and pieces that seemed to be historical in nature. I guess cleaning out her car isn't a top priority for her, but I already knew that. I found one pearl on her seat and five on the floorboards; twenty-six safely tucked into my bag, only twelve more to find.

I spent yet more serious time looking through the car, cleaning up the trash and gunk. I looked under each seat; all around the floorboards; in the folds of the seats. When I finished with the car, it was 02:30 am. I had spent four hours searching and was still twelve pearls shy.

I shined the flashlight on the ground outside of her door, and one precious pearl glimmered in the grass. I kept looking around and found another one. Only ten left to find. An extensive search through the grass yielded nothing. There had to be a couple out there.

I noticed a dirty round blip in the mud in one of her footprints. I carefully pulled it out, and yes, it was another one of my precious pearls! I used a rag from the trunk to wipe it off and put it in the bag.

I couldn't help thinking of the scripture that talked about throwing pearls before swine, which only made me angrier.

Was there more than one out here? I started digging up the mud, a handful at a time. It was hard and cold, but I didn't care. I dug out a handful of dirt and with the other hand, mushed through it, pulling out each pebble and stick until I had examined it all. I continued until I had checked the top layer of mud all along the path up to the front porch. That harvested me only one more precious pearl, which was cleaned off and put away. I still lacked eight pearls.

I had worked my way to the front door, and it was 04:15 am. I was exhausted and cold, and filthy from digging around in the mud. There was a spigot on the side of the cabin, which I turned on to rinse off my hands and feet. The ice-cold water and the forty-something degree air made this task one of the more physically painful experiences I can remember for a while. I then went into the cabin, gently put a couple of more logs on the fire, and headed for the bathroom to complete my ablutions.

After that, the only place left to look was on the floor in the main room, so I started crawling around. I used the flashlight to look under the beds. I found another pearl under our bed; none under the other one. If my exhausted brain was still working, then was still short seven.

I picked up the throw rug in front of the fireplace and uncovered one that was hidden in the fringe; six left.

I crawled around the floor shining the flashlight under the dresser, discovering one more against the wall; five left. One was under the rocking chair in the corner; four left. I raised up the front of the overstuffed chair and found another one; three left.

I was never good at hide-and-seek, but with Father's help, I was making progress.

I moved every piece of furniture, picked up every rug, checked in every corner, and nothing. I was still three short, and it was almost 6 am.

Then I had an idea to go check the pillows. I checked the four pillows on the spare bed and found one more precious pearl. Now I was only missing two!

I poured out the contents of the bag onto the spare bed and counted them all again. I was right: thirty-six heirloom pearls.

I went back outside and checked the grass with the flashlight. I checked the car again. I checked the bathroom again. I checked the dress again, the fringed rug in front of the fire, and under the dresser. But not one other pearl was to be found. I ground my teeth in frustration.

At 8:30 am, after ten hours of non-stop searching, I sat down on the edge of the tub and cried. My wife had lost two of the most precious pearls we had, and I could not find them. When I finished my pity-party, I took my pouch with the pearls out to the car and placed it in the bag with the dress. I brought the cooler with the food back into the cabin with me.

Then I threw a few more logs on the fire, started boiling some water for tea, and took out the crackers. That girl will wake up sometime, and she will need these items to help with her morning sickness. She'll probably try to weasel out of going to Church; no matter, I will go, anyway.

I'll have to think about what I'm going to do about the pearls. I debated not giving them to Lizzie in the first place. My stupid decision cost me two of them. I can't afford to make that mistake again.

I decided to finish fixing the tea and wake up the ungrateful wretch curled up in the bed.

I'll wait to see if she even mentions either the pearls or dress. If she doesn't, neither will I. One adage my dad told me as far back as I can remember said something about "letting sleeping dogs lie." At this very moment, what that means is starting to sink in. It would be so much easier to leave Lizzie be, asleep and stupidly unaware. I could leave her a note about going to church and she could laze in bed for a few more hours, something she would likely opt for over church anyway. She doesn't understand the legacy these pearls represent, the long line of love and sacrifice from which they came. Perhaps she never will. Her heart is walled up somewhere deep and remote and she is choosing to keep it there. Whatever happens between us, I'm going to make sure these pearls are locked away safe, too.

When the Pearls
Were Gathered

Part two

The First Morning

Lizzie

I awoke to daylight spilling through the open curtains, where I could see a sky devoid of clouds. And if I wasn't mistaken, the scent of mint.

Michael was no longer in bed. He was at the table by the door brewing mint tea, dressed in a white shirt, blue striped tie, and black pants. I was wondering how he'd managed to creep out of bed, take a shower, get dressed, and boil water in the electric kettle without me noticing. I must have been more tired than I thought. About then I saw that he'd brought the cooler in from the trunk of my car... no, *our* car. If I didn't know better, I'd have guessed I'd been drugged.

He looked over at me and smiled easily, "Want some tea and crackers?"

My stomach lurched momentarily. I'd forgotten the baby liked to make its presence known in the morning – and sometimes in the afternoon.

"That would be great," I said queasily. "What time is it, anyway?"

Michael checked his watch. "Fifteen before nine. We need to leave at nine-thirty. It shouldn't take more than half-an-hour to drive up to the Sea Ranch meeting house."

"That's barely time for me to – " I choked back a wave of nausea.

"You look like you need these crackers..."

I nodded, concentrating on not throwing up, and realized I usually ate breakfast at least two hours earlier. Michael brought the crackers over and I was about to prop myself up against the pillows and start nibbling when I realized I wasn't wearing a stitch of clothing. Oh, well, what did it matter now? I pushed the sheet down to my waist and maneuvered carefully to keep the nausea at bay, into a semi-prone position, laying back against the pillows. My discomfort could hardly have escaped Michael's notice, and it didn't.

"Hold this," he said, placing the plate over the dark fuzz of pubic hair visible through the sheet.

He searched around on the floor on my side of the bed and came up with my robe.

"Want this?" he asked.

I nodded, my mouth full of crackers, so he laid it next to me on the bed, being careful to not make it too obvious that he was checking out the goods while doing so. After a moment, he nonchalantly went back to the table to deal with the hot drink fixings and get my mug of herbal tea. While his back was turned, I wriggled into my robe. I didn't have the sash to secure it in front coupled with my inability to completely conceal the tidbits I knew he'd find most interesting, but at least having it around my shoulders and partially covering my breasts helped me to feel less conspicuous.

"Feeling better?" he said, returning with the mug. I took it gratefully and sipped slowly. "I asked my mom what to do for morning sickness. She said crackers and herbal tea did wonders."

"Would've been nice if you'd told me earlier."

"I figured you'd need something to be thankful for after the big day," he replied.

"You're a devious one, Michael Kerry, and you know it," I teased.

I felt the tension of last night draining away in the lucid light of the morning.

"And you were very nice to me last night, Mrs. Elizabeth Kerry," he said, still smiling.

My heart woke up from its slumber and hopped like a kangaroo in my chest at the mention of my new name. I willed it to be calm.

I must have betrayed my momentary alarm because he went on with, "Don't run away on me now, precious. Not now that we've taken down the battle lines."

We hadn't torn down the battle lines, I thought. I had surrendered. I had given Michael what he wanted for the sake of the baby. I couldn't, of course, tell him that. How many parents sacrificed this much, and more, for the sake of their children, I thought. I solemnly vowed to be kinder with his heart. After all, he'd sacrificed more than I did for the sake of my baby.

I sipped my tea, playing for time. I set the cup down on the nightstand and took his hand.

"You don't see me running, do you?"

"Not literally," he said, still eyeing me closely. One thing was for sure: Michael looked at me in ways Jason never did. I wasn't sure how I felt about that, but either way, it would take some getting used to.

"So come back to bed and I'll show you I'm not running," I challenged, trying to use a relatively sultry tone without sounding too over-the-top.

He knew I'd called his bluff then, because I knew that if there was one matter about which Michael Kerry was fully dedicated, it was his commitment to his religion. He wasn't going to miss church meetings unless he had a *bona fide* reason or there was a life-or-death situation, and self-gratification didn't meet those criteria.

"You know very well we're going to church, Lizzie Kerry."

That name again and my heart began a hopping frenzy.

"Then I better get in the shower and get going, hadn't I?" I responded with as much composure as I could muster.

I threw off the covers and robe, knowing very well Mister Michael Kerry would see more than enough to be tantalized, perhaps enough to sway him from going to church, and seductively sauntered into the bathroom.

After I'd taken the briefest of showers, I realized I had forgotten to bring my clothes in with me, so I leaned my head out the door to ask Michael to find them for me. I waited as he rummaged through my suitcase, and suddenly I realized I didn't like him going through my stuff. I just wasn't ready for him to know me that well, but it was too late now. He had set the suitcase on the extra bed.

"Let's see – dress, stockings..." he mumbled, riffling through my suitcase and pulling out the necessary items. "What color underwear?" He flicked his head in my direction with just a hint of a smile playing on his lips.

I closed my eyes, took a deep breath, whipped out of the bathroom, thumped the door closed with my trailing foot, and marched over to him, my wet hair disheveled and dripping all over the rug. "Black... as in your wicked wifey."

He did a double take, then another double take, and dropped the item of intimate apparel he was holding.

"So you want to play games with me on Sunday morning, Lizzie?"

"You're the one playing games," I accused.

"These what you're looking for?" he asked, ignoring my accusation and holding up a pair of panties just beyond my reach.

"Let me have those," I yelled, reaching up to grab them out of his hand.

"Kiss me first!" he challenged, sticking his hands behind his back.

"Fine, have it your way!"

I tilted my head up towards him and closed my eyes, but nothing happened. I was confused. I opened my eyes, took a step backward.

"You kiss me," he demanded. He hadn't moved – his hands were still behind his back, clutching my underpants. This was payback for tempting him to skip going to church or even thinking I could. Michael had his sacred cows and I knew what they were. He wasn't going to let me abuse them.

"Fine," I snapped. I took his head between my hands and gave him the best kiss I knew how. He did not, however, respond, and that made me even more furious.

"You got what you want. Now give me what I want," I demanded. My lips felt like I'd just smeared chili peppers on them.

He whipped my little black number around from behind his back and handed it to me. I quickly slipped it on. Somehow having on panties made me feel so much less naked.

"Yum... you look good in black," he teased.

"The followers of Satan usually do," I snapped back.

My wit did not dazzle him. "I'll be waiting in the car. Ten minutes or I leave without you."

He was already headed for the door. For a flash, I thought this might be a viable alternative – until I remembered I'd be stuck for hours without phone, TV, or companionship in a place I did not know. Being with Michael was infinitely preferable than being abandoned in this claustrophobic cottage that reeked of our post-nuptial activities, so I dressed at lightning speed, leaving my hair damp and barely combed, and skipping makeup entirely in favor of brushing my teeth. I was rewarded with a run in my new stockings for my pains.

Hell, I thought, I had forgotten my bra, so what did stockings matter? I yanked them off and tossed them in the trash. I flounced out to the car with water drizzling down the back of my neck and jumped into the passenger seat. The engine was already running and the inside of my car (no, *our* car) comfortably warm.

"One minute to spare, Lizzie."

I glared at Michael, brushing my hair out so it would dry faster and look better. "Please turn the heater up. I didn't have time to blow dry my hair."

"You got it." He adjusted the setting to high while I pulled strands of hair through my brush, wishing I had one of those hair dryers that plugged into the cigarette lighter like my mother had taken with her when we last went camping.

"Despite what you may think, Michael," I said, "I do have a testimony of the gospel and I do think it is important for us to go to church."

"I have never doubted that for a moment."

"Then stop acting as if you did."

"If I had doubted it, even for a second, I wouldn't have married you. So get that straight in your head, Lizzie Kerry."

This time my heart didn't try to reorient its position in the universe when he used my new name. I could get used to this, I told myself. I could get used to anything. Except those words spoken in the dark that now lay unspoken between us – no one is going to hurt you anymore and please don't cry, please don't cry.

"Then," I said, getting the last word in, "stop acting like it. People who say one thing and feel another are hypocrites." Except that I knew, if anyone was a hypocrite, that person would be me.

Sunday

Lizzie

We drove home from the Sea Ranch chapel in a more comfortable silence than we had shared driving to it. I let my eyes drift over the ocean as it boiled and heaved against the cliffs. I gazed at trees that clung to slopes so steep I doubted I could traverse them, and marveled that the trees had grown and flourished in such inhospitable habitat. I watched wildflowers sprout out of crevices in the rock, in defiance of nature. I watched waves crash against cliffs that had withstood their assault for unnumbered years and still survived.

I was beaten and broken but I had not surrendered. I had not allowed Satan to sift me as wheat, and Michael still believed in me, even if I did not believe in myself.

In Sacrament, the first talk had been on contention and its instigator, Satan. I'd had enough encounters with Satan to know that he was a formidable foe and wilier than the most knavish politician. Contention was the fuel for Satan's fire, and Michael and I had been working overtime loading up firewood. Perhaps more me than him.

The second topic had covered overcoming contention and dealing with anger. And I was working pretty hard at bottling up my angry feelings toward Jason, Michael, my parents, my unborn child, and life in general. It felt completely unfair to me that I had to take the heat for my actions when Jason didn't, and that I had married someone I didn't love to provide a father for a baby, and that I had to endure the rigors of pregnancy.

It was all totally, completely, grossly unfair, and I was angry – especially with God.

I wasn't sure I was ready to apply either lesson today – or tomorrow. I decided not to share my thoughts with Michael. He was intent on the road and had barely spoken a word since we left church. I considered that a blessing because I didn't know how to begin again. If I started out on the right foot, I seemed to end on the wrong one.

Reflecting on the short time we'd spent together at the cottage before we'd left for church, I realized that Michael and I were at odds because of me. Me. Just little old me. I tried to discern when the lines of communication had been cut, but I couldn't put my finger on it. I could not figure out when we had started fighting or if we were really fighting at all.

I'd awoken feeling hopeful and relaxed for the first time in days. Michael had brought me mint tea and crackers to alleviate my morning sickness. There was no guile in his actions. It always came back to me.

I'd implied that he ought to be paying more attention to me than to his allegiance to Heavenly Father and willfully tempted him to pay homage to me rather than his Father on this Sabbath Day. I ought to be cut off right now with all the other sinners in the world. Michael was like a grand Moses figure, and I was the rest of Israel, constantly whining and complaining. And I was as much trouble to him as the wandering Israelites had been to Moses. He'd been up at Mount Sinai communing with God to receive the Higher Law, while I'd been whoring around, sacrificing calves to heathen gods in the valley. Now he'd brought down the Ten Commandments and it was doubtful I could keep those.

Okay, those bitchy mental meanderings were a stretch. Michael wasn't Moses and I was not a useless whore. Still, Michael has always been the picture of piety and stout-hearted in his adherence to our religious standards. I rolled with the flow and let it take me where it wanted to.

"Lizzie," he said, bringing my attention back to the present. "You look awful serious. What's wrong?"

"Everything," I confided.

"C'mon, talk to me."

"Going to church is depressing."

"Only if you're feeling inadequate."

"Some of us are."

"That's Satan talking."

"I really don't want to hear any more about Satan," I said, sighing. We heard enough today."

"Scares you, does he?"

"If he doesn't scare you, he ought to."

"For being so flippant before church, you sure turned sober afterward."

"Who says I was being flippant?"

Michael shot me a knowing look, but whether it was disparaging or approving, I couldn't tell.

"So what's it gonna take to cheer you up, Lizzie?"

"A miracle, probably," I replied. Like you could show up as Jason but be a person like Michael, I thought. Or Jason could never have happened and you could be the love of my life.

"Like what kind of miracle?" he asked.

I mistakenly thought Michael was goading me again, so I decided to play right back at him.

"I didn't realize I was talking to God," I answered.

"All right, Lizzie – here's the deal. As soon as we get to Stillwater Cove, we're going for a walk on the beach. I refuse to join your pity party."

"Fine, we'll do whatever you want. I didn't want to come on this stupid honeymoon anyway."

"Whoa, whoa. Don't put this one on me. You wanted a father for your baby. You got one. Sometimes, just once in a blue moon, you could consider someone besides yourself."

"And that means you," I said, staring out at the leaden sky and finding no comfort in it.

"Lizzie, I'm trying to make you happy. We're in a beautiful place and the cottage is charming. It's not raining anymore. Now, please, for my sake, choose to be happy."

"Like it's a choice," I sulked.

I wondered then if happiness was a choice or you woke up one day and it materialized like the sunrise. I had never asked myself that question before, so I supposed that meant I had been happy – until I decided to dance with the devil in the form of Jason Dalton. I'd been hearing for years that even though repentance was a way back for those who'd sinned, it was far better never to have sinned at all. I was beginning to believe it.

Just then, we passed the Stillwater Cove sign and it was only minutes before we pulled up in front of the cottage. Michael and I made haste to eat a snack lunch out of the cooler and change our clothes.

I didn't even bother to closet myself in the bathroom this time. Michael knew what I looked like without my clothes and I was beginning to get used to this disconcerting fact. He seemed to like it, and I knew why: I had been blessed with the body parts men liked, and I knew Michael liked them. I had always known he liked them, but I'd never imagined him intimately entangled with them. Today, standing here almost naked in front of him, I was wishing I didn't have these body parts, but I couldn't change them anymore than I could change being pregnant.

Being clad in jeans and a T-shirt rather than church dress helped me feel more like my old self, the one who'd never been pregnant and never spent the night with her best friend Michael, and my casual clothes were a definite winner over the wedding gown, even if it had dazzled all eyes on my wedding day.

We walked down through the redwoods to the cove where the waves came in, waves that had traveled from parts unknown, crashed, and died right before our eyes. They looked fierce and foreboding, and the white water foamed and frothed up to the mouth of the creek, its fury petering out on the rocky beach. Seeing such savage energy made me think of Jason pounding up and down the lanes in the swimming pool, a force in constant motion, restless and never satisfied, destroying whatever fell into his path.

Michael took my hand and we walked up the creek on a well-defined path that wound along the bank among the fern and skunk cabbage. The smell of rotting wood and moss permeated the air. Redwoods and Monterey pine towered over us, making a canopy high above the forest floor and blocking most of the sunlight. I felt peaceful and safe in the shadowy light amongst the great trees. We crossed a bridge and stared into the muddy turbulent water rushing down towards the ocean.

"I like this," I said, smiling up at Michael.

"Finally!" he exclaimed.

Then he gave me a long, hot kiss that took my breath away and started my heart careening in cartwheels against my ribs. Just as quickly, he broke free and began walking fast up the trail.

"Check this out, Lizzie – wanna cross the stream over this log?"

I stared at the turbid, frothy water beneath the log and gauged its width. It had to be at least three feet wide. I was game for adventure, wasn't I? I'd fooled around with Jason Dalton.

"Sure," I said, feeling reckless.

Michael went first, making it look easy. The log was perhaps five or six feet above the creek. My balancing act didn't look nearly as graceful as Michael's, but I made it.

We started walking along the trail on the other side with me leading the way. I skipped out of Michael's reach and pressed forward among the ferns, sometimes stooping to circumvent overhanging branches. Michael caught up to me and grabbed me around the waist, trying to kiss me again. Feeling impetuous, I sidestepped him and started running down the trail with leaves and small branches grasping at my clothes as I careened by.

"Catch me if you can!" I yelled over my shoulder. Being in the forest with Michael chasing me made me feel giddy and playful, how we used to be before we decided to grow up and get married.

"Hey, not so fast, Lizzie!" called Michael over the noise of the creek, but I didn't stop to listen. I could hear the soft thud of his feet on the trail behind me, and I accelerated, heedless of the slick footing and proximity of the water. I ran helter-skelter for a minute or more, well ahead of Michael, who apparently wasn't buying into this game of chase or couldn't keep pace with me. I was practically at full tilt when I broke out of the taller undergrowth at a point where the path made a sharp curve. I didn't negotiate the turn fast enough and realized I was going right over the bank into the water. I shrieked, half from fear, half from exhilaration, and found myself flying over a three- or four-foot drop into the caramel-colored water. I hoped it wasn't deep, but I was darned sure it would be cold.

Luckily for me, the water was high enough to prevent injury, but not so deep that it swept me away. I fell onto my knees and panicked for a moment as I adjusted to the shocking cold. I held my breath, then scrambled for a foothold, glad of my hiking boots, and drew myself up out of the water shakily. The water was no more than waist high but running swiftly enough to make it hard to stand up. I searched the banks for a way out. Just yards away near the opposite bank, the water slowed and spun in a lazy circle along the curve of the bank, so I let the current sweep me downstream toward it and found my feet again in calmer water. I breathed a sigh of relief and waded towards the bank.

Then I realized Michael would be coming down the trail any second and I had the opportunity to execute the most perfect prank ever. It didn't seem so wicked to me at the time, but I was later to revise my opinion. The water under the bank was shallow and calm; all I had to do was float on my stomach with my face in the water, pretending to be a corpse, and he would totally freak out. It was freezing, but I couldn't have cared less. I couldn't get any colder or wetter.

I spread out my arms and placed my head inches from the water, just able to see the spot where I'd plunged into the creek out of the corner of my eye. It was no more than twenty seconds before Michael came marching down the path. I let my head go under the water and held my breath. He let out a blood curdling scream mixed up with my name and I heard a splash as he hit the water. I was hoping I could hold my breath long enough to make this look really convincing when I felt him grab my shoulder and yank up my head.

"Gotcha!" I yelled, choking back water and laughter.

He froze. It seemed to take him a moment to recollect himself and realize he'd been had. His hand was still gripping my shoulder uncomfortably hard.

"Goddammit, Lizzie – I thought you'd drowned!" he exclaimed and flung me back into the water. I lost my footing and went over backward, choking down mud and water.

I groped for a foothold on the bottom, found my feet, and stood up again. I spat out water and sputtered, "You're swearing, beloved."

"Don't ever do that to me again."

"You have no sense of humor, Michael," I went on impishly.

"And you have no sense at all. I should leave you here and let you figure out how to get out of this mess yourself, but because you're now my wife –" and he really winced when he used those words, as if it pained him to say them " – and you're having my baby, I'm not going to."

"It's not your ba –"

"Don't say another word. Not one," he reprimanded. His eyes looked dangerous.

Didn't he get that I had just been fooling around? I whimpered as he grabbed me by the shoulders and guided me toward the bank, knowing that his rough handling of me was intentional. "We'll get out here and find another way across. We're not going back into that current. Even though you may not be concerned about the welfare of our baby, I am. I'm in charge now and don't you forget it."

I didn't like the idea of Michael being in charge, but I wasn't going to argue with him while he was helping me scramble up the bank and out of the frigid water. We were both bespattered with mud and brutally cold. Michael hadn't noticed – or pretended not to notice – that I was shaking.

The walk back to the cottage had an unearthly quality to it. Michael marched me as if I were a prisoner and maintained an unsettlingly rigid grip on my arm. I couldn't tell him that I hadn't intentionally fallen in the creek. I wanted to say I was sorry but there was something about the set of his jaw that deterred me. When we reached the cottage, he opened the door and shoved me inside.

"Stand right there," he said, pushing me against the wall next to the door. "We're not going to spread mud all over this room. Take your clothes off – now!"

My teeth were chattering with the cold and my hands were stiff, but Michael ignored my discomfort. When I stood dumbly and didn't immediately follow his instructions, he added, "No problem. I'll do it."

I didn't have a chance to protest before he was dragging my T-shirt over my head, leaving me topless. He undid the button on the top of my jeans, tore open the zipper, and dragged them, along with my undies, down over my hips, leaving me almost naked. I thought about suggesting he go a little easy, he was going to rip off my skin with my jeans, but his demeanor was so intimidating that I couldn't get up the nerve. I picked up my feet so he wouldn't bring me down like a Raider's linebacker as he yanked my jeans over them. He removed my socks with each leg.

Without throwing me a glance, he stripped off his own clothes excepting his boxers, gathered up the heap of sopping garments from the floor, threw them over his left arm, and headed for the bathroom. I didn't know what I was supposed to do, so I stood in my underwear singeing with cold. If Michael wasn't taking the situation so seriously, it would almost be funny. Except that it felt like about twenty below zero.

Frigid water was oozing down my back as it drizzled out of my hair and for the second time on the same day, I wished I had my hair dryer handy. I heard Michael turn on the water in the tub and imagined that he was trying to wash the mud out of our clothes. No doubt he was taking a hot shower as well. I wished he would hurry and make up his mind about how long he was going to be mad at me.

The bathroom door opened, and Michael emerged with an armload of dripping clothes. He looked as though he'd taken a shower because his hair was freshly wet and he had a towel wrapped around his middle as well as one over his arm. He carefully draped the sodden clothes out over the backs of the chairs in front of the fireplace and placed the towel on the floor to catch the drips, not even acknowledging my naked and shivering presence by the door. He set to making up a fire, placing first the kindling, fanning the flames, and finally adding a small log. I hoped it would blaze up quickly because I was still freezing. Then Michael retrieved a robe from his bag along with his scriptures, wrapped it around himself, and settled himself in one of the chairs by the fire.

At last I had the courage to speak. "Mind if I take a shower?"

He didn't look up from what he was reading. "Go right ahead."

I grabbed my robe up off the bed on my way to the bathroom and closed the door behind me. I ran water into the tub as hot as I dared, noticing that Michael hadn't left a spot of mud anywhere. I dumped Bath and Body Works bubble bath into the steaming water and stepped in. I'd never had a bath this good in my life nor appreciated the meaning of "bone-cold" until now.

I spent a long time washing the silt out of my hair and scrubbing my nails, luxuriating in the steam and hot soapy water. I ought to be angry with Michael for leaving me standing by the door, stripped and freezing, but I was upset with myself for misjudging him. I thought it was a funny prank; his feelings for me surfaced and he had a severe emotional reaction. I would have to figure out some way to get back into his good graces.

I let the water out of the tub and watched it swirl down the drain, wishing that Michael's antagonism would disappear just as easily. Then I blew my hair dry and spent an inordinate amount of time fixing it up to look perfect. I didn't know what I was fixing it for, but I reasoned that I wanted to feel like a human being again. After a final rinse of the tub to make sure there was no ugly ring to offend Michael's sensibilities, I wrapped the robe around me and swished into the room.

Reconciliation

Lizzie

"I'm all cleaned up," I said in my most friendly manner.

It didn't get a rise out of him. He was still ensconced in the chair, bent over his scriptures. I was glad to see a healthy fire was gamboling in the hearth and the air felt warm.

"Michael?" I began tentatively.

"What, Lizzie?" He still hadn't looked up.

"Are you still mad at me?"

"Who says I was mad?" He flashed me a brief, inscrutable glance.

"It was only meant to be a joke."

"I think we have vastly different ideas about what's fun and what's plain irresponsible," he rejoined.

"Then I'll have to try harder to understand you," I conceded. I thought I understood him before. Perhaps I was mistaken. I moved towards him. When I reached the chair, I put my arms around his shoulders and cradled his head against my belly.

"Please don't be mad at me," I whispered.

I began massaging his shoulders. He was very warm whereas my hands were cool. I leaned down my head and nestled my cheek against his, my hair falling across his shoulders. He set aside his scriptures and leaned his head back into my bosom. He no longer appeared angry, just watchful, like a cougar staring out from tall grass. I sidestepped around the chair, curled up in his lap, and gave him the kind of wild kiss I'd given Jason when I was feeling really wanton. The cougar leaped, then withdrew.

"So, is this kiss-and-make-up time?"

"I guess," I murmured.

"Then I hope it's not just going to be kissing."

My heart lurched and I felt warmth surging back into my bones. He surprised me by flashing me a broad grin and I found myself smiling too.

"You're like the weather fronts off the Pacific, Lizzie, my love – one minute it's raining and the next the sun is out."

"I like to keep you on your toes," I teased, drawing my fingers through his hair, which had dried to a lustrous shine while I was cleaning up. He eased into my touch like a cat being stroked.

"Let's not guess now," he said, as he tumbled me to the floor.

After we made love in front of the fire, a late-afternoon rain came in, and we held each other and listened to the sound of raindrops on the roof and against the windows. This was my second time with Michael, and I realized that how he loved on me was as different from Jason's heated libido as the way Michael followed me with his eyes. I'm still going to have to get used to this nuanced, almost timorous manner of love making, but now I know I can.

We ate a dinner from the cooler of chicken tortilla wraps, raw vegetables with dip, and chocolate chip cookies washed down with sparkling water. Our wet clothes were starting to steam by the fire when we turned up the sheets on the bed and settled in with our scriptures.

"So what were you studying earlier?" I asked.

"Before you seduced me?" he said lightly.

"Did not!"

"I say you did," he cajoled. "And in answer to your question, I was looking up the topic from today's Sacrament talk – overcoming anger."

I bit my lip. "That was my fault."

"Let's not play he-said she-said. You wanna know what I was thinking?"

"Go ahead."

"First, if you're angry, the Holy Ghost leaves."

"That's assuming I had the Holy Ghost in the first place," I interjected.

"Now, Lizzie, you gotta quit being so hard on yourself," he responded, putting his arm around me. I shrugged. "In D&C 121:37, we read that if we exercise 'any degree of unrighteousness, behold the Spirit of the Lord is withdrawn.'"

"Then it's a question," I surmised, "of how you get the Holy Ghost back, isn't it?"

"Getting it back is the key," said Michael gently.

"You have to repent and pray for forgiveness from the Lord. In that, I acknowledge my deficiencies."

He chose to ignore my self-deprecating comment. "And our Sacrament speaker this morning had a couple of other suggestions, too. Read Proverbs 15:1: 'A soft answer turneth away wrath: but grievous words stir up anger.' "

"I'm good at 'grievous words,'" I said, scrunching myself up under the sheets.

"I know."

He put his arm around me and pulled me to him.

"You should think about following the advice in Proverbs 25:15: 'By long forbearing is a prince persuaded, and a soft tongue breaketh the bone.'"

"And for what reason would I need to persuade my prince?" I teased.

He kicked me in the foot affectionately. "I was more worried about you breaking my bones."

"Give me time, it could happen," I teased as I kissed his ear.

"How about a scripture on being made whole again?"

"Try the first three verses of Psalm 23. It's my favorite," I suggested.

"I know. Written because King David wanted to be accepted back into favor with the Lord after having sent Bathsheba's husband, Uriah, to the battle front and getting him killed," Michael explained as he flipped through the Old Testament to find Psalms. "Actually, Psalm 51 might be more significant. That was supposedly written after King David had lain with Bathsheba."

"Psalm 51? I don't know that one."

"Anyways, here's Psalm 23: 'The Lord is my shepherd; I shall not want. He maketh me to lie down in green pastures: he leadeth me beside the still waters. He restoreth my soul: he leadeth me in the paths of righteousness for his name's sake.'"

I curled up silently against Michael, thinking that there was one thing I desired that I should not, and my soul would not be restored nor would I find green pastures or still waters until I could let it go. The Lord had given me more than I deserved in Michael, and I should be thankful and happy that I was with a man who wanted me and cared for me. So why could I not be satisfied and accept that Michael was enough? Why did I want more when I had been given so much? I was like King David: he had the most beautiful wives in Israel, but he wanted someone else's. I was truly a wretched soul.

"Why so quiet, Lizzie?" asked Michael softly.

"I am sorry I can't be everything you want me to be in a wife," I replied, curling my toes under the sheets.

"Now what makes you think that?"

I couldn't think of a way to tell him without hurting him, so I shook my head.

"Let's say our prayers and turn out the lights," he suggested.

"Good idea."

"Your turn," he added.

I didn't want it to be my turn, but it seemed my turn was coming around a lot more often than I would like. Even if this evening by the fire hadn't been half so bad as I thought it would be. It was only hard because I still wanted Jason so desperately.

We hauled ourselves out of bed, kneeling by the bed sans clothing. I said a brief prayer. Then Michael switched out the light, throwing the room into shadow, and we clambered back under the sheets. Suddenly I felt claustrophobic and there was altogether too much of Michael entwined around my limbs, but I didn't have the heart to push him away.

"What's wrong, Lizzie?" he whispered. "You're tense."

"Thinking about stuff," I mumbled.

"This is hard for you, isn't it?"

"What?"

"Being with me – I mean, being married."

"It's just... different. I'll adapt. And I do have the benefit of my vastly greater experience," I said dryly.

"Now you're teasing me, honey," he whispered.

"Michael, why do you put up with me?"

"I'm your husband now. I have to."

"Oh," I said gravely. "I hadn't thought of it like that."

I disentangled myself from his embrace and leaned my head back against the pillow with his left arm still crooked under my neck.

"What are we, Michael, by your definition – love or lust?" He stiffened next to me, his arm still locked under my shoulder, our bodies touching from hip to toe. I angled my head towards him on the pillow and saw a vein pulsing in his forehead as his eyes traced some invisible line on the ceiling.

"Neither, Lizzie," he said. The rise and fall of his chest was measured, as if he were counting each breath like a person practicing yoga. "It's an experiment, a poorly designed and executed experiment, carried out by persons entirely lacking the prerequisite skill and knowledge for a successful outcome, and conducted with a reckless disregard for truth and honesty."

I shivered against him. "You're wrong, Michael."

"If you knew the answer, there was no point in asking the question. So which is it – in your wise estimation?" His face was a mask of coolness as impersonal as a statue.

"Love," I whispered, fingering the hollow of his hip.

"You don't know what love is, Lizzie." He flicked his gaze toward me, the sockets of his eyes casting round shadows in his face so that it was impossible to discern his expression.

"Then show me," I breathed, moving my free hand up to his chest under the sheet. He caught it by the wrist and restrained it.

"No, Lizzie. I told you this was an experiment, and an ill-conceived one at that."

I heard the wind in the treetops swaying in the wild weather and the waves charging up at the cliffs below. Shadows moved across the room as the firelight flickered and the cottage creaked as the elements combined against it, cracking against the onslaught of the wind and the storm outside. Michael's fingers were clamped against my wrist, and I felt my pulse beat under his grip. We were like two wrestlers locked in a struggle that neither of us could win but from which neither of us could back down. After more minutes had elapsed than I could count, Michael took the arm he was holding and twisted it back over my head onto the pillow, leaning across me and crushing his ribs into my chest. I held my breath as his nose touched mine. His eyes were dark and unfathomable.

"I thought you said no," I croaked, barely able to find the breath to get the words out.

"I'm experimenting," he whispered, his teeth flashing deadly as a shark's, "– with lust."

At that moment I realized there were parts of Michael I didn't know at all and that he was angry with me, angry with me in some monumental, cavernous way that engulfed me as surely as the gates of hell encircled the sinners in Dante's *Inferno*.

So I turned my head aside on the pillow and succumbed to Michael's onslaught in the same way that I had to Jason's relentless assaults against my body, and this time I wasn't sure I could tell the difference between them. Michael's experiment with lust, unlike the hell to which Dante's sinners were consigned, was mercifully short. He curled up against me and fell asleep with his arm across my waist. Now I knew what the emotion was between Jason and me, and I felt singed with guilt because I still wanted Jason. But I now had firsthand experience with what it felt like to have a man to pour love on me and to drive lust into me. I didn't like this new knowledge. It made it so much harder to sustain my dream of the unattainable Jason, knowing I had never experienced with Jason the tenderness of which Michael was capable.

It took much longer for me to me to fall asleep, but I finally succumbed with Air Supply's "Young Love" drifting through my brain, wondering if, like the words of the song, this was how love was supposed to be. I prayed for the oblivion of slumber, but once again my prayers were unanswered.

+++++++

I dreamed I was beside the river, and it looked even more vast and foreboding this time. Michael was making love to me violently on the shore, but I kept looking over his shoulder at the water, more afraid of what might emerge out of the deep than the thrashing Michael was giving me. And then up rose Jason, more glorious and terrifying than before, making powerful strokes towards the shore and I knew he was coming for me and I tried to break away from Michael's embrace, but Michael would not let me go. I tried to scream to Michael, to warn him we had to get away, but Michael couldn't hear me. Jason was crawling out of the water with his hair shining and showering droplets, and he grabbed my feet and I could feel my body slither down every inch of Michael's body as Jason tore us apart.

I made a last, violent effort to grasp Michael's feet but it was too late and Jason was towing me into the water and I began choking because I was still screaming for Michael to help me. Just before I went under, I locked on Michael's eyes. He was sitting on the shore staring at me, neither angry nor distressed, and I understood he had decided that it was up to me to choose, and he wasn't going to venture in and fight for me because I had to fight for myself.

I started screaming even louder, without a sound coming out of my mouth, and began pummeling Jason's chest and legs although my anger was not against Jason for taking me away from Michael but against Michael for not coming after me.

I felt myself drowning and wished with every fiber of my being that I might go whence I could not return, but I saw Jason ahead of me and knew I could not go where Jason was headed, and I would have to find a way out of the river without Michael's help and I was so livid I began to swallow great gulps of the black water. Then I realized I could breathe again so I must have made it up to the air and I was floating on the surface of the water.

I awoke with a start to the sound of torrential rain beating down on the roof in the darkness and found that I was sitting up in bed crying. I let the fear and anger well up out of me in great sobs, and wordlessly cursed Jason for ever being born.

"Lizzie, honey, what is going on?" came Michael's voice from the pillow beside me.

"Nightmare," I sobbed.

"Bad one, huh?"

"Pretty bad," I said, hoping the choking sobs would subside. I wasn't supposed to be crying like this. My father had drilled into both Lindsey and me that tears were for sissies and wimps.

Michael sat up beside me and put his arm around me. He began kissing my neck and stroking my back. It was both sweet and sad. I simply didn't know how to tell him, please don't do this now, Michael. It's bad timing and bad karma. This is not what I need. But Michael didn't know, and I wouldn't tell him.

How could I tell a man who would do anything for me, that I would not do the same for him?

How could I say that I wanted another man to hold me?

Or that I was receiving secret visitations from my forbidden, imaginary lover in my dreams?

How could I tell him like Jim Steinman from Meat Loaf that yes, he's hit two out of three: I wanted him and needed him, but I didn't know if I could ever love him?

How could I say no to eyes that smoked in the dark and hands that touched me as if I were an angel and a heart that beat so hard against mine that it practically leaped out of its ribcage? I wanted to protest but I couldn't because, in spite of myself, I responded physically to Michael's hands. I wanted to be his moonbeam dancing on the water, not venturing beneath it. Because, in the final analysis, I was safer in the cold, unloving, still place around my heart than I was in Michael's arms.

So I went through the motions and pretended he was Jason, knowing this was the worst kind of sin because I lusted for Jason in my heart while I was with Michael and this was the ultimate betrayal.

And I remembered how David and Bathsheba were punished for their misdeeds by the loss of their firstborn son, and I was horrified and terrified that God had the power to punish me in the same way and that everything Michael had sacrificed might be for nothing.

When it was over and we were lying quietly next to each other, I begged Michael to please forgive me, please forgive me, and he asked me for what and I had no words to tell him, so I held him next to me for as long as I could stay awake.

Because now I was more afraid of sleep than wakefulness.

In my dreams I was lost to Jason and Michael would not help me and I had to find the answers for myself.

I wanted to tell Michael how enraged I was that he was going to let Jason take me away, but Michael did not see nor did he know that he had been a participant in my dream, and he did not know that we had allowed Jason to come between us in our most intimate moments.

So I held on to Michael as if he were my lifeline and fought the waves of sleep that threatened to envelope me. I struggled against fatigue and fear, but in time, I surrendered to them and came to consciousness in the black river where I had fought with Jason.

I was alone in the swift current, not far from the bank where Jason dragged me away from Michael, and I began making strokes for the shore – not against the current, but across it. I felt my strength returning and soon my feet touched solid ground and I scrambled out. I heard screeching off in the distance but there was no sign of Michael so I began calling for him, searching everywhere, but I could not find him. The screeching grew louder and louder and I could not determine what it was, but it began to grate on my nerves.

I awoke with a start. The screeching kept on as incessantly as the whine of a crop duster.

"Hear that?" said Michael from somewhere over my shoulder.

"What?"

"The peacocks."

Damn the peacocks. I was going to go out there and rip their splendid tails to pieces, one magnificent feather after another.

"They were in my dream," I said dully.

"Scare you?"

"Something like that."

"Was it a bad dream, like the one you had earlier last night?"

I didn't want to remember my earlier dream or the bittersweet taste of Michael's lips after I awoke.

"Not as bad."

"What d' you wanna do today?" he asked.

Probably something that fell under the classification of sin, I thought, but I could always go for second best.

"Eat a big breakfast," I answered.

Michael smiled broadly. "Now that is something I can rustle up. You need some crackers right now?"

"Don't remind me. Maybe the kid will keep quiet this morning."

I slid out of bed, wrapped myself in my robe, went over to the table with the electric kettle, and broke open a packet of crackers. I nibbled them slowly, thinking that any day that didn't start out with my head in the toilet bowl held promise. Jason seemed a long way away in the brightness of the morning, and I hoped to keep him there.

"I'll shower first," called Michael.

"Go for it, I'll make hot water in the kettle," I replied.

"You did that last night."

"OK, lover boy, quit looking so pleased with yourself," I teased.

I'd forgotten that Michael and I had shared an easy camaraderie before Jason invaded my body and my senses.

Maybe I could pretend, just for today, that Jason had never happened and I wasn't pregnant or married to Michael, and we were just high-school kids heading out to the coast for a lark. Dream on, Lizzie, I told myself.

On Monday

Lizzie

On Monday, despite my misgivings, we did keep the fantasy alive. Michael took me north up to Sea Ranch for breakfast at a swanky hotel restaurant for breakfast. I ate a huge plate of eggs, bacon, and hash browns, as well as a side of fresh fruit.

I could see the ocean foaming restlessly against the cliffs from our table, and there were patches of blue in the sky, despite the threatening clouds.

Michael was at his most relaxed, confident, and charming. I could almost believe we were a couple on our honeymoon, head-over-heels in love with each other.

We walked on the cliffs above the beach to admire the view and made our way down a precarious path to the beach, which was equally stunning and deserted. I spent a long time gazing out to sea, savoring the impersonal stare of the horizon. I could get lost in a mind so vast.

Later, Michael took me back to the cottage for lunch out of the cooler, and we sat on the stoop of the porch, stuffing ourselves with the last of the salmon canapés and some fancy cucumber swans my mother had fashioned to grace the wedding reception.

The day passed more swiftly than I had imagined, and it looked as though rain was riding in on the wings of the night. Michael suggested we set up the foldout table in our closet and work on a 500-piece puzzle of the coast that he'd found on the top shelf. To my mind, the endeavor was overly ambitious, but I was game to try if he was. We challenged each other to fit pieces ever more quickly and found ourselves competing for who would be the first to fit a piece, acting like a couple of chickens scrambling for a morsel of food. We teased and laughed and played like a couple of kids. It was good to know there were vestiges of our friendship that had survived the momentous changes in our relationship.

As dark fell, we headed out for dinner to another fancy restaurant, this time south of Stillwater Cove. I wore a deep blue silky dress that outlined my figure, enjoying the fact that I still had one. Of course, I forgot my slip, so with nothing but the silky top, my ample endowment was easy to discern. Michael seemed to really like that, which was something I decided to file away for future use. He dressed up in his white shirt and dark pants again, making sure not a hair was out of place. When I caught a glance of us in a floor-length mirror in the foyer of the restaurant, I had to admit we were a stunning couple: Michael with his angular looks and flawless, gleaming hair, and me with my mysterious dark tresses and the mauve tinges under my eyes. As we sat down, I marveled at the crisp, white table cloths, the sparkling cutlery, and the plates as smooth as the inside of a conch shell. Even my father would be impressed at an eatery this upscale. I didn't dare look at the prices on the menu or think about the mission fund Michael was using to pay for this. He was sacrificing everything he held sacred for me.

It was a heavy burden to bear.

We spoke little on our drive back to the cottage, and I found myself dozing against the car window, awakening only when we pulled up outside and Michael told me we had reached our destination. The rain had arrived in earnest, and I was soaked and cold by the time we reached the shelter of the porch. We went in and Michael began stoking the fire yet again. He'd bought an armload of logs from the owner of the ranch for our last night. I undressed quickly by the meager light of the fire Michael was coaxing into flames and sat down behind him on one of the chairs facing the hearth. The air was cool but not as chilly as it had been on the night we arrived.

Our wedding night seemed to exist in a different time. I found myself drowsy with sleep again. The day in the fresh air and our sumptuous dinner were taking their toll. Michael had to wake me again for bedtime prayer, and I was barely alert during the prayer. I snuggled gratefully into the sheets, longing for sleep to overtake me. Jason was a dim memory, hovering at the wings of the stage.

"For doing nothing, I sure feel tired," I said.

"You're pregnant," he observed. I winced, not wanting to think about it. "And I've been keeping you up half the night. So go to sleep."

He pulled the coverlet up over my shoulders and slid in beside me. I was sure he was going to make a pass at me, but he didn't. Either he was restraining himself or he was dead beat too. My relief was overwhelming. I didn't want to think about anything or anyone tonight. Little did I know that Jason was waiting for me in the dark, in the pouring rain.

Jason

Lizzie

I awoke sometime after midnight. Once again, the rain had swept in on the night wind and was assaulting the walls outside. I heard the wind shift in the treetops and with it my thoughts swung back to the day only three months ago when Jason and I had first tasted the forbidden fruit.

This is how I ended up pregnant.

I arrived at the community pool to which Jason had an access key well before nine pm, two weeks after our first date, and waited in the still shadows under the trees at the edge of the parking lot, pacing back and forth.

I had spent the last five days fretting about what lie would suffice for my father, and picked Saturday morning at breakfast, because that was when he was at his most relaxed and I had half a chance of getting him to acquiesce. It had taken me ten minutes of reasoning and pleading to convince my father to let Michael take me out to see *Agnes of God* – because it dealt with religious and moral issues, had been critically acclaimed, was rated PG-13, and it wasn't like Michael was a boyfriend or anything.

By the time I got to the pool, I was edgy and irritated. I was dressed simply in a pale blue T-shirt, a black leather jacket and my favorite black jeans, because I didn't want to arouse my parents' suspicions.

I had brought a plain navy-blue bathing suit but I wasn't wearing it. I didn't know what to expect of Jason anymore and

I was tired of playing charades. I plopped down on the curb under a Chinese elm tree, figuring I'd wasted my time in coming. I felt as if I'd arrived for the main event but was only going to see the opening act.

Jason was late. He finally screeched into the parking lot at 9:22 pm, not that I was constantly watching the clock or anything. He rolled down his window and leaned out.

"You're late," I began tersely.

"Jeez, Lizzie, I'm sorry. The bus coming back was late and family dinners take forever." He stepped out of his car and added with a sly smile. "I'll make it up to you."

"Let's go in," I responded insouciantly, standing up. I slung the string bag containing my bathing suit over my shoulder and turned toward the building. I didn't expect him to move so fast, but I'd gone no more than a few paces when he came up behind me, seized my hand and spun me round. He got a fan of my hair across his face for his trouble. He blinked to regain his equanimity. I was still trying to find mine.

"Lizzie, I missed you." He gave me a quick kiss on the lips and led me up to the side door with exaggerated gallantry.

I was trembling from surprise and anticipation.

He fished the key out of his pocket and deftly opened the door, allowing me to pass ahead of him into the pool complex. The cement walkway between the buildings was unearthly quiet and cool after the warmth of earlier in the evening. We made our way across the concrete to the changing rooms without speaking, Jason towing me along beside him. The place was oddly empty without the footfalls of students, the splash of swimmers, and the monosyllabic shouts of swim instructors.

The glassy expanse of water, bereft of swimmers, shimmered eerily in the darkness. I felt a brief pang of panic; I should have paid attention to it.

"I'll meet you poolside," Jason said, "unless you wanna help me get ready."

"I'm not your mother," I snapped back, trying to look as disapproving as I felt.

"And thank the Lord for that! Suit yourself." He turned on his heel and disappeared into the men's changing rooms.

I swung my string bag a couple of times and made reluctant footsteps around the wall into the adjacent women's locker room. I had to switch the light on. I stared at my face in the mirror, trying to believe I was really here alone with Jason. I had better hurry up, get my suit on, and get out there.

This was my audition for admittance to Jason's heart.

It took me longer than him to get ready, so Jason was already making white water when I emerged from the locker room. He hadn't switched all the lights on, and the far end of the pool was in semidarkness. I walked towards the murky end. I had draped a garish beach towel with the symbol of a great sun on it around my shoulders. I was reminded of Adam and Eve in the Garden, when they used fig leaves to cover their nakedness.

The blue-and-white lane markers were still set up, and Jason was doing laps at a furious pace, making perfect flips at each end. His intensity was intimidating. He swam as if he were an animal pacing the borders of a cage. I was surprised he still had such vigor left at the end of the day after a long swim meet.

I sat down at the edge of the pool with my feet dangling in the water, picking the lane next to the one in which he was so ferociously working out his paces. He flipped over like a seal at the far end of the pool and began another lap of his flawless butterfly. I realized it was the first time I'd seen him in the water without swim goggles and swim cap, but it didn't seem to make a difference to the fluidity of his strokes. He must have seen me, but he didn't give any indication until he ducked under the lane markers and popped up between my legs. He placed one hand on each knee to lever himself up. He was staring right at my crotch, then he dropped back into the water.

"Hey, kiddo, you coming in?"

I flung the towel off my shoulders and hesitated. Jason didn't. He grabbed my arms and pulled me in. I came up gasping and spitting out water, which was shockingly cool to my overheated skin.

"Nice move, jock," I said, glaring. He still had hold of my arms. "Leave off of me!"

He ducked me under and held me just long enough to give me a scare, and then laughed when I came up sputtering. I took a quick gasp of air and slipped under the lane dividers into the next lane and made off swimming as fast as I could, freestyle. I credited myself with being a decent swimmer, but I knew I was no match for Jason. It didn't take him long to catch up to me. I felt his fingers scrape by my feet and I kicked hard towards the opposite end of the pool. I kept waiting for him to grab my legs until I realized he should have caught me by now, but he was pacing himself right at my heels. I tried to make my kicks splash more, and that must have annoyed him because he grabbed me by the knees and flipped me onto my back in a move worthy of an award for stealth. My head went under again and I choked down more water, but he wrapped his arm around my waist and hoisted me up. I coughed again. It was then I realized how strong he was. The thought was both scary and exciting. We were eyeball to eyeball, and he was grinning widely.

"Thought you could run away little girl, did you?" he teased. Still supporting me, he kissed my mouth. As he drew back, he added, "You are so hot, do you know that?"

I felt hot after the frenzied lap with Jason at my heels, that was for sure, even with the expanse of shimmering water around me.

"Float on your back, and I'll pretend I'm a lifeguard rescuing you. Don't try to swim, I'll drag you."

Suddenly I did want to be a damsel in distress and have him cup me in his arms. He adopted a lifeguard hold under my shoulders and I felt the water swirling underneath me as he stroked powerfully through the water with me floating above his chest. We reached the darker end of the pool and he released me.

"You made it," he said, and lifted me up by the waist and set me on the side of the pool like a doll. Then he used his arms to raise himself out of the water in front of me, placing his head at the level of my breasts.

"Oh, Lizzie, Lizzie, beautiful Lizzie. I think you need some mouth-to-mouth," he chanted. Without further to-do, he hoisted himself up, folded his legs up between his arms, and kneeled on the edge of the pool. I scooted back to avoid being kneed in the groin, feeling like a young seal who'd just been bested by an adult. I slid backward some more on the hard surface of the concrete, and he came crawling after me. A few more yards, then I bumped up against a pile of foam swim floats and rubber mats and scampered up them.

"Can't run away now, Lizzie," he grinned.

"I wasn't trying," I blustered.

"Good, then quit looking so scared," he added. He shook his hair to get the water out of it, and the drops went skimming through the air like a thousand pieces of crystal. Even in the half-light, he looked stunningly handsome with his sunny grin and his sleek muscles. I threw back my head to expose my neck. He knew when to make his move. He clambered on top of me and took my head between his hands.

"You are drop-dead gorgeous, girl. I want you so bad."

I felt powerful as a volcano, full of smoke and dark fire and lava I was aching to give up to the light. He dragged my soaked hair back from my face with his fingers and kissed me.

It was not how he'd kissed me before.

I had unleashed his animal instincts. My lips smoked beneath his. He slipped down the straps of my swimsuit, which I hardly noticed, and I certainly didn't protest. Then he seductively explored my breasts, one at a time, with long, sweet kisses, subtly working the bathing suit off my hips. Somewhere along the way he ditched his suit as well, if, that is, he ever had it on.

I knew I'd passed the audition for sure, but I wasn't certain I wanted to accept the starring role, although it looked like I was going to.

There was a five-alarm fire ringing at the periphery of my hearing, but I was so intent on playing the part that I totally ignored it. I was overcome with the acrid smoke of full-scale lust, and I gave myself to it completely. But when I lay there, afterwards, breathless and panting, with his head against my heart, I knew I would have to do this again and again to satisfy him, and he would never be contented with less.

I had tasted of the fruit; it was sweet and delicious to the palate, and the more of it one tasted, the more one desired it.

When I returned home a few minutes before midnight, I snuck in the door hoping no one had waited up for me but found my mother dozing in an armchair in the living room where she was reading the current copy of the *Ensign*. This monthly epistle from the headquarters of the Church in Salt Lake City, Utah was read avidly by most of the active membership, and my mother was no exception. In fact, I was supposed to give it a thorough perusal as well. The magazine had fallen open into her lap and her hair was splayed out against the back of the sofa, but she must have been alert for the sound of the front door opening, because she raised her head drowsily when I came into the living room. I hoped she was too sleepy to notice that my hair was slightly wet.

I'd pulled up the collar of my leather jacket to hide the marks from Jason's kisses on my neck, but I hadn't thought to bring a sanitary napkin for afterwards, seeing as it was my first sexual encounter. I hadn't known what to expect and I couldn't confide in another woman and I hadn't expected Jason to go all the way that night – or if I had, I wasn't prepared to admit it to myself. I felt exhilarated and confused and violated, shocked by how much it hurt the first time as well as empowered by the knowledge that I had entered a world both richer and darker than the innocence of childhood. I was terrified that my mother would see blood on my jeans even though they were black, and I felt marked, like Cain, with the stain of sin, even if it was invisible to my mother's eye. I moved shakily towards her, and bent to give her a quick kiss on the cheek.

"Hi, Mom, I'm home," I whispered.

"How was the movie?" she asked, brushing her hair back with her hand and gazing at the clock. I couldn't remember what time I had said I would be home and I almost asked "What movie?" before I gathered my wits together to cement the lie.

"Good. Really good. I'm beat so I'll head up to bed."

"See you in the morning, sweetheart."

"You too, Mom," I responded, backing away until I was beyond the circle of light from the floor lamp. I took the stairs up to my room quickly, without a backward glance, and fell asleep longing for Jason to take me again. It was both horrible and incredible.

In the days that followed, I became obsessed with him. I spent almost every waking minute burning to feel his embrace. His eyes would pop up at me out of a math problem, or his smile would slide into my dreams. He came to me in the middle of the day sauntering down the corridors of the high school with his hair glowing like a halo and visited me in the deep of the night with his wicked kisses as I wrestled for sleep. I was acutely conscious of his physical presence – I knew when he walked into a room, down a hallway, or into a church meeting room. When I watched him at his swim meets, which I was doing more frequently now at the expense of my homework, we seemed connected by an invisible but tangible cord. He had only to glance up at the stands, where I sat alone, enshrouded in a cloud of physical longing, to make my knees shake and my fingers tingle. Though I would not know it until years later, I was having a similar effect on him. Our passion was like the Tree of Life, standing at the entrance to the Garden, which no one must touch or they would be encircled forever in its flames.

To my amazement, in the seemingly brief interval between our first encounter and the pregnancy test, no one noticed us. How was it that his father Bishop Dalton, my parents, Janine and Shannon my best friends, and Michael my surrogate brother, didn't see it?

Jason and I would sneak finger touches in the hallways at church as we flew by each other, or he'd drag his hand along my waistline as I unloaded books from my locker at school. He left messages on my locker about where to meet him. He never called or spoke directly to me at church.

The secrecy itself added fuel to our fire.

It was a challenge to devise ways to outwit his parents and mine. It was part of the game we played with each other, coming up with different places to meet. On a day we knew my parents and Lindsey to be out, we had sex on the floor of my father's home office. I was too afraid to allow him into my bedroom. On a freezing day in October, we hiked up a local creek, laid out a blanket, and froze everything but our insides having sex on the leaf litter.

Our sultry affair was not to last long. Before I bought the pregnancy test kit, I was sure something had changed. I was queasy in the morning and tired early in the afternoon. My blood throbbed thick and slow in my veins. I felt like a languid, autumn afternoon – bursting, ripe.

When I read the test, I finally came to my senses.

It was like a satellite spiraling out of orbit and hurtling earthward. I could hear the atmosphere whistling by my ears as I spun helplessly away from the stars. I picked myself up from the ground and knew I was in pieces. There were bits of me all over the bathroom.

I spent two days and two nights trying to gather myself together, reliving every moment with Jason. I didn't know how to tell him, but I had to. I didn't know what I should do or what he would want me to do. Then I found a note stuck into the side of my locker door proposing another rendezvous. It was one we'd used before: the park behind Jason's house. I could stop there on my way home from doing homework at Michael's house, because it had to be dark. Jason and I would perhaps spend fifteen minutes satisfying our lust for each other in the shelter of the bushes and leave as swiftly as we'd arrived.

I was fairly trembling when I showed up. I was fifteen minutes early and spent the interim shivering in the dark in my thin black sweater, cursing myself for forgetting to bring a jacket. I hoped my parents weren't going to check what time I planned to leave Michael's; if they did I was going to have to do some fancy footwork to come up with a plausible explanation.

"Lizzie!" Jason brushed aside the branches concealing our little den of iniquity.

"It's freezing," I said, relieved that at last he had arrived. "Couldn't you get here any faster?"

"It's only eight-thirty – the time I said I'd be here," he replied.

The expression on my face must have told him something was wrong.

"We got a problem," I said, trying not to sound as shaky as I felt.

"Yeah, what?" he asked cockily. "Someone find out about us?"

"Sort of," I said wryly.

"Who is it?"

"The Almighty," I said.

"As in God-our-Heavenly-Father Almighty?" he asked, and I saw his teeth flash in the dark. "In case it has escaped you, He's known all along. So what's your problem now? You're not going to get religious on me, are you?"

That was when I realized the only thing Jason was really scared of was his father finding out about what we were doing. Personally, I'd pick Bishop Dalton any day over my own father. It didn't bear thinking about having to explain to him what I was about to explain to Jason.

"Jason, I'm pregnant," I said.

"No way!"

"Yes, way. You wanna see the test – I brought it with me."

There was a long, somber silence. Too bad I couldn't see his face in the shadows.

"You're going to get rid of it, aren't you?"

I thought maybe I'd misheard. "I'm gonna do what?"

"You know, like, not have it."

"Just in case you didn't know – it," and I placed heavy emphasis on the "it," "is a baby. The kind that gets blessed in church."

"I don't wanna get involved in this," he said, totally ignoring my last point. "You want it – fine, go ahead. But I'm not part of this. You screwed up, you figure it out."

"I screwed up?" I yelled, incredulous.

"Got your days of the month wrong, whatever," he said.

"Let's get this straight, Jason. You have been screwing me. You did this to me!"

"I'm sorry, Lizzie, I hadn't realized you were an unwilling participant. But, now that I know that, I'm leaving." He turned and bent down to get under the bushes.

"Not so fast, jackass," I screamed, grabbing the back of his jacket.

He turned so quickly he almost knocked me down. "You listen up, Elizabeth Sherringdon. My dad's the bishop. Who do you think they'll believe – me or you?"

"Believe what?"

"That you've been screwing around with several guys on the swim team. I found out what was happening – now I'm going to tell my father, Bishop Dalton, so you can correct the error of your ways."

"You wouldn't!" I exclaimed, horrified. My whole body was shaking, and it wasn't just for want of a jacket on this chilly night. He yanked me by my ponytail and backed me up to the wall behind us.

"I've got friends on the swim team, Lizzie. A lot of these guys would give their left nut to boast about getting laid with you. You have been going to all the swim meets, haven't you?"

"That was to see you."

"So you say."

I couldn't have imagined a worse nightmare: Jason was going to turn on me after everything we'd shared. They'd be taking my dad to the hospital in an ambulance if he heard this story. I would never live down the shame at school. Being branded as the "swim team slut" didn't bear thinking about. I wanted to cry but remembered that only sissies and wimps did.

"You're hurting me," I whimpered.

"I gotta go, Lizzie. You even mention anything about us, you'll regret it 'til the day you die."

I didn't doubt it. Until the day I died and probably for Eternity. Finally, he let go of me and strode off through the branches. I had no clue what I was going to do. I was absolutely, completely, and utterly screwed, and Jason didn't care. I flung the test kit, box and all, into a trash can on the way back to my car. Then I banged my head on the roof a few times, hoping I'd get a concussion and I wouldn't be able to remember who I was.

Back with Michael

Lizzie

Unfortunately, I knew all too well who I was and was acutely conscious of Michael breathing evenly beside me.

At length, I drifted off into a restless sleep. I awoke to the pearly light of morning rain and the sound of waves crashing against the cliffs, with Michael lying quietly beside me. This wasn't the end of a nightmare; it was just the beginning.

Today we were going home, except that I wasn't going back to the home I knew. I was going to a home already crammed to bursting and I was planning to add yet another member to it in a few months.

As far as I could tell, Michael's room didn't have any extra space for my personal effects, and I had no idea how I was going to fit in. I thought I'd better make a show of facing the day, so I slid my legs out from under the sheets and wondered if I should head for the bathroom for a quick inspection of the toilet bowl or eat some crackers to stave off the inevitable. Michael grabbed my wrist and drew me back towards him. I jumped, not realizing he'd been awake.

"Hey, not so fast," he said. "This is our last chance to be really alone."

I curled back around and gave him an indulgent smile. "I'll try not to throw up on you, then."

"In that case, let me get you some crackers and milk," he came back, looking somewhat crestfallen.

"Might be a winning idea," I responded lightly.

He stepped out on his side of the bed, went over to the table with the electric kettle, and nonchalantly tossed a packet of crackers over to me. Then he found the milk in the cooler and poured it into one of the coffee mugs.

"Here you go, sweetheart."

I'd already broken into the crackers when I took the mug and knocked back the milk. I sat for a few minutes with the covers folded on my lap, feeling my insides work it out. Michael was sitting on the opposite edge of the bed, not looking at me.

"You wanna get rolling, or what, Lizzie?" he asked.

I wasn't sure who was waiting for whom. For Michael, he seemed dispirited.

"You can come back to bed now, if you want," I said, realizing that I didn't want to disappoint him.

"Are you asking?"

Now I was confused. "You were asking, so I'm saying it's OK"

"I think I'll get a shower," he replied flatly.

Just when I thought I had him figured out, the cougar whisked away from me with a flick of his tail and disappeared into the tree line. The bathroom door shut with a click. I leaned back against the pillows, closed my eyes, and drew in a long breath. Fine; whatever. Next time I wouldn't be so accommodating. I flung the sheets off the bed and started gathering up my belongings and stuffing them in my suitcase. Might as well get this over with as soon as possible. I laid out my skinny pinstripe jeans with the leg zippers open, dry but looking somewhat worse for their foray in the stream, a long-sleeved sweater, topping them off with my underwear.

I charged into the bathroom and began an energetic tooth brushing routine in front of the sink to the singing of the showerhead as it drenched Michael behind the shower curtain. I was flossing when he turned off the water and pulled the shower curtain aside.

"Why are you in here?" he demanded with eyes as round as an owl's.

With barely a sideways glance, I stopped flossing and tossed the string into the wastebasket. Next I took a swig of mouthwash from my travel-size Listerine and began gargling. Realizing he was apparently waiting for me to make the next move, I grabbed a towel off the rack and flung it at him, just a little harder than I should have. It didn't faze him.

"Thanks, dear," he said mildly, and began drying himself off.

Avoiding his eyes, I spat out the mouthwash and turned on the faucet to rinse out the sink.

"You in a hurry or something, Lizzie?"

"You're the one in a hurry," I retorted.

"Don't let me stand in your way."

He stepped over the rim of the tub and skirted around me before making his way out the door. I decided I might as well go for a shower right now, even though I hadn't brought my clothes with me, so I hung my robe on the back of the door and turned on the water. I pulled the curtain closed. The spray revived me, and I spent several minutes enjoying the feel of hot water running down my body. When I was ready to get out, I threw the shower curtain aside, stepped out onto the bathmat and nearly jumped out of my skin when a towel hit me in the midriff.

"Don't do that!" I yelled.

Michael was sitting on the toilet watching me, fully dressed in khakis and a pale blue shirt that matched his eyes. I wondered how long he'd been sitting there. Damn cougar had sneaked up on me while I wasn't paying attention. I wrapped the towel around me, suddenly wanting to be alone.

"Can I get you something to wear?" he asked.

"Yeah – I set out a pair of jeans and a sweater by my suitcase. And I'll need my underwear. It's on top."

"Got it," he went on pleasantly. He disappeared out the bathroom door and I heaved a sigh of relief. Then he re-emerged with my garments, draped them over the sink, and sat down on the toilet lid again. I hoped he wasn't planning on staying while I got dressed, but he didn't make a move to leave.

"You're not gonna watch, are you?"

"I like watching you."

I didn't know what game he was playing now, so I dried off and dressed in a hurry. The cougar lay in the grass, staring out from his cover with hungry eyes, unmoving. He was crouched and ready to pounce, but he didn't. I combed out my hair and applied makeup, glancing at him out of the corner of my eye. I looked less tired today. Maybe the fresh air had been beneficial because there was a glow about my cheeks. I took a long time to blow dry my hair, figuring Michael would grow tired of my antics. He didn't.

When I was finished, I whirled around and said, "Ready to take on the world."

But not the cougar, I thought.

"You look ravishing," he exclaimed with admiring eyes.

That was the effect I'd been hoping for.

"Let's get breakfast," he added.

Looked like the cougar was hungry, but he had other prey on his mind besides me. He took my hand and led me out the door. We ate at a café within a couple of miles of the cottage, getting soaked in a downpour on our way back out to the car. The rain had arrived in earnest by this time, and it didn't look as though it would let up soon. It was going to be a long drive home, I thought morosely. I tried not to think about the next week and the fact that I would be spending Christmas with my new family and not my own. There were a lot of things I didn't want to think about, including impending motherhood, my new digs, the demands of my husband and, most of all, Jason.

My new home

Lizzie

It was mid-afternoon when we rolled on to Michael's street in the Nissan. If the day had looked unpromising at the coast, it was downright depressing in Solano County. Not only was the rain coming down steadily, but the fog had moved in off the ocean. Michael's house presented a particularly dreary aspect with its mismatched roof shingles and faded paint. I smiled at him wanly, trying not to look too disillusioned.

"This is it, Lizzie, showtime!"

I doubted the family would allow us to downplay our arrival. I didn't want to think about the next day when I'd be moving my belongings from my house to Michael's. We got out of the car, leaving the luggage in the back seat for the time being because of the rain. When we reached the front door of the Kerry family home, Michael inserted his key into the lock to open it.

"I have a house key for you. Sorry, I should have given it to you earlier," he noted.

"The devil is in the details," I said from behind his shoulder.

"Silly me, I thought the devil was dancing in your heart."

"Very probably," I muttered, wondering if he was trying to cheer me up.

"Hey, sweetie, I was only kidding." He turned to me, sliding his arm around my waist, and bent to give me a peck on the cheek. "Everything is going to turn out fine, you'll see."

But I didn't see any reason to be optimistic. Michael wasn't the one losing the comforts of his home, moving in with a new family, and pining for a lost love, albeit a phantasy. He wanted to be married to me – of that I was sure – but I was beginning to think I'd made a terrible mistake accepting his proposal and going through with it. The door opened, interrupting these moribund thoughts, and we were greeted by Alison and Sarah, who'd obviously been anticipating our arrival with considerable eagerness.

"Lizzie!" exclaimed the five-year-old. She ran up to me and jumped into my arms.

"Hey, bro," said Sarah, "how'd it go?"

"Just perfect, not too much rain," replied Michael, stepping inside and giving Sarah a big hug.

Sarah called into the house, "They're back!"

"Mom and Dad have a surprise for you in your bedroom," said Alison with eyes as bright as a kitten.

"More than our wedding presents?" I asked.

"Don't blow it, Alison," cautioned Sarah.

"Hey kids," said Anne, coming down the stairs. "How was your trip?"

She hugged us both.

"Very nice," I replied. "It really is a beautiful place."

Michael's father and Edward emerged into the living room from the garage.

"Hello, Lizzie, dear," he said. "Did you and Michael enjoy yourselves?"

Only Rachel was missing, and I learned that she was at the mall with a friend.

"We had a great time," said Michael.

He wasn't speaking for both of us. I was still wrestling with my demons.

"Mom and I have a surprise for you upstairs," went on Patrick. "Wanna come see it?"

"You bet, Dad."

We all traipsed up the stairs. Michael carried Alison and Sarah hung next to me.

Patrick was ahead of us when he opened the door to what was now our room with a flourish. Michael was rushed in behind his father and saw it first.

"Oh, Dad, that is awesome!" he exclaimed.

I pulled up behind him and looked over his shoulder. There was a new queen-size bed sitting on the rug, just begging for us to curl up in it. Our wedding presents were piled on Michael's desk and the floor around it.

"You shouldn't have done this," I said. It was obvious what the Kerry's considered important in a marriage. I hated to think of Michael's mission fund going toward a marital bed, but there was no other way they could have come up with the money. "I don't know what to say."

Patrick put his arm around me. "We wanted you to start out right."

"I don't know how I can thank you," I added.

Edward pushed by us, ran over to the bed and bounced on it. He did a quick roll and came up grinning. Michael set Alison down, joined Edward, and they began wrestling on the comforter. It brought a smile to my lips. Alison walked up to the bed more timorously, and touched the comforter near its foot. Then Edward grabbed her hand, pulled her into the melee and all three of them became a mass of arms and legs from which giggles and squeals emanated." That's enough rough housing, kids," Anne said in her motherly tone.

Edward was trying to pin Michael's head down under a pillow and he stopped. Alison was yanking Edward's foot and she sat up, her face shining. Michael's head came up, his hair awry.

"I guess we should let Lizzie try it out. C'mon, love," he directed to me.

Edward and Alison demurely picked themselves up off the bed and walked back to the group by the door.

"Go on," urged Sarah, pushing me forward.

I wished I wasn't becoming such a prominent member of the family, but there it was. Too many hopes were riding on me. I went over and sat down on the opposite side from Michael.

"Pretty nice. New sheets, I bet," I commented.

"I made it up!" interjected Sarah.

"That was very sweet of you," Michael replied.

I turned back the comforter and checked out the label on the sheets. Sure enough, Egyptian cotton, three-hundred-thread count. They might not be rich, but they knew quality. I did not deserve this. I was the wolf in sheep's clothing, but they treated me as if I were a little white lamb.

Before I had a chance to slip away, Michael rolled across the bed, grabbed me by the waist and wrestled me down onto the covers. "So how do you rate this big bed, Lizzie?"

I was so startled, for a few moments I couldn't speak and just blinked up at him like a mouse caught in the beam of a flashlight.

"Cat got your tongue?" he went on in the same teasing vein.

I felt as if I were blushing some horrendous shade of red. I glanced over at the rest of the family and Michael's parents were smiling broadly.

"It feels very comfortable," I said stiffly.

"Lizzie's so impressed, she just can't find the words to express her gratitude – which is unusual, since she's rarely at a loss for words," Michael added. I figured he did that just to goad me. His parents started laughing.

"Let's leave 'em to it, guys," said Patrick to the rest of the family. The five new members of my family shuffled out the door.

"We should unpack the car," said Michael, after they were gone.

"And open our wedding gifts," I said, recovering my equanimity. Michael was still holding me down. "So let me up."

"You're in such a hurry, Lizzie Kerry. What's eating you today?"

"Let me up!" I protested more loudly and began to struggle, but he pinned me down more firmly.

"How about a pretty please?"

I wished I had a venomous bite like a black widow. "How about you quit *holding me down*?"

"How about you kiss me?" he went on, taunting me.

"How about I don't?"

He didn't give me a chance for further protest – he simply gave me a taste of his lips and his tongue, leaving me breathless and fuming. But, as quickly as he'd moved in, the cougar slunk away. He was up on his feet, out the door and tearing down the stairs before I had slid off the bed and found my feet.

I spent a few minutes inspecting the bed, realizing that with three drawers built into the frame on each side for a total of six, that I had at least a fighting chance of finding enough room for my essentials. I hoped I could convince Michael to move some of his clothes out of his closet and into the drawers under our new bed so there would be room for me to hang my dresses. His closet wasn't very substantial.

Alison peeped in around the door.

"Mom wants to know if you want some herbal tea and cookies," she said.

"What I really want is a nap in this new bed," I replied, enjoying the thought of luxuriating in the new sheets.

"I'm sure that can be arranged," said Michael from behind her. He'd brought up his travel bag and my suitcase. "Want to unpack now or would you rather open wedding presents?"

Ignoring Michael's question, I turned to Alison. "Thank you, Alison. I can fix something for myself later, but tell her thanks for asking, all right?"

Alison turned tail and hopped off down the stairs as brightly as a bunny rabbit. Meanwhile, Michael had set down our bags next to the closet door.

Then I added, "I'd love to test out the bed."

"Really?" said Michael, regarding me with raised eyebrows and reaching over to shut the bedroom door. He flipped the lock shut and my heart did a couple of flips, just for good measure.

"I didn't mean that!" I exclaimed.

I sat back down on the bed and slid over to what I assumed was my side near the door, sighing. I took off my tennis shoes and socks. I should just indulge him and maybe he'd leave me be for a while.

"Wouldn't want you to end up in a sulk like this morning," said Michael.

"I was not in a sulk – you were!"

Michael threw his jacket onto his desk chair and began unbuttoning his pale blue shirt. "That's debatable."

I heaved another sigh and pulled my legs underneath the comforter. This bed was going to be magnificent but I would have to share it with Michael, which could a plus or a minus, depending on whether we were on fighting or friendly terms.

"Lizzie, it'd be a whole lot easier if you took your jeans off first."

I think he liked to be presumptuous deliberately to annoy me. "I'm taking a nap."

"Have it your way, then," he responded evenly.

Moving In

Lizzie

Later that evening, we wrote in our journals and opened our wedding gifts. Many of them we planned to store in the garage because they included a set of bath towels, kitchen utensils, saucepans, bakeware, flatware, and a set of dishes, all of which we would need when we moved into our own place. In a small box wrapped with gold foil paper and a glittery gold ribbon, with a name tag indicating my parents were the benefactors, I found five crisp one-hundred-dollar bills. I gasped and held them up for Michael to see.

"Must be nice to have rich parents," he said.

"Putting worldly treasures first does occasionally has its advantages," I answered. "Anyway, you can put them in the money box you told me about."

I hated giving them up, but I knew Michael would appreciate the gesture. At least he wouldn't be tempted to spend them as frivolously as I might.

"Thank you, sweetheart," he said, gently taking the bills from me and kissing me.

The following morning, a Thursday, Michael and I drove over to my parents' house to collect my belongings.

Mercifully, my father was working on some big corporate case involving millions of dollars that couldn't wait until after Christmas and he was not home. My mother greeted us enthusiastically and Lindsey came dashing down the stairs to extract all the gory details of my honeymoon from me. I placated her as best I could while she and my mother helped me pack. Michael stood around offering help where he could, but mostly he carried boxes from my room down to the car as fast as I could fill them.

He was going to work at the garden store from three to nine pm later in the day and wanted to make sure we finished in time. He had the same work schedule the next day. He'd given his employers notice, because he was going to start helping out at his father's shop in January for two hours a day directly after school, and Saturday mornings as well. The garden store was anxious for him to put in as many hours as he was available over the Christmas holiday, and Michael was anxious for the extra income, now that he was responsible for my incidental expenses.

I hated to think I was going to be dependent on Michael in this way, because I'd felt that I was an equal partner in our relationship before. If anything, I'd been the friend with more leverage, because I owned the Nissan and lived in the fancy house. It was hard for me to accept that the balance had shifted permanently, and I didn't like having to defer to Michael in matters of finance, but I knew that was coming. After all, he had been earning and saving money for several years, and I had never given money a second thought, because it was always available. Available like the air you breathe.

It took two trips with my car stacked to the limit with boxes to move everything to the Kerry's. Michael had been trying to get me to take less, so I compromised and left half my Sunday clothes hanging in the closet. Lindsey had her eye on them for ages, and I was betting I'd never wear them again. I gazed at the boxes on top of the bed. Rachel, Sarah and Alison decided they all wanted to help me unpack, but I suspected they were motivated more by curiosity than altruism. Rachel proved to be an excellent organizer, just like her brother. Michael had relocated his pants, underwear, and T-shirts from the closet to the drawers under our new bed early in the morning, leaving almost three-fourths of the hanging space in the closet for me. I thought it a particularly generous gesture.

Rachel fingered and admired my clothes as she hung them up for me, while Sarah worked on my more mundane sock and underwear collection. Alison was busy checking out my jewelry boxes. I was hoping she wouldn't lose anything valuable and was trying hard not to feel like I was being violated. But since Michael knew me in my most intimate parts, what did it matter that his sisters were rifling through my personal effects?

I had nothing of myself, not even my dreams, because Jason owned me in the night.

We didn't finish sorting out my worldly goods before Michael had to leave for work, so he kissed me good-bye and left us in the middle of a pile of boxes. Shortly thereafter, the girls discovered my boom box and spent the next fifteen minutes going through my country and pop tape collection deciding what music they were going to play while we unpacked. I told myself I didn't care because I liked all my tapes and it didn't matter what they selected.

Sarah started playing a Phil Collins album. I tried not to think about the words to "One More Night" but they echoed in my head anyway. I inwardly cursed Jason for so casually letting me go, and myself for not. I tried to focus on the task at hand. I was hoping I'd have everything stashed before Michael came home. I wondered how he was going to handle the Lizzie invasion.

We finally made it to the box of shoes. I wasn't Imelda Marcos, but I had about twenty pairs including heels, boots and even a pair of dress-up tennies with lace and pearls my mother had assembled at Home Making Night, a women's church activity for overburdened mothers to stress out some more to complete craft projects, learn how to knit or sew, or preserve food for the End Times.

"You're the same size as me," exclaimed Rachel. I hoped she wasn't headed where I thought she was.

On impulse, I said, "You can have those, if you like."

I must have been motivated by guilt, I told myself. Sarah looked crestfallen, so I added, "Tell you what, Sarah, why don't you and Rachel each find an outfit you like? Take anything. Looks like I have a surplus, anyway."

Besides, I reasoned with myself, I wouldn't be able to wear any of these gorgeous clothes in a month or so. Neither one of them was as well-endowed as me, but I was willing to bet any dress I had in my wardrobe was nicer than what was in theirs, because we shopped at Macy's, and Sarah and Rachel looked more like Ross and Target to me.

"That is so sweet, Lizzie," piped up Sarah. She ran over and hugged me.

They ought to have known I was the wolf in the flock, I thought. My offer started them on a frantic search amongst the piles of clothing for just the right outfit.

"And I'll give you something for helping too, Alison," I said, realizing that if I left Alison out, she'd be really hurt. I figured there must be a piece of jewelry she'd want. Since Alison was already tinkering with my trinket collection, I added, "See if you can find something you like in there."

"Thank you so much, Lizzie," cried the little girl. "You are the best sister."

She threw a frown over at her two blood sisters, as if to say, you never treat me this nicely, and I was glad they were so absorbed in rummaging through my stuff that they didn't notice Alison in the jewelry. With Rachel and Sarah preoccupied, I had a chance to make faster progress on the rest of the job of unpacking.

Two hours later, I had everything stowed away and shipshape. My computer was sitting on a rollaway stand and had elicited a great deal of excitement. I was thinking that after the baby arrived, I might as well move it downstairs so the whole family could use it and make room for the crib because I wouldn't need the computer for homework any longer. There was barely any walkable space in Michael's bedroom before, but now with the larger bed and two people, it was, well, claustrophobic.

The whole concept of being married and becoming a parent weighed heavily on my spirits as the day wore on. The grim realities were setting in.

Rachel selected a lime green sweater and flowing black skirt that complemented her dark looks along with the sling-back heels I'd offered her. Sarah was careful and earnest in her search, and finally chose one of my favorite outfits: a whimsical dress of blue-flowered print loaded with lace and ribbons. I bet that would impress the boys at church, even if she didn't have any cleavage to fill it out and needed highlights to set off her mousy brown hair. I wondered if she had suitable shoes to match. Hell, I might as well give her the pair I always wore with it. Her feet were smaller than mine, so I figured she could stuff the toes with paper.

"I've got some shoes to go with that," I suggested. I scrambled over to the closet and retrieved them from the shoe rack I'd brought. "If they're too big, you can always stuff the toes."

Again, she gave me a grateful smile and said she was going to wear the dress on Sunday for sure, even though it was better suited for spring than the middle of winter.

I thought I should offer to fix her hair, so I did. The intruder in their midst was already introducing worldly concepts like vanity, I thought to myself.

Alison had found what she wanted too: a pair of teardrop pearl earrings—the ones that matched my gorgeous pearl choker, unfortunately. But how could I say no to a five-year-old who must have talked her parents into letting her have her ears pierced? I decided not to let on they were real pearls in case Rachel and Sarah should fall prey to yet another of the seven deadly sins, envy. I still had the choker and probably another set of smaller genuine pearl earrings that would work with it. Unlike the necklace Michael had given me, which fell apart the first time I wore it. Who would even think of giving someone a beautiful necklace without the matching earrings? Come to think of it, I haven't seen those silly pearls since the night of the wedding. I guess Michael's fastidiousness came to the rescue and he cleaned up the mess in my car after I went to sleep: at least he's good for something.

٠٠٠٠٠٠٠

Now the girls had finagled shoes, clothes and jewelry out of me, they were a happy crew by the time darkness fell and we sat down to dinner. It felt odd not to have Michael sitting next to me and Alison in his spot. I was beginning to develop an intimate understanding of the concept "leech."

I went up to Michael's room after dinner to write in my journal, feeling the need for distance from this tightly knit family. I wrote about the honeymoon and my illicit desire for Jason and how I wanted to overcome it.

Michael came in around ten pm, looking worn out.

"Long shift?" I asked, looking up from my writing. I was propped up amongst the pillows on our new bed. "You look all in."

"Yes, I am. Christmas rush, you know how that is."

I didn't, because I'd never held a job in my life, but I wasn't about to tell him so.

"You're a quick study, aren't you?" he commented, surveying the room.

I hoped he now realized it felt like to be invaded. He opened the closet and stared at the array of dresses and skirts hanging there.

"Your sisters were a big help."

"Didn't know you had so many clothes," he said, looking at the array of clothes that had taken up residence. He began flicking the hangers down the rack and examining my outfits, one by one.

"Yeah, well, some of us do have the misfortune of desire for worldly goods."

"'Beware of pride, lest ye become as the Nephites of old,'" he quoted.

"You should see my jewelry collection," I went on mischievously.

He went over to his desk, opened one of my jewelry boxes, checked out a few of my baubles, and turned back to look at me. He pursed his lips together. "You leave my journal alone, understand?"

I hadn't even considered his stupid journal, which was lying out in plain sight on his desk. "Look, Michael, you've already told me, and I promised to keep my hands off the Holy Grail. Satisfied?"

He softened. "Sorry, I'm tired is all."

"Let's say a prayer and go to sleep," I suggested.

And sleep we did. On that night, I did not dream of Jason. I didn't dream at all – my dreams were all shattered.

That Saturday

Lizzie

By Saturday I was getting used to the routine of this new household and the fact that Michael was working way too many hours, but it gave me time to myself, when Rachel, Sarah or Alison weren't interrupting me for some reason.

We spent Saturday doing household chores. Edward had designed a circular wheel for the refrigerator that listed everyone's name and their assignment for the week. Michael was exempted because of working the entire day Saturday, so I took up the slack for him. I was grateful that all I had to do was dust and vacuum the living room, which took no time at all. I was beginning to understand the concept of "many hands make light work." It was amazing how fast seven people could clean up a small house. I tried to find places for Edward's construction projects and Alison's toys, but they just didn't fit in. Then there were Anne's craft and sewing projects that were strewn on shelves about the living room. I decided to dust around them; I doubted anyone would care.

We spent the late afternoon making cinnamon ornaments for the tree and fixing them to the branches with white, green and red ribbons. I had to admit the Kerry family tree, with its homemade ornaments, popcorn chains and endearing, home-sewn angel, even if it wasn't as fancy as my mother's designer tree adorned with silver-and-blue ribbons and expensive glass balls. I felt a brief pang of homesickness, but it passed in the bustle of helping Anne make dinner and reading Alison her bedtime story.

As we nestled on the couch, Alison said to me, "You know what I really want Santa to bring me for Christmas, Lizzie?"

I didn't have a clue. "You better tell me, I have no idea."

"A pair of real ballet shoes."

"And why is that?" I asked.

"I want to take ballet lessons," she whispered, "but I think it cost too much."

"I'll see what I can do, then."

"You mean it?"

I wasn't sure whether I meant it about the ballet slippers or the lessons, but I reassured her that I did. It didn't seem too tall an order for a five-year-old. The Kerry's weren't that strapped, were they? They'd taken me in. I probably shouldn't think about how I was impacting the Kerry household budget, because it couldn't be pretty. I decided I'd take up the subject of Alison's ballet lessons with my new mother-in-law the next day, Sunday, when she was most likely to be in a receptive frame of mind. I'd learned from my father that timing one's approach was everything. At least he'd taught me something useful in seventeen years, I told myself.

I waited up until after nine-thirty, when everyone in the household had retired, but with Michael showing no signs of coming home, I traipsed listlessly up the stairs and began preparations for bed. Michael and Edward shared the bathroom next to their parents' room, a wise decision because three girls in one bathroom were a crowd. I was sure Edward took no more than minutes to brush his teeth and slick back his hair, and I'd come to realize that Michael was equally efficient. I'd decided to leave my blow dryer and makeup in our bedroom, because I felt self-conscious taking up space in my in-laws' bathroom. I was sitting at Michael's desk, brushing out my hair, when he finally walked in the door.

"Hey, stranger, how's it going?"

"Another long day," he replied wearily.

It didn't help me feel any better that he was putting in all these hours for us.

"How was your day, Lizzie?" he asked, coming up behind me and wrapping his arms around me. I was not going to think about where he was putting his hands. He bent down and kissed me lightly on the neck. He moved his hands down to my belly. "How's baby?"

"Mercifully unobtrusive," I replied.

"I can't wait until you really have one of mine," he went on.

I wondered it if was male stupidity or if he realized how much a statement of that nature would irk me. I threw down my hairbrush, just so he'd know I wasn't happy about what he'd said. He took a step back away from me.

"Just in case you've forgotten, Michael John Kerry," I said as coldly as I knew how, "you've been saying all along this is your baby as much as mine. And just in case I hadn't told you, I'm not planning on having any more kids with you."

I should have known this would set him off. "You what?"

"I was thinking that when *our* baby starts kindergarten, I'd be able to go back to school and get my teacher's credentials."

"You're dead wrong, then. And what makes you think I wouldn't want to have more kids with you, Lizzie?"

"I don't plan on being a stay-at-home mom," I countered, ignoring his question.

"What you want doesn't matter, that's what you're gonna be. And just in case you didn't know it, that's what our Prophet and church leaders recommend, too."

I hated that he could always fall back on church policy. t was church policy that had got me here in the first place.

"Well, I'm still not making any more babies with you, so there!" I retorted.

"Fine, then go find another place to sleep," he yelled.

"Can't wait," I snapped back, flinging back the chair and marching for the door. "See if I care!"

Before I reached it, however, I heard a low knocking. We couldn't even have a decent fight without interruptions, I thought.

"I hate living in this family," I added injuriously.

I flung open the door. To my horror, little Alison was standing outside in her night gown. I hoped she hadn't heard my last outburst, but I was betting she had. I hadn't exactly been careful about keeping my voice down.

"I'm sorry," Alison said, turning away.

"Don't go, sweetie," I begged. "I'm the one who should be sorry. What's the matter?"

"I had a bad nightmare. Rachel and Sarah don't b'lieve me about the monster in the river."

A chill went through me. I swept her up in my arms. "You can stay with us, honey. I do believe you about the monster, OK? And we're gonna make him go away."

Alison hugged me and clung to me like a rose climbing up a trellis. I turned back to Michael and was ashamed to see such pain in his eyes. I closed the door gently.

"Are you and my brother fighting again?" asked Alison, looking from my face to his.

"You might say that," he replied tightly.

"Then we should say a prayer. That's what Mom and Dad say we ought to do to make Satan go away."

"Right then," Michael came back.

"Who would you like to say it?" I asked him, wilting under the furor of his gaze.

"Alison would be the best choice, don't you think, Lizzie?"

I nodded numbly. The three of us knelt next to the bed with Alison in the middle. She asked Heavenly Father to please make the monster go away and not be upset that her brother and new sister were fighting, because she knew they were really sorry and didn't want to fight. She was wrong; I was as angry as the Wicked Witch of the West in the *Wizard of Oz* and I wanted to change Michael into water as soon as my powers enabled it.

When Alison was finished with the prayer, she looked brightly up at us and said, "You have to shake hands and kiss, like Mom makes me do with Rachel and Sarah."

I was beginning to wish I hadn't invited Alison in. Michael held out his right hand and reluctantly I gave him mine. We shook over Alison's head.

"Now you have to kiss," she said emphatically.

I finally had the nerve to look Michael in the eye, and I didn't like what I saw. The cougar's eyes were smoldering like the streets of Sacramento on a scorching August day. I returned his look with as much defiance as I could muster, leaned forward, and offered him my lips. He responded by giving me a long savage kiss. If he was intending to hurt me, it worked.

"See, you're friends again," interjected Alison blithely.

Thank goodness for the gullibility of a child, I told myself.

"You girls get into bed now, and I'll be right there. Just going to brush my teeth and change," Michael said.

We scrambled under the sheets. I put Alison on the side nearest the window, so she'd be next to Michael. I wasn't cuddling up with him tonight, I told myself. I was going to nurse my anger and make him realize that he couldn't lecture me like the Stake President, who was the most senior religious authority in an area of the Church of Jesus Christ of Latter-day Saints. I waited until Michael had closed the door until I asked Alison the question that had really been tantalizing me.

"So, sweetheart, what's this monster of yours look like?"

"He comes out of the river and the water is dripping off his golden hair," she replied simply. My blood froze as hard as the glaciers in the last Ice Age. "He's gonna take me and drown me in the river."

I tried not to lose control. "Have you seen this monster before?"

"He's a new one."

Then I was terrified of what I'd done. I was putting this family in jeopardy as surely as if I'd taken them into a flood. I was being punished for letting Jason into my head and God wasn't just punishing me, He was going to take vengeance on the innocent.

I heard the door click and I clenched my teeth. I didn't want to deal with Michael right now. I didn't want to deal with a five-year-old's nightmare. I didn't want to deal with *anything*.

"Lizzie?" he said.

"Yes, honey," I answered, without warmth.

"Why don't you put Alison on your side? She'll sleep better that way."

Michael's tone was as lacking in conciliation as mine, so I thought I'd better follow his instructions. I grabbed Alison and rolled her over the top of me onto the other side of the bed. She giggled. I made sure my back was toward Michael and tucked Alison in under my arm.

"I love you, Alison," I whispered. "You're a real sweetheart, know that?"

"I love you too, Lizzie. 'Cept when you're mad."

I had to admit I wasn't too lovable when I lost my temper.

"I didn't mean that about your family, either," I added.

"I know – you gave us all that nice stuff when you moved in, so I know you didn't mean it," she replied, confirming my suspicions that she'd overheard the words I'd so carelessly spoken. "You said that to make my brother mad."

"I'm sorry, honey – you'll forgive me, won't you?"

"I already did. He still has to."

I winced.

"You could say you're sorry," she whispered.

"Shhh," I said for an answer.

"You still mad at my brother?"

"Yes, seething," I confirmed.

"What's 'seething?'" she asked.

I took a deep breath. "Like – real, real mad."

It took her a moment to absorb this. "Then you should say another prayer," she suggested.

"We'll figure it out in the morning," I sighed. "You go to sleep."

"Promise?"

"Yes, I promise." I had made so many impossible promises, what would one more matter?

Michael lifted the covers and slid in behind us. I hoped he hadn't overheard our hushed conversation. He wrapped his arm around both of us, and I stiffened, desperately wanting my own space, but finding myself trapped between Michael and Alison. He brushed his cheek against my shoulder and kissed the bare skin.

"Good night, ladies, sleep well."

I grit my teeth, hoping for the blissful oblivion of sleep, which I was sure would be long in coming. The words of Eagles' "Heartache Tonight," the song Rachel had been playing all day, echoed through my head. We had beaten it down in the bushes and gnawed it to the bone, but it wasn't going away.

"I love you, Lizzie, even though I'm mad as hell at you right now," he whispered.

"Ditto," I replied. I hoped Alison wasn't listening. It was bad enough that I was placating my husband with half-truths.

He tightened his grip around us, and I felt the clash of two wills as strong as those waves we'd seen crashing against the cliffs of the northern California coast battering against each other.

It was not Michael I should be fighting with at all, I thought, it was the Jason of my fantasies. He was coming for Alison and he was going to take her in the river and drown her and I would have to stop it, no matter what. Where was he? I said in my heart, I'm coming for you, Alison, and don't be afraid. I'll find you and I'll make him stop, I'll make him stop.

I'll Make Him Stop

Lizzie

I lay awake long after Michael and Alison fell asleep.

I knew Jason was waiting for me and I did not want to face
him, but I knew he was coming tonight. I found myself floating on
the river again under a grey sky in a pouring rain. I could hear the
waves pounding at the mouth of the river where it entered the
sea as the current carried me towards the ocean. I was afraid I
would drown in the white water but I had to find Alison because
Jason was taking her out to sea and I could not let him. The
water went over my head and I dove towards the blackness and
vowed I wasn't coming up until I found her.

It was Jason I saw first, then Alison, wrapped in his arms,
helpless and screaming wordlessly. Damn your soul, Jason,
damn your soul. You will not take Alison, you will not injure the
innocent. First I pleaded with him, to no avail. Come get her, he
said, come get her. I will, I replied, I will. Take me instead of her –
I'll go, but not Alison, not my baby, not the innocent.

I saw him let her go and Michael came from out of nowhere
and took her up to the surface with him and I knew she was
safe and it did not matter what happened to me, as long as
she was protected. You will not have me, I yelled at him, you will
not sift me as wheat. But I already have, he laughed in my face.
I've owned your body completely and I want your soul. You shall
not have it, I screamed at him, I have promised it to Michael
and you shall not have it. What do you know about promises,
he mocked. Your heart belongs to me, and me only. I can come
and take you in your dreams as I wish, and you come willingly.

Then you pretend I am Michael to soothe your denigrated soul. But we both know it is only me you desire. It is me you feel and me you want when you are making love.

Go away, I cried, you are a fraud and a vision; *you* are not real.

I am more real than the blood flowing in your veins and the air you breathe and the water in this river, he replied, and I live in the child in your womb.

No, the child is Michael's, I have promised the child to him just as Rebecca promised Samuel to the Lord and you will not have him, I bawled.

I will take the child, he replied, you shall see, I will take the child. No, no, I sobbed, not the child. Everything I have done is for the child. Take me, but not the child; not the child because the child is without sin and you will not take the innocent. Take me, but not Michael and not the child.

I gasped for air.

It was morning.

I wondered if the nightmares would ever end.

A new nightmare was emerging in which I was going to the bathroom to throw up, I thought. I wriggled free of my captors and made a desperate dash for the bathroom. I was glad no one was up. I retched into the toilet bowl Sarah had cleaned yesterday. It was a crying shame to mess it up, so after the heaving subsided, I scrabbled around under the sink for the toilet brush and scrubbed it as hard as I could. Then I crouched on the floor in front of the porcelain bowl as if it were an altar and sobbed wildly. I hated myself for my weakness, knowing my father was right and only sissies and wimps gave in to tears.

"Lizzie, what going--?"

It was Patrick. I couldn't get away from this family, no matter where I turned.

"Morning sickness?"

I nodded and sobbed some more.

"Poor baby." He picked me up off the floor and set me on his lap on the edge of the bathtub. I was so embarrassed that I sobbed even more violently.

"Michael and I had a fight. Then Alison had a nightmare," I blubbered.

"Shhh, let's not wake anyone else," he said. "You just cry all you need."

It took a while, but finally the nausea and the sobs subsided.

"I'm OK now," I said, getting up.

He grabbed a handful of tissues out of the box on the back of the toilet and handed them to me. I dabbed my eyes.

"You have your weekly meeting with Bishop Dalton this morning, right?"

"Yeah," I responded glumly.

"Get dressed and I'll make you guys breakfast. And Lizzie, if you want to talk, you know you can trust me. I won't say anything to Anne or Michael or anyone."

"OK."

I fled out the door and down the hallway, but there was nowhere to run. Michael and Alison were behind the bedroom door. I opened it gingerly and saw that Michael was propped up in bed scribbling in his journal.

"Hi," I said tentatively.

"You look pale," he said, only flicking his glance at me briefly. He kept on writing.

"Your dad said he's making us breakfast."

"Think you can keep it down?"

I shook my head. He put down his pen and set aside his journal.

"Come over here, you rebel."

I walked around to his side of the bed and checked to make sure Alison was still asleep.

"Don't worry about her, she's safe," he reassured me.

I knew she was out of harm's way. I had saved her from Jason, but I feared for the life within me. I sat down on the bed. Michael put his arm around me and brought my head up to face him.

"You practically bit off my tongue last night," I observed.

"That would have its advantages," he replied wryly.

He drew me close to him and hugged me, but we still couldn't apologize to one another.

"You still mad at me, Michael?"

"Yes, livid."

"Me, too."

"Truce?"

"No way."

"That's what I thought, but at least it's honest," he said heavily. "Get dressed and we'll go eat Dad's breakfast."

We had not called a truce, but it seemed we had stopped fighting while we went about our Sunday morning activities. We sat at the breakfast table opposite my father-in-law, avoiding each other's eyes and eating his walnut waffles in silence.

"You two fighting again?" he inquired.

"I guess so," I replied. "It's sort of a ceasefire so we can eat breakfast."

"What is it this time?" he asked.

"That's not a subject for discussion," I said quickly to prevent Michael from butting in.

"And neither one of you wants to back down?"

"That's about it, Dad," said Michael, stabbing a piece of waffle with his fork.

"Then you'll have to suffer the consequences of being stiff-necked."

My consequences arrived right after breakfast, when I tossed up the waffles in the bathroom fifteen minutes after I'd consumed them. Michael gave me an "I told you so" shrug when I came back to our room. Patrick might have been full of empathy in the bathroom earlier, but my he hadn't sounded the least bit happy with us at breakfast. I blamed Michael for saying neither one of us was backing down from our respective positions. The Lord was letting me experience the full brunt of my sins and Michael wasn't giving me any sympathy, which made me even madder. Michael was wrong and I had just as much right to have a job outside the home as he did. Unfortunately, Bishop Dalton would not agree with me.

Bishop's Lament

Bishop Dalton

It was less than a week since their honeymoon, and I had grave concerns about Michael and Lizzie Kerry.

Their wedding had gone off without a hitch, and I had a strong impression that they were supposed to be together, so I could not imagine what had caused this falling out. But it was patently obvious that they'd had a spat and were sitting on opposite sides of the fence when they came into my office for their weekly counseling appointment. They were holding hands when they entered, but it was to make a show of unity for my benefit, not theirs.

Lizzie was abnormally pale and looked as though she hadn't slept well. When they sat down, they didn't look at one another or smile at me, and the togetherness I'd seen before the wedding day had vanished. I wondered if something had gone wrong on the honeymoon. I knew these things could happen, but Michael and Lizzie were not innocent of one another. They had known what to expect. What was I missing?

I thought it best that I take the lead, so I offered the opening prayer. In my heart, I asked the Lord fervently to reveal what I might do to help this young couple.

"Tell me about your honeymoon," I began softly, hoping to set them at ease.

This brought a smile to Michael's lips.

"We went up the coast. Wonderful," he said.

"It's a beautiful place," added Lizzie, almost too quickly. "Big trees, spectacular waves."

"Were you getting along there?" I asked.

"Of course," Lizzie answered brightly.

"Good. Always helps to start off on the right foot. And what have you been doing since you came back?"

"Moving, for one," said Lizzie. Her voice was less steady now.

"How did that go?"

"My sisters were a big help," interjected Michael.

"Good." I took a deep breath. I might as well go for broke. "And why are you so upset with each other this morning?"

Their silence spoke volumes. We have a problem, Houston, I thought. I didn't miss the mark too often when it came to counseling couples, and the Lord had once again allowed me to see what was in their hearts.

"OK. Lizzie, you can go first."

She said nothing, so I waited. Michael fidgeted in his seat. I heaved a sigh, wishing that the responsibilities of a bishop weren't so onerous.

"I'd be happy to say another prayer with you, if you think that would help," I offered.

"We had a fight," she conceded.

"I gathered that. Want to elaborate?"

She shook her head.

"Then you won't mind if I ask Michael?"

"Whatever..." she said in the same surly vein, much to my disappointment.

"Yes, Bishop, we did," said Michael.

"Would you mind elaborating?" I asked gently. I didn't want him to think I was pushing, I just wanted them to get beyond the impasse.

"I came home from work late last night and told Lizzie I'd like to have more kids with her," Michael said.

Lizzie flashed him a look both pained and angry.

"That's not what it was –" she interrupted.

I intervened before she could finish. "Lizzie, I gave you the opportunity to speak first." I placed heavy emphasis on the "first." "Since you declined, you'll have to wait your turn."

She folded her arms across her chest and glared at me I was simply enforcing the rules, and if Lizzie didn't like them, that was too bad. I redirected my attention to Michael.

"You were saying?"

"I guess it's pretty stupid to say I want more kids, seeing as we didn't plan on having this baby," Michael acknowledged. "Lizzie just lit into me. Said she's not having any more kids with me, ever, period. Which made me pretty upset."

"You do want more kids someday, right, Michael?"

"Of course," he affirmed. I didn't find that unnatural, even if the first child was an accident. Michael's timing was bad, that was all, and Lizzie was overly sensitive. They just needed to stop stepping on each other's toes.

"Lizzie," I said, redirecting my focus towards her. "Have anything you want to add?"

"He said he wanted me to be a stay-at-home mom."

"That is what's best for your family."

"That's what's best for Michael," she rejoined. "I want to go back to school in the future."

"That's not an option," interjected Michael.

"Slow down, son, it's Lizzie's turn now," I cautioned. For Lizzie's benefit, I went on, "You decided to marry Michael and have his baby, right?"

"Right," she replied sullenly.

"Did you have other choices?"

"Yes."

"What were those?"

"I could have given the baby up for adoption and not married Michael."

"Correct. What else?" I went on.

"I could have kept the baby and not married Michael. But that wouldn't have been right."

"Why not?" I asked cautiously.

"Because a baby needs a mother and a father."

"I totally concur."

"So I chose what was best for the baby," she went on.

"And what is best for the baby when he or she is growing up?"

She knew where I was headed, and she didn't like it.

"For me to be a stay-at-home mom," she acknowledged, twisting her hands in her lap.

"Thank you," I said warmly. "Do you know what I'd call that?"

"No," she responded dourly.

"Sacrifice. That's what you do for those you love. It's part of the Lord's plan. It's what He did for us."

She sighed visibly.

"Let me ask you – is it conceivable that someday, sometime in the future, when your baby has grown up a little, you might want to have another one?"

"I don't know," she said. Again she flashed a harsh glance in Michael's direction.

"Do you care about Michael's happiness, Lizzie?" I asked, testing the tender thread that held them together.

"Of course."

"Is it more important than your happiness?"

"Yes," she said with conviction.

I felt that at last I might be making progress. I hung onto this thread.

"What would you do to make Michael happy?"

She hesitated to reply, then looked at me with such sorrow and tenderness that I thought I would break down weeping. "I would do anything. I owe him."

She shielded her eyes as if she were trying to hold back tears. Michael leaned forward in his chair and put his head in his hands. I was glad that one of them had finally broken down, and I was stunned that it was Lizzie, not Michael.

"I'm sorry, Lizzie," Michael interposed. "I didn't mean that stuff about having kids like it came out."

"Yes, you did. And you were right," she went on.

I was glad to hear they were finally engaging in a dialogue.

"Then will you please forgive me, Lizzie?" asked Michael.

"Sure."

He got up out of the chair, knelt beside her and whispered something I couldn't discern. I gathered it had the desired effect, because when she looked up at me, she was choking back tears. Michael went back to his chair and dragged it next to hers.

I saw that and the fact that they were now holding hands as a positive sign. But I still didn't understand why Lizzie was so gun-shy about having more children, given that they had decided to marry and raise this one together.

If I had only discerned the true state of affairs, I would have understood Lizzie's agitation.

"Look, why don't you two come over for Family Home Evening a week from Monday?" I suggested.

"Thanks, Bishop," Michael answered for them.

I detected the faintest hint of alarm in Lizzie's expression, but if that had been what I saw, she held it in check. I suggested Lizzie offer a prayer to close our interview and hoped fervently that they wouldn't come into my office so at odds with one another in the future. This was an uneasy start to a marriage, what with a baby on the way and their two families in opposition to one another.

———————— ‥✦✦✦‥ ————————

Lizzie

"You were wonderful in there," whispered Michael to me as we walked out of the bishop's office. I shook my head. He took my denial as a sign I was still miffed at him. "You're not still mad at me, are you?"

"No."

"You really meant it about making me happy?"

"Don't push your luck, lover boy," I said, trying to make light of it. I was feeling too much pressure and I was afraid I would blow. Then, because I sensed Michael would only be satisfied with a truthful answer, not a flippant one, I added, "Yes, I meant it, so back off."

"You are a spectacular woman, Lizzie, and you drive me totally up the wall," he said.

"That's because when you flirt with the devil, he always gets you in the end," I responded lightly.

"You just pretend to be wicked – inside you truly are good."

"That's exactly what Satan wants you to think, Michael."

"I'll prove you wrong."

"Let me know when you do."

"You're impossible, Lizzie."

"That's my charm," I teased.

Then I saw Jason coming down the hallway towards us and I froze in my footsteps, hoping Michael wouldn't see the effect Jason had on me.

"Honey, kiss me right now," I whispered, whirling to face Michael and putting my arms around his neck.

He must have realized my temperature had exceeded the limits of its internal thermostat.

"Lizzie, you're on fire," he breathed.

"Shut up and kiss me," I whispered more urgently. "Now!"

So it came to pass that as Michael and I smooched in the hallway of the chapel, Jason slipped by, dragging the fingers of one hand shamelessly across my buttocks. The audacity of the man! I nearly fainted from shock, and if Michael had seen it, he would have punched Jason's lights out. I wished he had.

First Christmas

On Christmas morning, the Kerry family held a gift exchange. Because of the size of their family and their desire to focus on the spiritual rather than the commercial aspects of Christmas, each member of the family picked a name out of a hat and was expected to buy a gift for that family member. The limit was twenty dollars. If you picked your own name, you simply tried again. The parents also gave each child a present and laid out stockings by the fire. The stockings were filled mostly with tangerines and candy.

I had the good fortune to pick Alison's name out of the hat, and I knew exactly what I was getting her. I talked to my mother-in-law about ballet lessons the same day Bishop Dalton resolved my latest fight with Michael. That meant I knew they had decided to consider letting Alison take up ballet. I'd even offered to take Alison to class in my car since Patrick didn't arrive home until after five pm and the lessons started at four-thirty. I went to the local Danskin store, found ballet shoes in Alison's size, and carefully sewed on the ribbons to tie them. I then broke the family's twenty-dollar golden rule and picked out a black leotard and tights for Alison as well. I thought I'd be able to persuade my mother-in-law to stuff them in Alison's stocking, and no one would be the wiser. Anne put the dance gear in her stocking on Christmas Eve.

We had a special breakfast of cranberry muffins, eggs, bacon, and hash browns on Christmas morning prepared by our favorite stand-in chef Patrick and his able assistant Edward. We were going to my parents for Christmas dinner later in the day. I wasn't looking forward to that meal with joyful anticipation, but I was hoping my mother would slip me some cash when my father was out of sight.

Alison's face when she opened her ballet shoes lit up like a sunny day and was the high point of my Christmas.

I was presented with two Phil Collins albums on tape, including *No Jacket Required*, and I knew that meant either Rachel or Sarah had picked out my name because they must have gone through my entire tape collection to figure out what I didn't have. One of the songs on the album was "Take Me Home," and I thought that was a suitably ironic context for me on my first Christmas away from the parental nest. I didn't want to be here and I didn't want to be married to Michael and I wished I had never fallen in love with Jason. And look where the whole mass of shenanigans had gotten me: I'd lost my lover, got my heart broken, become pregnant, messed up my best friend's life, and been banished from my childhood home.

It could be worse, I thought, Michael could be someone I didn't care about. Looking across at him as we sat amongst the discarded wrapping paper and gifts, I felt sad that I wasn't in love with him, because I thought he would have made some devout returned female missionary an upstanding husband. He wasn't handsome by the standards of the day, but he was tall and lean and had a winning smile, when he wanted to show it. He was a hundred times more committed to our faith than I was. He was also practical, conscientious and unselfish, and always stepped to the plate when it came to helping me out with homework, even if it meant getting up at the crack of dawn as he had just a few weeks ago. He had another side to him that I had only begun to appreciate on our honeymoon. For all his protestations of sexual innocence, he had some cool moves in the bedroom.

You might call it tender, but I felt like he never let down his guard. He had never said he loved me in our most intimate moments, and I wondered if he was deliberately holding out on me. I caught his eye from across the room as he looked up from helping Edward assemble yet another model train, and I was filled with a flush of warmth toward him. Maybe this was how couples felt when they'd been married for years and were no longer in love but still in like. I wished that could be enough.

Maybe this was what true love felt like, and Michael was right when he said I didn't know the difference.

Whatever it was that flashed between us, the connection was broken as irrevocably as the strand of pink pearls he'd given me before our wedding when the whole family decided to play a game of Uno with a double pack of cards. The contest lasted more than two hours. Anne even stopped cooking to join in. Edward proved to be the sneakiest player and finally beat us out to rid himself of his last card.

When the game was over, I said to Michael, "We should go now. My dad doesn't like dinner guests to be late."

We took our coats and headed out into the light of a dreary day. Rain was forecast for tomorrow, and the clouds had moved in ahead of the storm.

As he opened the door for me and we stepped into the grey winter day, Michael said, "You sure look happy today, Lizzie, sweetheart."

"That's because I am, but I'm sure Dad will put a damper on it."

"Be positive," he chided.

"You don't know my dad as well as I do."

"Happiness is a choice, Lizzie."

"So you keep telling me. When you get pregnant by mistake and marry someone you –" I stopped myself just in time. I really needed to learn not to say exactly what was on my mind.

"And marry someone who what?" he asked gently.

"Who's so wonderful and nice it makes you feel inferior all the time," I ad-libbed, "and you think you'll never live up to their expectations, it's a tough act."

I prized myself that I could still think on my feet. Michael kissed me sweetly. I had fooled him again.

"You are one fine woman, Lizzie Kerry."

"If you put people on pedestals, they're bound to fall off," I chided.

"Then don't build my pedestal too high, my love," he teased right back.

I decided Michael Kerry could match me any day when it came to sparring with words.

"Let's knock 'em dead," he went on playfully.

"What's our strategy?"

"Simple. Show them how happy we are together. They want to rain on our parade, let them. They can be as mad and upset as they want, but we don't let them get to us."

"Easier said than done," I mused.

"Quit being a naysayer."

"I wouldn't be here today if I'd been a naysayer," I added more seriously.

"Get over it, Lizzie. Accept what happened and move on. One of these days you're going to stop sitting by the road wallowing in your own personal pity-party and move on."

"I'm having a baby, that's moving on," I rejoindered.

"You'll have moved on when the happiness of others is more important than your own."

"Then I'm sorry I'm not the saint you are," I retorted. "And just in case you didn't know it, I have put the baby's happiness ahead of mine."

"You had to—or you wouldn't be keeping the baby," he added, flatly.

Why were we always ending up in a fight?

"Stop criticizing me, Michael Kerry. Just because you're so perfect." My tone was getting testier now.

"I wasn't criticizing you. I was merely trying to be helpful."

"You're not being helpful," I snapped.

"I guess it's impossible to help those who don't want to be helped. Suit yourself."

He opened the car door for me. I got in, grabbed the handle, and slammed the door as hard as I could, almost catching his fingers in the door. He walked around the front of the car and I could tell from the set of his jaw that he was fighting for composure.

When he'd slid in behind the wheel, he said, "Next time you want to avoid going to your parents for dinner because you're uncomfortable bringing me with you, make sure you get my fingers in the door when you slam it. Then we can spend the rest of Christmas Day at the Emergency Room."

I hated that he could be so cool while I barely was hanging onto my temper even on Christmas Day. "Screw you! It's not like you care about going either. Let's quit fighting with each other and save it for my dad."

"I'm sure you'll come up with a rearguard action when my guard is down," he remarked sardonically.

"Your guard is never down."

"Around you, Lizzie Kerry, that's a matter of survival."

I'd like to see someone take that smug grin off his face, I thought. I didn't know until later that the only person who possessed that power was me.

Christmas Dinner

Lizzie

My mother answered the door. She was dressed as if she were going out to the opera, in a cream, merino wool sweater with pearls and sequins at the neck and wrist, paired with a black pencil skirt that showed off her still-admirable figure. I was glad Michael had dressed up for the occasion in a shirt and tie because I looked decidedly dowdy in a bulky red sweater and leggings. Mom gave us both hugs and asked me how Christmas had gone at the Kerry's. Her effusive display of affection gave me the false impression that we would receive a warm reception from my father.

"If it's not Lizzie and her new hubby," came my father's voice from the hall behind my mother. "How was your little jaunt up the coast?"

"It was fine, Dad, very fine," I replied, my courage melting.

"It was about as romantic as you could imagine," chimed in Michael. "You should take Sally up there for a weekend. I'd be happy to give you the number."

My mother gave Michael the most dazzling smile. She almost looked happy. I couldn't believe Michael had the grit to suggest something so outrageous. My father was the most unromantic individual I knew.

"Sally and I," he said, walking up behind her and protectively placing an arm around her, "don't believe in self-indulgence.

We'd rather be home in our ward serving in our callings. Of course you two hedonists don't have callings now, do you?"

I'm going to spit on his grave, I thought. He knew darned well we were repenting and couldn't hold callings or even say prayers publicly in church. And he spent every spare second of his time at home on legal work related to his profession, not his church calling.

"We choose to serve in other ways," Michael went on, undaunted. "Like helping the members of our families. Our Prophet has said we should not seek the honors of the world."

"You're young, boy. You'll learn that putting food on the table for your family demands a certain amount of sacrifice and time away from home at a real job." My father stared pointedly at my belly and his meaning was unmistakable.

"Why don't we go in to eat?" suggested my mother.

She darted upstairs to call Lindsey from her room. My father showed us where he wanted us to sit. Mom had set the table with our fanciest gold-edged dinnerware and had laid out the Waterford crystal drinking glasses and hand-embroidered napkins. The cutlery was gold-plated with intricately carved handles of buffalo horn.

"You sure set out a beautiful table for us, Sally," said Michael.

I wanted to double over every time Michael used my mother's Christian name, because I knew it grated on my father's nerves every time he heard it.

"I'd appreciate if you'd call my wife Sister Sherringdon," my father interpolated as if reading my mind.

"Really, Derek," she said, coming back out of the kitchen. "Now that Michael is our son-in-law and Lizzie is his wife, we ought to be on a first-name basis. You go ahead and call me 'Sally' anytime, Michael."

My mother had won round one, I thought, but we had a long way to go.

"I don't suppose you have a spread like this at your house too often, do you?" my father continued, as my mother brought out one bowl after another of food. There were green beans with mushrooms and almonds, garlic mashed potatoes, yams topped with caramelized walnuts, broccoli au gratin, and Brussels sprouts. There was no way we were going to make a dent in all those vegetables. The stuffed duck came last, garnished with parsley and orange slices. My mouth watered. I had missed the gourmet food that was served in the home of my birth while living at the Kerry's.

My mother started sending the dishes around and my father began carving the duck. Lindsey threw me an accusatory glare although I couldn't figure out what I'd done wrong, other than leaving her with all the household chores.

"What are your plans after high school, Michael?" my father asked. He may have sounded affable but I knew him well enough to know he was mounting another attack.

"I'm going to work in my father's shop," Michael replied.

"Aaah. The family garage, right? Not going to college?"

My father knew very well Michael couldn't go to college, not with a baby coming.

"I decided it would be in Lizzie's best interests to put some money on the table."

"It won't be much, will it?"

"We'll manage," Michael said evenly.

"But not, perhaps, in the style to which Lizzie is accustomed," added my father. I didn't like him talking about me as if I wasn't present.

"Wealth is overrated," I interjected.

"I'm sure you'll be saying that when you're walking around a store wishing for something you can't afford," came back my father.

"There are other treasures in life besides money," I countered.

Then I reached over and fondled Michael's neck because I knew any display of affection would annoy my undemonstrative father. Michael's skin was hot to the touch and sent sparks down my arm. I didn't know why he kept evoking these physical responses in me. Michael threw me a sly smile and I returned it. In this moment we were united like warriors riding recklessly into the fray.

My mother offered a prayer over the food and there was a hush as we tucked into our plates. I ate heartily, knowing it would be a long time before I'd eat another gourmet meal like this one. At the Kerry house, dinner was a noisy affair, but here the vastness of the ceilings and the great white expanses of wall dwarfed us into silence. Michael complimented my mother on the exemplary nature of the cuisine. Lindsey made mild complaint about the hours she'd spent helping Mom in the kitchen, and I suddenly wished I was back at the Kerry's.

The women in the Sherringdon home worked to keep my father in the style to which he was accustomed. He wouldn't dream of lifting a finger to dust, vacuum, wash a dish, or chop vegetables. At the Kerry's, the family worked together to produce meals and accomplish the chores. No job was too humble for any member of the household. Patrick was just as comfortable doing the dishes as he was fixing cars. Moving out had given me a new perspective. I realized there were drawbacks to living with the Kerry family, but they were outweighed by the compassion and caring shared within the walls of that home.

I'd never known that kind of love in the house where I grew up.

I wouldn't have recognized it if it had hit me in the face unless I'd married Michael.

As I sat there, play acting for my parents and putting a brave face on my uncertain future, I wondered if Michael could be right, and I didn't know anything about love at all.

Dinner With Bishop Dalton

Lizzie

The next Monday, the 30th of December, we were on our way to another dinner, and I was twice as nervous about going to Jason Dalton's house as I had been about visiting my parents. I didn't dare decline the invitation because that would raise Michael's suspicions, and the last thing I wanted to do was provoke a confrontation about dinner with our bishop.

We arrived punctually and rang the bell. Of course Jason had to answer the door. I was sure his appearance to greet us was intentional.

"Hey, bro," he said, slapping a high five on Michael. "How's the new wife?"

"She's hot as ever, man," Michael replied in the same macho vein.

"Hey, Liz, how's married life?" His eyes were undressing me, but from where he was standing, I was sure that I was the only one to notice.

"Just peachy," I replied with a slight toss of my head.

My insides were like jello. The Jason of my dreams was swimming through my head while the live version was close enough for me to reach out and touch.

I dressed to kill: a short black skirt that hung tight on my hips, a black knit, form-fitting sweater, fishnet black stockings, and black shoes with sparkles on the buckles. I'd piled part of my hair up on top of my head, mussed and wild, Madonna-style, and snapped a black velvet ribbon choker with pearls and lace at its center around my neck. Finally, I'd painted my nails midnight blue, smudged on matching eye shadow that accentuated the blue circles beneath my eyes, and loaded up my lips with a dark shade of magenta.

Michael hadn't batted an eyelid. I claimed to be dressing up for him, although I'd made no such efforts for my parents' Christmas dinner. Michael had remarked that if I was going to dress up this hot whenever we went out for dinner, he was going to start sending a Lizzie-and-Michael dinner calendar around Relief Society like our missionaries did so that we could receive more invitations to eat out. I returned his taunt with a brittle, dazzling smile because inside I was feeling as churned up as the ocean up by Stillwater Cove.

My mother would have said I looked tarty, and she would have been spot on, but I no longer cared what she thought. My father would have forbade me to leave the house. But I didn't live with them anymore. I threw my overcoat over the ensemble so Michael's parents wouldn't see what I was wearing. I couldn't afford to upset this game, because I was all out of aces, and I was betting Patrick would know I was bluffing.

After Jason led us inside, he asked hospitably, "What would you like to drink?"

"Mineral water, if you've got it," replied Michael. I knew that wasn't in the refrigerator in the Kerry home.

"I'll have a gin 'n' tonic," I said saucily for Jason's benefit. Michael stepped on my toes and gave me an icy stare.

"My wife will have the same as I'm having," he added firmly.

"Gotta keep the women in line, dude," Jason said lasciviously and disappeared into the kitchen.

"Hey, kids," called Bishop Dalton, coming into the foyer. "Come on in and sit down. Dinner's ready."

"What the hell d'you think you're doing?" said Michael under his breath as we followed the bishop into the living area, gripping me by the wrist. The dining table was set to rival my mother's but toned down to convey elegance rather than ostentation.

"Just kidding around, Michael," I whispered back.

"Don't, Lizzie. I swear – not at our bishop's house, tonight or any other night."

"You're hurting my arm," I whimpered. He was hurting a bit, but not enough to justify the fake whimper.

"A lot more than your arm is gonna hurt if you don't stop it!"

I wondered what he meant, but something about the way he was twisting my wrist kept me from asking.

"Have a seat over here," said Sister Dalton, indicating two vacant chairs on one side of the table. The seat covers were slate-blue to match the couch where I'd sat watching *Red Dawn* with Jason only a few months ago.

The Daltons had three children besides Jason who emerged like mice after dark from various corners of the house as soon as dinner was ready to be served. Jason came back with our drinks and set them to the right of our place settings. Bishop Dalton and his wife sat at opposite ends of the table and the younger kids ranged down the opposite side.

To my consternation, I realized I was going to be stuck between Michael and Jason. I wanted to disappear into the floor. I looked around desperately, but there was no way out. It didn't matter what Michael said in the future, I was never accepting a dinner invitation here again, I thought.

Jason took his place at my right and the hairs stood up on my arm. God forbid Michael should notice. Sister Dalton offered grace and we began dinner. She'd made a lamb roast with all the trimmings including roast potatoes, Brussels sprouts, gravy, dinner rolls, and salad.

"So how was your honeymoon, Lizzie?" asked Sister Dalton.

"Very beautiful, and unbelievably romantic," I responded. I winked at Michael, hoping he would understand my lie was for his sake, and not to make Jason jealous.

Under the table Jason shimmied his leg up to mine and I wondered if the fishnet hose were going to burn permanent crisscrosses in my legs. If Michael saw this, I thought, the dining table was going to end up in the kitchen. I sipped my mineral water nervously.

"What about you, Michael?" Jason asked of Michael conspiratorially, leaning forward to address Michael across me. He was so close I could feel the warmth of his breath. "How was it for you, man?"

I couldn't look at either one of them. I leaned back in my chair and set my fork down because my hand was shaking so badly.

"Everything you ever hoped for in your wildest dreams," Michael said, so low that I knew only Jason and I could hear it.

Michael didn't know there was no need for Jason to dream wild dreams about me, but I was sure Jason appreciated the irony.

My skin was smoking, and I was sure my hair was going to burst into flame any minute. Sweat was rolling down my back. I tried to eat but my stomach wasn't agreeable. Maybe the kid had figured out his real dad was on the scene and wanted to get his biological father's attention.

I gulped more mineral water, catching only snippets of conversation. I was feeling light-headed and realizing I should never have come.

"What will you do after high school?" Sister Dalton was asking Michael. She didn't know I was pregnant, of course. Bishops didn't share matters of a confidential nature with their wives – or they certainly were not supposed to.

"I'm going to work in my dad's shop, actually," Michael responded cordially. "Got a three-week training course in Michigan in February."

I whipped my head around. That was news to me. I couldn't believe Michael had not said one single word about this to me.

I was fuming but I could do nothing but sit there, with Jason's leg pressed up against me and Michael's superior smile pinging off my eyeballs. I reached for my water. I was so hot I was ready to dump it over my head. Or Michael's. Or Jason's. I wasn't sure which at this moment.

"You planning to have kids, dude?" asked Jason.

I choked down a piece of ice.

"We want to, yes. Don't we, Lizzie?" Michael put his arm around me and smiled around the table. I couldn't believe Michael's composure or Jason's audacity. "Lots, as a matter of fact."

I was so angry I would have screamed at him at the top of my lungs if we'd been alone. I realized that the term 'churlish bastard' fit both of them.

As it was, my hands were shaking so badly I laid them in my lap. I willed myself to take in deep gulps of air, otherwise I was going to faint. Fainting sounded preferable, but I didn't want to cause a scene. I was saving that for the minute I got Michael alone.

I don't know how I survived the meal. I must have made polite conversation, but I never addressed Jason directly. I drank so much water Jason refilled my glass twice. My sweater wasn't clinging to me because it was tight—it was noticeably drenched with sweat.

Michael leaned into my ear and whispered, "Lizzie, is something wrong?" He touched the hand that lay in my lap while I fidgeted with my water glass. "You're hot."

"I'm not doin' so good," I whispered.

"You wanna go home?"

I shook my head. I'd dressed to get Jason's attention. Now I'd got it, and I was paying the price.

Family Home Evening
with Bishop Dalton

Lizzie

Bishop Dalton's voice interrupted my train of thought. "We're going to have the Family Home Evening lesson in the living room. Let's all move in there and get comfortable."

I needed to get out of the claustrophobic position between Michael and Jason, so I welcomed the change of scene.

"I'd like to use the bathroom, if you'll excuse me," I said.

I bumped Jason as I got to my feet and felt like I'd been hit with a stun gun.

"Sorry," I muttered, and fled.

I crossed the foyer and closed the bathroom door. Luckily for me I made it to the bowl before my dinner came up. I was glad I had hardly touched my food. I closed the lid of the toilet bowl, laid my forehead against its cool surface, and let the tears leak out of my eyes. In that moment, I hated both of them: talking about me like I was some kind of trophy.

And Michael could have told me he was going away for three weeks in February.

But I had to pull myself together. had to go back in there and face them. "Be strong and of a good courage," whispered Joshua. Feeling dizzy and disoriented, I staggered to my feet, washed my face with cold water, and drank some out of my hand. I was really fed up being nauseous from the pregnancy. I hoped it was going to stop soon. I didn't think I could endure another six months of this crap. I took some long deep breaths and wiped the exposed portions of my arms and neck with a corner of the hand towel soaked in cold water. A brief examination of my face in the mirror revealed a more tragic appearance now than when I'd done my makeup earlier. There was a strange cast to my skin and a derelict look about my expression. I turned, set my jaw, and unlocked the door. Back to face my tormentors – again.

"Lizzie," Bishop greeted me. "We're all ready for our lesson. Would you like to offer the prayer?"

One did not refuse a bishop, so I simply nodded and took my place next to Michael on the loveseat where Jason and I had watched *Red Dawn*. I said a quick prayer, my voice sounding small and husky. Afterwards, Michael put his arm around me in a proprietary manner. His message to the assembled company: she's mine and everyone else keep their hands off her. I wondered if it was possible for him to be subconsciously aware of my interaction with Jason. But I did note that his actions were received, loud and clear, by both Jason and the bishop.

When I allowed my gaze to take in the rest of the room, I discovered Jason lounging in an armchair opposite me, allowing his eyes to roam freely over my body. Once again, I hoped his actions passed unnoticed, but realized the bishop was taking it all in.

"I've picked the topic of chastity for tonight," began Bishop Dalton.

Jason rolled his eyes at me and I let my gaze slide away to the floor. Either Bishop Dalton had a cruel sense of humor or he had no clue about the traces of passion permeating the room.

"Anyone want to define it for me?" he asked, looking around the room.

"That would be complete abstinence before marriage and total fidelity afterward," piped up Michael. He ought to know, I thought.

There were other ways to be unfaithful, I thought, and I was entirely too familiar with them. And I was going to be eternally damned for letting Jason get mixed up in my relationship with Michael.

"It also means avoiding pornography and sexually explicit material," added Becky Dalton. "Because those things can incite men and women to make wrong choices. In his Sermon on the Mount, Jesus said that to lust in your heart was a sin."

This was a sin with which I was all too familiar, I thought.

"Becky is going to read you a scripture about Alma's advice to his son. In case you don't recall, Corianton had forsaken preaching the gospel to the Zoramites to pursue the harlot, Isabel. For you littler ones"—addressing the younger children—"that's a bad woman. Alma told his son Corianton that to commit sexual sin was second only to the sin of murder."

Sister Dalton promptly read from Alma 39:5. "'Know ye not, my son, that these things are an abomination in the sight of the Lord; yea, most abominable above all sins save it be the shedding of innocent blood or denying the Holy Ghost?'"

"Lizzie, what is the advice for married couples?" asked Bishop Dalton. I jumped at the sound of my name.

"If you hand me the scriptures, I think I can find it." I could look up "cleave" in the Topical Guide section at the back of the standard work and I was sure I'd find the reference I was thinking of. Sister Dalton passed me the scriptures from which she'd just read. It didn't take me long to find what I was looking for.

"Here it is in Doctrine & Covenants 42:22," I said, "'Thou shalt love thy wife with all thy heart, and shalt cleave unto her and none else.' And that goes for wives with respect to husbands also."

"And why do you think this commandment is so important?" asked Bishop Dalton.

"Our bodies are sacred," said the Dalton's ten-year-old daughter.

"Very good. Anything else?"

"It's the power to create life," spoke up Michael from beside me.

I was all too familiar with that aspect, also.

"There can be bad consequences if you don't keep the law," added Jason's fourteen-year-old sister. "Like disease and pregnancy." She'd obviously learned something from her high-school sex education classes.

"Remember King David?" asked Bishop Dalton. "He was a great king and a great leader. But what happened?"

"He wanted someone else's wife for himself," said the ten-year-old. "And he had her guy killed."

The irony of Jason lounging across the room and eating me up with his eyes was not lost on me. Neither was my own aching for him.

Michael was stroking my neck softly. I told myself to get a grip. I tried to concentrate on the pleasant feeling of Michael's fingers against my skin, but it was Jason legs under the table and his scathing eyes that kept coming to the forefront of my mind.

"Good – Bathsheba's husband, Uriah, was sent to the front of the battle so that when he died, David was able to marry her. But the Lord was displeased about what David had done and He punished David for the rest of David's life. That might be something to keep in mind when we are tempted to commit sin. We can repent, as David did, but we will have to face the consequences of our actions."

There was no doubt in my mind that the Lord was going to punish me for the rest of my life for having known Jason outside the confines of marriage and for wanting him when I was within them. I wiped my eyes and Michael realized the lesson had finally got to me, so he pulled me against his shoulder.

"Don't beat yourself up anymore, Lizzie," he whispered.

I did not want Michael in my head at this moment than I wanted Jason in it. And if Michael knew what I knew, he would not be sitting so peacefully next to me; he'd have Jason pinned down on the carpet and the cougar would be ripping his guts out.

"I think that does it for tonight, unless anyone has any questions?" Bishop Dalton said.

I wondered if he'd noticed that Jason had been a spectator and not a participant. I guess I was the only person present with whom Jason had made a connection.

Becky Dalton offered us dessert and Michael demurred. "Lizzie's not feeling her best and I think we should go home. We've got an early start as we're back to school tomorrow."

Becky Dalton nodded with mutual understanding and retrieved our coats from the coat rack in the foyer. Michael helped me on with mine.

Jason had disappeared, and it was the second-to-last time I would see him socially outside of church before the baby arrived. He didn't even bother to say good-bye. It was altogether dreadfully depressing.

Every cell in my body yearned to be home in the big bed in Michael's bedroom, even if it wasn't with the person I dreamed about.

It was odd that I now thought of the Kerry's place as home. It was one of many changes I was to experience in the coming year.

The Trip Home

Lizzie

When we finally had a chance to be alone in the car, I'd intended to confront Michael about not telling me he was going away in February and telling the bishop's family we wanted "lots of kids," but the fight in me had evaporated by the time we got out to my Nissan. It was, after all, still "my" Nissan since the title had not been changed.

"Would've been nice if you'd told me first that you're planning to be gone in February," I said after Michael had fired up the engine. I tried to keep my tone neutral.

"Sorry, Lizzie, it slipped my mind. I was meaning to tell you. You're not mad about it, are you, sweetheart?" he answered. He let the engine idle and gave me a long, searching look.

"Actually, I'm mad as hell at you about it. You are damned lucky I didn't stand up and walk out at that moment," I said. I wasn't intending to be mad or antagonistic, but that's how I felt and that's how it came out.

"I just forgot," he said.

"No, you didn't, Michael Kerry. There is simply no chance that you 'just forgot.' Forgetting something that important is not in your nature. You didn't tell me. You knew, and you didn't tell me. It is that simple." I was surprised that my tone of voice was as calm and matter of fact as it was. It didn't sound like me talking. I am way too hot-headed. I can only attribute it to being exhausted as a pregnant mother who just had an encounter with the devil incarnate.

He sat there in silence. I had him, and we both knew it.

"And," I continued, "not only did I never say I wanted lots of children, I specifically said I did not want any more at all! So that was a lie."

"It was a kind of a figure of speech," he said, in the same calm tone of voice I was using. "You did say you'd do anything to make me happy."

"Within reason," I cautioned.

"I'm a reasonable kinda guy, Lizzie, in case it has escaped you."

"Usually. Well, sometimes," I pouted.

"Are you upset?"

I shrugged a bit, and said, "Honestly, yes. Your performance tonight sucked. You will have to make up for your actions."

"Did that lesson get to you?" he offered, seemingly trying to change the subject.

"Yeah," I said, letting the question float by.

"Perhaps that's what Bishop Dalton intended," Michael suggested.

It would have been more appropriate if the lesson had found application for his son, I thought. I was miserable and suffering the consequences of my misdoings. Jason was getting off scot-free, thanks to my letting him off the hook.

"Perhaps Bishop's lesson should have been on not assaulting your spouse, then it could've made you think about *your* actions," I countered.

"What is that supposed to mean?" His response was instantly tense. I had caught him with his lies; now that I had the upper hand to twist the conversation around to my way of thinking, there was no possibility he would be prepared for what was coming next.

"When you grabbed my arm, squeezing my wrist like you did, and threatened me, that was an assault. You have done that to me at least three times. I am not going to put up with such behavior. You may never grab me in anger or threaten me again. Understood?" I was matter of fact and firm, but not yelling at him. He was stunned into silence.

"I have heard my father talking about clients and assault for years. When you grabbed my wrist earlier, and twisted my arm around, then stuffed your face into mine and threatened me, you crossed the line. Physical abuse and threatening physical abuse can get you jail time. I'm not going to put up with it again, so you need to come to terms with your anger—and quickly."

We drove the rest of the way in a profound silence and trudged up to bed quietly. The rest of the family had already gone to sleep. Our evening prayer was brief. Michael was nonplussed but seemed to fall asleep the instant his head hit the pillow.

As for me, sleep was longer in coming, despite my weariness with the world. I still couldn't get the feeling of Jason's leg pressed against mine out of my mind. It was clear that I needed to stay away from him. Jason in the flesh – the real Jason -- was harder to resist than the Jason in my mind. The real Jason made the bad memories seem real, and my memories of us were bad enough. I didn't know what it was going to take to get over Jason, but I wished the Lord would hurry up and fix it.

Bishop Dalton Ponders

Bishop Dalton

After dinner, our Family Home Evening, seeing Michael and Lizzie off, helping clean things up, loading up the dishwasher, and starting yet another dishwasher cycle, I finally had some time to ponder the events of the evening.

I have seen Michael and Lizzie in some very uncomfortable situations and conversations. I have noted their actions and reactions; I have watched how they sit together and how they struggle to keep their composure. In short, I understand them at a level nobody else in my family would. As soon as I saw how they acted this evening, I knew something was up.

I noticed how my son was flirting with Lizzie, and not even being subtle about it. I noticed that when he did, she would blush and get flustered.

I had already suspected the baby wasn't Michael's, but Michael and Lizzie were so sincere when they spoke to me that I actually believed it. Now that I see how Jason and Lizzie acted at dinner, I believe I know more of the story.

After pondering on the whole situation, a painful potential came to mind and caused me to rethink all of it: could it be possible that my son Jason, who was constantly talking about Lizzie Sherringdon several months ago, was the father of the child Lizzie was now carrying?

That would explain why Jason couldn't talk about anything but Lizzie, and then refused to even acknowledge her existence.

That would explain why Michael, the least likely suspect on earth, whose "secret love" for Lizzie was the worst-kept secret imaginable, made him the perfect fall guy for people to anticipate as the father of Lizzie's child.

That would explain why Lizzie, whose feelings for Michael were, at best, friendly and familial, more like a kid brother than any kind of boyfriend, didn't jibe with them being sexually active.

Combining these ideas, it is now easy to see how Jason could have gotten Lizzie pregnant and abandoned her, and in sheer desperation, she went to Michael, whose love for her was as unconditional as it was boundless, and Lizzie talked him into marrying her.

I hope I'm wrong, but I can't help but think that I am depressingly right.

I originally planned the lesson on chastity for Michael and Lizzie, with my kids as ancillary targets. But now I realize the inspiration for that lesson was because Jason needed it.

With what I now suspect, I'll have to go to our new Stake President to talk to him about what I should do. He's been involved in Church leadership positions for nearly twenty years, so he will know how to counsel me about what to do.

Winter

Lizzie

The grey days of winter that had begun before Christmas settled in on the Sacramento Valley. Fog rolled in and stayed, turning the air damp and weighing on my spirits.

I'd finally gone for my first prenatal doctor appointment without Michael in attendance, and the baby and I had been pronounced healthy. They'd asked me if I wanted to listen to the heartbeat and I'd said no, maybe some other time. I wasn't ready to acknowledge the presence of the life inside me yet, nor did I want to know whether I was having a girl or boy in advance. The middle-aged, grey-haired doctor had just shaken his head, and told me he couldn't discern gender at this gestational stage, but if I wanted to know ahead of time like most of his patients, he would be happy to inform me later on.

In spite of my attempts to be inconspicuous, I was becoming an important player in the Kerry household. I now helped Rachel and Sarah fix their hair on Sunday mornings. My new sisters were turning heads as they graced the hallways of the chapel. I had miraculously convinced Michael's parents to allow Alison to take ballet lessons and consequently had become her protégée, now that I was taking her to class every Wednesday. And Patrick had of course asked me to teach Family Home Evening on two occasions, because he liked the content of my lessons.

Michael was spending a couple of hours each day after school at his father's shop, mostly learning the computer system, swabbing floors, and shuffling paperwork. He'd later help with the repair work, but Patrick knew Michael's real abilities lay in organizing and managing, so he was assigning Michael the tasks best suited to him. Michael had a locked box in one of the drawers on his side of the bed where he was stashing the money that he'd earned for a deposit on an apartment for us. He said he wanted to be able to count it from time to time, much like a mission fund. I thought he just liked the idea of having his treasure chest under his feet rather than in the impersonal vault of a bank. He hadn't given me the key, and I was afraid to ask for it. I needed $40 to get my hair styled at my usual salon but I hadn't been able to conjure up the nerve to request the money. It was on my list of things to bring up the coming weekend.

Michael had a glow about him, and I supposed that had to do with spending his nights in my arms and physically expressing his affection for me, which he did frequently. I tried to find happiness in being the object of his desire, but, in all honesty, I was depressed. I didn't want Michael to see it because the last thing I wanted him to know was that I was still pining for another I would never hold. Sometimes I'd get up in the night, steal down the stairs, plug my boombox in next to the TV, and listen via the headphones to Madonna or Elton John or Eurythmics playing songs like "Love Don't Live Here Anymore," "I Guess That's Why They Call It the Blues," and "Here Comes the Rain Again" over and over, because wallowing in misery was better than lying next to Michael trying to hide it.

On a Saturday morning sometime after midnight as I lay hunched on the couch in a pool of tears, I realized someone had come down the stairs and I was not alone.

"Lizzie, what's up?" came Rachel's voice.

I wheeled in surprise and wiped my eyes.

"You're crying, sis," she said softly.

The tears fell faster.

"You and Michael have a fight?"

I shook my head.

"What's wrong?"

"It's too hard to explain," I blubbered.

She sat down on the couch and put her arm around me.

"It's not us, is it?"

"What d' you mean?"

"Us, the family, you know."

"No, Rachel. You've all been spectacular."

"So it's Michael, then?"

"It's not him either." A renewed flood of weeping ensued.

"He loves you a whole lot, Lizzie."

"Sure," I replied, none too confidently.

"Just because he's working and studying and can't be with you all the time doesn't mean he's not thinking about you."

"I'm sorry I can't explain, Rachel. It's complicated."

"If you wanna talk or whatever, let me know. Or I can just be a shoulder to cry on."

I took her up on her final offer and having her there, in some bizarre way, did seem to help. When I was calmer, she suggested I go back to bed and we traipsed upstairs, hugging outside Michael's door before making our separate ways to bed.

The next morning before we went downstairs for breakfast, but after I'd had crackers and milk, and indulged Michael's romantic inclinations, I told him I was flat broke and needed forty bucks from the funds in the kitty for my hair cut. After all, I had entrusted him with the five one-hundred-dollar bills my mother and father had given us for a wedding present, and I knew they were in the box.

"Forty dollars, Lizzie?" he exclaimed. "Where are you going – Vidal Sassoon?"

"It's my regular hair stylist."

"My mother and my sisters never spend that much on their hair. Anyway, your hair looks gorgeous."

"Look, there's plenty of money in that box," I protested.

"I know – and we're going to need all of it when we move out. You don't have a clue what it costs to run a household, do you, Lizzie?"

I didn't, but I wasn't about to admit it. I was sure Michael was prepared to give me an education.

"Tell you what, Michael – I'll find some jobs babysitting in the ward and I'll pay for it."

"No."

"If you're not going to give me the –"

"You're not doing any babysitting. You'll have plenty of that in six months' time. Saturday night is our date night and you're dead beat on Friday. This is non-negotiable."

"Then just give me the money. And it's not fair that you keep the key to the box all to yourself. It's *our* money."

"Find another hair stylist."

"No! I like the one I have."

My father's prophetic words about Michael not being able to keep me in the style to which I was accustomed echoed in my head.

"I'm going down to breakfast," I said, flinging back the sheets and throwing on my robe. I wasn't going to have another fight with Michael. We'd been on good terms for at least a month and I didn't want to start anything.

"You're not wearing anything under that robe," he observed, rolling his eyes.

"I don't care!" I flounced out of the room, taking care not to slam the door. Even if I was furious, I wasn't going to give Michael the satisfaction of knowing it.

Patrick was flipping pancakes in two large saucepans on the stove when I arrived downstairs. I gave him my best fake smile.

"Top of the mornin' to you, Lizzie. How are you today?"

"Didn't sleep well, but otherwise fine," I responded, wrapping my bathrobe more tightly around me.

Anne appeared from the laundry nook. She'd already started another load of clothes from the huge volume the household generated. I hated to think how much a baby was going to add to the laundry.

"Hi, Anne," I said.

"Where's Michael, Lizzie?" she asked.

"On his way. He'll be down any minute."

Michael and I usually came downstairs together, fully dressed. They exchanged a look, but I couldn't decipher it. I was hoping they didn't notice my eyes were red from crying and that I wasn't in the happiest of moods. I wasn't getting my hair cut today, I thought, but I was going to my hair stylist as soon as I could earn some extra money babysitting. It would only take a few calls to Relief Society to find someone in need of a babysitter for tonight.

Screw the Saturday night date – Michael would have to sit this one out on his own.

Rachel

On a Saturday morning in mid-January, my new sister-in-law, Lizzie, announced she was going to the mall with her girlfriend, Shannon, in the afternoon. Shannon had been one of Lizzie's bridesmaids like me. I was surprised that my brother decided to get married so young, but I knew he was nuts about Lizzie. Maybe he just couldn't wait. First thing when he came home, he'd find her, put his arms around her, and give her a long smooch.

Kinda like my parents, come to think of it. My dad has always been real sweet to my mom. I hoped I'd have a husband like my dad someday.

Michael made some snide remark about Lizzie not having any money to spend at the mall, so why was she going, but it didn't make an impression on me that they might be having a spat. I figured Lizzie was window shopping because that's what I like to do. I didn't have money to spend there either, but sometimes it was fun to look.

While we were hanging out watching a video about three pm, as the rain came down outside, Lizzie called from Shannon's house. I took the call. Lizzie said she wouldn't be home for dinner because she had a job babysitting for Sister Clay's three brats. They really were, I'd taken care of them myself. She had me write down the number and I hung up the phone. My mom was taking a break on the couch with the church magazine the *Ensign*. I forgot that Michael was in the room too, helping Edward with another of his silly models. That kid would never stop tinkering.

"Mom, Lizzie has a babysitting job after she gets done at the mall."

Michael interrupted. "Lizzie is doing what?"

"Babysitting," I said. I had no idea what he was so stoked up about.

"I told her not to do that," he said turning red. He looked like he was about to blow up.

"What's the big deal?" I asked, curious.

"It's our date night," he replied.

"I'm sure she had a good reason," interjected my mom. "Sister Clay probably needed someone on short notice."

Sister Clay always needed someone on short notice, I thought, it was tough trying to find any young woman in the entire stake willing to watch her kids.

"You can call her if you want, Michael," I offered, waving the slip on which I'd written down the number.

"No thanks, sis." If my brother *was* real mad, he wasn't letting on. He continued smoothly, "Say, Mom, mind if I go over to Jeremy's tonight, since Lizzie won't be here?"

My heart leaped. This was my chance. "Can I go too?"

Michael frowned at me, but no one had said no yet.

"Why do you want to go, Rachel?" asked my mom.

"She's been angling to get a date with Jeremy since the wedding, if you must know, Mom," replied Michael.

I wished he wouldn't butt in where he wasn't wanted, but I needed him if I wanted to see Jeremy.

"I see," said Mom thoughtfully. "OK, Rachel – since Michael will be present, you can go."

I rushed up to my mom and gave her a big hug. "Thanks, Mom."

"You really shouldn't let her," Michael went on.

"I don't see the harm in it. It's not like she's going to marry him," replied my mom coolly.

Michael must have objected because he was mad at Lizzie, not because he felt strongly one way or the other about Jeremy and me. Michael phoned Jeremy and told him we'd be over around seven, and I was skipping around with anticipation. Jeremy and I had been hanging out together at lunchtime and breaks at school, but I hadn't gotten up the nerve to ask my parents if we could go on a real date. Firstly, I wasn't eighteen yet and secondly, Jeremy wasn't a member of our church. That was two strikes against any one-on-one date happening.

Jeremy and Michael usually played chess, but since I was tagging along, Jeremy told Michael he'd rent *The Natural* for us to watch and said to tell me hello. I was mentally jumping up and down, but I didn't want the rest of the family to know it. I didn't care for baseball but I couldn't wait to spend time with Jeremy, even under my brother's disapproving eye.

When we arrived at Jeremy's in Dad's Suburban, which Michael had to borrow because Lizzie was driving her car, Jeremy let us in and introduced me to his parents. They were going out and he was watching his eleven-year-old sister. He had been Michael's best friend for ages so they had no qualms about leaving us home together.

Jeremy was bundled up in a dark grey sweatshirt and black corduroy pants. He had naturally dark curly hair and soft brown eyes. Maybe his nose was a little too pug-like, but he had a sweet mouth. Just looking at him gave me bumps in the stomach. He offered us sodas and asked if we wanted popcorn now or later. We agreed later would be better, since we'd just finished dinner. Then I sat on the couch next to Michael. Jeremy's sister wrapped herself under a blanket in the armchair. Jeremy started the movie and positioned himself on my vacant side. He slipped his arm around me while I sidled up next to him. It was the first time I could remember us touching other than dancing at the wedding, and it made me feel warm and tingly all over. I snuggled into Jeremy and wished desperately Michael wouldn't look so disapproving because I was dying to play with Jeremy's curls. I thought I better not push my luck with my brother, because he was still out of sort about Lizzie babysitting.

When the movie was over and Michael and I were heading for the door, Jeremy got up and took Michael aside to say something out of my hearing. Michael grudgingly agreed to whatever it was Jeremy had asked. I was soon to find out.

"Wait up, Rachel," Jeremy said under his breath. He looked out of breath and was fidgeting with the belt loops of his corduroys. Then he went ahead of us towards the door and opened it for us. The rain had temporarily abated. Michael strode out to the Suburban and climbed up into the driver's seat while Jeremy drew me aside under the porch. He kept looking at the Suburban out of the corner of his eye.

"It was nice, having you come over," he said. His brown eyes were as soft as a teddy bear. They gave me a warm feeling inside. I smiled at him, feeling giddy.

"Can I kiss you?" Jeremy asked.

"I never kissed anyone," I confessed.

"Me neither."

We both flashed a look at the truck, which was now idling in the driveway.

"OK," I said.

He didn't put his arms around me, just leaned into my face. It felt so weird, feeling someone's lips pressed up to mine and the wet taste of his tongue. It must have been just moments, but the sensation of his lips on mine lasted a long while afterwards.

"Did you like it?" he whispered with his hands behind his back. He had gone all red in the face.

"Yes!" I gave him a huge smile and skipped out to the truck. I was on top of the world.

"Thanks, bro," I told Michael as I climbed in.

"I knew I should not have brought you," he responded.

"He's your best friend, you should be happy for him," I exclaimed.

"I dread to think what monster I've unleashed now."

I didn't think Michael was as upset as he pretended to be – at least, not with me.

"We're not getting home too late, are we?" I asked. It was ten-thirty, and I was usually supposed to be back before ten. I was betting I wouldn't sleep tonight for thinking about Jeremy.

"Mom and Dad will be fine with it, now that I'm a responsible, married man," he said wryly. He steered the truck out of the driveway and we headed towards home.

"How do you like being married, Michael?" I asked.

"I like it fine."

"So why is Lizzie sad?"

"She's not sad," he said, looking at me quickly, as if he didn't believe his own denial.

"She was down in the living room last night sobbing her heart out on the sofa – that's sad in my book."

"She was what?"

Shit, I'd just blown it. Michael didn't know. I didn't think I'd be able to worm my way out of this one, so I decided to elaborate.

"I came downstairs because I was awake and the light was on at, I guess, one o'clock in the morning, and she was on the couch, just crying. Like, really crying, you know. And she wouldn't tell me why, either. I tried to cheer her up."

Michael wiped his eyes. I wondered if he was choked up. I thought I'd try changing the subject. "Why did you get married so young, anyway? Seems kinda crazy to me."

"That's none of your business," he said sternly.

I didn't realize I'd touched a nerve. "It's not like she's pregnant or any – "

I stopped. Oh my God, maybe she was.

Michael's jaw tightened.

There was only one reason people got married so young, I thought. I wondered why it hadn't dawned on me before. I guess I wouldn't have thought Michael capable of it, that was why.

"She is pregnant, isn't she?" I paused, waiting for him to deny it, which he didn't. "Oh, Michael, that means she and you, like, did it before the wedding day."

"You get one hundred percent for deductive logic, sis," he replied gravely. "And don't be telling anyone, otherwise I will really wring your neck like I should right now."

"I promise." It was great to be keeper of a big secret, but I didn't think it would be a secret for long. "I'm real sorry for Lizzie. I guess that would be a good reason to be sitting on the couch in the middle of the night bawling my eyes out. No wonder she wouldn't say. Do Mom and Dad know?"

"Yes."

I couldn't believe there were so many secrets being concealed in our house. I was at a loss for words after this interaction, so I laid my head back against the seat and dreamed of Jeremy until we arrived home. Lizzie hadn't gotten back yet and Michael said he'd wait up for her. He didn't sound the least bit happy, either because I'd found out their big secret or because Lizzie still wasn't home. I wouldn't want to be in Lizzie's shoes, I thought, expecting a baby in her senior year of high school.

⁺⁺◆◆⁺⁺

Lizzie

When I walked in the door on the Saturday night that I'd been out babysitting at Sister Clay's, I didn't expect Michael to be sitting on the couch in the dark in the living room waiting for me. Pretty stupid of me, really, when he'd already expressed his opinion on me earning my own money. I knew I was in trouble the moment I caught sight of him. I shut the door gently and dropped my keys in my purse.

"Well, look what the cat drug in," he began.

I shivered. My hair was wet from the latest batch of rain. I took off my coat and threw it on the coat rack near the door.

"Hi, love," I began lightly.

"Forgot you had a date, did you?" His tone sounded ominous. I didn't like what I was hearing. "I told you, you didn't need to go out and earn money to get your hair done."

I didn't see the need to argue with him. He'd made himself absolutely clear on that point.

"And I told you I need to get my hair done," I protested, not looking at him. "Anyway, since we're gonna fight, let's do it in our bedroom so the rest of the family won't have to listen to us."

I walked over to the couch, offered him my hand, and he stood up. I kept my eyes focused on the small square of shag carpet by his feet. We went up the stairs together in silence.

When we had entered our room, he flipped on the switch by the door, closed the door carefully behind us, and stood with his back to it. I was just a few feet in front of him, facing him and concentrating on the floor.

"Look at me when I'm talking to you," he ordered.

I turned my eyes up to him defiantly, not liking what I saw. The cougar looked ready to go on a killing spree.

"I told you not to do this," he went on, without raising his voice.

"Yeah, well, I don't take orders." I wriggled my toes. "We are a couple, not a dictatorship."

He pursed his lips together, skirted around me to reach the bed, and bent down to access the drawer where we kept the money box. He took it out, placed it on the bed, and went over to his desk to get the key. I watched mutely, feeling my heart rate increase.

"Round one to you, Lizzie," he said. "Take the money – and the key, for that matter."

He tossed the key at me, and it hit me and fell to the floor. It took a moment to spot it, then bend down to pick it up.

"Rachel figured out you're pregnant, Lizzie, but she's not going to talk."

"Just like the rest of this family."

"Since we are talking right now, I have one question for you," he added.

"Happy to oblige, since you're being so generous," I replied, inwardly seething but thinking that I didn't want this disagreement to go over the top, especially as I had got what I wanted.

"Why is it that you're sneaking downstairs in the middle of the night and sobbing your heart out on the couch?"

My heart bounced off the baby on its way down to my feet. The room swayed. Damn Rachel, why did she have to tell him? But I couldn't blame her for being concerned about me.

"Rachel told you," I said, deliberately ignoring his question.

"Not intentionally. It just slipped out – she thought I knew. It would be nice if you'd talk to me, Lizzie. Why don't you tell me if something's upsetting you?"

"Because when I do, you take it personally and we always end up in a fight." I walked over to the bed and sat down, realizing there was no way I was going to stop myself from crying—yet again—and I didn't want Michael to see it. But the floodgates were going to open no matter how hard I tried to stop them and they did. I hated being pregnant and weepy. My dad was right that tears were for wimps and sissies.

Michael sat down next to me and put his arm around me.

"Is it me?" he asked softly.

"Yes. And no." The tears started in earnest.

"My family?"

I shook my head.

"Is it the baby?"

"No."

There was only one person left, and I hoped he wasn't going there. If he knew, he didn't say so. "Lizzie, I wanna make you happy. Please tell me what I can do."

I thought of a Janie Fricke song, "I'll Need Someone to Hold Me when I Cry."

"Just hold me," I whispered.

"Promise me one thing, Lizzie."

"All right," I said reluctantly. I'd already made so many promises I was afraid of breaking, what would one more matter?

"If you're feeling like this in the middle of the night, wake me up and I'll try to make it better. Fix you something hot to drink, play whatever you want."

"You're gonna lose a lot of sleep," I protested, feeling marginally more cheerful.

"I can handle that. I think we should talk to Bishop Dalton about this tomorrow."

"No."

"He might have some suggestions."

"All right," I said reluctantly, "since you're letting me go to my hair stylist."

I actually smiled at my own dig.

Suddenly, sitting next to him on the bed, listening to his soft entreaties and feeling his gentle arms around me, I ached for him to fill up the void left by my unreal Jason.

"Michael, wanna kiss and make up?" I whispered. I wiped my eyes with the back of my hand.

"We're not fighting. And what kind of 'kiss and make up,' anyway?"

"The kind where you treat me very, very nice under these sheets."

He swung me into his lap and laid my head against his shoulder. "They're very nice sheets."

"You're teasing me," I whispered.

"Lizzie," he said, tilting my head up so that I was looking directly into those fierce eyes, and I knew he wasn't teasing anymore. "If this helps you to get over him, fine. But if you're doing it out of obligation, or because of some misplaced sense of gratitude, let's not."

My reply was barely audible. "I do enjoy it."

He hadn't mentioned guilt and I was feeling as guilty as Judas right now.

"Is this gonna be one of the times when it helps?" The cougar looked like he was contemplating a retreat, but I wasn't ready to let him go.

"I don't know; probably."

"Why is it you don't know?"

"Because it changes," I said, biting my lip. I never knew if Jason was going to be there or not, or if I would be wishing for Jason or not. I only knew I wished for the unreal Jason less now than I had a month ago.

"Can you please turn out the light, Michael?" I begged. I didn't think I could endure his eyes anymore, or perhaps it was that in the dark I had more room to hide.

He slipped me off his lap, went over to the door, and flipped the light switch. Then he returned to the edge of the bed and encircled me in an embrace. I started undressing in his arms. I was too tired to go down the hall to the bathroom and brush my teeth. I was too tired for everything.

"Those Clay boys were a serious handful," I said. "I really earned my twenty-dollar fee tonight."

That haircut was feeling a lot more expensive tonight than it had this afternoon.

I continued to undress wrapped in Michael's arms, throwing my clothes in a heap by the desk. I was usually much less careless about leaving my belongings lying around, in deference to Michael's need for order, but he didn't seem to mind. The hall light spilled through the space above and below the closed door, keeping the room from being in total darkness. I watched

Michael's eyes scan me up and down, and I was gratified to see the captivated look on his face. I pulled him into the bed with me and we laid down on our sides facing each other. Michael seemed content lying next to me in my birthday suit, which he called his "favorite outfit."

It was moments like this that drove the images of Jason out of my mind. I spent a long, contemplative moment, soaking up this feeling, hoping to add it to my arsenal. I needed all of the weapons I could to fight the unreal and undead Jason who continued to haunt the corners of my innermost world.

I seemed to spend a lot of time around Michael in his favorite outfit. What at one time felt unnatural and perverse was now liberating. Especially when I focused more on the look in his eyes than on what his eyes were beholding. I'd had more than enough males tell me they thought I was beautiful to be reassured that I was, but it was more of an intellectual understanding: you were never sure they weren't just saying it to make time with you. Watching the face of a young man who had sacrificed so much for me and my baby, scanning my bulging figure, seeing the adoration and love expressed in his eyes, drove that understanding deep into my heart. I was beautiful to Michael, whatever the time of day or night, and that was good enough for me.

After several moments of laying side by side, Michael got up and undressed. I crawled under the sheets, holding them up so he could get in. He began kissing me slowly, starting softly at my mouth, traveling down my neck, running his hands gently over me, massaging and playing with his favorite parts. He toyed with my hair along the way.

"You're still wet from the rain."

"Yeah," I murmured, feeling the tension drain out of me. "I should've listened to you about the babysitting. I'm sorry."

"Shhh." He placed a finger over my lips and kept stroking my body. "You don't have to be sorry for anything tonight."

But I was sorry – sorry for allowing lust to overpower common sense, for giving up my body to flesh-and-blood Jason, for conceiving a baby out of wedlock, and for letting thoughts of fake Jason into the marital bed.

If only there could be no past and no future and no tomorrow, only now, in this moment, I thought. Let there be no you and no me but only the beating of two hearts. Let there be only the sound of the two souls who found each other in the ocean of the night. Let there be no space between you and me but the river of eternity in our eyes. Let me be one in you, and you in me, and let us find a place in the window of time where we can meet and not be afraid. Let us be one.

The Search for Happiness

Bishop Dalton

It was time to see Lizzie and Michael Kerry again. Another Sunday morning of many Sundays when I would spend less time with my wife and family than I wanted to. I kept telling myself it would all be worth it when I looked back on my life. I sighed as my counselor ushered them in and they sat down. They seemed unusually quiet, and I was unsure if this boded good or evil.

Lizzie had the same tragic cast to her eyes that I had noticed in the past few weeks, as though a great sorrow weighed on her, but she had not unburdened herself in our meetings. I remembered that sin brought upon the perpetrator its own agony and hoped that in time she would allow the Savior to heal her pain. I asked Michael to say an opening prayer, and when I resumed my place in the chair behind my desk, I began.

"How are you two doing?"

"Better," said Lizzie.

"Actually, there is a matter we wanted to ask you about," interjected Michael.

"*You* wanted to," flashed Lizzie, but softly.

I realized that they had discussed whether or not they wanted to bring up this topic with me, and that although Lizzie had not concurred with Michael, she'd given him permission to address it.

"Lizzie is not happy," said Michael. "My sister found her downstairs on the couch the other night in tears. And I gather it's been going on for a while." It was his turn to flash her a look of reproach. "I don't get why she wouldn't talk to me."

I ignored Michael's mild rebuff and directed my next question to Lizzie.

"What is the source of this unhappiness?" I asked her simply.

She sat silently regarding me, gentle but unflinching.

"Is it something between you and Michael?"

"It is and it isn't," she stated slowly. If I had only known how truly she spoke.

I found myself smiling. That's an oxymoron, Lizzie. If you want me to help you, then you'll have to be more specific."

"*He* understands," she went on, momentarily glancing over at her husband.

"Bishop," interrupted Michael, just when I thought I was getting somewhere, "I think Lizzie's just having a tough time growing up: being married, expecting a baby, everything."

I had the odd feeling he was coming to her rescue so she wouldn't have to tell me what was really on her mind.

"Lizzie, sometimes we have a difficult time accepting the Lord's will for us. You must have faith that, in time, what seems hard now will become easier. It's how you grow. I can make a suggestion, though."

"What?" she asked, looking more hopeful.

"You two both write journals, don't you?"

They nodded in unison.

"Not every day," added Lizzie, "but at least once a week. I usually work on mine on Sunday afternoons. Michael is more diligent than I am."

"Great," I continued. "Here's what I want you to do – and since I'm going to ask Lizzie, I'm going to ask you to do it too, Michael. At the end of every day – and I do mean every day – write down at least one thing that made you happy. If you can only think of one thing, that's fine. I don't care what it is: a beautiful sunset, a great hamburger, or whatever else you can come up with; I want you to write it down in your journal and share those thoughts with each other. Does that sound like something you could do?"

"Easy," replied Michael.

"Works for me," said Lizzie.

In spite of the fact that my intellect reasoned that I should adjourn our meeting, I felt as if there were unfinished business between Lizzie and Michael.

"Is there anything else you want to talk to me about?" I asked.

"Can I talk to you alone, Bishop?" Lizzie asked.

I realized from Michael's expression that he'd not been expecting this, but it didn't seem to perturb him.

"I'll go," he offered. He stood up, took her hand, leaned down and kissed her on the cheek very briefly and sweetly. I saw that he wanted to convey to her that her unexpected request had not upset him.

When he'd shut the door, I waited for her to explain.

"Bishop," she said, "I don't know how to say this, but I'm just not in love with him."

Now that would be a reason to be unhappy, and I would wager she hadn't shared this revelation with Michael. I wasn't a betting man, per se, because our church did not believe in gambling. Still, it seemed a pretty solid bet.

And although Michael hadn't expressed himself, I think he knew, in his heart, exactly what was wrong and didn't want to face it. I had seen Lizzie and Michael together for so much of their lives that there was no doubt in my mind she cared for him, so it was difficult for me to understand why the inevitable changes that occur in a long-term relationship were making her so miserable. It probably had a lot to do with the fact that she was seventeen and pregnant. The young were impatient.

"I think there are many ways to be 'in love,'" Lizzie," I said, choosing my words carefully. This wasn't the first time I'd heard one or both members of a couple express their frustration with the waning of passion. Passion was like the spark that started the fire, but it wasn't what kept love alive in a relationship. Love came from a lifetime of shared experiences, both joyful and sad.

"You may believe there's a difference between 'in love' and 'love.' 'In love' is simply a facet of the emotion 'love.' The world places undue emphasis on the experience of being in love, but little on the true grit that cements relationships together. I want you to look for the true grit. Michael was your friend for a long time, right?"

"Yes."

"And do you still like him now that you're living with him?"

"Yes, except when he's controlling – and sarcastic. And he is maddeningly neat."

"Let's not focus on the negatives," I warned.

"He's so much better than me – I mean, in a spiritual way." She dropped her head, regarded her long delicate fingers, and twisted her hands.

"This isn't about comparing your spiritual progress to Michael's."

"He's so far ahead of me, I don't think I'm even in the same race."

Her insistence surprised me.

"You wouldn't understand," she went on.

"Why not?"

"I can't explain it, that's all," she replied doggedly.

I was sure she could explain it, but for some reason she didn't want to, but I decided not to press the issue.

"Do you find that he has some admirable qualities?"

"Lots."

"Lizzie, there are so many couples who come in here absolutely disliking each other. It's hard for me to get them to list even a few positive attributes about each other. You're way ahead of the game, and you don't even know it."

"Why do we fight, then?"

"Most fights are about who's going to run the show. Is that what's making you sad?"

"We haven't really been fighting, except for once about a month ago and last night. Anyway, that doesn't count."

They hadn't looked on the outs when they walked into my office this morning, so I figured they must have made up.

"I didn't want to fight anymore, so I tried real hard for the last month."

"Seems to be working, Lizzie."

"Then why am I so blue? I thought if you tried to be more righteous you'd be happy."

"Maybe you haven't addressed what's really wrong," I suggested gently.

Depression is anger turned inward; that's what came to mind as I sat looking at her. And I wondered what she was so angry about because it didn't seem to be Michael. It might be the fact that she was on her way to having a baby in a few months.

"I know what's wrong. I'm working on it," she answered vehemently, before I could probe more deeply. She may not have told me where the anger was coming from, but I knew it was there.

"Then keep working on it. Most situations can't be resolved in a New York minute."

"Or ever," she interjected bitterly.

"You have two choices, Lizzie. You can change the situation or you can change the way you feel about it. If there's no way to change the situation, then option number two is the only one open to you. Usually, if we look really deeply into our hearts, we can learn to accept what we cannot change. Now, I have another suggestion for your journal. You don't have to share this with Michael – it's just for your own benefit."

Lizzie brightened. "Try me."

"I want you to list every night in your journal something about Michael you like or something he did that you liked during the past day."

"That's it?"

"Think you can do that for me?"

"He's such a saint, that shouldn't be hard," she rejoined, but without a trace of sarcasm.

"I'm glad to hear that," I said, smiling. Then I added, "You and Michael are going to be all right, Lizzie. Just hang in there a little longer. Can we invite Michael back in?"

"OK."

"Why don't you get him?"

Lizzie tripped out the door and came back holding her husband by the hand.

"Must be a good sign that Lizzie's not crying for once," Michael remarked as they sat down.

Lizzie punched him good-naturedly in the ribs and smiled for the first time that morning. "See what I mean about the sarcasm, Bishop?"

Michael responded calmly to her jibe. "See what happens when my back is turned, she puts a knife in it."

"It's a matter of survival," Lizzie cut in.

Suddenly I realized they were playing an intricate game with one another, the kind of game couples usually play when they're courting, so I played right along with them.

"Funny, Lizzie was saying you were such a saint, a minute ago."

Lizzie swung her eyes from me to Michael, and they shared a profound look of understanding. You're playing me, Bishop, her eyes said. Michael almost fell on the floor laughing, before Lizzie and I joined in.

"I take it we're making progress," Michael said, when he'd recovered from his fit of laughter.

"I'm making progress, but I can't speak for you," smirked Lizzie.

"OK, kids, I think it's time for a closing prayer," I said, in an attempt to close our meeting. I was still chuckling. It looked to me like Lizzie Kerry was head over heels in love with her husband, and he with her, and neither of them had a clue how to tell each other without letting their guard down. Whatever was standing between them, it had to be gargantuan.

Lizzie

As we walked down the hallway after our conference with the Bishop, Michael said, "Honey, I'm dying to hear more."

"More about what?" I asked unsuspectingly.

"More about my saintly qualities."

"That was a private conference," I responded, turning my head away from him.

"I could always check out your journal," Michael said mischievously.

"You wouldn't! After the threats you laid on me!"

"I'm just teasing," he said gently. "You are too serious, Lizzie."

I sighed. "Somebody has to be."

We walked towards the chapel.

"Thanks for last night, by the way," I added.

"The money for your hair? My mistake – I owe you an apology."

"I didn't mean that," I whispered.

Michael whistled softly. "I should be thanking you."

"You were very nice to me, Michael Kerry."

He stopped my forward progress, drew my hand to his lips, and kissed my fingers. "The pleasure was all mine."

I felt like I had hailstones in my chest.

"You are quite wrong," I said demurely, and we walked on into the chapel to take our seats with Michael's family.

Gloominess

Lizzie

My gloomy outlook didn't turn around right away. A few nights later I woke up in the middle of the night unable to sleep for thinking about Jason and feeling bummed about breaking up with him and being pregnant, I slid out of bed and sat at Michael's desk in the dark for a while instead of going downstairs. I didn't want to bother Michael but I couldn't toss in bed any longer. The hell with it, I'd made another ridiculous promise, so I owed it to him to honor it. I went over to the bed and sat cross-legged on the floor on Michael's side.

"Honey," I whispered. "I can't sleep."

I reached up and touched his face, feeling the stubble on his chin. He came to consciousness slowly.

"Michael, I'm real sorry but I can't sleep and you made me promise to wake you up. Otherwise, I would have left you alone."

"Lizzie, baby. Where are you?"

"Down here on the floor."

He shifted back to make room for me. "Get back in bed, you'll get cold."

I put up my arms and he took me into his embrace.

"I'm on the wrong side," I complained.

"Change might do you good. So why can't you sleep, my precious pearl?"

"Thinking about stuff."

"You wanna talk about it?"

"No."

"Didn't think so. What would you like to do? We could read scriptures, play some music, or I could give you a back or neck rub."

"I could go for the neck rub. It's not going to lead to something else, is it?"

"Only if you want it to."

"All right," I said cautiously.

"Sit between my legs and throw your hair forward."

We readjusted our positions and Michael loosened my nightgown, so it didn't impede the action of his hands on my shoulder muscles.

"You are tense, my love."

I let Michael work on my neck, telling myself to relax and not think about Jason because there was nothing I could do to change what had happened.

"I hate that I'm gonna be fat," I said after a while.

"You are not gonna be fat. It's a baby, remember? And you'll still be a gorgeous woman to me."

"But not to anyone else," I countered, thinking of the unreal Jason. I wanted the real Jason to ache for me like I ached for my unreal version of him.

"You don't need to be gorgeous to anyone else but me." Michael's hands stopped massaging my neck. He leaned forward and whispered in my ear, "Or do you wanna be?"

The room was suddenly too quiet, and I felt sure Michael had picked up on my train of thought. I had to think of a way to backpedal – fast.

"Lizzie?" His voice sounded tight.

"I guess you may be right, I don't need to be attractive for anyone else," I said, worried that my words would not convince him.

There was a means to convince him, and although I was reluctant to use it, it would allay his suspicions. I twisted to face him, put my arms around his neck and started kissing him. He pulled away from me.

"Whoa, Lizzie. You just said you didn't want the neck massage to lead to anything."

"Changed my mind." I could tell he wanted to buy it but my rapid turnabout had made him skeptical. "You did say you wanted to make me feel better."

He took the bait, and I praised myself for covering so skillfully.

Afterwards, when I was once more sitting with my back to my husband, curled up in a tight fetal position, knees almost under my chin, a position that would soon be infeasible with my growing pregnancy, with Michael's arms wrapped around me and neither of us was wearing a stitch of clothing, as usual, I wondered how long into a marriage it was before couples quit sleeping naked together as often as we did. Laying there, I wondered if I had discovered something I could use, because Michael had put Jason temporarily out of my mind.

"Lizzie, sweetheart," Michael whispered in my ear. "Next time you want me to make love to you in the middle of the night, why don't you just say so?"

"That really was not my intention," I remonstrated.

"Why the change of heart?"

I had better come up with a reason quick, and my brain was moving none too adeptly at this dusky hour of the night. "You took advantage of me."

He wrapped his arms around me tighter. "And that, my precious pearl, is a bold-faced lie."

"You," I whispered with my head turned slightly towards the side of his face, "said we were an experiment characterized by, and I quote, 'a reckless disregard for truth and honesty,' unquote. So I'm not kissing and telling."

His whole body went taut. "You kiss well enough, Lizzie, but you don't tell."

"Then stop asking," I replied.

I might have dropped the words over a sheer cliff. The silence was so complete and suffocating that we were pressed together inside it like two atoms forced together in nuclear fusion. If he was breathing, I could not hear it, and my own breath was caught inside my lungs, unable to find release. We were skin-to-skin but separated by a vast chasm filled with half-truths, misconceptions, and unexpressed frustration. He laid his forehead on my right shoulder and let out a long sigh.

"All right, Lizzie. I got it."

He kissed my bare shoulder and my skin pricked as if I'd been tattooed. Then he withdrew his arms, extricated his legs from around my body and got up from the bed. He searched on the floor for what must have been his pajama bottoms and pulled them on while I rolled over, leaned my head sleepily on my knees and watched. I knew I had made some dreadful and terrible miscalculation, but I was too exhausted to figure it out.

He went over to his desk, sat down with his head buried in his arms, and remained motionless there for a long time in the dark while the house breathed all around us. I don't remember how or when I curled back under the covers and fell asleep. Or how I ended up on his side of the bed bent into his pillow with his pajama top clasped in my hand. Or if he ever slipped into the bed on my side. Nothing. I was, however, haunted by that image of him, silhouetted at his desk with his back folded over and his head resting in his hands, because it was the image of someone beaten and broken.

I wished I had gone to him and got down on my knees and told him the truth, begged his forgiveness, given him some reason to hope, but I did not.

⋅⋅✦✦✦⋅⋅

Lizzie

I did begin to sleep better, but it was quite the contrary for Michael. I kept him up making hot chocolate downstairs, awakening his mother in the process; playing Madonna tapes despite the fact that he didn't care for her music; and reading me scriptures with bleary eyes. Knowing Michael would share them with me made me less afraid of the nights when I lay sleepless, and the less I feared them, the more hopeful I became that I would survive the breakup with both the real Jason and the one of my imagination and learn from my mistakes. Following Bishop Dalton's advice about enumerating the positive events of my day was also lifting my spirits. Or maybe it was that Michael and I actually talked about the minutiae of our daily lives.

I did not know what Bishop Dalton's motives had been: to get us thinking about the blessings in our lives or to get us talking, but it helped us to stop fighting. And we steered clear of the deep, dangerous questions about the identity of the baby's biological father, when and how it was conceived, where we stood in our relationship, and what our expectations of each other were.

On a Wednesday night a couple of weeks later, when we were in bed in our pajamas propped up against the pillows, I read Michael my positive experiences for the past day.

"We had pancakes for breakfast – yummy good. I took Alison to ballet practice where she excelled and was radiant about her progress. Rachel got permission (finally) to go on a real date with Jeremy. I got an A on my English essay."

"You always get an A on your English essays," interrupted Michael.

"So, it still makes me happy."

"You've got grade fixation," he joshed.

"Like you don't."

"I'm the one planning to go to college."

"How were you planning on doing that while you're supporting me and the baby?" I asked.

"Night school," he replied without skipping a beat.

"No way," I said, dropping my journal onto the bed and drawing my knees up as close to my chin as possible. I rested my cheek on my knees and looked sideways at him, giving him my full attention.

"Yes, way. Watch me do it. I don't intend to spend the rest of my life working on cars."

"But then the baby and I will never see you," I complained.

"Sure, you will," he countered.

"Like when?"

"On the weekends."

"In your spare time? When you're done with homework or your church calling?" I demanded, stretching my legs out and folding my arms across my bosom.

He put his journal down. "You saying you're gonna miss me?"

"No!"

"Then it won't be a problem, will it?"

I could have hit him. I didn't know how he *always* managed to twist my words around and use them against me.

"Read your stuff for today," I said, attempting to change the subject. I wiped my forehead which had unexpectedly turned hot.

"Right then. Lizzie kissed me good morning."

"I always kiss you good morning."

"Shut up, it's my turn." Michael paused. "Lizzie did not burn Alison's cookies.'

"Wait a minute – those were Alison's cookies, why am I getting credit?"

"You set the timer as well as taking them out of the oven and off the cookie sheets."

"That doesn't count."

"If I say it counts, it does. Moving right along... Dad said I did a good job today. Lizzie's hair looked gorgeous. Mom made stuffed cabbage, which I love... and Lizzie got an A on her English test."

"That was my happy event."

"It made me happy too."

"You can't use my stuff. That's cheating!" I exclaimed.

"Lights out time," he said, ignoring me and reaching for the light. Then I realized, for the first time since we'd been sharing what made us happy, that almost all of his entries were about me, and having someone's happiness depend on you was a tremendous responsibility.

Two steps forward, one step back

Rachel

The second Sunday in February, not long after my third date with Jeremy, my brother left for Michigan to take a three-week mechanics course. Jeremy and I had been able to go to the movies or rent a video to watch at Jeremy's or our house with Lizzie and Michael, because my parents wouldn't let us go on a one-on-one date. One of those stupid Church rules about not going on solo dates until you were eighteen.

They were worrying about the wrong person. They should have been watching my brother while he and Lizzie were pretending to just be friends when they were really making babies. Because of my brother's violation of a very sacred law, which was in gravity second only to murder in the eyes of the God, I was being held on a tight leash. It was all extremely unfair.

But I did like Lizzie, even if she and my brother had broken some major rules. I was always hoping she would go out with us, because she had a car and at least she would let us sit by ourselves in the back row at the movie theater. She was sharp at fixing hair, gave me nice clothes, and loaned me some sparkly nail polish to set off my fingers. One night she did my hair in an elegant French braid with a ribbon woven through it and Jeremy went nuts over it.

While there were advantages in having an older sister-in-law, with Michael gone *she* was driving me nuts. She kept hanging about the phone waiting for him to call and pacing around the living room. She took me to the mall the first Saturday he was gone and drove Janine, Shannon and me barmy dragging us around all the stores. Michael had told me to keep an eye on her for him while he was gone because he was worried about her getting blue. She didn't look blue to me, she was simply maddening, asking all the time if Michael had called. My dad wanted to find out how Michael's classes were going but could hardly get Lizzie to relinquish the phone to him.

Lizzie was upstairs doing homework when Michael called on the Thursday night of his second week away, and Dad took the call.

"Hi, son. How's it going?" Dad cupped the mouthpiece and said to Mom, "It's Michael."

He paused while Michael spoke.

"How's Lizzie? Great, I think she's missing you big time."

Michael said something that made Dad smile.

"Yes, I know it's her eighteenth birthday next Monday and we'll do something nice for her."

Michael must have been relaying instructions. He'd given me the assignment to stick a wrapped present on her bed while she wasn't looking.

"Vanilla cake with chocolate frosting. Got it. Yes, I will remind Rachel. You wanna talk to Rach? Sure."

Dad handed me the phone.

"Hi, sis," came Michael's voice.

"Hi, kiddo. How's it going out there?"

"Cold. Please remember my present for Monday for Lizzie, all right? How is she, anyway?"

"We went to the mall last weekend with Shannon and Janine."

"Buy anything?"

"Shannon and Janine did. Lizzie said you'd kill her if she spent anything out of the savings bank."

"I would not."

"She listens to you more than she lets on. She's gonna be really pissed that we haven't told her you're on the phone yet. She's got it bad for you, Michael."

"Nice to know I'm missed. Can you run up and get her, please?"

"Sure." I put the phone down, bounded upstairs, and knocked on Michael and Lizzie's bedroom door. "Lizzie! Phone call."

The door whipped open in my face. "I'll be right there."

Lizzie rushed down the stairs and picked up the phone.

I understood. Jeremy was doing strange things to my heart too. I was counting on Lizzie to accompany us to the movies tomorrow night and without my brother along to censor us, it was a certainty that we could sit in the back by ourselves.

She cradled the phone into her ear and lounged against the counter.

"Hi, Michael. How's life treating you?"

She smiled as he spoke.

"You heard I'm missing you? Who's tattling – Rachel or your dad?"

She paused again to listen.

"Look, I'm fine. I went to my doctor's appointment and everything is OK."

Another pause.

"No, I didn't spend any money at the mall. Think I was brought up as a rich kid or something?" Lizzie was smiling now. I was glad she wasn't moping around anymore like she had been in January.

"Yes, Jeremy is going on a date with Rachel Friday night and I'm taking them."

Lizzie twirled her hair.

"I am not encouraging insanity. They're high-school kids."

As if, because she and Michael were married, it somehow implied they weren't.

"All right, I'll get your mom. So long." She set the phone down and told Mom that Michael wanted to talk to her. I wondered why she didn't say "I love you." Come to think of it, I hadn't heard her say it, even once, in all their conversations. For a girl acting so gooey-eyed, Lizzie sure wasn't letting on.

Lizzie

It was Friday around two pm during the second week that Michael was at his training class when I was summoned to the high-school office to take a phone call from my father, who turned out to be Patrick Kerry rather than the real thing, which was infinitely preferable.

"Hi, what's up?" I asked, shocked that Patrick Kerry was calling me at school. It probably meant something bad had happened.

"Here's the deal, Lizzie — Anne just went into hospital this morning with gallstones and they'll be operating this afternoon. I need you to take charge at home. I'm gonna stay down here until she comes to. Can you fix dinner and make sure the kids are all right?"

I was relieved to hear the call had nothing to do with Michael. "Sure. Jeremy and Rachel were going on a date with me to the movies but it's OK if he comes over, isn't it?"

"Yes, as long as you supervise. Make sure Jeremy doesn't bring a movie rated above PG-13. Think you can handle everything?"

"Of course," I said easily. Hopefully I won't make a mess of this like everything else in my life, I thought. "Can you talk to the office so I can go home, otherwise Alison will be there ahead of me?"

"Yeah — lemme talk to them."

I handed the phone off to the administrator and waited while Patrick Kerry gave an explanation of why I needed to leave early. With permission granted, I walked out to my car and wondered what was on the dinner menu. I had a sinking feeling there was nothing pre-cooked or canned or frozen in the Kerry household that I could throw together in fifteen minutes or less. Almost everything we ate was prepared from scratch. At least Anne Kerry had her recipes organized in a binder, because I was going to need it.

I arrived home ahead of Alison and walked to the school bus stop to collect her. She was surprised but elated to see me, albeit I gave her the news her mother was in hospital. I asked Alison what she thought was on for dinner and she reminded me that Friday night was pizza night (home prepared, of course). That meant all I'd have to do was make the dough and throw it together. I mixed up yeast, flour, and water in the bread machine and set it to "knead" before leaving the dough to rise while I dug up topping ingredients from the refrigerator. I'd lived in the Kerry household long enough to know it took two pizzas to feed everyone, although we were minus Michael, Anne, and Patrick. About this time, Rachel, Sarah, and Edward walked in the door wanting after-school snacks and I relayed them the news that their mother was in hospital. They took it in stride. I was the new mommy and this didn't faze them in the least. Then I discovered we didn't have any after-school snacks because Anne Kerry usually made batches of granola bars, cookies, and other treats on Fridays, so they ate apples instead and demanded that we make treats for tomorrow.

"Let's make lemon bars," suggested Sarah.

"And chocolate chip cookies," added Edward.

"Tell you what, if you can find the recipes and lay out the ingredients, I'll throw everything together."

I thought it would be unwise to have too many kids under foot in the kitchen. If they could get me to a starting point, I could take it from there. I suggested Rachel call Jeremy and invite him to pizza since it looked like we'd have extra and asked him to see if he could rent *Out of Africa* on his way over. That would take care of the entertainment for tonight. I resumed my search for pizza toppings in the refrigerator, falling over Sarah and Edward who were assembling the ingredients for treats. I located the salami, bell peppers, onions for one pizza and ham for the other. I grabbed a can of pineapple off the shelf so I could turn it into a Hawaiian, which was the younger kids' favorite. I checked the bread machine and calculated what time the dough would be ready.

Then it was time to switch on the oven and start on lemon bars and chocolate chip cookies. The cookies were easy to throw together in the mixer, other than the fact that I had to dig eggshell out of the dough when I dropped a piece into the bowl.

The lemon bars were a real pain because I had to make the crust first, melting butter in a pan and mixing it with granola (the real stuff out of a bin in the Kerry's food storage), press it into a glass dish, and then prepare the topping, which required both lemon zest and juice. I grated some skin off my fingers along with the zest, so I hoped nobody minded extra protein in their lemon bars. I almost curdled the lemon topping while heating it on the stove because I forgot you shouldn't let it boil, a fact Sarah was quick to observe and correct.

I understood now why Anne Kerry didn't work outside the home: she had her plate full here. I realized with a sinking feeling that she wouldn't be up to running the household even when she did arrive home. That meant only one thing; the rest of us would all have to pick up the slack, and being the most capable person here, the brunt of the burden was going to fall on me.

The bread machine alarmed that the pizza dough was ready and it was time to roll it out on the pizza round. Alison helped spread canned pizza sauce and cheese on the crust, and Edward did an exacting job of adding the toppings, laying them out with the careful symmetry of an engineer. Just after the pizzas hit the oven, Jeremy arrived. Rachel had been preening in the bedroom and danced down the stairs to greet him. Seeing her so over the moon about him made me think how foolish it was to be young and in love. I looked at my belly and it reminded me of all the reasons not to go down that road again.

As I dropped teaspoonfuls of chocolate chip cookie dough onto baking sheets, I wondered about the laundry that was probably piling up with a house crammed so full of bodies, so I asked Sarah if she would bring down the girls' clothes so that I could get a load started after dinner. The kitchen was crammed with utensils and bowls from preparing dinner. I stared at the mess forlornly and began unloading the dishwasher so I could reload it with the latest dirty dishes.

I was hoping I'd be able to sit down by the time dinner came out of the oven when I felt the baby gurgle in my belly. It wasn't the first time I'd felt my little one. I was starting to develop a bulge in the lower abdomen and my clothes were disconcertingly tight. I'd really gone to the mall to look at maternity wear last weekend, but

I'd dragged the girls all over the place to hide my real intentions. I ought to talk to my mother about getting some clothes. I could probably get castoffs from the mothers in the ward and, if I acted nice, I was betting my mother would take me on a shopping spree at Mervyn's. It was entirely depressing to think about being huge and pregnant in high school.

Not to mention the thought that Michael might no longer find me attractive. I didn't know why I was worrying about being attractive to him because he'd said it made no difference to him whether I was pregnant or not. I had heard that stupid "love is blind" line as long as I could remember, but it didn't make sense before. I did have to admit that watching Michael look at me during one of our increasingly frequent moments sans clothing, helped. But sensing this was coming from somewhere down inside of him, perhaps even a place he did not fully understand, was starting to make the line more believable. Could he actually love looking at a pregnant woman? Really? I'd have to wait and see, but not for long.

With the extent of my new responsibilities, I realized I had actually not thought about Michael for at least a few hours. I hated to admit it, but I was missing him in a major way. I didn't realize how nice it was to have someone cuddle up to you every night and wake up with you in the morning. I was relying entirely too much on his companionship, I decided, and now that he was away, I needed to learn to be separate again. It wasn't healthy to depend on a person this much for my sense of well-being, I thought. I'd done that once and I wasn't doing it again.

But was I starting to depend on Michael? Michael was nothing like Jason – either Jason in the flesh or the Jason of my imagination. Michael thought about me and cared for me, and he showed it. I knew I could trust him in ways I could never trust Jason. I concluded that depending on Michael might not be a bad thing. But still...

The timer rang and I realized the pizzas were ready.

"Dinner's ready," I called. I put on the oven gloves and carefully slid the large rounds out of the oven. Edward offered to slice the pizzas and made some careful cuts that gave us even-sized slices. Rachel set out glasses and a pitcher of red punch. I let everyone come up one by one to make their selections. When they were done and were seated at the table, I took one slice of each pizza for myself and sat down at the head of the table. I asked Sarah to say grace. Jeremy and I exchanged smiles as we ate.

"Sure nice of you to invite me here, Mrs. Lizzie," he said, with cheese dripping from his chin.

I realized I'd forgotten napkins and jumped up to get them.

"You're welcome, Jeremy," I replied, handing around the napkins.

"So how did you talk Michael into working for his dad?" he asked. "He was supposed to go to college."

"It was a joint decision," I said cautiously. "Of course I want him to go to college. He's thinking about taking night classes to get his degree."

Rachel looked at me oddly, as if she knew more than she should.

"I want to be just like my dad when I grow up," interjected Edward.

He was already, I thought.

"I wanna be a doctor," Jeremy said.

I could imagine him as a physician since he had a way of looking at people that made you realize he cared.

"Med school? Wow! I hope you do it," I said.

"What kind of doctor?" asked Rachel from beside him.

"I like kids. Pediatric oncology, maybe."

Jeremy knew the lingo already, and I hoped Rachel was going to study her biology texts diligently so she could keep up with him.

"Sounds like serious stuff," I responded. "Good for you."

The phone rang and I jumped up to get it. Couldn't Michael time his calls so that they didn't arrive in the middle of dinner?

"What the hell are you doing calling in the –"

"Hello, this is Sister Stern from the Relief Society Presidency."

I gasped and began again.

"Sister Stern," I said graciously. "So sorry, I thought you were someone else."

"Which daughter are you?" she asked cautiously.

The black sheep, I thought, and replied, "Lizzie."

"Well, Lizzie, we heard about your mother and wanted to see if we could offer some help at home."

"I don't need any help. We're just fine," I protested.

"We thought you might be in need of a few meals next week."

"Meals? Oh, yes, like dinner," I said, backpedaling. "I wouldn't want to impose..."

"Look, dear, just tell us how many people and I'll send around a signup sheet on Sunday."

"I should ask my father-in-law first," I said.

"Oh, you're that Lizzie."

I hadn't a clue what "that Lizzie" meant, but I was sure it couldn't be positive.

"How about we bring dinner on Monday night?" she continued.

Reluctantly, I acquiesced, told her we were seven since Michael was away, thanked her profusely, and hung up the phone. I hoped my in-laws wouldn't be upset with me. I had barely replaced the receiver when the phone rang again.

"Kerry residence," I answered. I wasn't going to get caught out thinking I was talking to Michael this time.

"Lizzie, my love, how are you?"

I stared at my second piece of pizza which was going to be cold by the time I ate it. My heart started clamoring in my chest. "Michael?"

"You sound stressed. How are you, my precious pearl?"

"Your mom's in the hospital with gall stones and your dad's with her. I'm holding down the fort here. We're in the middle of pizza."

"You – in charge?"

"You don't think I'm capable?"

"Rather like having a lamb leading the flock, isn't it?'

"That was unfair," I countered.

"Lizzie, sweetheart, I'm teasing."

"It's no easy job," I went on. "And I *am* perfectly capable."

"How's Mom?"

"I don't know. Your dad hasn't called yet. I guess she'll be OK after surgery."

There was a long pause. "Lizzie, I miss you."

"I'm here waiting for you," I said.

"Have Dad call me when he has news about Mom. I'll talk to you then."

"Sure."

"Lizzie, hang in there. I'll be home soon."

"Bye, then."

"Good-bye, my love. Sweet dreams."

I heard the click as Michael hung up and stared at the receiver, as if by a miracle it would conjure him up out of nowhere. I detected a trace of disappointment in his voice. I should have said something appropriate, like I missed him too or I couldn't wait for him to come home. Suddenly I did miss him and did wish fervently that he were coming home tomorrow and not next Friday.

But I would not allow myself to become emotionally dependent on him; I was never going to give anyone that power over me again. If I did, I would no doubt get my feelings hurt all over again. Even if I could trust Michael, I wasn't so sure about our situation. Too many folks told us we were doomed, and I couldn't argue with them.

At this moment, I realized that five pairs of eyes were fixed on me. I hated not having a place I could talk on the phone to Michael without the rest of the household listening in.

"What are you looking at?" I asked.

"Don't be sad, Lizzie, he's coming home next week," Sarah said softly.

"I'm not sad," I objected.

"You look sad," added Edward.

"You could be nicer, Lizzie," said Rachel.

"What d' you mean? I was nice!"

"You never say you love him," remarked Alison.

"I'm sure she will next time she talks to him," Jeremy said, with a quizzical look in his soft eyes. "I would want my wife to say she loved me if I talked to her on the phone."

He was looking at Rachel when he said it, and I wished the phone would swallow me up like a magic lamp.

"Does anyone want any more pizza?" I asked, trying to change the subject.

That started a second feeding frenzy that I was hoping would help them all forget about what Alison and Jeremy had just pointed out.

Patrick came home around 11 pm with the news that Anne would be in the hospital until Monday and would need to convalesce at home for a few weeks. That meant I'd be baking my own cake for my eighteenth birthday, because I doubted Anne would be feeling up to it. I tried not to be annoyed with Michael for being gone and his father for sending him and his mother for getting gallstones. It wasn't like they'd done it intentionally. The fates were merely conspiring against me, as they had done last fall. Anyway, my eighteenth birthday was hardly the most significant event to occur in my life. There were other rites of passage in which I'd already participated that were supposed to happen after you were eighteen.

The rest of the time before Michael's return went by in a haze. I buzzed through Saturday in a blur of chores, cooking, laundry, and homework. I decided running a household was a seven-day-a-week job that I was ill prepared to assume when I was trying to keep my high-school GPA above 3.9. Patrick gave me two hundred dollars and told me to go grocery shopping on Monday after school. I wished it was birthday money I could go blow on maternity clothes because practically everything I had didn't fit. Anne helped me with the list and planned the menus for later in the week. Relief Society delivered meals until Thursday, including my birthday dinner on Monday night. Anne must have leaked the fact that I was turning eighteen, because not only did dinner show up, but along with it came a great big cake topped with pale pink roses and whipped cream, complete with trick candles that set the entire family into peals of laughter when I couldn't blow them out.

The Kerry's gave me a new journal and a bunch of school supplies, as well as a twenty-dollar gift certificate to Target. I was sure Patrick and Anne were expecting me to shop for clothes appropriate to my condition, and I was sorely in need of them. My parents sent a card home with me from church and invited me to dinner, which I declined. I was more at ease with my new family these days. In the card from my parents was a one-hundred-dollar bill – manna from heaven! Rachel and Sarah gasped, and I felt guilty that my in-laws could probably never spend this much on their kids for birthdays. I thought it would be nice to go to the Solano Mall in Fairfield next weekend with Michael and pick out clothes together, if Michael had the time or inclination for it.

Michael phoned shortly after dinner and told me he had a surprise for me, but I'd have to wait until I went to bed, so I fussed all evening wondering what he was up to. Nothing had materialized by the time 9 pm came around, so I set off for the bathroom to complete my nightly toiletries. While I was gone, another member of the family placed a card and a small package wrapped with silver bows in the middle of the bed. I snatched it up eagerly and undid the ribbons. Inside was a heart-shaped locket on a gold chain. I ripped open the card and he'd written, "Rejoice, O my heart, and give place no more for the enemy of my soul. 2 Nephi 4:28." Underneath this scripture, he'd added, "Work on the heart," the words he'd said while we were dancing at the wedding when I'd sarcastically told him I had the face of an angel and the heart of a devil. Below it he'd drawn the shape of a heart and signed it simply "M." I rummaged in the bottom of the closet for our wedding album, found a group shot with Michael in it that was about the right size for a locket, cut his head out of the photo, and stuck it in the locket. Then I snapped the chain around my neck. I determined not to ask him what the locket cost and not to tell him I had already put his picture in it.

Michael's Homecoming

Lizzie

Friday was not far away, but by the time Michael arrived home, I expected I would be doing most of the cooking. I took charge of the laundry after Anne came home because she wasn't supposed to be lifting anything for six weeks. I seemed to spending an inordinate amount of time folding clothes and pairing socks. At least Patrick didn't need any shirts ironed, except for Sunday.

On Friday evening I had an apron over my rapidly growing belly and was grating cheese, rolling out pizza dough, and making fruit pies for tomorrow's dessert. I was still wearing the locket Michael had given me for my birthday. Edward wanted to show me how he could spin the pizza dough instead of rolling it out, and managed to drop one of the crusts on my head, so my hair was covered with a fine layer of flour interspersed with the bits of dough Sarah hadn't been able to remove. Edward had expressed his apologies and I decided it was better to laugh than cry, so Sarah, Edward and I all ended up in a heap of giggles on the floor.

Anne was upstairs resting and Patrick was still at the auto shop, even though it was past 6 pm. I guess Michael contributed more to the workload at his father's business than any of us realized. Alison was watching cartoons on TV and Rachel had gone over to Jeremy's. I was beginning to think they were getting in too deep for high-school kids, but I wasn't exactly in a position to disparage high-school romances.

"It's Michael!" yelled Alison from the couch and rushed to the door.

I had dough for the cherry pie crust wrapped around a rolling pin and was just about to drape it over the cherry pie filling that Anne had canned last June. My heart rate went through the ceiling and I had no hands free to wipe the sweat off my forehead.

"Hello, everyone!" Michael called as he walked in the door.

Edward was busy laying out pepperoni on the pizzas in a perfect geometric design. Sarah got up from the table and gave her brother a welcome home hug while I made a desperate effort to finish crimping the edges of the pie before Michael got to me. I picked up a knife and made two slashes in the center of the pie.

"Where's Lizzie?" I heard Michael ask Sarah.

"Cooking in the kitchen," Sarah replied.

Michael came up behind me, wrapped his arms around me, and kissed my neck. Husbands really shouldn't be allowed to assault their wives in the kitchen when the wives couldn't defend themselves, I thought. But I did have the knife in my hand.

"Lizzie," he whispered, "you're showing."

"I know," I said under my breath, setting down the knife. "Most of my clothes don't fit."

"Let's tell them tonight."

That was the last thing on my mind right now, but I saw no reason to delay the inevitable. Most of the family knew already.

"Dad's not home yet?" asked Michael.

"Still at the shop - he called and said he'd be late. He'll probably show up about the time the pizzas come out of the oven."

"What kind d'ya make?" he asked, rocking me gently.

"One is pepperoni, black olives and mushrooms; the other ham and pineapple."

"Mmmh. Sounds good. What happened to your hair?"

"Edward was experimenting with twirling pizza dough. He's improving but he has a ways to go."

"Could be the new fad in hair styles. Yummy enough to eat."

"If you like hair."

"I like yours."

"Look, you're distracting me. Can you please leave me alone so I can finish up in here?" I protested because Michael was taking serious liberties with his hands. I didn't mind, but, still.

"First, tell me you missed me. That's what my spies inform me."

"All right, I missed you," I conceded.

He whirled me around to face him. "Now say it when you're looking at me."

"Yes, already," I flung back offhandedly.

He searched my face, kissed me on the lips, and I wondered if I was going to be able to hold it together to finish up the pies. Then he noticed the locket.

"You're wearing it, so does that mean you like it?" he asked.

"Yes, very much. It was sweet of you."

Before I had time to stop him, he seized the heart and snapped it open. We were standing very close now and I felt his breath on my neck. He flashed me an enchanting smile.

"Didn't waste any time, did you?"

I felt like I'd been caught with my hand in the cookie jar. He snapped the heart closed.

"I've been working on the heart, like you suggested," I said softly.

He dropped his hands from the chain and took a step back. "I hope you're not toying with me."

I was unsure whether he was rebuffing me or merely warning me that he didn't take my words lightly. I didn't know what he expected next, but he spared me the trouble.

"I haven't seen Rachel. Where is she, anyway?"

This was the question I'd been dreading. "Jeremy's."

"I told you not to encourage them."

"It's a high-school romance," I contradicted. "They never last."

"I hope you're not applying that generalization to us," he responded evenly.

I winced. "We're different."

"It's reassuring to hear that from a girl with your experience."

I ignored the jibe. "I have to finish up in here. Can't you find something useful to do with yourself?"

"If you've got half-an-hour to spare, I could," he replied.

I dissolved in laughter. Perhaps it had something to do with the fact that I looked a fright and I was so glad to see him. "Get lost, lover boy. I've got a family to feed."

"Do you burn pizza as well as you burn cookies, my love?"

"I'm gonna carve you up and serve you on the pizza if you don't get out of here right now," I retorted.

"You'd live to regret it, so I'd better make tracks," he answered, and turned on his heel to go upstairs. At that moment, Patrick walked in the door.

"Hey, Michael, how'd it go?" he asked of his son.

Michael walked up to him and gave him a hug. "Thanks, Dad. Really good – I might actually be able to do the job now."

"All I can say is, I'm glad you're home. Lizzie has been driving us nuts."

I walked out of the kitchen, ready to refute Patrick's last statement. Michael and his father were both enjoying the joke at my expense.

"I have not!" I exclaimed.

Michael picked up his bag and headed for the stairs. "Feel free to join me if you want to," he flung over his shoulder.

I looked at Patrick and shrugged. "In case you hadn't noticed, I'm trying to fix dinner. And Michael," I called after him, "I'm sure your mother would appreciate if you looked in on her."

"Give me a holler when pizza's ready, Lizzie, so I can take some up to her," he replied coolly.

I was ready to fling a whole pizza in his face. "I already planned on it."

———— ·+++++· ————

The pizzas turned out perfect, and Michael did take some up to his mother. There was no sign of Rachel or Jeremy, so I gathered Patrick was going to pick her up or Jeremy's parents were giving her a ride home. We had just eliminated the last piece of pizza when Michael addressed Sarah, Alison, Edward, and his father. He wrapped his arm around my waist as he spoke.

"Lizzie and I want to let you know we're expecting a baby."

There were gasps, but not from Patrick, as we expected.

"That was fast," remarked Sarah. "Did you plan it?"

"Does that mean I'll be an aunt?" asked Alison.

"Are you having a boy or a girl?" chimed in Edward.

The questions were dropping as thick as hail and I couldn't answer them fast enough.

"It was kind of an accident," I said cautiously, "but we're excited. And yes, you'll be an aunt, Alison."

I flashed a glance at Michael and he gave me a brilliant smile, infecting me with his enthusiasm. I told myself I was feeling giddy as a reaction to his homecoming. Or was it his expression when he saw his picture in the locket? The phone rang and jingled my nerves some more. Michael answered the call.

"Jeremy, how're you doing?" asked Michael.

He paused while Jeremy asked him something.

"A dance? Next Friday night? And you want Lizzie and me to make it a group date? Sure we'll do it." He cupped the receiver and looked at me. "You will, won't you, Lizzie?"

I signaled in the affirmative.

"Of course she will, Jeremy. Sounds like a blast. Rachel wants to talk to Dad? All right, put her on and he'll talk to her."

My father-in-law had a sotto voce conversation with Rachel, from which I gathered he was none too happy about the persistence of Jeremy's pursuit of Rachel. I deduced that Michael and I were obligated for next Friday night, which suited me fine as long as I could find a dress that fit me. I figured I would use the one hundred dollars my parents had given me for my birthday to purchase a dress and some other clothes that would fit me. Then Patrick hung up the phone and we resumed our consumption of the pizzas in silence.

Later that night, Michael and I had a protracted conversation about the fact that he thought I wasn't eating enough because my cheeks looked hollow and my limbs were looking thinner as my belly grew. I didn't dare tell him the doctor concurred with his opinion and had advised me that I wasn't gaining enough weight. I was dead on my feet and jetlag had finally caught up with Michael, so it wasn't until the next morning he showed me how much he'd missed me. I wondered if he knew that I had actually missed him just as much.

••••••

Despite Michael's commitment at his father's shop, he did find time to take me to the mall to pick out a dress for the following Friday's youth dance. Technically, since we were a married couple, we ought not to be going, but we were making a foursome with Jeremy and Rachel and I didn't think anyone was going to stand on protocol. The dress we selected was a shiny dark blue and fell in a straight line from my breasts to my knees. The bust was well enough done that I wouldn't have to wear that increasingly uncomfortable bra. The neckline was trimmed with white lace and cut perfectly to show off Michael's locket. The skirt was constructed so that it flared outward as I twirled, and displayed enough leg to tantalize, although I didn't think Michael needed any encouragement. I knew better: I absolutely knew he didn't.

On Friday night, we set out at 8:30 pm for the Fairfield Stake Center, picking Jeremy up on the way. Michael looked particularly well turned out in black slacks and a grey shirt with subtle stripes. Rachel and Jeremy were in high spirits, and their merriment was infectious even though I was more ready for bed than dancing. If the baby hadn't been moving around and I hadn't been so tired, I would have forgotten I was pregnant. By the time we arrived at the building, Michael's qualms about Jeremy and Rachel had temporarily subsided.

We paid our entrance fee and went into the hall. The lighting was muted, in contrast to the music, which was blasting out Dire Straits' "Money for Nothing." There weren't many young people dancing, so we hung at the periphery of the floor, snacking on chips and dip and sipping water.

When "For Just a Moment" off the album started up, Michael said to Jeremy, "I think it's time we get the ladies out there, Jeremy. Lizzie's going to fall asleep if we don't start dancing."

"I'm taking care of two people," I reasoned.

"You're taking care of a lot more than two right now," Michael added.

We walked out onto the floor and started a rumba, though the beat was a little fast for it. I was hoping I could still remember the variations. As I listened to the words of the song, I reminisced about the dazzling blue of Jason's eyes and his hard, hot embrace. I had soared too close to the flame and been burned, but that feeling was addictive. Somehow, I had to get over Jason; this unreal Jason that haunted me from the depths of hell in the dark recesses of my mind. Passion like that was the stuff of movies and hit songs and not for everyday life.

Rachel and Jeremy moved into the periphery of my vision, and I realized from the way he was holding her and the way she was looking at him that they were deeply in love. As much as I didn't want to admit it to myself, I wanted what they had. I heaved a subtle sigh and Michael picked up on it.

"I appreciate what you're doing for my family, Lizzie."

"Praise like that could go to my head," I responded. "You wouldn't want that, would you?"

"What I want," he said emphatically, "is for you to be happy."

We did a backwards Cuban walk, staring each other down.

"I'm fine," I went on evenly.

"Does 'fine' mean happy?"

"It means whatever you want it to mean," I said, lightly tossing my head and avoiding his eyes.

He whirled me around him in the fancy turn we had learned. The music was fading.

"You're avoiding the question, Lizzie Kerry, and you know it."

I stepped away from him, turned, and headed for the sidelines, flipping my skirt in the process. He wasn't going to pin me down tonight, unless it was after we got home.

"If you're happy, I'm happy – how's that?" I threw over my shoulder.

"Lizzie, why do you have to be so impossibly enigmatic?" he sighed, catching up with me.

"Because you're so impossibly pushy," I flashed.

Michael looked over at Jeremy and Rachel and his displeasure was evident. "Let's go break in on Jeremy and Rachel. They're getting far too serious with each other."

"They look happy."

Ignoring my comment, Michael walked up to Rachel and Jeremy and cut in. He handed me over to Jeremy and slipped off to the sidelines with Rachel, much to my annoyance. I thought a Youth Dance was no place to have a discussion with Rachel about Jeremy.

"Sorry about that, you know Michael," I said to Jeremy as "Rhythm of the Night" began to hammer out of the speakers.

"He's looking out for his sister."

"He's going to tell Rachel she shouldn't be dating you," I continued.

"That's not going to be any kind of deterrence for her," he mused with a faint smile.

"It is rather like the War of the Worlds, you and her," I suggested, having to yell over the music. "We believe Christ has already come and you're still waiting for Him."

"We have other beliefs in common," countered Jeremy.

"Look, don't get me wrong. I like you, Jeremy. You need to realize you're going to encounter opposition from both sets of parents. Don't get yourself into something you can't get out of."

Great advice, coming from me, I thought.

"Now tell me what you really think, Lizzie."

"As long as you promise not to tell Michael."

"What makes you so afraid of his opinion? He's crazy about you."

"Who says?" I demanded.

"After I heard you were pregnant, I asked him if he didn't think he'd gotten married too young. He said, "'There isn't any woman I'll ever want but Lizzie.'"

I sucked in my breath. "He never says that to me."

"It's a guy thing, Lizzie." When it appeared I didn't understand, he added, "You have to tell him you're crazy about him first."

"And then he'll reciprocate?"

"Aren't you guys there yet?" asked Jeremy, incredulously.

"Of course we are! I'm just upset about him interfering with you and Rachel." I decided it was time to change the topic of the conversation. "Where you and Rachel are concerned, I'd tread softly. Most opposing religions have spent more time making war than making love."

"Are you telling me I shouldn't date her?"

"I'm telling you, there may be irreconcilable differences." Then, seeing my last statement had upset him, I added, "Jeremy, who d'ya think has been trying to help you two get together?"

He smiled. "You're just telling me not to get her pregnant."

"Let's not go there," I said wryly.

The music came to an end, and Jeremy and I walked over to where Michael and Rachel were talking. The first bars of yet another rock song turned up a little too much sounded out of the speakers. Now I knew where the "loud" in "loudspeaker" came from. Rachel was not looking happy, but she brightened as Jeremy and I approached.

"C'mon, Lizzie," Michael said to me, "let's dance."

"You said something to upset her," I suggested as soon as we were out of earshot.

Michael ignored my observation and said, "Let's try a cha-cha to this."

"You've got to be kidding!"

"Are you telling me you can't or won't?"

"Of course I can," I countered, snatching his left hand and raising it up like a stop sign in a Latin hold. We glared at each other with our eyes inches apart. I followed his lead, making small steps with a lot of hip action to prove I was up for the challenge.

"I told Rachel she's on a train headed over the edge of a cliff," Michael said.

"You always had a soft touch," I replied, whipping my head around for a turn.

"She deserves honesty from me," he responded, guiding me into a turn.

"If it's true love, they'll find a way."

"I'll be watching," he replied, narrowing his eyes. I was sure he wasn't just referring to Rachel and Jeremy.

I deserved honesty from him, and I couldn't understand why I wasn't getting it. If this marriage was an experiment defined by a reckless disregard for honesty and truth and I had been responsible for its design, I wanted to change the rules. Because ever since that night when he'd sprawled over his desk with his head in his hands, sitting in the dark for hours without speaking, he had stopped asking questions about where my feelings lay and if I still thought of the child's father.

He never said he loved me in our most intimate moments. Perhaps he had he grown tired of pursuing me and was going through the motions just as I had been. He was a lion in the bedroom but I couldn't tell if his heart was in it. My growing belly hadn't deterred him. Could it be that I was young and female and I didn't turn him down. It was probably all about satisfying his lust, as he'd suggested that night on our honeymoon. He'd told Jason I was everything he'd ever imagined about in his wildest dreams, but that had most likely been a boast, not an expression of his undying devotion.

If I'd been nothing more than a sex object for Jason, why should I be anything else to Michael? He'd accused me of being enigmatic tonight, but he was nothing if not a complete mystery to me.,

The night he arrived home from Detroit, I had thought our relationship was making progress, but he immediately started sidestepping me. If I got close, he skittered away. Trying to find harmony in our dance steps, I gave myself to the music and the determined motion of the dance and felt the heat rising between us.

I realized I was beginning to want Michael in the way that I had once wanted Jason last fall. I had no clue how it had crept up on me. Michael was nothing like Jason. He was nerdy and Jason was handsome. Michael was always mindful of my feelings whereas Jason completely disregarded them. He was kind where Jason had been cruel. And mostly, unselfish in the bedroom whereas Jason had satisfied his appetite at my expense.

I was desperate to know what Michael was thinking, and it didn't look like he was going to own up to me anytime soon. But there was one way to find out what went on inside Michael's head. I could sneak a peek in his journal. Just a couple of pages, nothing more, the next time he was out home teaching. He'd never be the wiser.

Michael's Journal

Sunday, March 9

Lizzie

I was in a state of tense anticipation by the time Michael and Patrick left to visit two of the families on their home teaching route after lunch on Sunday afternoon. I knew I had at least a couple of hours and I figured ten minutes ought to be adequate, but I underestimated how compelling it would be to take a tour inside Michael's head.

I sat down at his desk and picked up his journal, turning it over to examine the rear cover and placing it back on the surface of the desk. I felt like Eve about to taste the proverbial fruit of the Tree of Knowledge of Good and Evil. At least I wasn't going to get caught and have to confess to my husband like Eve did to Adam, I thought. As long Michael had decided to keep playing these mind games and holding me at arm's length, I was determined to find out for myself.

I picked up the journal again and opened it with trembling fingers. I flicked through the dates until the middle of October, the time he'd proposed to me. I wonder what he'd written about that.

Sunday, 20-Oct-1985. I can't believe what happened today. Lizzie asked me to talk to her after church so we went to the park. Then she told me she was pregnant and that her boyfriend dumped her when he found out. She had obviously decided against an abortion, and there are only two other "righteous" options in that situation: marry the father (out of the question) or put the baby up for adoption. But in some stunning flash of inspiration, I thought of a third: I could marry her. Without giving it a second thought, I proposed. She begrudgingly accepted, but at least she accepted. It was probably the least enthusiastic acceptance of a proposal anyone could imagine. It was so insulting that I wanted to retract the offer. I still might.

I tried to get something out of her about the guy, but she wouldn't give it up. As far as I can tell, he's a church member, which makes his reaction even more despicable. And I kept asking myself how come I didn't even know she had a boyfriend and if she had to get pregnant, why couldn't it be me instead of some jerk who was going to dump her? I ought to know the answer to that: if it had been me, she wouldn't have gotten pregnant because I wouldn't be screwing her.

I've been in love with Lizzie for years, but I never made a move because I knew she only thought of me as a kid-brother or friend. After today, I wonder how she thinks of me. Am I her hero or her fool?

I knew I'd be going on my mission and I didn't want to start something with her that I couldn't finish. I always thought that when I got back from an honorable mission, that would be the time to ask Lizzie out. That was when I would be ready to be there for her.

I still can't believe I suggested getting married as an option today. Frankly, I can't believe Lizzie accepted. Now, as I write this, I don't see how I can withdraw my offer. I don't even know if I want to.

Marrying her means I will have to say I am the father of the baby, so I'm going to bear the burden of someone else's sin. I seriously wonder if I am making the right decision, but it's too late to go back now. I always wanted Lizzie and I guess if this is the only way I can have her, I'll take it.

Then Lizzie threw up, as if to prove she really was pregnant. She didn't want to see Bishop Dalton right away, but I told her we had to — no ifs, ands, or buts. The problem with Lizzie is that she doesn't always have the courage of her convictions, but we cannot delay the inevitable. First we went home to talk to my parents, which, of everything I expected I'd have to do, it felt like it would definitely be the worst.

They took the news surprisingly well, and I'm amazed my father didn't light into me. I'm lucky to have great parents. It felt weird telling my father I loved Lizzie and never having said so to her, but that's the way it went down.

Later in the afternoon, Lizzie and I went to see Bishop Dalton. We were immediately barred from public prayers and church callings, as I expected, which probably hurt me more than Lizzie. She seemed upset that he wanted to see us on a weekly basis, but that's the drill with our leaders. They don't want us to slip up again.

Wow, that was enlightening. I knew my reaction to Michael's proposal was tentative but seeing it in writing made me cringe. I kept reading.

Wednesday, 23-Oct-1985. *Last night I met Bishop Dalton with Lizzie and her parents. I didn't expect the meeting to go well and it didn't. I felt awful having to look Lizzie's father in the eye and tell him I got his precious daughter pregnant. Especially when I hadn't. But that was what I signed up for.*

I am trying not to be mad about the whole ruckus around lying about being the father, or at the pathetic jerk who she screwed, or even at Lizzie. I'm not sure which of those points I'm most mad about.

Lizzie better not let me down now.

To make matters worse, Lizzie's father said we couldn't live in their house. This was hardly a surprise to me. I would have been shocked if he said it was OK. But it was obviously a real blow to Lizzie. I hadn't told her then, but I didn't want to live with them. At all!

I was sort of hoping we'd end up with my folks, but convincing Lizzie of the wisdom of moving in with them wasn't going to be easy. When I told her my plan in the truck on the way to my house, she called my house 'a dump' and that made me really mad. She was acting like a stuck-up, spoiled little girl and I told her so. I have always known that about her but hoped that she would have grown up by the time we got married. Her impulsive, spoiled nature screwed that up, too. Maybe I should have been gentler on her but hearing that sneer about my family really hurt. Lizzie's family wouldn't give us a place to live; I was betting mine would jump at the chance.

On that score, I turned out to be right. Mom and Dad took it in their stride. Dad is such a cool cat that he asked Lizzie to give our Family Home Evening lesson next week. Then I took Lizzie upstairs to make sure she understood that no matter how she felt about moving in here, she wouldn't let on to the rest of my family. I really hope she'll stand by that promise.

Then I did something really stupid. I had her pinned up against the door because I wanted to make her notice me – in the way a girl would notice a guy. She was looking over my shoulder at my bed, no doubt realizing that in less than six weeks we'd be in it – together – and I wanted to kiss her so badly that I just did it. Her lips looked so kissable when she was pouting. Then I realized how stupid I'd been and I hadn't even asked her if I could, so I apologized, which probably made me look even more ridiculous. She colored up all red and didn't say anything.

I asked when she was coming by again because I couldn't bear to see her leave. Actually, I was ready to take her into my bed right now. Of course I wouldn't have, but that was the first time I realized I wanted Lizzie in a major, big-league kinda way and I was going to get her and I had no frigging idea what I was doing.

I couldn't believe what I was reading. I felt like I'd leaped out of an airplane on a parachute jump and discovered I was without my chute. I remembered that day in his bedroom the first time he'd kissed me, and that I had been as shocked at my response as he was at his, despite the fact that he'd been unaware of the effect he had on me. I traced my finger down the page and found the next entry on the following Saturday morning.

Saturday, 26-Oct-1985. *Lizzie came over Thursday ostensibly to do homework but spent most of the time going over arrangements for the wedding, which is a big pain in the back side. Weddings are a big deal for girls, or maybe their mothers, but as for me, the wedding day isn't nearly as tantalizing as the prospect of the wedding night. I thought Lizzie might be obsessing over the wedding arrangements because she finds that idea equally daunting, but not for the same reasons as me. At least Lizzie knows what to expect. I, on the other hand, have never made it with a girl and I want it to be good for both of us on our wedding night.*

Lizzie apparently has no idea what a big wedding is going to cost. I am praying her parents are going to foot most of the bill. After all, that is what the bride's family does, right?

I just hope she's not going to be a spendthrift after the wedding, because I don't know how I'll be able to cope if she is. I thought she could make her dress and the bridesmaids' dresses – now that there are four, counting my sisters, Rachel and Sarah. Nice of Lizzie to include them. Then I realized Lizzie hadn't sewn a garment in her life and my mother is Lizzie's only hope of getting it all done.

We also have to go down to the courthouse with Lizzie's parents and have them sign the marriage certificate because Lizzie will still be underage in December – her birthday is in February. Not an event I am looking forward to.. Then Lizzie asked me who I wanted for best man and I suggested Jeremy Stein. An argument ensued about whether we should have a Jewish best man, but since Jeremy is my best friend, I decided to insist.

She scorned my belief that experiences like this with non-members were missionary opportunities because everyone would soon know she was pregnant and we were no example for non-members. That upset me – she was the problem, not me. Lizzie and I hadn't committed any sin. I was so upset I used the 'D – ' word, which I can't remember having ever used it before. I deliberately didn't take time to help her with her chemistry homework, and I repented on my knees that night for swearing and for being so short with Lizzie.

Seeing my actions in his writing really tugged at something down inside of me. I guess I really am the devil.

Sunday, 27-Oct-1985. *One thing I do like about the fact that I'm now dating Lizzie is that I can finally put my arm around her and hold her hand when I want to and show everyone that she is my girl, even if she doesn't seem to like it. She let me know her displeasure after church by complaining about where my hands were ending up. She simply would not understand that it was driving me nuts that I had barely kissed her, but I was expected to act like her husband in five weeks.*

Then she made this weird promise that I could touch her as much as I wanted after we were married and embarrassed the heck out of me.

I wasn't some jock who was going to jump his wife if she didn't feel like it. We drove back to my house in an uneasy silence. Then I told her I wasn't going to force myself on her, and she started crying and I wanted desperately to hold her, but of course I couldn't because she scares the heck out of me, so I played with her hair instead. Lizzie has the thickest, most lovely hair I've ever seen. I didn't know what else to do to console her, so when she calmed down, I left her in the car. It's awful not to know what I can do to help the person I love more than my church standing, my mission, and my life.

Oh, Michael, I thought, why were you making cuts and turns so fast I might as well have been chasing a hare through the scrub brush? Why didn't you tell me you wanted me like that? And would it have made any difference if I had known?

Michael's Journal; Inside Michel's head

Lizzie

Now that I was inside Michael's head, it was so compelling that I couldn't stop reading. I turned over to the next page, rested my head on my cheek, and kept going.

Tuesday, 29-Oct-1985. *Last night Lizzie taught our Family Home Evening lesson. I guess Dad had it all figured out because he asked her to teach on the Atonement. She did a great job, but I realized she was having a rough time with the subject and I was wishing that we had studied the Atonement in private together rather than under the public scrutiny of my family. I wanted to take Lizzie in my arms and tell her that Heavenly Father loved her and I loved her and we didn't care what she'd done, because I knew she was sincerely sorry and she hadn't shirked the consequences. She might not believe she can be forgiven, but I do.*

Next thing I know, Dad looks at me expectantly and says Lizzie and I have an announcement to make, and I tell everyone we're getting married.

Then Rachel comes out with this line about me being a 'wonderful kisser,' which is a shock to me because I have only kissed Lizzie once – briefly – and Lizzie is hiding her head in her hands from humiliation. I can't imagine why Lizzie is making up this story unless she wants for me to kiss her, but I have to endure a discussion about Lizzie's wedding dress, the bridesmaids' dresses, Lizzie moving in with us after the honeymoon, then drink sparkling apple cider in celebration of our upcoming nuptials, followed by pears covered in chocolate mousse, before I can get Lizzie alone outside the front door.

I immediately quiz her about the 'wonderful kisser' story and she admits she made it up for one of her girlfriends. Then I suggest we not make it up and I push her up against the stucco and kiss her. This time I feel her respond and she lets me ever so briefly have a taste of her tongue. But afterwards she rebuffs me by deliberately and convincingly wiping the kiss off her lips with the back of her hand. Now I don't know whether she was teasing me, or I have offended her, or what.

She walked down the driveway without looking back and I practically cried, which thankfully she didn't see. I wonder if I will ever figure her out.

She runs scalding hot and frigid cold like a faulty water faucet.

I'm dreading tomorrow, the day before Hallowe'en. I'm going to the courthouse with Lizzie and her parents. On the upside, I have a ring to give her. We're not supposed to place emphasis on rings as symbols in the church because they are worldly, but no matter what, my Lizzie is going to have a ring – a ring with a history, in fact.

I'd talked to Mom and Dad about getting Lizzie a ring and they had suggested a family heirloom that Mom had received from her mother. It sounded like a winner to me. When I saw it, a ruby surrounded by a swirl of real diamonds, I was captivated by its intricate design and delicate features. That's how I see Lizzie: she is the center of my universe and makes everything around her glitter and sparkle.

I set down Michael's journal and stared out the window. A bluejay winged by with a flash of fierce blue and I wondered how, after knowing Michael for so many years, I'd understood him so little. I turned to the next page and resumed reading.

I felt tears sting my eyes as I read Michael's words. That day when I'd looked up the scripture he was reading.

Thursday, Halloween 1985. *I gave Lizzie the ring yesterday after we went to the courthouse with her parents and I actually think it made her happy. Short-lived victory, unfortunately. This evening we had a big row because I forgot to meet her to pick up the stupid wedding invitations. She lit into me for not caring about the wedding. I thought her complaints petty, considering what I was giving up. I should have been thinking about what I was getting – the girl of my dreams – but I wasn't. Then she dumped the entire box of wedding invites over my head and they spilled all over the floor, so I was standing staring at her amongst a pile of paper. I retaliated by pointing out that it was her fault she was in this predicament and she ought to have known a possible consequence was getting pregnant. To make it worse, I told her I was regretting having made the commitment to marry her.*

OK, so I felt that way at the time, but I made that observation in the heat of the moment and I wished I could take it back instantly, especially as she got even by telling me she didn't want to marry me either and threw the wedding ring I'd just presented her with down on the rug in front of me. I do believe what she said and I'm crushed. I wish Lizzie didn't have the ability to make me lose my head. I guess that's what being in love does to a guy.

However, when I ponder it, I'm not sure if what I am feeling is love. If it is, then someone screwed up, big time. This feeling both gives me clarity and fogs my whole brain, is exhilarating and exasperating, makes me feel whole and rips me apart.

Luckily for us, Dad averted a major disaster because he just happened to hear Lizzie slam my bedroom door so hard that I thought she was going to break the frame. I knew I was in for it because Dad never lets any of us get away with temper tantrums. He marched Lizzie right back into my room and told us to kneel. In Dad's world, you don't wait to repent when you have an argument with someone. He doesn't believe in letting resentment fester. I was feeling real sorry by this time so I prayed sincerely for forgiveness, both from Lizzie and the Lord.

When it was her turn, she made us wait – I've couldn't believe this, but Lizzie is a tough nut to crack – about twenty minutes before she said her prayer. When she was done, she burst into tears and I thought that it might be possible this cloud had a silver lining. After Dad went downstairs, I read her a scripture from Joshua about overcoming fear and doubt with the idea that it might give her courage, but my hopes for a positive outcome for our relationship remain solidly at the bottom of the river into which they have sunk.

My mood didn't improve during dinner, and I vented my frustration on Lizzie with as many sarcastic remarks as I could muster to humiliate her. I made sure she knew there are certain things I expect of her after we're married and I'm going to get them.

After dinner, I was feeling really sorry about everything I said, so I fixed the fan belt on her car for her, which I'd been meaning to do for weeks, and cleared up the wedding invitations that she had dumped all over the floor of our room, while she went up to my parents' room to try on Mom's wedding dress. Then I laid out my completed chemistry problems on my bed so Lizzie could check my answers if she got stuck. I felt so despondent about Lizzie that I started looking up all the scriptures on hope. Hope comes from faith, according to what I read, and I have no faith that Lizzie will ever love me. Not in the way I love her, and probably not in any real way. I am convinced that all my hopes for this marriage are an illusion.

I'd totally missed the point. All Michael had needed the day we fought over the wedding invitations was for me to let him know in some minor way that I cared about him and not just the wedding. He had no hope for the future because he did not believe in my affection. Honestly, I guess at the time, neither did I.

I had to stop writing because Lizzie came back into my room after trying on the wedding dress. She looked entirely too pleased with herself and I did my best to ignore her, although it's difficult to ignore Lizzie when my heart rate soars every time she walks into the room. She curled up on my bed to do her homework and I am back to completing this journal entry. I'm having a hard time concentrating because what I really want to do is jump on top of her and pin her down on the bed and make her forget about her lover. I hate myself for thinking like this.

As the moments ticked by with absolute silence between us and without really being aware of it, I found myself staring at her. She wasn't doing homework as I expected but was engrossed in studying my scriptures. Finally, she realized I was watching her and looked up. She said she was reading the chapter in Joshua I'd quoted from earlier. I said some stuff to belittle her – something about her needing to go to war or part the Sacramento River. I can't remember exactly what I said, but I'm kicking myself now. I could see she was indignant, so I laid it on even thicker and told her I hoped she wasn't going to get religious on me, because I'd been looking forward to battling Satan. She looked positively crushed, which is what I intended, because I wanted her to feel as crushed as I did. I told her she couldn't spend the night now, but she'd be able to as soon as she was my wife, and that did it. She left.

The minute she was gone I regretted everything I'd said and wondered how I could be so callous to someone I love so much. I will have to think of a way to get her back.

Well, at least he can admit when he is wrong. I'm not the only devil in this relationship.

Michael's Journal; November

Lizzie

Inertia kept me reading...

Friday, 01-Nov-1985. *I thought of something, though it wasn't much. I got up as dawn was breaking, walked to school, and talked the janitor into letting me into the cafeteria at 6:30 am. Then I dialed Lizzie's house from the pay phone and offered to help her finish her chemistry homework. I was sure she wouldn't have completed the assignment. That was when she admitted to having morning sickness every day"* (Michael underlined the last two words), *"and I felt as low as a junkyard dog. I couldn't imagine what it would be like to wake up every morning needing to throw up. Lizzie reluctantly agreed to meet me after I offered to buy her breakfast. She showed up at seven without makeup and her hair looked like she'd barely had a chance to drag a brush through it, but it was still the best-looking hair in the world to me on the best-looking girl. I gave her a long hug and told her she looked terrific, a compliment she didn't believe even though she did look terrific, and I apologized for last night's hostility after our row. I told her I was sorry for not helping her with her homework like I usually did, and that I appreciated her turning to the scriptures for guidance. Then I said if my repentance had been true, I wouldn't have kept making jibes like I did last night at dinner and I told her I needed her forgiveness. She smiled ever so sweetly and said of course she'd forgive me, and would I please buy her breakfast like I'd promised so we could get on with the homework? While we ate eggs and sausage and worked on the homework problems, I kept thinking how much I wanted to hold her and cover her with kisses, but I couldn't* *because we were in the high-school cafeteria. I wished it was our wedding night and I could have her all to myself.*

It was getting on eight-thirty when we finished, almost time for classes to start. She packed up her books and, just before turning to go, put her arms around my neck and kissed me lightly on the lips. I pulled her to me before she could break away and held her, brushing my lips against her cheek and ear. She didn't struggle to get away. I finally had to release her when the bell rang. Does this mean there is hope?

I flipped the page and kept going...

Tuesday, 05-Nov-1985. *Lizzie was over to sew the bridesmaids' dresses tonight and I told her we were going to take ballroom dance lessons with Mrs. Gurnsey so we'd be able to dance at the wedding. She wasn't too upset that I had set it up without consulting her, but she took it in stride and thankfully agreed. Those lessons will be about the only time I get her undivided attention now that she's engrossed in preparations for the wedding, and it's the only time I feel like she can accept me touching her. I feel like I'm going to be a fixture at this wedding, not the groom. She barely gave me a moment's consideration tonight when she came over to work on the bridesmaids' dresses, albeit she came up to wish me good-bye before leaving. I was doing my nightly scripture study and I decided to pay her back for overlooking me by ignoring her. So she waltzed up to the bed and leaned over me with her lips pursed up and her tits practically hanging out of her top. If I looked at her now I was going to grab her and get her on my bed and rip her clothes off, which I know I'm not allowed to do, so I forced myself to stare at my scriptures even though I couldn't read a word with her female accoutrements still visible in my peripheral vision.*

I made a snide comment about how flaunting it may have worked for her lover, but it wouldn't work for me, which put her on the defensive. She told me to keep him out of it, but I didn't think he was out of it, seeing that he got her pregnant, and I made that point blindingly clear. I hadn't ever had it out with her about where she stood with regard to her ex – was she in love with him still or had she put it behind her? I'm not even sure I want to know the answer. But I asked her point-blank anyway, and she wouldn't give me a straight answer.

That seriously confirmed just how much I was treading in deep water. Not responding was an answer in itself: it meant she probably was still hankering after the guy. I wanted desperately to know if they'd made out more than once, or if she'd had a fling and immediately regretted it, or what exactly happened...

Those three words underlined. Not knowing was torturing Michael as much as keeping the secret was torturing me. But I had to keep it a secret.

...so I went ahead and asked. This time she did reply, and I didn't like what I heard. I couldn't believe they'd met in a bunch of places, a bunch of times, and she said she'd wanted it and enjoyed it. I was not impressed. I was downright scared – as if it were not bad enough to be getting married in my teens, I think I might be marrying a girl who's pregnant with someone else's kid, still in love with the kid's father, and nursing a broken heart.

Next, Lizzie asked me if I was going to obsess about her affair on our wedding night. I thought, I'm going to obsess on it until the day I die if she doesn't come clean and I don't find out who this loser is. I want to punch his lights out. I had told her before I didn't care who he was, but I was lying. I wanted to know, and bad. I'd made a deal with the devil when I agreed to let her keep his identity a secret from me. She accused me of not understanding her feelings, but I know well enough what it feels like to be left out in the cold! I couldn't take her getting in my face about it, so I grabbed her wrists and practically flung her to the floor. I cannot believe how she can make me so ferociously and blindingly mad. It took a few seconds for the both of us to comprehend that there were some lines we couldn't cross and that we had just made complete asses of ourselves.

She recovered faster than I did, making some smart-ass remark about our wedding night and I told her I was gonna find a way to shut her up when the time came (I think she had a pretty good idea what I meant).

What I really want to do is to find a way to make her want me like she wants him, whatever it takes. I'm seriously thinking I need to go look up some books in the library on how to take care of a woman in the bedroom. I would ask Dad, but he thinks I've already made it with Lizzie so there's no chance of getting advice from him. It's killing me that Lizzie knows more about sex than me.

My innuendos about our wedding night had the intended effect, though. They sent Lizzie running for the door. Now I'm cursing myself because I didn't want her to leave at all and she was (maybe) going to kiss me when she arrived and I made sure to drive her away. She's confused and upset because I've sent her a mixed message yet again and scared her off.

I don't know why I can't get this right.

I glanced at the alarm clock on Michael's side of the bed. Time was catching up with me and decided to skip some pages in the journal so I could fast forward to the day of our wedding. I couldn't believe Michael had consulted some kind of sex manual to figure out how to please me on our wedding night. That sly son-of-a-bitch. Yeah, sure I had more actual experience than him on our wedding night, but he had the benefit of expert advice. No wonder his hands were so steady when he was unbuttoning my dress.

But I shouldn't be complaining one little bit. I have to admit I like how he treats me in the bedroom. He is kind and gentle and loving. Probably more than I'll ever deserve.

Michael's Journal; December

Lizzie

I scanned forward, and found an entry dated on the morning of our wedding day.

Saturday, 14-Dec-1985. I woke up at seven today and I thought I'd better write down my thoughts. Forty years from now, when I'm old and grey, I might want to remember how I felt on the day I married Lizzie.

I went over to Jeremy's last night because I was so restless that I couldn't stay home. I wasn't having a stag party, but I needed to do something. I wanted someone to hang out with and that's the best man's job, as far as I know. We did what we usually did on Friday nights before Lizzie became my fiancée: played chess. Jeremy won with some wily moves because I wasn't concentrating on strategy like I usually did. He asked me what our church's position on sex before marriage was. I told him it was a big no-no, second only to the sin of murder. He thought the comparison to murder eccentric but didn't argue that chastity was outmoded as most of my other friends did. The Jewish faith also preached celibacy before marriage. Since he'd brought it up, I could only surmise that he was obliquely trying to find out if Lizzie and I were an item before the big day, or if we'd been saving ourselves for each other. Technically we hadn't jumped the gun, but no one was going to believe that fact in a few months, least of all Jeremy. He could do math; he was a chess whiz after all. I decided to leave him in the dark about Lizzie and me, though I'm assuming he thinks we are waiting for the big day.

He asked me about the ceremony and what we planned for our reception, and I told him the arrangements were mostly in the hands of Lizzie's mother, who needed a capacious wedding to impress her friends and show off her daughter. He said I wouldn't be so upset about throwing a big party to celebrate our marriage twenty years from now when I looked back, which reminded me of a comment Lizzie had made about pictures of our wedding. Jeremy wanted to know why I wasn't in favor of a glitzy wedding so I could show off to everyone that I'd captured the queen, but I didn't enlighten him. The only person I need to impress on our wedding day is Lizzie, and she is proving to be a hard sell.

It was late, nearly ten pm, when I snuck into Lizzie's place with the pearl necklace handed down from my great-grandfather. I hope she appreciates it; at least she seemed to. Then I got kicked out by her father and had to call my dad from a payphone to a get ride home. Dad must have known I was nervous, because he tried to be reassuring. He told me everything would work itself out in time, a comment I couldn't quite understand in light of the fact that Lizzie and I had told no one that the real father of the baby wasn't me.

Today, I seriously doubt I will have Lizzie's heart, even if I am going to possess her body. If I had the choice, I don't know what I'd choose. I'll take her body for now, I guess, but I want it all – body and soul.

I stopped reading Michael's journal to take time out to visit the bathroom. All was quiet in the living room. Sarah, Rachel, and Edward were in their rooms, and Alison had fallen asleep on the couch. Anne Kerry was nowhere in evidence. I crept back to our bedroom, desperate to read more.

Michael, you do have me, body and soul, I thought, and I must tell you as soon as you get home. Why has it taken me so long and why did I not see the light shining right in front of me? Forgive me if I hurt you, my love, I'll make it up to you.

Thursday, 19-Dec-1985. *I did not take this journal on our honeymoon. I wanted to let the experience happen, and then digest it, and record my impressions later. So here I go. Frankly at this point, I have no idea what to write.*

We stayed in a cottage on an isolated part of the northern California coast. The morning after the day I married Lizzie, I feel like everything is unraveling. Yes, she is beautiful beyond anything I imagined and I knew she wanted to please me that first night but I am afraid she's not ready for me, or anyone besides the bastard who got her pregnant. I guess I should say she's not ready for anyone "else."

I think I am being selfish about wanting to possess her so badly, but I can't stop myself. Almost like she expects it of me and will feel rejected if I don't pursue her so I'm in a Catch-22: damned if I do and damned if I don't.

As she walked up towards me on her father's arm in the cultural hall of our chapel yesterday in my mother's updated wedding gown, she looked so stunning I thought she was a princess in a fairytale. And yet she looked so fragile I thought she'd break if I touched her. There were dark circles under her eyes as if she hadn't slept well and her eyes seemed to be imploring me to help her keep going.

That's why I let her sleep as long as possible that first morning, after I spent most of the night retrieving the priceless pearls of my family's heirloom. Lizzie has no idea of its real worth and I don't think she deserves to wear it ever again.

I'm don't know if I can do this: being strong enough for the two of us. After the chapel wedding ceremony, when we were in the lineup, I thought she was going to faint or throw up but she held on. She can be a rock when she wants to be.

I was betting she hadn't eaten so I found her a plate of food as soon as I could break away. Then she rallied and I left her in

Jeremy's care while I told the DJ to play a song I thought she'd like to dance to, since I knew she liked Air Supply and it seemed appropriate for a wedding.

I really went to town on the rumba since we'd practiced it ad nauseam and I wanted to show her off and show her that I could take charge. I don't know what happened but there were all kinds of sparks between us, not the kind where we get mad at each other. It was more like challenge and play. I knew what it meant for me.

Despite the rapport that happened when we were dancing, by the time we got to the car we were already having a fight about Rachel and Jeremy. Jeremy is my best friend and a great guy. He wants to go to med school for all the right reasons. But when it comes to him and my sister dating – that's a disaster waiting to happen.

There are enough problems when two people of the same faith get together—take a look at Lizzie and me—without blending the complexities of two vastly different religions. Lizzie told me it's prejudiced of me to believe this. But honestly, I don't want Jeremy or Rachel to be hurt someday down the line. I'm hoping it's a high-school romance that will run its course. I am intending to not encourage them. Which, it seems, Lizzie obviously is. It's my parents' decision to make, which is to say my dad's, because he is not going to be happy about it. He's only inflexible about a few issues and one of them is dating outside our faith, so we'll see if Rachel, Jeremy, and Lizzie convince him otherwise.

Chastity before marriage is high up there on Dad's list of important principles, and he already thinks I've broken that law and hasn't evicted me from the household, so I guess my sister dating a non-member ought to be the least of my concerns.

Whatever... There we were, saying good-bye to Rachel, and Lizzie almost refused to get into the car. I was about ready to throw her in I was so miffed at her. We didn't talk for a while after that. I know Lizzie could not possibly be in love with me, which is both mind-numbingly crushing and heart-wrenchingly devastating. But that is all on me, and I'm gonna have to suck it up and take it. I thought that perhaps I had been too harsh with Lizzie (again), and I should be more sensitive to her feelings, so I tried to start a dialogue with her about her ex. I wanted her to put it into perspective and see that the affair was physical attraction at its worst. I would have expected her to hate the guy's guts after what he did, but I am convinced she is still stuck on him. I tried to explain that when you commit a sin, you can't expect to feel good about it. In fact, if you know it's wrong, at some point you're going to feel major guilt and major pain, like Alma the Younger when he realized the gospel was true. Part of what Lizzie is going through is feeling bad about what she did even though she denies it to me. She told me while we were dancing that she had the heart of the devil and I was just being deceived by a pretty face. I don't buy that. I told her, in all seriousness, she needed to work on the heart. She's so broken up over this guy (and I want to crack him in pieces for hurting her like this), she doesn't want to trust anyone.

I keep telling myself I need to give this whole marriage thing sometimes because we seem to be working out OK in the bedroom. If I'm wrong, then Lizzie's the best actress I know because there's some stuff that even she cannot fake. I can't see her marrying me to keep the baby or being so tender with me that first night if she wasn't trying to make progress towards a real relationship.

I probably shouldn't keep pointing out to her that she made the choice to be with this guy and she made the choice to break the law of chastity and now she will have to face the consequences. I want to slap her sometimes for being so impetuous and screwing up her life like this, but maybe that's part of what I love about her. She makes me think of Marianne in Jane Austen's Sense and Sensibility, which I was forced to study for English Lit two years ago.

Our conversation on the way up Stillwater Cove: somehow, we ended up in a 'Truth or Dare' challenge and I told her about my crush on Kathy Foster last year. I tried to tell her what she and her ex had going was lust not love, but she didn't get it. She said it felt the same, so they might as well be the same, which was tantamount to her admitting that she still had feelings for the bastard.

Then she managed to break the pearl necklace I gave her, and the pearls flew all over the car! Does she have any clue what this heirloom means to me and my family? I am so pissed off about it I can barely write these words. I mean, seriously, as precious and valuable as she knew this necklace is, and without a thought, she ripped it all apart. I'm beginning to think this marriage is headed in the same direction: broken into a gazillion bits like the pearl necklace.

To top it off, she started crying. I wished I hadn't pushed her that much and did kind of feel like a jerk for making her cry unhappy tears on her wedding day, so I told her I would somehow fix the necklace. I need to be more patient. I knowingly married a girl who was pregnant with another guy's baby from a passionate sexual liaison. I took this upon myself and am taking the lie with me. If the lie frustrates me, that is my fault.

I don't want to even think about our marriage being screwed up already, and knowing that Lizzie is still in love, or at least still in lust, with some bastard who left her high and dry. I don't know if I can bear it. I cannot handle her not being in love with me and wanting someone else.

I was hoping the nap Lizzie took on the drive would help because she has been looking exhausted, but I can't say her temper improved by the time we got to the cabin that first night. I tried not to react because I figured it was pre-wedding night nerves. I worked on the fire for a while hoping she'd settle down and took most of my formal wear off while she was in the bathroom, hoping to make it easier when the time came. She was taking a long time about undressing or whatever it was she was doing in bathroom, but I figured she was fixing herself up for our big moment or, more likely, buying time.

I wanted to start things off right so I remembered to have a bedtime prayer with her and hoped it would soothe her nerves, but the prayer did not have its intended effect. I was so stoked about being alone with her that I didn't feel nervous. It's easy when you're in love and you know you're getting the love of your life. I fear Lizzie is neither in love (at least, not with me) nor getting the guy she wants. I can only justify my actions by the fact that she agreed to marry me and she knew what she was signing up for, at least this part of it.

By the time I unpinned her veil, let down her hair (such fantastic hair!) and helped her out of her dress, she was visibly shaking. I almost felt sorry for her, but at the same time, she had been naked with that "other guy" in who knows how many times and places, so what's her problem?

I wanted to hold her at arm's length and look at her a while since I had never seen a grown woman naked, but I didn't want to make her any more uncomfortable than she already seemed to be. I helped get the dress off her and carefully set it on the second bed, while she stood with her back to me. She hadn't turned around by the time I came back to her, so I knew she was embarrassed about the next step. Thus it fell to me to turn her around and uncross her arms from her breasts, and then I took her right into bed.

Except I was unprepared for what happened next. This was supposed to be a magical moment on our wedding night and she was freaking crying and shaking and I had no idea what to do. All I could think of was to hold off on consummating the marriage until this outburst of emotion subsided. I kept telling myself patience is a virtue and she'll calm down eventually. I reminded myself she'd done this a whole bunch times before by her own account, so she knew what was coming and, shoot, she'd known me since kindergarten and had nothing to be afraid of. I can only surmise that she doesn't want me to see the real person behind the facade and making love to a woman is as close as a man can get to being inside another soul, other than his mother's womb.

I wish Lizzie could see the person I see inside her: the one who is caring and fun-loving and generous. Getting herself into this mess has made her defensive and angry and hurt, and it seems I'm gonna be the fall guy who bears the brunt of her bruised feelings. I am so not ready to fill that role.

Her tears were wet against my chest and all I could do was tell her, please don't cry, Bethie, please don't cry and I won't hurt you, when I should have told her I loved her. I couldn't, or wouldn't, say those three magic words because I believed then, as I do now, that Lizzie cannot possibly be in love with me and is likely in love with the jerk who got her pregnant. Frankly, I can only handle one broken heart at a time in this marriage. I am going to wait until she says "I love you" first, whenever that time comes, maybe never. I want to believe she does love me, or will love me at some level, or she wouldn't have agreed to this sham of a marriage. I kept holding her, waiting, waiting... until it didn't even look like this rocket was gonna launch and we both fell asleep.

When I woke up an hour or so later, the sheets next to me were empty and for a minute I panicked and thought Lizzie had abandoned this whole enterprise. She was only a few feet away, pacing the floor in the moonlight with a tragic expression on her face, and I watched her a long while, trying to assess her mood. I wanted to comfort her, so I invited her back into bed. Before she climbed in, as if she had read my mind, she dropped her gown and stood in front of me in the moonlight not wearing a stitch of clothing so I could finally look at her. She was some sight to behold, and I was aroused all over again.

She seemed calmer this time when she slid under the sheets and I put my arms around her while I practically begged her to let me make love to her. She looked at me with great mournful eyes and accepted me into her embrace. I knew it was up to me to take of her first, like the books said, so I sort of fumbled under the bedclothes and murmured about was this good or did she like it this way? I just had to pretend like I knew what the hell I was doing and she seemed to go with the flow, and suddenly I realized she was moving and responding to me in ways I'd never dreamed she would. Then it was my turn and that's when she called out, over and over, Michael, don't hurt me; Michael, don't hurt me, and I knew it wasn't about losing her virginity because that water was way downstream.

I should have told her how much I loved her right then and how overpowering and magical the union of our bodies was for me, how grateful I was for this moment and how much I wished she might feel the joy I felt to be in her arms. For all her claims that she is a miserable sinner, Lizzie is the sweetest, noblest soul for giving me the most sacred and finest provinces of herself.

My tears were falling all over Michael's words, but as he was using a ballpoint pen and the ink had dried months ago, his handwriting did not smudge. I was glad now that I hadn't rebuffed him during that second attempt to consummate our marriage, and that I'd promised him he would always be welcome in my arms. That was when a man felt a woman loved him, when she gave him physical intimacy. I had gone through the motions and spared Michael's heart.

There were, however, times when I could have behaved better, or been honest without being hurtful. I should not have danced with Jason at my wedding because I knew what that would do to me, and I should not have kissed Michael right in front of Jason to incite jealousy. I should not have dressed deliberately to entice Jason when we went to the Daltons for dinner. I should have told Michael who the baby's father was so we would be better prepared to deal with the social ramifications. I should have told Michael about my infatuation with Jason in a non-confrontational context, with the stated intention that I was working on getting over him rather than pining uselessly for a relationship that would never be and should never have been. I wondered how many times since Michael proposed that I had undertaken a course of action I should not have and had omitted the things that needed doing. I was filled with a terrible sense of my own worthlessness, despite the fact that Michael held me in such high regard and saw in me so much more than I saw in myself.

I wanted to read more, because as imperfect as I am, it was nice to know that someone as decent as Michael thought so highly of me. I certainly know Michael is no saint, but it longer matters. The entry for Thursday continued.

I think that morning started out all right because Lizzie invited me back to bed. I was not sure of her motives, because she knew I was all dressed for church and time to get there was getting seriously lacking. And I was bleary-eyed from lack of sleep after the "pearl hunt." I don't know if it was a challenge to find out what was more important to me, or a deliberate tease because she didn't expect me to take her up on it, which, of course, I didn't. I teased her right back when she forgot to take her clothes into the bathroom. I made her kiss me for her panties. I didn't respond to her lips because they were as luscious and tempting as ever, and I knew if I had, we wouldn't have made it to church – and we were sorely in need of all the heavenly help we could get, as events later in the day attest.

She managed to make to the car before my patience ran out and we attended a spiritual church service. But, on the way back to Stillwater Cove, despite the stunning beauty of the coastline, she was as gloomy as a rainy day. I couldn't seem to snap her out of it. I hoped she wasn't bummed out about being there with me, or our nocturnal activities, or something I said or did not say. I decided to take her on a walk after lunch although I really wanted to make love to her again. Given her despondent mood, I thought it unwise since she might have thought I was taking advantage of her.

Being in the redwood forest cheered her, and at that moment I didn't think she minded me kissing her, because she started acting like the fun-loving Lizzie I used to know. Only then she decided to play a horrible trick on me, and so we were at cross purposes again. She fell into the creek (she says by accident) while I was chasing her down the trail beside it, and when I came upon the spot where she went over the edge, I saw her lying face down in the water. I thought she was drowning or hit her head or something, and how in the hell was I going to explain to everyone that I'd let my wife die on our honeymoon? I think I yelled as I leaped in and got to her as fast as I could, only to find out that she wasn't in danger at all.

After I lifted her head out of the water and realized I'd been had, I was so mad I threw her back in again. Doesn't she know it would kill me if something happened to her? I found another way out so we wouldn't have to risk getting swept away in the current and marched her back to the cottage like a prisoner, just so she'd know how upset I was. I stripped us down because we were both freezing, rinsed out all our clothes in the bathroom, and took a shower, leaving her standing by the door in nothing but her underwear. That might have been the most jerkish thing I could have done. I should have taken care of her and got her in the shower first, but I was afraid I wouldn't be able to keep my hands off her and I was way too mad to think straight. Considering that we had talks in church just that morning about contention and overcoming anger, I completely failed to apply the gospel principles I know so well. I really should not let my ego get in the way of being nice to Lizzie, especially on our honeymoon. I need to remember she is only seventeen, she is pregnant, she does not really love me, and she is scared to death of me. Once in a while, she just has to act like a wild teenager instead of the woman she needs to become.

Oh, Lizzie, I married you for all the wrong reasons and to gratify my own desires, and I don't know why you're so good at pushing my buttons, but sometimes I wish you weren't.

Even if he didn't know it, Michael was a master at pushing my buttons, too. I wish he would have said what was on his mind instead of erecting walls between us. We were so busy protecting our feelings that we hadn't seen what was right in front of us. I vowed I wouldn't hide out from him anymore, even if he was going to hole up his feelings in the den of his mind. I went on reading; I was hooked.

Friday, 20-Dec-1985. *As unbelievable as it seems, Lizzie was the one who initiated overtures to make up after our adventures in the creek at Stillwater Cove! What a reunion it was when we made out in front of the fire. She is certainly full of surprises, my precious pearl. In the early hours of Monday morning, she woke up crying after a nightmare. She cuddled into me, and, once again, started the process, so we made love in the secret places of the night. She kept asking me to forgive her and I don't know* for the life of me why. She keeps saying she's not the wife she should be, and I say she is everything I want in a wife and more.

Tuesday, we went up to Sea Ranch for breakfast and walked along the cliffs. In the afternoon, we worked on a puzzle because it was raining again and ate dinner at a swanky restaurant. Wednesday, our last day alone together, arrived. When I awoke, Lizzie was still asleep. I snuggled up to her, enjoying the feel of her skin against mine. I wanted her, as usual, but on different terms. More than anything, I wished she would be like Sunday night after she fell in the creek and she'd say she wanted me. Technically, she hadn't actually said it, but she'd certainly implied it. She was not going to accept any romantic gestures that morning, so I turned the tables on her and headed for the bathroom to make preparations to leave. I guess that annoyed her. I still wanted her just the same, so I settled for second best and watched her get dressed in the bathroom, which annoyed her even more. I should have backed down and admitted to her I wanted to take her back to bed but I wasn't going to step out of the corner I'd painted myself into. My stubbornness got me precisely nothing.

Bully for me.

Lizzie was real quiet on the way home, and that started me worrying about how we were going to do this for the next twenty years. Luckily, we had a wonderful surprise awaiting us: my parents splurged on a new double bed for us complete with sheets and comforter. I'm not so sure Lizzie was as thrilled about it as me, but we did lie down on the bed later in the afternoon when everyone left us alone.

By that time, I had a major burn for my wife but she wanted to take a nap. I guess sex means something different to the two of us: she is my one and only to me; I am just the next guy to her and her ticket out of being a single mother. Somehow, I managed to persuade her to indulge me, and I happily indulged her. I wish Lizzie could know what this means to me. I think I'm winning her around, but she is still going to say "I love you" first.

I do have to admit, Michael does take care of me most of the time. Maybe all the time where sex is concerned. And, no, Michael is not just rescuing me from being a single mother: he has rescued me from everything!

Sunday, 22-Dec-1985. *It is almost Christmas. I've been working too many hours at the garden store, to save up as much money for Lizzie and our future as possible. Her parents gave us five hundred dollars as a wedding present and Lizzie impressed me by entrusting me with the money.*

Although Lizzie has been raised with everything money can buy, I bet she would have preferred a simple wedding if her mom hadn't been so stuck on showing off her daughter. Lizzie has moved her stuff in, and boy, does she have a lot of gorgeous clothes! My sisters never had duds this nice. She surprised me by giving Rachel and Sarah outfits for helping her, which is pretty sweet of her. Plus she's doing my Saturday chores since I'm putting in so many hours at the store. Lizzie is awfully tolerant of my sister Alison, who is practically glued to her side when I'm not around, and she's going to take care of ironing my Sunday shirts and doing my laundry with hers. There are a lot of great things about having a wife, especially one who wants to please me like Lizzie. That's what I'm telling myself now—because Lizzie and I had a real blowout last night.

Right now, Lizzie has disappeared into the bathroom and Alison is sleeping in our bed next to me. Last night when I got home late from work, I made the mistake of telling Lizzie I couldn't wait for us to have our own kids. I do think of this baby as mine in a spiritual sense, and everyone else is going to think he or she is mine in the biological sense, but I do want Lizzie to have my kids someday, too. She flat out told me she wasn't having any kids with me and was going back to school when her baby starts Kindergarten! So I stupidly told her she could go sleep somewhere else; she said that was fine with her and marched right out the door.

At which point, Alison showed up. Alison has nightmares from time to time, and she used to end up in my parents' bed, but I guess she's adopted Lizzie as her new mom and we couldn't very well turn her out, even if we were in the middle of a fight. Anyhow, Alison made us sort of make up, which just goes to show that Jesus was right when He said we each needed to learn to become like little children, humble and submissive. Lizzie and Alison cuddled up in bed while I went down the hall to brush my teeth, and Lizzie made sure to stick Alison in the middle, so she was between us. When I returned, I told Lizzie there was no way Alison was going to sleep between us, because I know Dad would expect me to make peace with my wife and I shouldn't let the sun go down on my wrath and all that. I put my arm around Lizzie and told her I loved her. I doubt she believed I was being sincere, not after our hurtful interchange earlier. She said, 'Ditto.' God, I hope she means it.

Who does Michael think he is, being so superior? The kid took on a pregnant woman, knowing he was going to have to accept the child as his. Blindsiding me with that demand was totally uncalled for! He knew what my goals and aspirations were! What a jerk!

Sunday evening, 22-Dec-1985. *Lizzie and I have made up. When we met with Bishop Dalton this morning, Lizzie saw reason. I didn't mean to push Lizzie about having kids; I was seriously talking someday, sometime in the future. I didn't mean tomorrow and I didn't mean never. Who the hell does she think she is talking about going back to school and getting a job instead of staying home to raise our family? She can be such a hypocritical diva!*

At least Bishop Dalton can get through to her. He got her to admit that staying home was the best thing a mother could do for her kids. He made her see that since she'd decided to keep the baby, that's what she needed to do. What really surprised me is that Lizzie admitted she'd do anything to make me happy, and she didn't put any conditions on it like she usually does. She started crying and I asked her forgiveness, which she tendered. Then I crouched down on the floor in front of her and whispered that I wouldn't make her do anything she didn't want to do, ever, and she said she was sorry for not considering my feelings and would I please be patient with her? How is it I ended up feeling like a jerk again?

I hoped Michael's patience hadn't run out now.

Michael's Journal; January

Lizzie

I flipped forward through the first couple of weeks of January. There were a number of entries about working with his father, his disappointment about not going on a mission or attending college, his impressions of a convert baptism in early January, and notes about his home teaching visits. He invariably sang my praises, but the entries were sparse. He hadn't had much time for journal writing since he'd acquired a wife, I thought. I found a long entry for January 19.

Sunday, 19-Jan-1986. *Last night Lizzie and I had our first fight in almost a month, and I found out from Rachel that Lizzie is in a major tailspin. Yesterday morning, Lizzie asked me for forty bucks for a haircut, which I think is entirely excessive when a normal one costs less than fifteen, but Lizzie has been accustomed to living in a higher economic sphere. I told her no, she ought to change hair stylists and she said fine, she'd just earn extra money babysitting, and walked out the door to go down to breakfast. I thought she would get over it, and I gave her a twenty-dollar bill after breakfast. But by yesterday afternoon, the issue had re-emerged when Rachel took a phone call from Lizzie to say she wouldn't be home until late because she was babysitting somewhere. That made me really mad, but I wasn't letting on to anyone. I was saving all of it for later when Lizzie got home. I decided to wait up for her.*

In the meantime, since Lizzie had skipped out on our weekly date, Rachel and I went to Jeremy's to watch a movie. I would have preferred to go to Jeremy's without Rachel if Lizzie wasn't going to be there, but somehow Rachel conned my parents into letting her tag along, so Jeremy and I missed our chess game and watched The Natural *instead. I felt like the odd man out because Jeremy and Rachel were all over one another, and it would have been better if Lizzie had been there to keep me company. Seeing them snuggling up on the couch was making me madder and madder that Lizzie had skipped out on our date night.*

I wasn't prepared for what happened next. On the way home in Dad's Suburban, Rachel told me she'd found Lizzie downstairs on the couch crying in the middle of the night. And I don't think this is the first time it has happened; it's the first time someone has caught Lizzie in the act. Now I felt like a real louse. My wife's miserable as hell, and I'm in the middle of a big money row with her, and I find out she's depressed in a major way. Probably something I did, but I'm so crass I don't know it. All the way home, I was trying to decide which subject I should broach first. I didn't know whether to feel angry or sad.

I waited up for Lizzie in the dark on our living room couch and confronted her the minute she walked in. She suggested we take it to our room. Fine with me. I knew what she'd been doing: earning the difference between what I thought necessary for a haircut and what she considered necessary. I had already decided the hell with it, there were some battles a guy couldn't win and this was one of them, so I gave her the amount she needed (although she probably didn't need it anymore) as well as the key to the money box. I don't care about the money; I just want Lizzie to be happy. We can stay with Mom and Dad as long as we want. What really bothers me is that she's up in the middle of the night bawling her eyes out and she won't talk to me about what's bugging her. When I asked her, she said it wasn't me, or the baby, or my family. That means it must be that jerk who screwed her last fall, and I don't know if I want to go there. I made her promise she'd wake me up anytime she's feeling blue and that we'd talk to Bishop Dalton about this (which we did, today). I would do anything to make Lizzie happy, anything. I'd leave her if that's what she wants. I don't know why it happened last night but I ended up making love to her, despite my misgivings. I know that something happened between, but I have no idea what it is. I don't know if she's using me to get over him, or I'm using her, or we're using each other. I don't know if I can go on loving her with this uncertainty or if she can go on pretending to love me when she doesn't or if she's falling in love with me in spite of herself. I don't know how to love her – should I stop trying or should I keep trying or should I pretend everything is OK and someday it will be?

After our meeting with Bishop Dalton today, I am more hopeful. He told us to share what makes us happy each day. Waking up with Lizzie and falling asleep with her is what does it for me. Nothing else matters. I can endure anything as long as Lizzie is there to share it with me. She talked to Bishop Dalton alone for a while and seemed more positive afterwards, so I think she made some progress, whatever it was. Then Bishop Dalton said Lizzie had been telling him what a saint I was, and I started laughing because I couldn't believe it possible that Lizzie, knowing me as she did, hadn't seen through my façade and didn't know that I was no better than her, just better at hiding my faults. Lizzie is the saint for agreeing to be my wife for her baby's sake and for pretending to be happy when she isn't and for taking care of me like she does. I didn't know what she was up to, so I quizzed her on the way into Sacrament meeting, but she wasn't letting on. Except that she thanked me for last night, and I thought she meant me giving her the key to the money box, but she told me that I had it all wrong. Does this mean I am getting it right? What game is Lizzie are you playing? When she holds the key to my heart, why does she hesitate to open the lock?

Michael's Journal: Discovered!

Lizzie

I was so moved by what I had just read that a river welled up in my eyes and poured down my cheeks. I sat for a long time with my head bent in my hands, letting my tears fall onto the pages of Michael's journal, heedless of the steady fading of the light and the minutes drifting down through time. I don't know how long it took for me to become aware of a presence in the room behind me. It could only be one person. My heart felt like it was a stone that someone had taken a hammer to and smashed into a thousand pieces when I realized Michael was standing silently, watching me. I did not know how long he had been there. I turned around slowly, keeping my eyes on the floor.

"Lizzie, what are you doing?" His voice was barely recognizable.

I couldn't answer him. There were stones choking my lungs.

"Is that my journal you're reading?"

I couldn't breathe. He was going to kill me.

"Look at me when I'm talking to you!" he yelled.

My eyes swept up to his face and, seeing his expression, my whole body shook. He was as white as the paint on the walls, tight-lipped and seething. The cougar looked ready to tear me into shreds, slowly, so that the drawn-out tearing of my limbs would maximize my suffering. If I were a deer, this is what I would feel right after the cougar had brought me down and I knew I was going to be torn apart, limb from limb.

"You don't understand," I whimpered.

"What don't I understand?" he demanded.

"It's not what you think."

"Really."

He moved a few steps closer.

"What have you read?"

Does the deer look in the eyes of the cougar as she feels the razor cut of his teeth in her neck?

"The stuff about us."

"What stuff, Lizzie?"

The claws were unsheathed now, ready to slash and rip.

"Most of what you wrote since you proposed to me," I confessed weakly.

"You deceitful, despicable, dishonorable bitch!"

Slash one.

"You low-life, lying, two-timing, faunching fake!"

Slash two.

"You're gonna pay for this." He looked towards the bed deliberately. "Let's see. You keep your journal on the nightstand, don't you?"

My blood began spilling from my wounds onto the ground.

"Don't go there, Michael," I begged.

He spun around. I looked into the jaws of the cougar and it was terrifying.

"We're sharing everything with each other now, aren't we? All our shameful, dirty secrets. Lacking the prerequisite skill and knowledge for *communicating* with me and recklessly disregarding any standards for truth and honesty, you decided to conduct your own sordid little investigation. I think I'm entirely within my rights to review *your* thoughts about us, too, don't you think?"

Slash three.

"Please, don't hurt me like this," I pleaded.

"Hurt you? What would you know about pain, except how to inflict it?"

He had his hands on my journal now. He bounced onto the bed and began flicking through the pages.

"D'you read what I wrote about our wedding night?"

"Yes, it was beaut –"

"Shut up, Lizzie. Let's see what you wrote. I'll read it to you."

"No!" I shrieked. The knowledge would destroy him. He must not find out what I had written about Jason on our wedding day. I couldn't allow him to see the dark places in my heart where I had tendered my lust for Jason. I didn't love Jason anymore – there was no reason for Michael to know that I had once wanted Jason when Michael made love to me.

I love you, Michael, I love you, I intoned in my head, don't do this.

My knees were shaking so badly I couldn't stand up, so I crawled to the bed. Michael was still searching for the right page. He shifted over to my side of the bed and scrambled to a standing position, holding my journal above his head.

"Come 'n' get it, Lizzie," he mocked.

My adrenaline finally kicked in and I moved with surprising swiftness for a lumpy pregnant woman. I leaped onto the bed and grabbed him by the shoulder, trying to pull down his arm. I got a hand on the journal – I had it now, I thought. I pulled. Michael and I were in a tug-of-war. Then, with a vigorous jerk of his hand, Michael wrenched the journal away from me. The force of his action sent me flying backwards through the air. I hit the left side of my head on Michael's desk with a nauseating thud. Blood began to flow.

The cougar sliced the air with a bone-chilling scream as the deer lay with its neck broken in a pool of blood. They disappeared in a veil of purple rain before everything went black.

The Accident

Lizzie

I am going to throw up again, dammit, I thought. Why do I still have morning sickness?

"Lizzie, Lizzie, can you hear me?"

Who was that? Michael or his father? I tried to speak but I couldn't get any words out.

"I've killed her Dad, I've killed her." That was Michael. There was something I needed to tell him – what was it? Why were my thoughts trudging as slowly through my head as a person wading through a muddy swamp?

"She's not dead, son. Anne, if he can't help, get him out of here."

"I'm not leaving," Michael protested.

What was I supposed to tell him? I asked myself again.

"Michael, dear, get a blanket off the bed," said Mama Anne.

"Do you know where her health insurance card is, Michael?" asked Patrick.

"Yeah, Dad."

"Get it and stick it in your pocket."

I coughed and choked and my stomach emptied its insides. Patrick held my hair while I retched.

Then the pain hit.

I thought someone was raining an avalanche of rocks down on my head. I groaned. My hair felt sticky on the left side of my head. It must be sweat.

"Lizzie, can you hear me?"

I tried to say 'yes,' but it came out more like a gurgle.

"Good girl."

"She's got an awful gash on the left side of her head," came Mama Anne's voice.

I wanted to say 'it hurts,' which only came out as another gurgle.

My voice was a whisper. A whisper coming from a long, dark tunnel.

"Anne, go downstairs and get Lizzie's car started. I think it will be easier to get her into her own car than the Suburban. Michael, we're gonna lift her up and I want you to support her neck, just in case."

Just in case of what, I wanted to know. I heard the jingle of keys.

"Let's see if she can feel her fingers and toes, Dad," suggested Michael.

"You do it," answered Patrick.

Someone pinched the toes on both feet hard and I winced. That must be Michael. Next he squeezed the fingers of my left hand, then the right.

"Ooush," I croaked.

"She seems OK," said Michael.

I have to tell you something, I need to tell you now. Don't go away.

"She's cold, son. Got that blanket?"

I wanted to say, I'm not cold, I'm burning up. My head is wet with sweat. I don't want a blanket. But I couldn't get my tongue around the words. And why couldn't I remember what I was supposed to tell Michael?

Michael placed the blanket over me, and I had no power to throw it off. The rocks raining down on my head hurt even more.

"It hurts," I wailed, at last finding I could pronounce two words intelligibly. Then I realized tears were streaming down my cheeks. I had no idea why I was crying.

The room came suddenly into focus, went blurry, then swam into focus again. Michael was wiping my tears with a tissue, looking so scared I thought he would start crying too.

"Bethie, my precious pearl, you're gonna be okay," he whispered.

What was I supposed to tell him? I asked myself again. I was pacing up and down the walls of my mind trying to figure it out, but the hammering of the rocks was so intense I couldn't fix on it. The tears kept pouring out of my eyes in a silent stream.

"Lizzie, we're gonna take you down to the car in minute or so, all right?" said Patrick gently.

I swung my eyes in the direction of his voice and had to concentrate to make him stay in focus.

"Think you can stand up, with some help?" he went on.

I nodded, feeling my head swim as I did so, and I bent up my knees. Patrick put an arm under my right shoulder and Michael under the left.

"Is the baby going to be okay?" I asked tremulously.

"I'm sure we'll find that out when you get to the hospital," answered Patrick. "On three, Michael."

I took a deep breath.

"One, two, three!"

I was encouraged to discover my legs worked, and it was just my head that was messed up. I felt so dizzy I didn't think I could stand without help. We started for the door. It looked a long way away to me, but we were through it and down the stairs in moments.

"Rachel, would you please get some ice from the freezer in a bag and wrap it in a dish towel?" said Patrick. "On the double. Sarah, please bring the blanket on the floor in Michael's room down to Lizzie's car."

"What's happened to Lizzie?" I heard Alison say. "Her head's bleeding."

"She's gonna be all right, Alison. She fell and hurt her head," Patrick responded.

"Who's gonna watch us?" came Edward's voice.

"Rachel," said Patrick.

A shadow that was Rachel flashed across my line of sight and we kept walking across the living room, through the front door, down the driveway and out to my car. The light outside felt so bright it hurt.

"How you holding up, Lizzie?" asked Michael.

I had to concentrate to form the words, but it was getting easier now.

"Fine," I answered. "Head hurts."

What was I supposed to tell him? I asked myself again.

"Let's get her in the back seat, Michael. You sit on one side and I'll have Sarah sit on the other."

The rear door was already open. They helped me carefully into the back seat. By this time I was feeling less groggy so I was able to assist.

"Here's Rachel with the ice pack," said Michael, scooting in next to me.

He placed it against the left side of my head and the cold felt as painful as the pounding of the rocks on my head. I still couldn't remember what I wanted to tell him, and I gave up trying.

"That hurts," I whined.

"Sorry, sweetheart, it'll help stop the swelling," assured Michael.

I wasn't in a position to contest him. Sarah opened the door on the opposite side and threw a blanket over me. Then she slid in next to me on my right, and she and Michael adjusted the blanket. She slammed the door and my head rattled. She took my hands in hers.

"Your hands feel cold, sis," she said softly.

"I'm okay. It's only my head."

I leaned back against the seat and closed my eyes, but it seemed to intensify the pain and make my head spin like I was on a roller coaster, so I opened them again. Mama Anne climbed into the front seat and Patrick settled himself behind the steering wheel.

"Everyone got their seat belts on?" he asked, looking backward over his shoulder at the three of us squashed into the rear of the Nissan.

"There are only two belts back here," announced Michael.

"Forget mine," I offered. "I'm screwed up already."

Patrick Kerry gave me an ironic smile. Sarah and Michael belted themselves in and Patrick Kerry pulled away from the curb.

"What happened, Michael?" asked Sarah.

"We were fighting over Lizzie's journal," he answered, which did little more than confuse Sarah.

"You were reading her journal?" Sarah continued.

"No, she was reading *my* journal."

"I don't get it."

"I came home and found her reading my journal, so I decided to take a look at hers."

"Wait a minute – she was reading your journal – without your permission?"

At least they now knew me for the rat I was, I thought. I wished they'd throw me out of the car so I could put an end to this misery.

"Yes, I was," I added, as if to reemphasize Michael's point.

"Shoot, Lizzie, don't you know any better?" she asked me, nudging me in the ribs.

I leaned my head back against the seat wearily and my field of view fluttered like a mirage.

"No, I don't," I said defensively.

I wondered that Anne and Patrick hadn't inserted their own commentary into our interchange. I was sure they were listening in.

"Let's not talk about who was reading what journal and why, Sarah," said Michael tightly.

"Lizzie's in no shape to talk. What happened is that we were both standing on the bed with our hands on her journal in a tug-of-war – and I won. She went flying and smacked her head on the desk. Got it?"

"Sure, Michael," Sarah said soberly.

"I didn't hit her, Dad, I swear it," added Michael, loudly enough so his parents could both hear.

"I know that, son," replied Patrick. "Let's concentrate on getting Lizzie taken care of and the rest we'll figure out later."

The car made another turn and I saw a sign for the hospital. I hoped they dispensed strong pain meds, but I doubted I would get anything because I was pregnant. I hoped the baby was OK, even though I'd wished him or her dead five months ago.

"I'm so sorry for what happened," whispered Michael to me. "Please forgive me."

"Not your fault," I replied softly. "I wish you could make my head stop hurting."

I wished for a lot of things: that I had never fallen in love with Jason Dalton, that I wasn't expecting a baby, that I hadn't read Michael's journal, but mostly I wished Michael would put his arms around me and tell me he could forgive me for violating his most sacred boundaries.

At the Hospital

Lizzie

The car stopped at the entrance to Emergency. Mama Anne leaped out and disappeared inside to fetch a wheelchair. I wanted to protest that I was perfectly capable of walking, but I couldn't be sure of it.

"Michael, you despise me now, don't you?" I asked him, under my breath so that Sarah wouldn't hear. He knew exactly what I was referring to.

"No, Lizzie."

"You're never gonna forgive me for reading your journal, are you?"

"Here's Mom," he said, ignoring my question, as Anne emerged pushing a wheelchair. She had a small hospital blanket draped over one arm. "Let's get you out of the car, Lizzie."

Michael opened the door, set aside the blanket from our bed, and helped me out of the car and into the wheelchair. Anne laid the hospital blanket over me because I was visibly shivering, and began wheeling me into the Emergency Room, followed by Michael. Patrick drove away with Sarah to park my car.

"I'll speak to Admissions, Michael. Give me Lizzie's insurance card, please. You sit with her."

Michael fished my credit card-sized medical identification card out of the pocket of his jeans and handed it to her.

"Tell them she can't take Vicodin.Remember when she broke her arm when she was twelve? She doesn't need anything that's gonna make her throw up."

"Okay, just take her over there and I'll be right back. She'll have to sign a bunch of paperwork."

"Remember to tell them she's pregnant."

"I know, Michael," Anne reassured him.

Michael pushed me across the waiting area and sat down facing me with his elbows on his knees.

"Why won't you talk to me?" I asked. His face was scrunched up as though he were mulling over a problem.

"This isn't the time, Lizzie." He looked around the waiting room and then in the direction of the admissions desk, avoiding my gaze.

"I am truly sorry," I added meekly.

"I think we both know you're feeling the sorrowing of the damned and not the sorrowing of the truly penitent right now," he said menacingly.

I wanted desperately to tell him that he was wrong, but one of the office staff interrupted us with paperwork for me to sign. I scribbled my signature half a dozen times and handed the paperwork back to the woman. Then a man in blue scrubs came out of the double doors leading to the innards of Emergency Department, and indicated that I should go with him. His name tag read "Dan." He spun the wheelchair around and I was whisked away through the double doors before I could remember what I had been meaning to tell Michael. Then it hit me as solidly as an ice block and I cursed myself for not being able to remember. I love you, Michael; that's what I had been meaning to say.

I was transferred to a rollaway bed and the attending physician immediately placed some kind of clamps along both sides of the gash on my head to stem the blood flow. The physician then drew a small blood sample from the vein in my left arm and sent it off stat for analysis. They were worried about blood loss, especially as I was obviously pregnant.

The pressure from the clamps made my head hurt even more, but they wouldn't give me any pain meds because of the pregnancy. After attending to the immediate medical concerns, the physician took a detailed medical history and account of the accident.

I was not quite sure they understood my explanation about what had caused the gash on my head, but they told me I was going to need stitches and they would clean up the wound first. They took my vitals, asked me how bad the pain was on a scale of one to ten and how long I had been unconscious (which I didn't know), shone a small flashlight into each eye and evaluated my reflexes. They checked the baby's heartbeat, found it to be normal, and asked me if I wanted to listen, but I declined. It didn't take a medical genius to tell me what I already suspected: I most likely had a concussion, and would need a couple of days rest, but they wanted to keep me in the hospital overnight for observation. Dan hooked up an IV. They were debating whether or not to send me for a CT scan, and decided it would be safer to keep me overnight for observation because of potential risks to the baby. It was a good thing they didn't know my father was an attorney, because any hint of legal action would be sure to motivate them to conduct a battery of further tests as proof that they had considered every medical angle. The doctor, who introduced himself as "Dr. Teague," also informed me that the other danger was a hematoma, bleeding into the skull that could put pressure on the brain and the brain stem, but since I had been bleeding profusely at the site of injury, it was unlikely. I was then left with a female aide who didn't look much older than me to help me undress and put on a hospital gown. She told me in an accent with soft Hispanic inflections that the team would be back to attend to me.

It wasn't long before Dr. Teague and Dan returned. Dr. Teague said, "You should feel all right in a day or so."

He was in his mid-thirties, had eyes the color of blue Kool-Aid, hair clipped close to his head in a crew-cut, and looked as if he'd just stepped out of a military hospital. I must have looked unconvinced. He went on, "Post-concussive syndrome occurs in about ten percent of head injuries and yours doesn't look too severe, other than that nasty gash on the head. Hit the edge of a desk, you said?"

"Right," I said forlornly. I stared at my fingernails, realized I'd broken a couple in the fall, and wondered if I dared lay out the cash at the manicurist to get them fixed.

"We'll shave the hair around the wound, wash it up with Betadine scrub, give you a local anesthetic, and put in some stitches. You're not allergic to lidocaine, are you?"

I finally came out of my daze, whipping my head up. "You're gonna mess up my hair? No way!"

"Just the area around the cut," he responded encouragingly, looking up from the clip board where he'd been scribbling notes that were indecipherable to my untrained eye.

"No!" My voice sounded loud, even to me, almost as loud as the pounding in my head.

"Look, Elizabeth, this is routine. Your hair will grow back."

"It's not fair," I moaned, putting my head in my hands and beginning to cry.

"Dan," he said, addressing his assistant, "why don't you go talk to the husband and get him in here? We'll leave you alone for few moments, Elizabeth, all right?"

"It's Lizzie," I snapped.

"Yes, of course, Lizzie," Dr. Teague responded, completely unfazed by my outburst. "I'm sorry you have to go through this, I really am, especially in your condition."

I stared at my belly in dismay. Dr. Teague squeezed my hand, but his gesture did little to comfort me. I didn't fit into any of my clothes because I was pregnant and now my hair was going to look a fright for a very long time. I wanted to rip out my IV and disappear into the labyrinth of hospital corridors, but I didn't think I would be able to stay on my feet. Dr. Teague and Dan pulled the drapes shut and left me to myself. I went on crying quietly until I heard voices approaching. I was glad my father wasn't here to witness my ridiculous tears.

"I'll talk to her, just gimme a minute," said Michael.

"She's pretty upset." That was Dan.

"That's normal for Lizzie."

"You want to stay while we sew her up?" came Dr. Teague's voice.

"Sure."

Just so you can witness me being completely and utterly miserable and enjoy it, I wouldn't doubt, I thought. But being angry had its advantages – it had stemmed my flood of tears. I wiped my cheek dry with the back of the hand not sporting the IV and watched the solution dripping inexorably into my veins.

Michael parted the curtain and gave me a sympathetic smile. "Hello, my precious pearl. How are you feeling?"

"Been better," I said sullenly, looking away.

He pulled a chair up to the bed and took my hand. "I know this is a bummer, but they need to clean up the cut and put in some stitches."

"They're gonna screw up my hair," I mumbled.

Michael sighed. "I know, but you'll still look beautiful to me, honey."

He would be the only one, I thought.

"C'mon Lizzie, let's get it over with. Please cooperate – for my sake."

Michael did know how to exploit my weaknesses. He ought to be ripping my heart out for reading his journal, but he wasn't. He was probably saving that for later.

"I'm sorry they have to do this," he added.

He was not half as sorry as I was, I thought. He lifted up my hand, leaned his elbows on the sheets of the bed, and kissed the palm. My skin sizzled where his lips had touched it, and a shot of pain zapped through my head like a shooting star. I wished I didn't want to make it up to him so badly.

"Tell them they can start, then," I said reluctantly.

"I'll stay while they're doing it."

I wasn't sure I wanted him to stay, but I had no strength for arguing. I felt brutally tired and wished I could fall asleep so the hammering on my head would stop. Michael disappeared behind the curtain and came back with the medical team and Dr. Teague. They rolled up a tray with a variety of instruments that I thought it would be inadvisable to scrutinize too closely, propped me up on the pillows, and began prepping the wound for suturing. Michael stood at the head of the bed out of my line of sight, stroking my arm. I grimaced as they held my hair out for the razor and I felt strands falling away under its blade. Michael squeezed my arm and I told myself that tears were weakness, as two of them rolled out of my eyes.

"I'll be injecting a few cc's of lidocaine around the wound, we'll wash it up and then I will put in some sutures," said Dr. Teague, eyeing a small needle. "It will sting just like a shot, you'll feel some pressure – and then nothing."

I wanted to feel nothing, nothing at all. I wanted to be as blank as the white sheet covering my legs.

"Are you ready?" he asked, hovering like a bee about to inject its stinger.

"Sure," I responded. He focused a bright light on a metal swivel to the left side of my head and I closed my eyes against the glare. The needle stung in multiple places as he injected the painkiller into several sites around the wound and then all sensation on my scalp went dead as the anesthetic took effect. It took a few minutes to wash the wound before they were ready to proceed with the sutures.

"It looks clean," remarked the doctor, leaning in for a closer inspection. To his assistant, he said, "I'll be removing the clips as we go, Dan."

Dan handed him some sort of needle with black cord, and Dr. Teague went to work on sewing me up, which didn't take long.

"Eighteen stitches, Lizzie, one for every year of your life," he said triumphantly. "You'll want to get these out in seven to ten days. How are you feeling?"

"OK," I said glumly.

"You'll want to watch for any swelling at the site of the sutures and if you have a fever over one hundred, then you'll want to see your regular MD right away. Cheer up, young lady, you'll be out of here tomorrow. Dan will give you and your husband some written instructions and finish up while we arrange to admit you for the night."

Dan began the work of bandaging my head, which was still throbbing miserably. He also brought me a glass of milk and some extra-strength Tylenol.

"It ain't much, kiddo, but it's the best we can do for you in your current condition," he said, trying to cheer me.

Michael had been as patient as the desert waiting for rain through all the medical procedures and hadn't griped once about missing Sunday dinner or the dread subject of his journal, but finally he spoke up and said he thought it best if the rest of the Kerry family waited to see me until I came home, and he really should be going. He'd already called my parents and they were on their way over. I didn't take comfort from this news.

I wanted to tell him I hated him for what had happened, but my injury wasn't his fault and I didn't hate him at all. I was hopelessly afraid he'd never forgive me for perusing his journal and violating his trust, but in the pain and confusion of the accident, I couldn't bring myself to tell him that, somewhere between our honeymoon and our latest confrontation, I had fallen completely and desperately in love with him and I didn't think I could stand being rejected a second time.

It must have been around seven-thirty pm by the time I was wheeled into a private room, apparently arranged by my father who couldn't handle a pregnant daughter but whose sympathies did extend to daughters who'd split their heads open, and I promptly fell asleep despite the dull throb in my head. I awoke to find my mother sitting next to me. She looked anxious and tired.

"Lizzie, you're awake," she said.

"Mom, what are you doing here?" I asked.

"Family can stay until nine pm, so I thought I'd wait in case you woke up. How's your head, sweetheart?" Visiting the sick was one of the things my mother did best, along with organizing wedding receptions, Relief Society socials, and Elders Quorum progressive dinners.

"Improving," I said, managing a smile. I felt only a dreary ache, heavy as a cement block, which matched the crushing ache I was developing to see Michael again, even if he did think of me as a "dishonorable bitch." I couldn't remember the other eloquent adjectives he'd used to describe me after his fury at finding me pages deep into his journal, but I was sure they were all well deserved.

"Your father's pacing the hallways," added Mom. At least he wasn't pacing this room, I thought. "He told the doctor he wants the police to investigate."

"What?" I asked, incredulous. I felt my faculties returning. "It was an accident, Mom. You don't think Michael hit me, do you?"

"No, dear, but you know your father, always looking for some legal angle," she said.

"We were fighting over a journal," I went on, by way of explanation. She stared at me, nonplussed. "I had hold of one side and he had the other – he yanked it out of my grasp, then I slipped and hit the desk. End of story."

"What were you doing playing tug-of-war over a journal?"

"Mom, let's not get into it. A minor disagreement, that's all." could still lie with the best of them when it came to my mother.

"Your hair's going to be a sight, I imagine," she said, fingering a strand of hair on my shoulder.

"I don't need to be reminded I'm gonna look like a freak, Mom."

"We'll figure a way to fix it up, sweetheart."

"Thanks, Mom."

"Anything I can do for you?" she asked.

"I broke a couple of my nails, so it would be great if we could go to the manicurist together." Mom didn't skip a beat because, of course, she knew I wanted her to pay for me, but she was that kind of mother. "And can you please call Michael's house and tell him.... Oh, tell him... I'm feeling better."

That wasn't what I wanted to tell him at all, but I couldn't have my mother convey the message he needed to hear.

"You've got a phone – call him yourself," she suggested, indicating the table to the right of my bed. "I'll be going now, honey. I hope you feel better soon."

I stared at the nightstand and noticed not only the phone but two large flower arrangements. My mind was fuzzy at the edges, like watercolor paint petering out at the edges of a drawing. "Who sent those?"

"The pink and yellow arrangement is from us. I don't know who sent the other one."

"Thanks, Mom. Tell Dad thanks as well." She kissed me good-bye and sailed out.

I stared at the second arrangement of white lilies and burgundy roses interspersed with baby's breath, a replica of the bouquet I'd held on my wedding day, and I knew exactly who had sent them. I looked for a card and found one. It read, "See what happens when you let your heart rule your head. I shouldn't have called you all those names. I'm sorry," followed by the outline of a heart about the letter "M." I dialed the Kerry house and Patrick answered.

"Hey, Lizzie. Feeling better?"

"Lots," I said. "Can I talk to Michael, please?"

"Here's the man himself."

I heard the phone being handed off and Michael asked, "How's my baby?"

"Which one?" I countered. I heard him chuckle.

"You're sounding chipper."

"Sore head, but I'm better. At least I know what I gotta do to get flowers from my husband – and thanks."

"You're welcome."

"I can't remember all the names, but I'm sure I deserved them."

"No, you didn't."

"Yes, I did. We'll have to agree to disagree. When are you busting me out of here, anyway?"

"About nine tomorrow morning, as soon as I can raise the bail."

"What's the price?"

"I'm working on that." I detected an edge in Michael's voice, as though I was venturing into forbidden territory.

"I'm real sorry, Michael. Please believe me." I was being serious now.

"I believed you when you promised me you wouldn't go places you didn't belong."

"I'm busted, all right. I don't know if it's possible, but I'll make it up to you."

"See you in the morning." If he was willing to buy it, he wasn't letting on.

"Aren't you going to school?"

"Not until I get you out of there, Lizzie."

"Thanks, hotshot. You're a trooper."

"So now I'm a hotshot? Anyhow, sweet dreams, love."

"Only if you're in them." I hung up, feeling elated just by the sound of his voice even though my head felt like it had been kicked in by a horse.

———— ·•✦✦✦•· ————

I drifted into sleep and found myself in the great river where I had successfully tackled Jason for Alison. I dove down into the darkness but found no one. I returned to the surface and drew in long, ragged breaths of air. My head hurt from the freezing water. I rested briefly before striking out resolutely for the shoreline where I had last seen Michael. The sandy beach gleamed under the light of a full moon yet was deserted. Though the current in the river was swift, I reached the shore easily, feeling my strength grow with each stroke. It seemed that the faster I swam, the stronger I became, as if the energy in my limbs was powered by another, unseen force. As the shore rose up ahead of me, I checked for bottom with my feet and was grateful to find it. I waded out of the water, strode up the sand and into the treeline barefoot, and began calling for Michael.

Where had he gone?

I searched for what seemed like hours, but I could not find him. When I had almost given up, I came upon a clearing where a large animal lay prone in the moonlight. Its teeth flashed white as it uttered a low, mournful snarl. I hesitated, unsure whether to investigate further or seek cover amongst the trees. Unable to overcome my curiosity, I stepped out of the safety of the forest and gingerly approached the creature, a huge cougar. Then I saw the cause of his injury: an arrow was stuck in his shoulder and the wound was bleeding profusely.

I came around to the animal's head and stroked his shoulder in spite of his growling and the terrifying size of his teeth. I took the arrow by its shaft and pulled it out, ripping flesh and skin in the process. More severe bleeding ensued, and the cougar swung his head around as if to vent the full force of his wrath upon me, but did not attack. I felt the full blaze of his eyes on mine and shared his rage and pain.

Who has done this to you? I wanted to know, but the cougar could not tell me. The wound needed stitches, and I found a needle and thread in my hands. I sutured the tear to a steady accompaniment of growling and groaning, and in time the bleeding ceased. At last the cougar was quieted, and I placed my arms around its neck, no longer afraid of the dreadful teeth and claws. I embraced the powerful, sleek animal, my body enveloped by his under belly and his front paws around by shoulders, claws sheathed.

Exhaustion overtook me, and I slept in the protection of the cougar's embrace. When I came to in my dream, daylight was streaming down through the forest and Michael was holding me, but I screamed in alarm as I awoke to consciousness in the real world in a hospital bed with an ache in my head as large as a cave.

I wanted Michael with his arms around me, holding me as he had in my dream, but I was alone until a nurse looked in and informed me I had a visitor, who was none other than a police sergeant. The visitor introduced herself as Sergeant Litalia and explained that she was here to follow up on a possible case of spousal abuse. She had creamy light-brown skin and indigo circles under dark eyes and hair that was neatly swept up into a chignon. The creases in her uniform crackled with stiffness. I speedily corrected her statement regarding spousal abuse and gave a disjointed account of the events leading up to my cracking my head open on Michael's desk. She took down copious notes and indicated that as my head injury was apparently an accident, she was going to close the inquiry. I inwardly cursed my father for being an insensitive, intolerant parent, and hoped that he would get his just desserts sooner rather than later, preferably before he died.

After Sergeant Litalia left, I was served breakfast and then Michael arrived. I decided not to tell him about the visit from the police officer. Michael was cordial and solicitous but holding back. I was desperate to tell him once more how sorry I was and was he going to forgive me for delving into the secrets of his journal, but his detached manner deterred me.

At length I got checked out of the hospital and Michael drove me home. He departed for school in my car immediately after dropping me off, so I was left to my own devices for the remainder of the day. I spent much of it sleeping on his side of our bed, drinking in the smell of him from the sheets, and wishing I had never been so foolish as to consider snooping in my husband's journal.

By the time we went to bed that night, Michael and I had not spent a moment in private conversation. He retired to our room directly from the dinner table, saying he had a lot of homework to catch up on and didn't want to be disturbed. I watched whatever was on TV distractedly, making no sense of any of it, periodically entertained by Alison with snippets of ballet, until it was time for bed. I went up the stairs wearily, heading down the hallway to the bathroom to complete preparations for bed before making my way back to our room. My head had been growing steadily more painful as the day progressed, and the doctor said I should try not to use prescription painkillers because the effects on unborn children were unknown.

"Lizzie, how's the head?" asked Michael as I closed the door behind me.

"So-so."

"You ready to call it a night?"

"Yeah, definitely."

"I'll be right back. Excuse me," he said, barely brushing me as he slipped by me out the door. I donned my nightgown with miserable slowness and knelt down by the bed to await our evening prayer, saying a distraught one of my own, asking the Lord to soothe Michael's hurt feelings. My hopes of an answer, however, were not high. The Almighty seemed to prefer for me to suffer awhile after I made a mistake.

Michael returned and flipped off the overhead light, plunging us into darkness. He knelt by me and offered our bedtime prayer, asking for the Lord to help my head heal quickly, to keep our baby healthy, and to forgive him for causing my accident.

When we were both under the covers, he rolled over towards the window with his back to me, an ominous sign, because he had never done that before. I draped my arm around him.

"It wasn't your fault I hit my head," I said softly.

"Yes, it was," came the emotionless reply. "I wanted to get back at you by reading your journal. If I hadn't taken it, you wouldn't have been trying to wrest it out of my hands."

I sighed. "If you must see it that way, fine – I forgive you, no strings attached."

"I'll sleep easier now. Thank you."

"Michael?"

"What?" His voice sounded weary, as if he had been dealing with a recalcitrant child all day and was losing his patience.

"I love you, Michael, in case you were wondering," I said.

He squeezed the hand I had flung around his chest but did not speak.

"Are you ever gonna forgive me?" I asked gingerly, thinking that trust, once betrayed, was not easily regained.

"Go to sleep, Lizzie."

"Why can't we talk about this?" I protested.

"I said go to sleep. Now leave me alone."

"All right, if that's what you want," I replied meekly. He still held my hand cupped underneath his, next to his heart. I could feel it throbbing steadily against his chest, even though it ought not to be beating at all because I had broken it, and all the king's horses and all the king's men weren't going to be able to put it back together again.

Forgiveness

Lizzie

The next morning when I awoke with a dull pain in my head and a heavy ache in my gut, Michael had already gone downstairs. I crept out the door and leaned over the railing to find out what was going on in the kitchen. As far as I could discern, Michael and Patrick were in the midst of a serious discussion.

"Look, Dr. Teague from Emergency told me she hasn't gained enough weight for where she's at in the pregnancy."

"Michael, it hasn't escaped our notice. Your mother pointed this out to me weeks ago. We've just got to get her to eat more."

"Here's what I think we should do..."

My eavesdropping was interrupted by Sarah.

"Hi, Lizzie."

"Morning, Sarah." I hoped she hadn't thought I was listening in on Michael and his father. "Just on my way to the bathroom."

"How's your head feel?"

"Like I just got eighteen stitches – it hurts."

"Hope you feel better soon."

"Me, too," I added. I smiled reassuringly and whirled to head down the hallway just as Michael appeared at the bottom of the stairs. I didn't want him to find out I'd overheard his conversation with his father. It wouldn't matter: I found out what they intended later that evening.

At breakfast, Michael told me we were going grocery shopping and I should pick him up at his father's shop at six pm sharp. I showed up as requested, list in hand, and we headed over to Food 4 Less, where we made speedy progress up and down the aisles, loading up the shopping cart and checking off items as we went. My head was seriously hurting because it was the end of the day, but I didn't want to break Michael's concentration by complaining. We'd found all the items on the list when he led me into the canned milk section and pointed at the cases of Ensure.

"Vanilla, chocolate, or strawberry?"

I stared at him in bemusement. No one in the house was on a diet that I knew of.

"You're gonna drink two of these a day as a morning and afternoon snack. Full of vitamins. Did the doctor tell you that you haven't gained enough weight?"

Honesty wasn't highest on my list of favorite policies, but I thought it might be the best option here. I stared at the floor.

"Yes, actually."

"And you've been concealing that fact from me, haven't you?"

Busted again, I thought.

"I don't see why I need to gain twenty-five pounds having a seven- or eight-pound baby," I protested, still avoiding Michael's eyes.

"You may wish to fly in the face of medical science, but since you're my wife, I'm not going to allow it. 'm paying for these. Now pick a flavor or I'll pick one for you."

Michael knew very well I didn't like taking orders from him like this. I was ready to throw a case of the cans into his face but I was also desperate to earn his approval.

"Vanilla, then."

"Miracles will never cease." He placed a carton into the shopping cart. "Let's go."

When we'd proceeded through the checkout, he asked, "When did you last eat?"

"Lunchtime, when d' you think?" I snapped back.

He ripped open the carton containing the Ensure and tossed me one. "Drink one now. Don't you know you're feeding two?"

"It'll spoil dinner."

"Lizzie, do you think, for once in your life, you could do something I ask you without objections?"

I started pushing the cart outside as fast as I could, holding the unopened can in one hand. Michael increased his pace to keep even with me.

"You didn't ask," I remonstrated.

"Neither did you."

And I knew Michael could only be alluding to my reading his journal, and he was right: I hadn't asked and I hadn't been invited and I'd violated his trust in the deepest and most hurtful way imaginable. He's never gonna get over this, I thought. I've really screwed myself this time.

The problem, I thought to myself, still struggling to get thoughts together through the throbbing discomfort in my head, is that he discovered me reading a private and personal record. I had planned on making so many changes from the things I discovered. I now saw our relationship in a different light, and I wanted to be a different wife for this man who I now saw as a different husband. But all of that was ruined by him walking in while I was still reading. If I had only kept up with the time better.

He unlocked the trunk of the car and began stowing groceries. When he was finished, I said, "Look, Michael, I don't know what you want from me, but name one thing you want me to do and I'll do it, and I promise I won't argue."

He jerked his head up to look at me.

"Drink the contents of that can right now," he replied, indicating the can of Ensure he'd tossed me that was now lying next to my purse in the shopping cart. I took it, popped it open, and slugged down the thick milky liquid. "And do that twice a day, every day, until you start looking less like you just got back from Auschwitz."

I was going to protest that this amounted to two things, but I decided against it. I didn't need to sweat the small stuff, did I?

The next morning, Michael placed two cans of Ensure in my backpack as we were on our way out the door, and at the beginning of chemistry lab that afternoon, he checked it to see if I'd consumed them.

"You don't have to act like the Gestapo," I complained under my breath as we headed for our spots at the bench. "I promised you I'd drink them."

"You haven't always kept your word," he returned.

At least I'd earned his distrust honestly, I thought.

"I guess you have a point," I conceded. "Check my backpack all you want."

Oddly enough, he never checked it again. Perhaps he was not gonna sweat the small stuff after all, either.

The Big Stuff

Lizzie

Michael was, however, definitely and absolutely sweating the big stuff. Five weeks had gone by, and he hadn't touched me in the bedroom. I couldn't bring up this fact in our meetings with Bishop Dalton because I was too embarrassed to talk about it, and I knew it would only bring to light other issues I wasn't ready to discuss with Michael or anyone else.

Bishop Dalton was having us work on scripture study together and setting a goal to prepare for being sealed in the temple sometime in the next twelve months. If you were a member of the Church of Jesus Christ of Latter-day Saints, a temple marriage was your ultimate goal. But for me, that's where Michael would have been married.

The coveted "Temple Recommend," which gave you access to the most holy of places on the earth, at least in the eyes of church members, had strict prerequisites: you had to have a testimony of Jesus Christ and gospel principles; the restoration of the gospel through Joseph Smith, the first prophet; you had to be a full tithe payer, donating ten percent of your gross income to the church; you had to accept the current prophet and all ordained leaders as called of God; attend all your church meetings; keep the Word of Wisdom by abstaining from alcohol, drugs, coffee and cigarettes; you had to be honest in your dealings with others, including being up-to-date on financial obligations such as child support; you had to obey the law of chastity, which meant no sex outside marriage; and your conduct had to be in harmony with all the teachings of the church. It was a tall order for anyone to manage, but most of the regular Sunday attendees were making a fair job of it. The credit card-sized piece of paper that admitted you to this hallowed place was issued to an individual after interviews with both your Bishop and your Stake President, who was the head of the Church in your area. It was considered such a sacred obligation that members planning to attend for the first time had to take special classes to prepare them for the big day. So, yes, it was a big deal that Michael and I were planning to do this. Marriages sealed in the temples of the Church of Jesus Christ of Latter-day Saints could only be undone by order of the First Presidency, the presiding body of the Church that included the Prophet himself.

Michael and I were able to take the Sacrament again and had both been offered and accepted callings – me teaching the Stars (five-to-six-year-olds, whose class members included Alison), and Michael in the Young Men's organization. I didn't dare voice my concerns about our future temple marriage because Michael hadn't repudiated the plan and that could only mean he wanted it for us – as he always had.

Fortunately for me, "lusting in one's heart" didn't disqualify me from getting in the temple door, but Jesus had condemned it and I was sure it did qualify as one of the unspecified reasons that a member could decide they weren't worthy to enter this consecrated place. But I was over Jason, and while his memory was occasionally painful, he no longer occupied my thoughts as he once had. I wanted whatever Michael wanted for us, or whatever I thought would make him happy.

But I could not reconcile the persona Michael presented to the world and the one I saw in private. In public, he treated me as if I were the love of his life. He helped me with chores, opened doors for me, ate lunch with me at school, took me out on our weekly date (usually accompanied by Rachel and Jeremy), danced with me, held my hand, and put his arm around me when we sat on the couch to watch movies at home or at Jeremy's. He kissed me on the cheek or lips before we parted for class at school and greeted me similarly when he came home from the auto shop. But the minute we were alone, he withdrew into himself. He would study scriptures with me in bed as long as I didn't try to curl up against him.

On the first occasion that I became aware of his intention to avoid physical contact with me when we were alone, he simply got up, walked over to his desk, and sat down in the chair, offering no explanation. The hard glaze in his eyes told me I had better not ask questions and if I didn't know why he was doing this, I ought to. I knew all too well. He avoided me on Sunday afternoons when I took a nap by being sure to have at least one home teaching appointment scheduled during time we might have spent one-on-one time in our room. Michael and I became so adept at playing our roles that we even had our bishop fooled. Bishop Dalton said he felt we had made so much progress that we no longer needed our weekly meetings with him, and he thought we could resolve any issues that arose between us without his help. One look from Michael was enough to convey to me that I had better not contradict this pronouncement.

I kept being as nice to Michael as possible. I kept trying to make the changes I decided upon while reading his journal, but since they all seemed to fall on deaf ears, what did it matter?

The stitches in my head had been removed and I no longer suffered the after-effects of my concussion, except for the fact that my hair didn't look right, no matter how I teased it. To Michael's satisfaction, I did lose my gaunt look and my cheeks filled out along with my belly. Michael even took me to the mall to shop for maternity clothes and to get another haircut to repair the damage done at the hospital, but it was going to be months before I was going to look decent in any outfit and my hair didn't look any better to me after being styled than before. Mama Anne was on the mend and the burden of running the household had shifted back to her, relieving me of the responsibility so that I was feeling slightly better than dead on my feet. Spring was coming and the pear trees were white with blossom, but the promise of the season did little to lift my spirits.

Every time it was my turn to say our bedtime prayer, I prayed for Michael's forgiveness, but my pleas had no effect. He treated me with kindness and deference in the public eye of his family, but when we were alone, he turned away from me. Every night I wrapped my arm around him and told him I loved him. If these words had any effect, he wasn't letting on.

On a Tuesday in the second week of April, I cornered Patrick in the garage while Michael was doing homework in our room. I needed some advice and Patrick understood his son better than I did.

"Can I talk to you a minute?" I asked.

Patrick was cleaning up his workbench. He stopped what he was doing and looked up. "Sure. What's on your mind?"

"Things aren't right with Michael and me."

"What d'you mean?" he asked quizzically.

The words rushed out. "We haven't made out since I snooped in his journal."

I found myself blushing. Patrick sucked in his breath.

"Was everything all right before?" he asked.

I didn't know how to answer him. How would I know what was "all right?"

"Does he treat you nice?" Patrick prompted.

"Yeah, real nice."

"How about you?"

"You mean, am I nice to him?"

"Basically."

"I haven't turned him down, if that's what you mean," I said cautiously. I felt myself blushing again.

"And you two didn't have a problem before this?"

"No."

"Sounds like my son is a young man with some mighty hurt feelings."

"How do I get him back?" I lamented.

"You haven't lost him."

"He doesn't love me anymore."

"Of course he does, Lizzie."

"What can I do?"

"Love him," he said simply.

"And how do I do that? If he's not – you know..."

"Everything you've been doing since you two got married." He narrowed his eyes. "List the things you do to make Michael's life better."

"I do his laundry, iron his shirts, try to keep our room up to his standards of neatness, help out around the house, read scriptures together. So what?"

"And you cooked and cleaned for the whole family while Anne was sick – kept this household running, as a matter of fact. You give Family Home evening lessons, take Alison to her ballet class, fix hair for Rachel and Sarah on Sunday mornings, and chaperone Rachel's dates with Jeremy."

"But that stuff isn't for Michael," I protested.

"Sure it is – if it's for Michael's family, it's for Michael. You've come a long way since December, Lizzie."

"Michael doesn't notice that stuff."

"Yeah, he does."

"How'd you know that?"

"The way he looks at you."

Had I been missing something?

"Right after you got married, he was just smitten; now it's more like smitten with admiration."

I found myself smiling, and Patrick grinned back.

"It's dangerous to put people on pedestals. They might not live up to your expectations," I said.

"And then again, they might surprise you," countered Patrick.

"I let Michael down, and I so want to make it up to him," I added softly.

Then he said, almost as a whisper, "Why did you and Michael get married when you're having someone else's baby?"

My heart did a major lurch and dropped to my toes. I grabbed hold of the bench to steady myself.

"How d' you know?" I gulped.

"Lizzie, I didn't spend eighteen years raising my son without knowing him well enough to recognize when he's lying to me.

And he certainly wouldn't go getting a girl pregnant before he married her. That's not Michael. What I don't understand is how you two had the guts – or is the stupidity? – to come up with this cockamamie scheme and think you could fool me."

Obviously, we hadn't. Now I understood why he had not reacted with anger when we first told him.

"It worked for everyone else," I pleaded lamely. "You won't tell, will you?"

"It's a secret I'll carry to my grave."

"I'm sorry, Patrick, truly I am. I'm an impostor and I shouldn't be a part of this family and you've all been so good to me and I don't deserve it." My words tumbled out like water bubbling in a brook. I felt myself choking up.

"That's where you're wrong, Lizzie. You are a very special part of our family."

"Except for Michael," I protested.

He walked over to me and gave me a bear hug. "I have an idea. I haven't come up with next week's Family Home Evening topic, but I could assign Michael a lesson on forgiveness."

"He's gonna sweat blood over that one," I said in a muffled voice from his coveralls.

"That's the Atonement, Lizzie," he rejoined, releasing me.

We both laughed.

"Don't give up now, kiddo. He'll come around."

"But how long is it gonna take?" I asked in more serious vein.

"How long did it take you?"

We exchanged searching looks, and I thought that Patrick knew far more about me than I wanted him to know.

"Too long," I replied, turning for the door.

––––––––––––– ⋅⁺⁺⧓⁺⁺⋅ –––––––––––––

Michael didn't breathe a word to me about his assignment, but I knew he was working on it because he asked me to find a rock that would fit in the palm of your hand for every family member. I wasn't sure what he had in mind (except, perhaps, to throw them at me), but I complied without question. I was hoping that by acceding to whatever he requested I might somehow repair the damage I had done.

The Sunday before Michael was scheduled to present this lesson, his father, the man with whom I had just shared the most intimate details about my relationship with his son, was called as the bishop of our ward. I had been so wrapped up in the complexities of my marital drama that it hit me as shockingly as a major California earthquake; Michael merely raised his eyebrows and nodded at me as my face reddened. My own father had been certain his name would rise to the top this time around. Served him right for being so mean to me about getting pregnant before I was married. Payback might be a bitch in court, Dad, I thought, but it's a real corker when it comes down from the Almighty.

Bishop Kerry—my father-in-law! That was something to wrap my head around. I knew Mama Anne would have been asked if she could support him in this calling, and he would not have accepted it unless she had responded in the affirmative. They would have been counseled to tell no one until the calling was officially ratified by the members in the chapel on Sunday (by raising the right arm to the square). No confidential voting in the Church of Jesus Christ of Latter-day Saints. Still, extending the call was always made in confidence and members did have the right to dissent, which I'd never seen in my lifetime. Did that mean my father-in-law—no, Bishop Kerry—would learn the identity of our baby's father? It was too much for me to think about right now. As long as Bishop Kerry didn't tell his son, which I knew he could not and would not do...

Monday night duly arrived, probably sooner than Michael wished. Alison and I made Michael's favorite dessert, lemon meringue pie. After the dinner dishes were cleared away, Patrick offered the opening prayer and we sang the hymn "Lord, I Would Follow Thee." Then Patrick turned the time over to Michael for our lesson.

"Tonight's lesson is on forgiveness," began Michael, looking around the table to make sure he had everyone's attention, but avoiding my eyes.

I glanced over at Patrick (Bishop Kerry) and caught a trace of humor in his expression.

"Anyone want to give me examples of stories from the scriptures where this principle applies?" asked Michael.

"There's tons," I replied.

"Go ahead and cite them," he challenged.

I wished I hadn't been so glib, but I could think on my feet. "Here goes: Joseph and his brothers in the Old Testament, the Prodigal Son in the New Testament, the parable Jesus taught about the man of whom he forgave a debt, but that man would not forgive his debtor, and Nephi and his brothers in the Book of Mormon. Also Pahoran forgave Moroni for his angry letter about Pahoran's failure to provide military reinforcements in time of war."

"You're quite the scriptorian these days, Lizzie," Michael said.

I flashed a look at Bishop as if to say this is getting me nowhere, but my father-in-law put a forefinger to his lips to urge silence.

"Also, the woman taken in the act of adultery who was brought before Jesus," Michael went on smoothly.

"What's adultery?" asked Alison.

I put my head in my hands and sighed heavily. Why did sexual sin always have to insinuate itself into lesson topics?

"When you sleep with someone you're not married to," Michael responded tersely.

"That's fornication," I corrected him, raising up my head. "It's more like if I went out with another guy even though I'm married to your brother."

"But 'went out' might be putting it mildly," Michael interrupted.

"She's five," I spluttered.

"Almost six," Edward ventured.

"Guys, let's get back to the lesson – if you wanna argue, you can do that later," interrupted Bishop.

"We are not arguing," I responded emphatically.

As if to prove it, I put my arm around Michael and laid my head against his shoulder.

"Sorry," I whispered. "I was trying to be helpful."

I felt him relax against me.

"I know," he acknowledged. "Got your stones ready?"

They were in a cache under my chair. I disentangled my arm from around Michael's shoulders and scrabbled around at my feet to get the rocks.

"Lizzie's going to hand you each a fist-sized rock," Michael went on.

I passed them around and realized that I had one rock for every family member but hadn't considered Michael in my calculations because he was giving the lesson.

"You don't have one for me?" he said.

"I thought you meant one for everyone *except* you," I said under my breath. "We'll share."

I placed the last rock halfway between us, took his hand, placed it over the rock, and laid my hand on top of his.

"All right, everyone, imagine that you were going to stone someone to death for committing a grievous sin –"

"What's 'grievous?'" asked Alison.

"Really bad," I said quickly, not wanting to detract from Michael's object lesson.

"That's what the punishment for this woman's sin would have been in Israel at the time. I'm sure this rock would hurt pretty bad if I threw it at someone." Michael extricated his hand and the rock from under my fingers and lifted it as if to throw it at Edward across the table. He mimed throwing the rock and Edward cringed. "As you can imagine, being stoned to death would have been a horrible death."

"All of the Old Testament is so barbaric," interjected Sarah.

"So were all the ancient peoples," I added.

"And your point, Michael?" asked his father.

"If you withhold your forgiveness from someone, it's like you're holding a bunch of rocks in your hand ready to throw at them," he said.

Okay then, Michael, apply your damn lesson, I thought. I knew what I had done was worse than bad, but he owed me another chance.

Mama Anne said, "What did Jesus tell the woman, Michael?"

"To sin no more," replied Michael evenly.

"Fact: Jesus didn't condone the sin, and he wanted the elders of Israel to acknowledge that they were also sinners. Jesus taught that we should apply forgiveness to everyone," added Bishop.

"Sarah, want to read the scripture for that?" asked Michael.

He handed her his own scriptures, where he'd marked the page in Mosiah 26, verse 31, and she read it.

"Mom, would you please read Matthew 6, verse 14?" Michael went on.

Anne Kerry read from her own scriptures, "'For if ye forgive men their trespasses, your Heavenly Father will also forgive you.'"

"Two points here: one – we forgive because the Lord has commanded us and He didn't put any constraints on whom we should forgive; and two – that we obtain forgiveness for our own wrongdoings when we forgive others."

I thought of how miserable Jason had made me. I should forgive Jason, even if he didn't love me anymore and had never wanted me to have the baby. I guess Michael wasn't the only one who had work to do on forgiveness.

"That's it for tonight. Is that okay, Dad?"

Michael looked expectantly at his father.

"Good job, son." Bishop invited Sarah to give the closing prayer.

When it was over, Alison said, "Let's have dessert. It's your favorite, Michael – lemon meringue pie."

"Thanks, Mom," Michael directed at his mother.

"Don't give me the credit," she answered. "Lizzie and Alison made it."

"Oh, well thank you two, then," he added, and kissed me lightly on the mouth, making my heart go pitter-patter.

"Peace offering," I whispered, "not that it will make any difference, but I figured it was worth a try."

Why couldn't he be like this when we were alone? I asked myself.

I put my hands in my lap and hung my head. Mama Anne arose from her chair, retrieved the pie from the counter, and began serving slices to us. My appetite had all but evaporated, along with all hopes of a breakthrough, so I left the pie untouched. This caused Michael to remind me I was feeding two and I said with a smirk if he wanted me to eat my pie, no problem, he could feed me like a baby bird, which caused him to relent and tell me whatever I wanted was fine. What I wanted was his forgiveness and he was withholding it, I thought.

Conversation turned to homework, school, and a discussion about our former bishop and why he'd been released so suddenly. I was trying to remember the last time Jason had passed the Sacrament in church, but I couldn't. Had it been days, weeks, or months? Bishop Dalton's release couldn't have anything to do with his wayward jerk of a son, could it? I'd heard that Jason had dropped out of the high-school swim team. Perhaps he wasn't hitting his grades like before? I didn't even know if he had a girlfriend—at least, I hadn't seen him hanging around with anyone at school—and I almost didn't care. I guess he wasn't going on a mission like his dad had expected either, not after what he'd done.

I sat in queasy silence. Rachel piped up to say that Jeremy had invited her to the Senior Prom and since I had experience sewing fancy dresses, would I help her make an appropriate gown?

"Sure, Rachel, anytime. We can go to the sewing store Saturday and pick out a pattern and material," I replied. "The spring sales are on, so you'll probably be able to get a great deal. Do you have money saved?"

"Jeremy said he'd pay for it."

Of course, Jeremy's family was going to pay for him to go to med school, so I guess they could afford a prom dress for his girlfriend.

"Is he going to help choose it, too?"

"You bet!" she exclaimed.

Great, I mused – another opportunity to chaperone Jeremy and Rachel. We could go shopping before noon so that Michael would be at the auto shop and we wouldn't have to endure his condemnation.

"What are you making for your prom date with me?" asked Michael.

I did a double take and whipped my head around to look at him with an impudent stare. "We're not going."

"Why not?" he asked.

"I'm gonna be nine months pregnant and you wanna go to the prom with me!" I exclaimed.

"You can't be nine months along, Lizzie – you and Michael only got married in December," cried Sarah.

Everyone realized exactly what she'd implied. It was a miracle they didn't all take their rocks and throw them at me right now for being an idiot, I thought.

"That means you and Michael –" she ran on.

"That's why they were seeing Bishop Dalton every Sunday," added Rachel, but of course Rachel had already figured it out.

Sarah and Edward were staring at Michael incredulously. At least they weren't looking at me.

"We're busted, Lizzie," Michael said ruefully. "We couldn't keep it under wraps forever."

"Enough said," cautioned my new bishop in an authoritative tone. "We all know what it means."

"What does it mean?" interjected Alison.

There were times when having a very innocent, younger sister was a serious liability. This was one of them.

"I'll tell you later, Alison," I offered, hoping I could make a gracious exit.

"Is it a grievous sin?" asked Alison.

"Yes, very," I said gravely.

"Then I'm real sorry, Lizzie," said the five-year-old.

"Since we just had a lesson on forgiveness, I don't want to hear anyone condemning Michael and Lizzie for what they did," added Bishop. "Everyone in the ward is looking up to us now. That means no gossiping and no tattling."

His latter comment he directed at Rachel and Sarah, who looked as though they wanted to start playing "Twenty Questions."

"We're going up to bed – now," Michael said, taking my hand.

"It's only eight pm," I protested.

"Fine, I'll go without you."

"No!"

"Suit yourself, Lizzie."

Michael was already on his feet when I sprang up. I was going to tell him he didn't have to issue orders as if he were a military commander, but I thought better of it and flounced up the stairs after him.

"You could ask nicely," I said breathlessly, catching up. Lugging this parasite around in my belly was making the stairs heavy going.

"It doesn't make any difference if I do 'ask nicely,'" he retorted.

"You willing to fork out the cash for me to make a prom dress?" I asked bluntly.

"Yes," he replied, his back to me.

"Then I'll be honored to be your date, all right?"

"Thank you."

He opened the door and I followed him into the bedroom. After we had both paid a visit to the bathroom down the hall and made preparations for bed in unfriendly silence, I donned Michael's favorite night gown: the one that unbuttoned in the front. It had been his favorite night gown once upon a time, I thought, before I was stupid enough to read his journal. I sat down at the desk to brush out my hair, wishing that it wasn't so hopelessly screwed up, along with everything else.

"I'm gonna write a short journal entry, Lizzie, if you don't mind waiting."

"Fine," I flashed back.

Michael propped himself up against the pillows on top of the comforter, picked up his pen, and began writing. When I was done brushing my hair, I sat watching him from the chair near his desk, hugging my knees under the nightgown, wondering what I could do to make amends. I didn't want to go to the prom nine months pregnant, but I was going because he wanted me to be his date, and I didn't want to turn in early tonight because it would just mean I would spend an agonizing hour curled up against his unresponsive frame until I fell asleep. I sighed and picked my journal up off the desk. Michael glanced up from writing.

"What's on your mind, Lizzie?" he asked, narrowing his eyes.

"The rocks in your lesson tonight – nice analogy," I said. "Why don't you throw the ones you've been holding onto at me and get it over with?"

"I don't want to hurt you."

"You want to read my journal, fine – here it is." I tossed my journal onto the bed.

"You should treat journals with greater respect, Lizzie," he said evenly, retrieving it off the coverlet and carefully closing it. "Why don't you distill what's in here to the key points? I'll listen."

"I don't want to hurt you," I answered, sounding like his echo.

"I just want to know what goes on in that head of yours."

"You won't like me."

"Try me."

"Promise you won't be mad."

"Lizzie, Lizzie – always these conditions."

I got up from the desk and settled on the bed cross-legged at Michael's feet. He was going to wish he wasn't my husband after I got done with my confession, I thought, but he wasn't like my husband now so I might as well take the leap.

"All right – no conditions," I began. Michael put down his journal and regarded me thoughtfully, twiddling his ballpoint pen between his fingers.

"Here is your bedtime story, Michael. Last fall, as you know, a girl in our high school had the hots for a guy at our high school. And yes, he's a member of her church, which she knows you already figured out. She had a real crush on this guy and wanted to go all the way, so she did."

"She doesn't like to play by the rules," Michael mused.

"Yeah, I know. Good way to get burned. She fell in love and didn't think about getting pregnant or anything except being with this guy. They sometimes met in the park on her way home from her best friend's house."

"Geez, Lizzie, nice to know I was the cover story. And where did you, I mean, 'she' do it for the first time?"

I covered my face with my hands. "Let me finish the story. Her first time, they snuck into the school swimming pool."

"Interesting choice of venue."

"And don't laugh, it's not funny." I looked up at Michael and he was grinning.

"It is easy to fool around in the pool. There's less stuff to take off when you are ready to go further and there are a few places you can have privacy," I added for good measure, deciding it would be better to find the humor than the pathos in the account of my affair with Jason.

"Then the girl finds out she is pregnant, tells the father, and he becomes a villain by breaking up with her. Enter the hero of this little story, with his brilliant proposal. Problem is, the heroine is still in love with the villain. She stupidly figures, if she can't have the villain, at least she can have a piece of him in the baby." I take a deep breath before continuing.

"So the hero and the heroine are going to get married and live happily ever after, despite the fact that she is still entertaining romantic thoughts about the villain. More like lustful thoughts, if she is being honest. So she dresses to kill at her wedding to the hero, since she knows the villain will be there and is secretly hoping to make the hero jealous as hell, which, of course, he is. Our hero is blissfully unaware of the situation." It is amazing, I think, how many words you can fit into a single breath of air.

"And she is so nervous on her wedding night because she can't think of the hero as anything except her best friend, more like her kid brother. But she has to, now that they are married. After all, even heroes have righteous expectations. The first time they are together, she wants to tell him she can't do it and, as it happens, she can't pull it off. But she knows has to some time on their first night because she knows she belongs to the hero now. He is very nice about it. Very nice. Nicer than he has to be. And that makes sense, because, after all, he is the hero." I look to see what kind of reaction I am getting. Michael's face is unreadable.

"Now she is all confused between the villain and the hero when she is making love to the hero—on their *wedding* night—so she starts crying, which is utterly bewildering to our hero, who has gone so far out of his way to be sweet and caring. There's no way for her to explain that she wants the villain to be the hero to be the villain, and everything is mixed up and wrong. Jesus said it was a sin to lust after another in your heart, and this was her wedding night, for goodness' sake, and what the hell is she doing thinking about someone other than her hero husband? And though she doesn't know it at the time, the hero has more smarts than she gives him credit for. He's looked up some books about sex and he turns out to be an intuitive expert at applying theory in practice and damn it all, he manages to turn her on like she has never been turned on before."

The trace of a smile crossed Michael's lips. "You shouldn't swear, Lizzie."

I was tempted to say I would swear if I damn well wanted to, but I swallowed my pride and contained myself. "So our hero thinks everything is fine because he'd have to be blind, deaf and dumb not to know what he's doing is working its magic."

"I didn't think everything was fine, Lizzie."

"Hush, I'm not done with the story. The problem is, the heroine is still desperately in love with the villain, but she can't tell the hero because she's promised herself she's going to do her utmost to make the marriage to our hero work. She's miserable as hell because she wants a man she can't have and has a man she doesn't want, but she has decided to sacrifice herself for the sake of the child. Marrying the hero was the only way to keep the baby."

"Not the only way," Michael said gently.

"The only righteous way she could think of. We both know that," I countered. "Then the hero and heroine head back to the castle, where they are often at odds with one another because although she's been trying to hide it, the hero suspects the heroine is still madly in love with the villain, so he doesn't actually tell her he's crazy in love with her, although he does write every single tidbit of that down in his journal."

I gave Michael a mildly accusatory stare, then reflected on my hands where they lay in my lap. "Our hero is waiting for the heroine to take the first step, which is absolutely a mistake on his part. Because our hero has decided he's not going to tell the heroine how he feels either. To add insult to injury, our heroine did make this stupid promise to the hero before the wedding that he could make love to her as much as he wants and she does keep *that* promise and do her best to please him, even when she really wants to be in the arms of the villain."

"You know I wouldn't hold you to that promise, Lizzie," Michael interjected. At least he wasn't throwing his rocks at me yet, I thought. He would probably throw me out of here for good when I was done, so I took a long look at what I might be losing.

"She was holding *herself* to that promise. She had to," I replied fiercely, "because it's about the only thing she was doing right."

Michael was still contemplating me quietly and his expression was so deep I might be looking down a well. He had mastered the ability to hold a face with no emotion in it whatsoever.

"Then our hero has to take a trip to fight some dragons and suddenly she's missing him big-time, but she's so scared of getting her heart broken again, she fails to inform him that somewhere in all this, she has fallen in love with him. Major *faux pas*. When he arrives back at the castle, our hero and heroine are starting to make progress and then she makes another big blunder. Instead of *talking* to him to find out where his head is at, she decides to investigate the hero's journal without his permission and breaks the golden rule. She violates the hero's trust. Trust is a principle way up there on our hero's list. He's so mad and so hurt he won't forgive her and she doesn't know that she's ever going to be able to regain his trust."

I cupped my chin in my hands and waited. When Michael still didn't move, I realized I was going to break my father's golden rule yet again and start crying. "Michael, I'll go to a less expensive hair stylist and I'll stay home and have as many babies with you as you want, just please say you'll give me another chance."

"Come over here, Lizzie," he whispered.

I crept across the bed and as I was doing so, Michael flipped off the light switch and plunged the room into moonlight.

"It's nice to know the real Lizzie," he went on, cradling his arm around me and holding my head next to his chest.

"No, it's not," I choked.

"And I want you to go to that hair stylist you like – especially now, since I'm responsible for messing up your hair – and I do want you to stay home and raise this baby, and have some more with me, when we're both ready for it. And I'm not mad at you anymore even though I am still licking my wounds. You did hurt me, but I can get over it."

"I love you," I said.

"I know. You've been telling me that for a while and I think now I actually believe it."

At that moment he made his move and pushed me down onto the coverlet, pinning me with one hand by holding my wrists above my head. He unbuttoned my nightgown so fast I thought he was going to rip out the buttons and he managed to get his pajama bottoms off with only one hand. He placed the entire weight of his body on top of mine and kissed me with such fury I was sure he drew blood from my tongue. This was a Michael I didn't know, and I knew I was responsible for the savagery and the rage and the pain. If this was how it had to be, I thought, he could do anything he wanted tonight. Then I understood what he wanted was for me to feel his pain and give myself to him utterly and completely so that there was no doubt in his mind of my loyalty.

I let him take me into the river, into terrifying rapids that beat me against the gritty riverbed and sharp stones and I had to trust that he would get me out. This was not about satisfying me – it was about me letting go and giving in and driving the imaginary Jason from my heart forever. It was about hurting me as Michael had been hurt and showing me that he was a force more powerful than the rapids and hearing his song over the rushing water: I love you, I love you, over and over, until it drowned out all thought of anyone but him.

I am yours, Michael, forever and always.

⋅⋅✦✦✦✦✦⋅⋅

When he was finished, still positioned on top of me with his hands clamped on my wrists, he whispered, "Did I hurt you, Lizzie?"

"It hurt good," I whispered, limp beneath him. "Was that in one of your more advanced books?"

He laughed with a flash of teeth in the silver shadows. "No. What I researched was how to *please* a woman, not *take* one."

He released his grip on my wrists, suddenly hanging his head and shifting his weight off to one side. "I'm sorry, my love, I shouldn't have done that."

I lay still, docile, my arms still above my head, although I wanted badly to wrap them around him. "It was okay, Michael. I understand. But can you please explain, if you wanted me this much, how'd you manage to restrain yourself for six weeks?"

"Excessive amounts of pride and stubbornness."

It was my turn to laugh. "I thought that was my prerogative."

"Yeah, well, you needed some competition."

I lifted my hand to stroke his cheek.

"Now let me give you your turn," he murmured, "if you're not too beat up."

"Go slow," I said softly.

"I hope you weren't planning on getting much sleep tonight."

"You gonna make up for lost time?" I asked playfully.

"If you're game," he answered.

"As long as I'm not prey."

"Conditions, always conditions."

"No conditions, then, hotshot," I countered.

"I propose one," he said. "I do for you whatever you want."

"Is this gonna be out of one of those books?"

"I'm not telling."

"I thought we weren't gonna have any more secrets," I teased.

"We won't – not after I show you."

"All right, hotshot, if I can stay awake."

"I guarantee you'll stay awake."

"Then shut up and kiss me."

We finally fell asleep, exhausted, in the ragged light of dawn. We stumbled downstairs at seven-thirty knowing we were late for breakfast and not caring. Six pairs of eyes swiveled to survey us as we took our places at the table.

"Morning, kids. You look tired – rough night?" asked Mama Anne.

"No, Mom, it was just fine," Michael replied with a smile curling his lips. We'd rushed to get dressed and he hadn't had time to fix his hair, which was sticking out at all kinds of odd angles. We exchanged glances and couldn't stop ourselves from giggling. I felt light-headed and giddy.

"Am I missing the joke?" chimed in Sarah.

"No joke," I said between giggles.

Then I caught Bishop's eyes and he started grinning and I mouthed "thank you," hoping Michael wouldn't see it, which of course he did. Rachel asked us why we were so happy today and we told her that's what being in love did to you, which she ought to know. Sarah said she was glad we weren't fighting like last night and I denied that we had been fighting; then Alison chimed in to give us her opinion that we had looked like we were, but Michael's lesson must have helped, and it was sure nice that we'd made up and we shouldn't fight anymore. I couldn't have agreed with Alison more, and I told her I'd have a talk with her tonight about the baby.

We were too late for the bus, so Michael drove me to school, and he didn't spare a second to ask me what was going on between his father and me.

"What was that all about with you and Dad?"

"That's our secret," I answered.

"Uh-uh. No more secrets. Come on, 'fess up."

"On one condition..." I began lightly.

"We're not going there. No conditions." He flashed me a devious sideways glance. "I could keep you up all night until you tell me."

"You'll probably do that anyway," I protested, but I knew I was blushing while I smiled. "All right, hotshot, since we have no secrets. I told your father you and I weren't – you know..."

"Weren't what?"

"Being intimate," I replied, looking out the passenger window.

"You told my dad something like that! You have no shame, do you?"

"Not after last night, now that you know all my secrets," I went on. "Anyway, I told him I wanted to make up for hurting you and I didn't know how to win you back, so he came up with the idea of assigning you a Family Home Evening lesson on forgiveness. The rest was up to me."

I toyed with my fingernails, wondering if he was going to take offense.

"Never underestimate the power of a wife when she connives with her father-in-law—I mean Bishop—against her husband," he said. Then he threw back his head and laughed.

"You're glad it worked, aren't you?" I asked, still unsure of myself.

"Oh, Lizzie, queen of my heart, you're bold enough for the both of us and you have my dad totally bewitched, and I don't know how you do it, but it's impressive."

It was my turn to laugh.

"And just in case you were wondering, he knows it's not your baby and he's known all along you're not a miserable screw-up like me."

"He knew?" asked Michael, incredulously. "And he let me feel as low as a skunk for letting him believe I did this to you. He's a sly one, my dad."

"He's like the Lord, he works in mysterious ways," I rejoined.

"You're not a screw-up, you know," he added, turning serious.

"Yes, I am. You of all people should know that now."

"If you don't take it back, I'm gonna keep you up all night again."

"I'm not taking it back because it's true."

"Then you do want me to keep you up all night?"

"No!" I protested as we pulled into the school parking lot.

"Well, yes, if it will be as good as last night," I whispered.

He killed the ignition, stepped out of the driver's side, grabbed both our backpacks off the back seat, and came around to the passenger side to open the door for me. He closed the door, pushed me up against the car, and gave me a very long, hot kiss. I wondered if I was going to melt into the paint and hoped the emotional roller coaster of the last twelve hours wasn't causing undue stress on the baby.

"Stop," I exclaimed. "We're at school!"

"You're my wife and I'll do whatever I want with you."

He still had me pinned against the car, but I didn't struggle.

"I do take it back about being a 'miserable screw-up!'" I whispered.

"Too bad, I was so looking forward to tonight."

"That's still an option, in case you were wondering," I came back. "Now I have to get to class so please let me leave."

Michael stepped back with his arms up as if I were pointing a gun at him. "Lizzie, you are a wicked, wicked girl to tease a guy this way."

"That's why you're crazy about me," I countered, throwing my backpack on my shoulder and walking away. But for all my banter, Michael must have known he had me wrapped around his finger and I would jump over waterfalls and scale mountains for him.

The Senior Prom

Lizzie

Expressing my love for Michael for so many weeks without him reciprocating and being honest about my feelings during the first few months of our marriage had finally allowed me to regain Michael's trust. His affection I suspected I had never lost, although he had needed time to soothe his hurt feelings or, as he'd so aptly explained it, to overcome "excessive amounts of pride and stubbornness." It was a great burden to have someone's happiness depending on you, but what I hadn't realized were the rewards I reaped by gratifying his needs. The more I gave, the more he returned the favor. When I wasn't trying to impose my will on his and he wasn't trying to run the show, the fights stopped. If one of us grew strident or insistent, they resumed.

I began working on Rachel's prom dress in early May, a long gown in shimmering royal blue satin with a high waist and a demure neckline, before I started on my own dress because I'd promised to help Rachel first. It was difficult for me to cut it out on the floor of the living room now that I was close to eight months pregnant, but Rachel held the fabric patiently while I placed the pattern pieces and bent over to use the scissors. In a single weekend, I ran up the seams on Mama Anne's ancient sewing machine and sewed on the rhinestones. When Rachel tried on the dress, it fit perfectly and sparkled in all the right places. I thanked God for giving me steady hands and an able advisor in the person of Rachel's mother. I decided to loan Rachel one of my many pairs of heels for prom night because I had a pair that were perfect for the dress.

I had much greater difficulty finding a pattern and selecting material for myself. I wasn't sure if Michael cared about what color I chose, but I consulted him anyway. Red seemed too flashy for a date who was nine months pregnant and white too pure. Michael liked me in black (or at least, in black underwear, by his own pronouncement on our honeymoon), so I dragged him to the fabric store and showed him a black satin cloth imprinted with a flower pattern. The only problem was it ran nine dollars and ninety-nine cents a yard plus tax and I needed at least five yards to make a maternity gown fit for the prom (not to mention the trimmings). I thought he'd balk at the cost, so I quickly figured the total for him. He responded by saying that he was quite capable of doing the math, thank you, and stood regarding me thoughtfully for a while before rendering his decision. He said that since this dress represented about eight hours work for him, he trusted that I'd get more than one-time use out of it. I didn't discern his meaning right away, until he started smiling at me and shaking his head and saying I still had a stubborn streak. Only then did I realize he meant he hoped I'd be wearing it again in another pregnancy, and I wasn't sure whether I should smack him or embrace him.

I told him, no problem, we could have another kid right away as long as he wasn't going to balk at the cost of two kids in diapers, which was going to be exorbitant, because I could handle the lack of sleep. He knew then I'd called his bluff, and I knew I'd made great strides in his esteem, because spending this much on a frivolity such as a prom dress to satisfy my need to look good was a big compliment coming from Michael. I wasn't too confident I would look stunning or attractive at nine months pregnant, but Michael said I would. Judging by the fact that we hadn't slowed down in the bedroom, I ought to believe him.

Of course, there are other changes to a woman's body besides the bulging abdomen during pregnancy, and Michael was more than pleasantly ecstatic about those. His wide-eyed adoration more than made up for my feelings of horror at my expanding girth.

The Saturday before Memorial Day weekend, on a day when it looked like God had thrown dollops of Cool Whip into the sky for clouds and painted the Sierras west of the Sacramento Valley the color of blueberries, Janine and Shannon threw me a baby shower at Shannon's house. Five young women were in attendance, as well as my visiting teachers. We played ridiculous games like guessing the size of my waist (which I didn't want to divulge to a soul), and who could put a cloth diaper on a Cabbage Patch doll the fastest. Lynn, my visiting teacher, won that race – hardly surprising, as she was the only mother present. I stuck my finger trying to fasten one of the pins and thanked God for modern miracles like disposable diapers. I wondered if the Nissan was going hold all the presents, which included a stroller, receiving blankets, diaper bag, diapers, highchair, car seat, and a supply of baby clothes that looked like they'd be enough for twins, which I was extremely thankful I wasn't having. Michael showed up around two pm to pick me up, still wearing his mechanic's coveralls. I gathered he'd been struggling with a front-end repair that couldn't wait out the weekend and from his expression, I gauged he wasn't ready for the flurry of activity generated by his arrival.

He sat down for cake and lemon punch, waited on by four or five girls. I felt like telling them to keep their hands off my husband, but I could see he was enjoying the attention, so I decided to hold my peace. He probably wouldn't be able to keep his hands off me, later, when we were alone.

We stowed the baby items in the Nissan as best we could, with the help of the young women. Michael said it was great to live amongst saints who were so generous although he was daunted by the prospect of finding space for the baby items in our bedroom, which was crammed with just the two of us. He suggested I move some of my wardrobe out of his closet and back to my parents' house and I told him where he could stick that idea. He said no problem, either I could decide what clothes to eliminate or he'd do it for me. Janine turned traitor and offered to help me relocate my belongings. To top it off, Shannon said she was sure that the baby's welfare was a priority for me, and she couldn't see why I would mind housing my clothes somewhere else, temporarily, especially as I had a wardrobe that would outfit three young women and none of my clothes fitted me anyway in my current condition. I couldn't believe my girlfriends were siding with Michael, unless they were hoping for castoffs, and I consoled myself by eating a second piece of cake while wishing I could toss the remainder of it into their laps, whipped cream and all. Michael gave me one of those smug smiles he liked to use on me when he knew he'd won an argument, and I glared back at him licking bits of pink-and-blue frosting suggestively off my lips.

When the gifts had been loaded into the car, I could see Michael mentally totaling their cost, figuring how many hours he would have had to slog to afford such luxuries, and how much sooner this meant we'd be able to move out from his parental home. The girls gave us an exuberant sendoff, and I could almost look forward to the baby's arrival with carefree anticipation after a celebration as whimsical as this one.

School classes flew by in a blur as the early-June senior prom and my due date approached. I was cramming for finals and wishing I hadn't decided to take so many hard sciences in my senior year, while Michael was running an exhausting schedule at the auto shop, doing his homework, helping me with mine, preparing lessons for the Young Men, and home teaching, not to mention taking prenatal classes with me. It was a miracle we had energy left for each other, and I wondered how we would manage with a baby in the mix.

Rachel and Jeremy were still a hot item and didn't show signs of slowing down, much to the chagrin of both sets of parents. Michael chided me sorely for encouraging them in the first place. I resolutely stood my ground and proclaimed that if it was God's will, they would find a way, as we had, which did much to deter further objection from his corner. Jeremy had been accepted to UC Davis as a biology major in preparation for med school four years down the road. Michael signed up for a summer class at Solano Community College that would keep him away from home two nights a week for eight weeks, and I tried not to think about how much I was going to miss him. He reassured me by pointing out that I would have my hands full by then (and I rather thought other parts of my body than my hands would be involved, but I decided not to correct him).

⋯ ✦✦✦✦ ⋯

Michael and I couldn't come up with a name for our baby, mostly because every time he broached the subject, I put him off or declined all suggestions. I still wasn't altogether ready to deal with the stark reality of parenthood, despite the fact that I couldn't ignore the image of my swollen belly in the mirror and we were taking classes to prepare me for the big day.

Our wedding day didn't seem nearly as daunting as it had last year compared to this. Weddings were fun, even if you were in love with the wrong guy, and I'd known which day and what I'd be wearing and what was planned for the ceremony. Hell, I'd even had a foretaste of what to expect on the wedding night. I hadn't a clue what it was like to have a baby, and I was uncomfortable talking to my visiting teachers about it. So I read the birthing class manual and books on childbirth and pamphlets at the doctor's office and felt thoroughly confused.

I didn't want to tell Michael about my misgivings, because I didn't want him to know how scared I was. I didn't want him to know I was worried that I would end up with terrible stretch marks and my body wouldn't go back into shape and he wouldn't be attracted to me anymore, because I couldn't let him know I was that vain.

I channeled my nervous energy into shopping sprees with my mother for baby items, organizing space in our room for the baby, and producing a perfectly sewn dress for the senior prom. I decided not to let Michael see me wearing it ahead of the prom, much like I had with my wedding dress.

By the time prom night arrived on a warm evening in early June under a half-moon, my doctor had informed that I was twenty-five percent effaced and he expected me to deliver in the next couple of weeks, right on schedule. I decided that at least for tonight, I would not think about having a baby in the next couple of weeks, which was going to be difficult because the baby made sure his or her presence was acknowledged regularly by constantly kicking and turning.

Michael brought me a heavenly scented white orchid for my corsage and sported a carnation himself as we walked out to the Nissan. He had me execute a few twirls on the sidewalk so he could take a good look at me in the black dress, and he said I was as alluring as I had ever been. I'd flipped my hair away from my face, Farrah Fawcett style, and let fall loosely over my shoulders in large, springy curls with the aid of my big-barreled curling tongs. I wore very red lipstick, dark blue eye shadow, extra-thick mascara and royal-blue nail polish. My eyes looked dramatic and inviting, and Michael was ready to accept their invitation before we made it to the car.

"Come here, Lizzie, sweetheart. I want to kiss you before we leave."

He slipped his arm around my waist, except his arm didn't fit halfway around it anymore.

"Oh, no, you don't, lover boy," I said, sidestepping him.

"Is this going to be another night when you're difficult?"

"I am never difficult, and you know that very well," I answered playfully. "I'm wearing a lot of very red lipstick and I don't think you want it all over your face."

"Later, then..." he mused.

"Now go find out what is taking Rachel so long because we still have to pick up Jeremy."

Michael opened the passenger door and I settled into the passenger seat. Then he went back into the house to find his sister while I made myself comfortable. I couldn't achieve complete comfort no matter what I did now that I had a baby sitting on my bladder. I felt a contraction – another one of those Braxton-Hicks jobs they kept telling me about that I'd been experiencing in the last couple of weeks – and told myself to relax. The excitement of going to the prom must be affecting my body, I thought.

Rachel and Michael returned shortly, and she slid into the back seat. I'd worked on her hair for a while, piling most of it on top on her head and leaving just wispy curls around her face and neck. Rachel looked lovelier than she had as a bridesmaid at the wedding. I told myself once again that Rachel was only seventeen (she'd had a birthday in April), not yet a senior in high school, and this fling with Jeremy wouldn't last through his first year of college. He'd have ample chances to meet fine Jewish girls in college, I was sure. I wasn't going to take the heat for getting them together.

We picked up Jeremy and headed over to the high school. It was close to nine pm by the time we arrived and the dance hadn't begun in earnest yet. There were extra police cars cruising the neighborhood, but they wouldn't need to be concerned with us. We weren't members of the drinking crowd, but I was sure a few students would be sitting behind bars tomorrow wondering why they'd been fools enough to mix under-age drinking, prom dates, and driving.

Janine and Shannon both had dates: Janine with Joey, the DJ from our wedding, and Shannon with a classmate who wasn't a member of our Church. I had been meaning to tell her that going out with a non-member was begging to get her into hot water, but I didn't have the heart because I knew it didn't take a non-member to get one into the devil's stewpot. Shannon classified all the guys in our ward as "dweebs." I certainly knew one who was (although "jerk" might be more appropriate), and I had heard he was bringing his new girlfriend from Fairfield. I hoped I wouldn't run into him. He didn't send me into fits of lust anymore; nonetheless I felt distinctly self-conscious sitting in

Sacrament with his eyes boring into me from wherever he was sitting. His eyes still dripped with hunger when he looked at me and I found this observation distinctly disturbing, especially now that I was a married woman in the advanced stages of pregnancy and he was supposedly dating another girl.

I was carrying his baby, of course, even if no one knew it except the two of us. I didn't think of the child as his anymore. This "bundle of joy" belonged to Michael and me, no matter what circumstances had given rise to the child's existence. We were going to be the parents, legally, morally, and in the eyes of the Church, no matter who the sperm donor happened to be.

As if to remind me of his or her presence, the baby punched me in the ribs with a foot and I felt another contraction that was stronger and more painful than the ones I'd had before. Prom night high jinks, I told myself, checking my reflection in the window.

When we entered the rec hall where the dance was being held, we split off from Rachel and Jeremy to hang out with our lab partners from chemistry and discuss our impressions of the final exam. Naturally everyone was talking about what they were going to do after graduation, now that finals were over and we were on easy street. At least half the chemistry class was going on to college. Standing in the group, hugely pregnant, I felt out of place and disappointed that I wasn't boarding the college train like everyone else. Even Michael had that option.

I shouldn't be thinking like this. I'd made my choices months ago last September and I shouldn't be moping about having to live with them. I had many blessings to be thankful for, not least of which was a guy who cared about me and loved me in spite of my shortcomings. Michael must have picked up on my train of thought or noticed that I wasn't sharing the exuberance of the rest of the crowd, so he announced it was time we started dancing and took me out on the dance floor. It wasn't easy dancing with a baby between us, but we managed.

"You're quiet for Lizzie," he said softly as we danced cheek to cheek to the sound of Huey Lewis's "The Power of Love."

"Count your blessings," I replied lightly, not wanting to cast gloom on the celebrations.

"Feeling bummed about not going to college like everyone else, sweetheart?"

"No," I lied.

"Lizzie, lying is included in the Big Ten," he went on, and I knew he wasn't talking about college football.

I tossed back my head and looked him straight in the eye. "Quit playing Moses."

"Your turn for college will come, if that's what you want."

"I guess," I said, unconvinced.

"I promise," he countered.

"So you say," I returned, and thought better of it. "But at least you've got a better record at keeping promises than I have."

"Is this Lizzie's fragile ego showing itself at our senior prom because she's very noticeably pregnant?"

"Nobody else is," I complained.

"That, my love, is because they probably took a trip to the abortionist and at least you had the courage to have the baby."

"Courage, stupidity – same difference."

"There goes that fragile ego again."

"I just hope *he's* not here," I remarked, trying to change the subject. We both knew which "he" I was referring to.

"Probably is, not that you'll point him out to me," Michael said, tightening his grip on my shoulder.

The identity of the baby's father was, after all, still a point of contention between us even if Michael was pretending not to make a big deal of it. I'd read his journal and I knew he was burning to know the truth, but I couldn't or wouldn't give him the satisfaction of my knowledge. Need to know basis, I told myself, and there were certain truths I thought Michael could live without.

"I'll make you a deal. You quit bumming about not knowing who got me pregnant and I'll quit bumming about not going to college this fall."

"I never said I was bummed out about it," he returned evenly.

"I read your journal," I answered with a superior smile. That argument was sure to win him over, you idiot, Lizzie, I thought.

"An ill-advised venture if ever there was one." He wasn't smiling now and he was digging his nails into my shoulder through the silky fabric of my new dress. I hoped he wasn't going to tear it, because I had invested a considerable amount of effort and sacrificed sleep to have it sewn in time for prom night.

"Like teenage weddings when the bride is pregnant before the wedding day." I was in trouble now so I might as well dig the hole deeper. "And going to the senior prom with your teenage wife when she looks like she's about to have a baby on the dance floor."

"Don't tempt fate," rejoined Michael.

"I thought you believed in God."

"I thought I was dancing with one of Satan's minions."

"I don't wanna be a member of that club anymore."

"Good, because I was hoping I wouldn't have to spend the rest of my life dancing with the devil."

"You are teasing me, Michael Kerry."

"You're smiling," he replied, and I was. I kept smiling, because the tension had eased out of Michael's fingers and he had been trying to cheer me up without my realizing it.

We danced for a while, until Michael said I looked tired, which I wasn't going to own up to for a second because dancing was easier than hanging out with our high-school crowd talking about their wonderful plans for the future. We found Janine and Shannon, met their dates, and had a long conversation with Janine's date, Joey, about music. He played in a rock band and had wangled his way into a job at a local radio station through his father's connections in the advertising business – that is, until he went on his mission in a year. He sported a mustache and his hair was down to his shoulders, so I was guessing the mission hair cut was going to be a real sacrifice for him.

It was about eleven pm by the time I acknowledged that the contractions I'd been having earlier weren't exactly diminishing in intensity. We'd just hooked up with Rachel and Jeremy and were dancing in a foursome with them when a big one hit.

"Michael," I said, swaying slowly and taking deep breaths because this contraction felt like someone was sticking a needle into my cervix, "you know what you said about tempting fate?"

"Yeah, what?" he asked.

"I think you did."

He didn't get it.

"Remember what I said earlier about having a baby on the dance floor?" I yelled. Rachel and Jeremy could probably hear this.

Michael grabbed me by both wrists and stopped us, right in the middle of Rod Stewart's "Rhythm of my Heart." "Lizzie, I know you think it's funny to play tricks on me, but this better not be one of them."

"It isn't," I protested. The contraction was still going. I put my arms around his neck and leaned on him to catch my breath.

"Shoot, Lizzie, you are serious!"

"I've been trying to tell you," I gasped from his shoulder.

"Rachel, Jeremy! We gotta go – like now," he yelled above the glare of the music. "Lizzie's gonna have the baby!"

I could've hit him. I didn't want the impending event announced to our entire high-school class at the senior prom. A few nearby couples stared at us in astonishment and I colored up as bright red as one of the neon lights shining down on the dance floor.

"Shut up!" I spluttered. "Just tell them we have to go."

Michael grabbed his sister's arm, Rachel took Jeremy by the hand, and the couples around us parted to make way for us to leave the dance floor. I was hoping we'd make it to the car before I had another contraction. Michael told me to wait out front with Jeremy and Rachel while he retrieved the car from its parking space. I had another contraction while we were waiting, and this time I hung onto Rachel.

"What's it feel like?" she asked.

"Scary," I panted.

"Rachel, this is not the time to research what it's like having a baby," warned Jeremy.

"Why isn't he here yet?" I moaned.

"It takes hours to have a baby," Rachel interjected for my benefit.

"It doesn't feel like it's gonna take hours," I remonstrated.

"How long have you been having contractions?" she asked more sympathetically.

"I dunno. I wasn't counting. Like since we left home."

"No shit, Lizzie," said Jeremy. "Would've been nice if you'd told someone."

"I thought it would stop," I wailed, as the contraction subsided.

Michael pulled up in the car, leaped out, and walked around to open the passenger door for me.

"C'mon, Lizzie. Get in."

I flopped down like an ungainly seal, while Rachel and Jeremy ensconced themselves in the back seat. I was trying to remember my breathing exercises.

"You been timing these, Lizzie?" asked Michael.

"You're the one wearing the watch," I snapped back.

"If you woulda said something..."

"I didn't want to ruin your senior prom," I responded caustically.

"This could be the highlight," he said wryly. "Jeremy and Rachel, just in case you get tempted to try something before the wedding day: this could be you and Rachel, next year, at *her* senior prom."

We all started laughing and kept it up as Michael drove towards the hospital until another contraction hit.

"Can't you go any faster?" I breathed.

"No, Lizzie. I didn't want to attract the attention of the cops by speeding on senior prom night and get pulled over for a sobriety test."

"Great," I replied sarcastically, "then I hope you know how to deliver a baby."

"Don't be ridiculous. You know it takes hours."

"It's not gonna be hours," I yelled back.

"Calm down, you two," came Jeremy's voice from the back.

"We're almost there, Lizzie. Do you have your medical ID card?" asked Michael.

"Sure, lover boy. I was planning on having a baby tonight right in the middle of the senior prom, weren't you?"

"Shoot, Lizzie, I'm sorry," said Michael, tapping his fingers on the steering wheel as he drove. I guessed he was at least as nervous as me, even if he wasn't going to admit it.

"Do they ever stop fighting?" asked Jeremy, presumably of Rachel.

"Only when they're kissing and making up," replied Rachel, "which they do often enough."

"We are not fighting," I said with as much force as I could muster, as the contraction petered out.

"What do you call it, then?" Jeremy continued.

"Shut up, Jeremy," said Michael testily. "We're at the hospital. Now would you please find a spot for the car so I can walk in with Lizzie?"

"Sorry, bud. No problem."

"He shouldn't drive my car," I objected.

"Our car," corrected Michael. Then he added, "Fine, Lizzie, you park it."

"You know damn well I can't do that when I'm having a baby."

"Don't you two ever stop?" interjected Jeremy.

"Everybody be quiet right now!" ordered Rachel. "Lizzie, you shut up. Concentrate on having your baby and for goodness' sake, Michael, quit jumping down her throat and help her. Jeremy's gonna take care of the car."

I was glad somebody had finally come to their senses.

"I had a bag packed for the hospital at home..." I whimpered.

"Jeremy and I will pick it up right away, then," replied the capable Rachel, "and don't say a word about him driving your car or we won't do it! We'll get your medical ID card while we're at it and call your folks. Now get out of here, you two."

Michael and I made it into Admissions before the next contraction, but this one lasted a long while. I leaned on the counter, staring at the receptionist, unable to respond to her questions while Michael answered for me. I was furious that I wasn't able to speak for myself.

When this one stopped, I said, "I think I'll have a seat."

Michael and the receptionist, whose hospital ID proclaimed her to be Constance Willow, had a protracted conversation about the fact that I didn't have my ID card with me, but he argued convincingly that they had my records on file anyway and his sister was on her way over with it as we spoke, so they waved us on through. I felt like telling her, no problem, I could have the baby right here in the reception area if they didn't mind. The contractions were three to five minutes apart and lasting longer than a minute. It wasn't supposed to happen this fast, according to the books; but when had I ever done anything by the book?

We were walking down the hallway towards the delivery room when my waters broke.

"Michael, I hate to tell you this but I just ruined my prom dress," I said, feeling warm fluid pouring down my legs. This is disgusting, I thought, couldn't God have come up with a better design? Then I remembered the passage from the Old Testament about multiplying Eve's sorrow during childbirth because she ate of the Tree of the Knowledge of Good and Evil. Stupid Eve had to go and screw it up for everyone.

"What's this about your dress, sweetie?" he asked, because I'd stopped walking.

"My water just broke, idiot!" I yelled. I didn't have the chance to say more because this contraction swallowed me up in pain. I must've missed the part in the childbirth books about increased intensity for contractions after the amniotic sac lost its fluid and the baby's head bore down directly on the cervix.

"I wouldn't have had this baby if I'd known it was going to be like this!" I wailed when the contraction had passed.

"Sure you would, honey. You're doing fine, just try to relax."

He put his arm around me and hugged me.

"Easy for you to say. You're not having it," I protested.

"Lizzie, you're gonna do great. Women have been doing this for thousands of years. How d' you think we got here?" I didn't want to think my arrival on earth more than eighteen years ago, but I did have a lot more compassion for my mother now that I was starting to have a clearer understanding of what she'd gone through to bring me into the world. Mama Anne had done this how many times – five? Obviously pregnancy caused amnesia.

A nurse came scurrying down the hallway like a white mouse. "I'm Rhea, the labor nurse. Let's get you into the labor room, and we'll move you into the birthing center as soon as you get close. It'll probably be a while."

"No, it won't," I retorted.

It might be the first time for me, but I knew this one wasn't going to take hours, no matter what the medical staff said. Call it the woman's intuition, wishful thinking, or the Holy Ghost.

"Her water just broke," Michael said.

"Well, my, it might not be too long, then, kids. You look like you just came from a night out."

No kidding, I thought.

"Senior prom," I replied, sticking out my hand. "Call me Lizzie."

"I'm the dad – Michael," added my husband for her benefit.

We entered the labor room. There was a woman down at the other end making a lot of noise, sounding like she was enduring medieval torture. Another one was sitting quietly next to the bed where they placed me with a man who must have been her husband holding her hand.

"I'm not gonna scream," I whispered to Michael.

"I'm sure you won't, unless it's at me," he rejoined.

We smiled at each other. "I'm not gonna do that either, promise."

He kissed me on the cheek just as another contraction hit, but I didn't feel like collapsing on the bed. It seemed easier to stand up and hold onto Michael.

"Let's get her out of those clothes," suggested Rhea, when I was ready to follow her instructions. Michael was very adept at getting me out of my clothes, I thought. He helped me out of the prom dress and into a hospital gown. Before the next contraction arrived, Rhea had taken my pulse and blood pressure, listened to the baby's heart, snapped on a wrist band, and advised us that the doctor on call would be down right away. My regular doctor wasn't working this shift.

A young female OB/GYN showed up surprisingly soon. She couldn't be older than thirty, so she must have been a chemistry whiz in high school to get through med school at such an early age. I doubted she had kids. She was devoting her life to watching other people's suffering. The staff made me lie down on the bed even though I didn't want to and informed me I was at seven centimeters. I think that meant I was in transition – whatever it was, it was definitely transition from tolerable to excruciating pain.

"I told you it wouldn't be hours," I informed Michael with an arrogant smile, but that was just before a contraction started so I lost the smile. As long as I remembered to breathe slowly and deeply, I could handle it.

They were going to hook up an IV but I said no way, I didn't need pain meds, thank you, and didn't they know that was bad for the baby? Michael took the doctor aside and must have convinced her that it wasn't worth arguing with me.

"If you're okay with this, we're okay with it, Lizzie," she said, seating herself next to the bed. "We like to have all the options available, and you're doing fine. Your husband says he doesn't want us to upset you."

I rolled my eyes at Michael.

"He would know," I managed.

"You look great, kiddo," she added. "Baby's heartbeat is strong, so hang in there and it might not be too long. I'm going to check on some other patients now and we'll get back to you. Rhea will be monitoring your labor. She'll let me know if anything changes."

"Can I get out of this bed?"

"If you want to. Don't wander off too far."

"Lizzie, you wanna walk around?" asked Michael.

"It feels better."

"Whatever she can handle is fine, Michael. Hang in there with her – it gets intense towards the end."

What was she talking about, "intense towards the end?" It was intense now. What did she know? – she hadn't had any kids.

Pop Goes the Weasel

Lizzie

Michael helped me out of the bed and we paced around the labor room for another hour or so (although I lost all track of time), with Rhea or Michael timing the contractions and the intervals in-between. Yeah, they hurt, but I focused on taking long, slow breaths and listening to Michael's heart as he held me against him.

Rachel and Jeremy showed up with my medical ID card and overnight bag, and Jeremy wisely dragged Rachel off to the waiting room saying that Michael was all the help I needed. He was. Visions of Stillwater Cove kept coming to me: waves pounding on the ocean shore, the whirling of the seagulls, the mist trailing through the tree tops, and Michael's eyes as he looked at me for the first time in the moonlight with my robe falling off my shoulders.

Before I knew it the cries of the woman in the bed at the end had subsided into low moans, and they were wheeling me into the birthing center. Michael had changed into scrubs. I couldn't talk anymore, because the time between contractions was too short, so when Michael asked me if I was okay, I could only nod.

I no longer felt frightened, I just wanted to get this baby out. Rhea was telling me to please hold up because Dr. Cherry was on her way in right now, but I couldn't. Screw this, Rhea and Michael would just have to deal with it. Didn't they know you can't stop a baby or the tide coming in? I shook my head when Rhea told me to hang on and she shrugged at Michael. I felt as if I was going to burst like an overripe watermelon and spill seeds out all over the birthing room. I hoped I wasn't going to tear but there was no stopping now, so I pushed and felt the baby's head slide out of me. Everything got easier after that. Although Rhea had been waiting for the doctor, she knew just what to do, and eased one shoulder out followed by the other, and the whole squiggling mass appeared between my legs. Michael leaped to the foot of the bed to take a look.

"We have a boy, Lizzie."

"Thanks for being here with me, Dr. Kerry," I murmured. I heard a cough and a gasp from our new son as he took his first breath, then a thin wail penetrated the air.

Rhea tied off the cord and let Michael cut it. After Rhea had checked our son's Apgar score (8), pulse, and breathing rate, she wrapped him in a receiving blanket and handed him to Michael to show me.

"Told you I wasn't going to scream," I said, staring wide-eyed at the pink mass of flesh bundled into the blanket that was a whole person with miniature fingers and deep blue eyes.

"Here's Mommy, son; best Mommy in the world," said Michael, handing me our son. "Nice, quiet Mommy, too; but I can guarantee you it won't always be that way."

I glared at him and wished he wasn't such a savage tease. Dr. Cherry came flying in at this moment and had a brief consult with Rhea.

"Baby wouldn't wait," I heard Rhea say to her.

"She tear?" asked Dr. Cherry.

"Minor lacerations."

I had to put my legs up while they examined me.

"You're looking good, Lizzie. We're gonna take care of your little boy now, clean him up, and put some drops in his eyes. You still have to deliver the placenta but it'll be a lot easier than the baby. After that and getting this little guy cleaned up, we'll give him back to you, let you guys hang out for a while, and move you to a room."

Michael handed the baby back to Dr. Cherry and a pediatric nurse came in to take care of him. He was still covered in vernix, which was there to lubricate his passage into the world.

"How you doing, sweetheart?" Michael asked me.

"Feeling thinner," I said. I wondered what time it was. The adrenaline must have worn off because I was beginning to feel like I'd done too many laps in a very large pool. "What time is it?"

"Four am. Nice timing. Looks like we're not going to church today."

"You don't say, I finally found a way to get you out of it," I teased.

"Next time you better tell me when you start labor. It's supposed to be faster the second time around."

"You better hope there's gonna be a second time around, lover boy."

"I figure I'll be able to sweet talk you into it."

"It'd better be some seriously super scrumptiously sweet, sweet talking."

He gave me a blistering kiss, as if to prove it, then said: "Some... seriously... super... scrumptiously... sweet... sweet... What are you now, the alliteration queen?"

"Hey, you two, you just made one baby so you better leave off makin' another until you got this little guy taken care of," joked Rhea.

She placed the baby in my arms. Our son looked peachy pink and his skin was as smooth to the touch as the Egyptian cotton sheets on our bed. His head was covered with a blonde fuzz. Everyone would think he had Michael's hair. I wasn't going to correct them.

Within moments, with some gentle help from Rhea, he was happily nursing.

"What are you guys planning to call him?" asked Rhea.

"We couldn't agree on a name," I said.

"I'd like to use my grandfather's name – Ian," suggested Michael. We'd talked about this name before but I hadn't capitulated. I didn't feel like arguing now and I didn't want to call our son "baby" for the next few days while we deliberated.

"That's fine, as long as his middle name can be 'Michael,'" I replied.

"Conditions, always conditions," he said.

"Let's not argue," I pleaded. "You have an unfair advantage right now, but so be it."

"You're so much fun as an opposing force," he teased.

"I don't wanna be an opposing force," I came back, regarding him seriously.

"Me, neither."

"Let's hope Ian Michael Kerry isn't gonna be one," I rejoined.

"With Lizzie Kerry for a mother, the poor kid doesn't have a prayer."

"Thanks, lover boy." I slapped him gently in the ribs.

"Luckily for him, he has one sane parent."

I was going to offer a rebuttal, but I had another contraction and realized it was time to push out the placenta, which was a hell of a lot easier than Ian. Dr. Cherry spent a few minutes examining it to make sure I didn't have pieces retained, and then left to deal with other patients.

I kept working on nursing Ian Michael, but he really didn't seem to take to it. Spending all night dancing at the senior prom must have worn him out. Rhea assured me he'd be hungry within hours, if not sooner, and to just keep offering him my nipple.

I was moved to a regular room, once more a single, courtesy of my father, who would no doubt be ecstatic that there was finally a boy in the family. Ian Michael was going to be worth sacks of forgiveness for his wayward mother, I thought. Michael went off to call his parents and mine to inform them of the happy event. I was betting my father would be first to show up, and I was right.

Ian and I dozed off until dawn tipped its pink fingers over the horizon. Michael hadn't left and was sleeping in a chair next to my bed. They gave both of us breakfast and reminded me that if I was planning on breastfeeding, my body would be demanding 3,000 calories a day and I shouldn't skimp on meals. I was sure Michael wasn't going to let me forget it. Ian finally found his appetite along with his voice, which I thought pretty lusty for a kid who weighed only seven pounds, three ounces, and was about ten days early. I guess he was following his mother's example: he just couldn't wait until the time was right to find out about the mysteries of the universe.

My parents arrived at eight am sharp, the earliest hour visitors were allowed to see patients. My father was clad in a swanky, grey silk suit and tie, my mother in a pale blue lacy number. They looked as if they'd dressed up for a photo shoot, and Dad had even brought his camera. He didn't waste time getting down to business; that's my Dad. I wanted to protest that Ian Michael didn't want his eyeballs burned with a flash since he was just getting used to the idea of sunlight, but I could see it wasn't a point worth arguing. Roll on the doting grandparents, I thought.

My father gave both Michael and me big hugs as well as a huge box of chocolates and a baby congratulations flower basket covered in blue bows that matched the color of my mother's dress. I guess it was okay to shop on the Sabbath when it came to buying gifts for the daughter who'd just delivered his grandson, though I'd never seen my father tank up the Audi, even once, on a Sunday before.

It was nice to know I could get him to break some of his rules. My father had never shown his appreciation for me like this before, even when I made straight A's two years in a row in bishop. I had finally done something to impress him, and I wished I didn't feel so thrilled about it. I hadn't known I wanted my father's approval so badly.

After they left and Ian had fallen asleep again, I said to Michael, "I produce a son and I finally earn my father's respect. And it sucks that I feel happy about it."

"He might actually forgive me for knocking you up now," added Michael with a sly smile.

"I'm not sure his newfound appreciation extends to forgiveness. You're still the guy who screwed over his daughter, and I'm still the daughter who should've known better and deserves to rot in hell."

Michael sat next to me on the bed and put his arm around my shoulders. "Sounds like a ton of anger and resentment towards your dad, Lizzie."

"He earned it righteously," I replied defensively.

"You're gonna have to work on that, you know, sweetheart." He tousled my hair. The combs I'd put in last night before the prom were still fastened in it. Michael removed them one at a time and re-pinned my hair with them, being careful around the place where I'd had eighteen stitches in my head.

"It's easy for you. You've got the most spectacular dad in the world."

"And he doesn't let me worm my way out of forgiving others their trespasses against me," he went on.

"Yeah, well, you knew I loved you when you forgave me."

"Your dad loves you, Lizzie. Don't you know that?"

"Sure he does. That's why he's always treated me like a serf."

"You're worming, Lizzie."

"I just had a baby, I don't wanna do this now."

"You gotta do it some time. If you think it's not affecting your life, you're wrong. Your affair with Ian's biological father was all about pissing off your dad."

"No, it wasn't!" I protested. "It was about falling in love."

"Lust, Lizzie, lust."

"Fine, whatever, Mr. Psychologist."

"Hey, I'm not the enemy, sweetheart. I wanna help you, I really do. You have all this anger and it's not going away."

"I do not!" I yelled. I could have cursed him for his coolness.

"You're gonna wake up little Ian, Lizzie," he whispered, kissing my head.

I put my head in my hands and wished Michael wouldn't stick daggers in my heart when I was vulnerable and tired. Maybe it was just that he was afraid to approach me on other occasions because I usually had my sword drawn, ready for combat.

"I'll go home now and let you sleep some more," he added.

"Don't go," I begged.

"I'll stay, on one condition," he replied.

I hated it when he used my own lines on me. "Shoot, lover boy."

"It's Sunday, so we'll look up some scriptures on forgiveness together. I had Jeremy stick my scriptures in your bag. And you can tell me everything your dad ever did to make you mad."

"And how is that gonna help?"

"You need three things to restore a wounded soul: repentance and sorrow for disobedience to the Lord's commandments, unconditional love for your friends and family, and unconditional forgiveness for your adversaries."

I wanted to tell him my soul was fine: I'd repented of my errant ways, I loved him and his family as if they were my own, and I'd forgiven Jason for abandoning me. Besides, I was trying to be everything he wanted in a wife and *I* didn't need fixing.

But down in those invisible, dark corners of my soul, I knew there were places in my heart where resentment still smoldered like the lava underneath an inactive volcano.

"You have a son now, Lizzie. If you bottle up all that anger, you're gonna end up taking it out on him. Or me."

"You think I already do?"

He put a finger over my lips. "Shhhh. Please give us a try, for my sake."

If he was going to ask that sweetly, I could hardly turn him down. "I love you, Lizzie."

"I love you, too, more than you can possibly imagine." I responded. There was one question I had wanted to ask Michael for a long time. "Are you still mad at Ian's father, Michael?"

"Yeah," he admitted.

"You'll have to work on that," I said

"I know."

Epilogue

Two weeks after Ian was born, as Michael and I were on our way out of our ward building, in his official capacity as a bishop, Patrick Kerry handed me a plain envelope. Michael was lugging Ian in his carrier, and I had the diaper bag slung over one shoulder.

"This is for you, Lizzie," he said. "Some of our ward members wanted to help you and your new family get a head start. Good luck."

"Thanks very much, Bishop," I replied.

"What is it?" asked Michael.

"Let's open it in the car," I suggested.

We walked over to the Nissan, unlocked it, and strapped Ian into his car seat.

"Think he's gonna start crying on the way home?" I asked.

"He usually does if his mommy isn't holding him," replied Michael.

"You're jealous because you can't have me all to yourself now."

"I'll take as much of you as I can get then, my precious pearl."

He put his arms around me and kissed me before opening the passenger side door for me. I felt as hot as a mid-August day in Sacramento. I thought of last October, when I was terrified if he touched me and didn't like him driving my car. It seemed a lifetime away.

After we settled ourselves in the front seats, I ripped open the envelope and gasped as six one-hundred-dollar bills fluttered into my lap.

"Do we have to pay tithing on this?" I asked.

Michael grinned at me. "We didn't earn it, Lizzie. But it's nice that you thought about it."

"I wouldn't want to upset the priesthood holder in this family. I seem to do that a lot."

"Bethie, my love, repeat after me," he said, leaning back in the seat with his eyes half closed.

"What?"

"I will do the best that I can, every day, to make those around me happy, because I know that they love me just as I am."

It sounded like a good maxim to live by, especially for an imperfect soul like myself, so I repeated the phrase for Michael's benefit. Then I asked, "He can't hurt us anymore, can he?"

I knew Michael would know which 'he' I was referring to: that slithering snake with blue eyes who was Ian's biological father.

I didn't want anything or anyone to burst the bubble of happiness we'd built around us.

"Of course not, and I wouldn't let him."

This time, Michael was wrong. Some earthly foes were destined to seek retribution, even though the Lord had declared that vengeance belonged to Him alone.

About the Author

The author is a convert and long-time member of the Church of Jesus Christ of Latter-day Saints. She brings experiences from both inside and outside the Church into her writing. She earned a PhD in epidemiology from the University of California-Davis. She has worked for local and state health departments and resides in northern California. She has four grown children and enjoys swimming and walking her dog.

About the Editor

David Lee Crites provided insight and perspective as "the dude" with suggestions for Michael's side of the story. He loves the creative spirit and camaraderie that comes from writing and editing as a team.